American Ornithologists' Union

The Code of Nomenclature and Check-List of North American Birds

American Ornithologists' Union

The Code of Nomenclature and Check-List of North American Birds

ISBN/EAN: 9783337177072

Printed in Europe, USA, Canada, Australia, Japan

Cover: Foto ©ninafisch / pixelio.de

More available books at **www.hansebooks.com**

THE CODE OF NOMENCLATURE

AND

CHECK-LIST

OF

NORTH AMERICAN BIRDS

Adopted by the American Ornithologists' Union

BEING THE REPORT OF THE COMMITTEE OF THE
UNION ON CLASSIFICATION AND
NOMENCLATURE

Zoölogical Nomenclature is a means, not an end, of Zoölogical Science

NEW YORK
AMERICAN ORNITHOLOGISTS' UNION
1886

PREFACE.

AT the first Congress of the American Ornithologists' Union, held in New York, September 26-29, 1883, the following resolution was adopted:—

"*Resolved*, That the Chairman appoint a Committee of five, including himself, to whom shall be referred the question of a Revision of the Classification and Nomenclature of the Birds of North America."

In pursuance of this resolution the following Committee was appointed: Messrs. Coues, Allen, Ridgway, Brewster, and Henshaw.

The Committee, having held numerous sessions in Washington and New York, presented its Report at the second Congress of the Union, held in New York, Sept. 30 to Oct. 2, 1884, when the following resolution was adopted:—

"*Resolved*, That the Report of the Committee on the Revision of the Nomenclature and Classification of North Ameircan Birds be accepted and adopted, and that it be recommitted to the Committee, with instructions to complete and submit it to the Council as soon as practicable; and that the Council be empowered and instructed to accept and adopt the Report as finally rendered, with such modifications as they may deem necessary, and to publish the same, copyrighted, in part or in whole, and in one or more forms, in the name and under the auspices of the American Ornithologists' Union."

The Committee, having continued its sessions, presented its final report to the Council at a meeting held in Washington on the 21st of April, 1885, when the Report of the Committee was accepted and adopted, and was referred again to the Committee for publication, the Committee to exercise such editorial revision as might seem necessary.

Pursuant to the foregoing resolutions of the Union and Council, the Committee now offers to the public, in the name and on behalf of the Union, the result of its labors, consisting of a List of North American Birds, preceded by the Code of Rules adopted by the Committee for its guidance in the preparation of the List.

The Committee ventures to hope that the new Code will find favor, not only with ornithologists, but among zoölogists generally.

ELLIOTT COUES.
J. A. ALLEN.
ROBERT RIDGWAY.
WILLIAM BREWSTER.
H. W. HENSHAW.

TABLE OF CONTENTS.

	PAGE
I. INTRODUCTION	1
II. PRINCIPLES, CANONS, AND RECOMMENDATIONS	18
A. GENERAL PRINCIPLES	18
B. CANONS OF ZOÖLOGICAL NOMENCLATURE	22
§ 1. Of the Kinds of Names in Zoölogy	22
2. Of the Binomial System as a Phase of Zoölogical Nomenclature	29
3. Of the Trinomial System as a Phase of Zoölogical Nomenclature	30
4. Of the Beginning of Zoölogical Nomenclature proper, and of the Operation of the Law of Priority	32
5. Of Names Published Simultaneously	40
6. Of the Retention of Names	41
7. Of the Rejection of Names	47
8. Of the Emendation of Names	51
9. Of the Definition of Names	51
10. Of the Publication of Names	54
11. Of the Authority for Names	56
C. RECOMMENDATIONS FOR ZOÖLOGICAL NOMENCLATURE IN THE FUTURE.	58
§ 12. Of the Construction and Selection of Names	58
13. Of the Transliteration of Names	65
14. Of the Description of Zoölogical Objects	67
15. Of the Bibliography of Names	67
16. Of the Selection of Vernacular Names	68
III. CHECK-LIST OF NORTH AMERICAN BIRDS	71
I. PYGOPODES	73
a. Podicipedes	73
1. Podicipidæ	73

		PAGE
	b. Cepphi	75
	2. Urinatoridæ	75
	3. Alcidæ	76
II.	LONGIPENNES	84
	4. Stercorariidæ	84
	5. Laridæ	86
	6. Rynchopidæ	96
III.	TUBINARES	97
	7. Diomedeidæ	97
	8. Procellariidæ	98
IV.	STEGANOPODES	106
	9. Phaëthontidæ	106
	10. Sulidæ	107
	11. Anhingidæ	108
	12. Phalacrocoracidæ	109
	13. Pelecanidæ	112
	14. Fregatidæ	113
V.	ANSERES	113
	15. Anatidæ	113
VI.	ODONTOGLOSSÆ	130
	16. Phœnicopteridæ	130
VII.	HERODIONES	131
	a. Ibides	131
	17. Plataleidæ	131
	18. Ibididæ	131
	b. Ciconiæ	133
	19. Ciconiidæ	133
	c. Herodii	134
	20. Ardeidæ	134
VIII.	PALUDICOLÆ	138
	d. Grues	138
	21. Gruidæ	138
	e. Ralli	139
	22. Aramidæ	139
	23. Rallidæ	140
IX.	LIMICOLÆ	145
	24. Phalaropodidæ	145
	25. Recurvirostridæ	146
	26. Scolopacidæ	147
	27. Charadriidæ	160
	28. Aphrizidæ	164

			PAGE
		29. Hæmatopodidæ	165
		30. Jacanidæ	166
X.	GALLINÆ		167
	f. Phasiani		167
		31. Tetraonidæ	167
		32. Phasianidæ	177
	g. Penelopes		178
		32. Cracidæ	178
XI.	COLUMBÆ		178
		34. Columbidæ	178
XII.	RAPTORES		182
	h. Sarcorhamphi		182
		35. Cathartidæ	182
	i. Falcones		184
		36. Falconidæ	184
	j. Striges		197
		37. Strigidæ	197
		38. Bubonidæ	198
XIII.	PSITTACI		205
		39. Psittacidæ	205
XIV.	COCCYGES		206
	k. Cuculi		206
		46. Cuculidæ	206
	l. Trogones		208
		41. Trogonidæ	208
	m. Alcyones		209
		42. Alcedinidæ	209
XV.	PICI		210
		43. Picidæ	210
XVII.	MACROCHIRES		219
	n. Caprimulgi		219
		44. Caprimulgidæ	219
	o. Cypseli		221
		45. Micropodidæ	221
	p. Trochili		223
		46. Trochilidæ	223
XVIII.	PASSERES		228
	q. Clamatores		228
		47. Tyrannidæ	228
	r. Oscines		238
		48. Alaudidæ	238
		49. Corvidæ	240

TABLE OF CONTENTS.

		PAGE
50.	Sturnidæ	247
51.	Icteridæ	247
52.	Fringillidæ	254
53.	Tanagridæ	290
54.	Hirundinidæ	292
55.	Ampelidæ	294
56.	Laniidæ	295
57.	Vireonidæ	296
58.	Cœrebidæ	300
59.	Mniotiltidæ	300
60.	Motacillidæ	319
61.	Cinclidæ	321
62.	Troglodytidæ	321
63.	Certhiidæ	330
64.	Paridæ	331
65.	Sylviidæ	338
66.	Turdidæ	341

IV. HYPOTHETICAL LIST 343

V. THE FOSSIL BIRDS OF NORTH AMERICA . . 359

INDEX 369

THE CODE OF NOMENCLATURE

AND

CHECK-LIST OF NORTH AMERICAN BIRDS.

I.

INTRODUCTION.

IN beginning its work the Committee found it necessary to examine particularly those rules, precedents, and practices of nomenclature respecting which leading authorities differ, it becoming immediately obvious that no substantial and satisfactory progress in the preparation of a List of North American Birds could be made until various disputed points should be settled. This necessity led to the discussion of the general principles of zoölogical nomenclature, in their special application to the subject in hand; and ultimately resulted in the formation of a Code of Rules for the guidance of the Committee in fixing the name of every North American bird. These rules were considered in their bearing upon Zoölogy at large, as well as upon Ornithology alone; it being obvious that sound principles of nomenclature should be susceptible of general application. Furthermore, since in the nature of the case there can be no personal obligation, and no court of appeal with power to enforce its decision, canons of nomenclature should derive their weight wholly from their merit, and should acquire the force of law only by the common consent of zoölogists. Since nomenclature is a means, not an end, of science, the merit of a code of rules for naming objects rests upon its utility, its availability, and its efficiency in meeting all necessary and reasonable requirements of a system of classification, — in a word, upon its practical convenience.

Fortunately for the interests of science, the tendency of naturalists has latterly been toward substantial agreement upon most of the fundamental principles involved in nomenclature, variance of opinion coming mainly in the application of those principles in minor details. To prepare an acceptable and entirely available code of rules, the compilers of to-day have therefore to do little more than clearly formulate the current usages of the best naturalists, and consistently apply them to any given case.

Without undertaking to give in detail the history of zoölogical and botanical nomenclature from the Linnæan period to the present day, the Committee deems it proper and needful to advert to certain moot points. While binomial nomenclature may be considered to have originated with Linnæus, who propounded and established its fundamental principles with admirable sagacity, these have in the course of time and to some extent been necessarily modified to meet the requirements of the progress of zoölogical science, by restriction in some directions and extension in others. So radically, indeed, has the aspect of the science changed since the Linnæan period, and so profoundly do modern conceptions in biological science differ from those then held, that a strict binomial system has probably had its day, and may be abandoned, with great benefit to science, in the not distant future. But, assuming that the binomial nomenclature, with some modification, is still to be retained for a while, in its general features, the whole course of scientific nomenclature has shown that the *law of priority* — *lex prioritatis* — is the one great underlying principle ; and the nearly universal tendency is, to hold this principle inviolate, to adhere to it with the utmost possible stringency, and to tolerate the fewer infractions as time advances.[1] But there is unfortunately no

---

[1] A signal exception to this is found in the just published 'History of British Birds,' by Mr. Henry Seebohm, — an ingenious and thoughtful ornithologist, — who discards the *lex prioritatis*, substituting therefor an *auctorum plurimorum* principle, according to which his method is to use for every bird that specific name which has

unanimity in fixing the date of the beginning of the operation of the law of priority, naturalists being nearly evenly divided in opinion upon this point. The so-called 'Stricklandian Code' fixed the date at 1766,[1] — that of the twelfth edition of the 'Systema Naturæ.' This has been generally accepted by British zoölogists; while many others, especially in America and of late years, consider 1758 as the fittest starting-point, this being the date of the tenth edition of the 'Systema Naturæ,' in which Linnæus first methodically and consistently applied the binomial nomenclature to zoölogy. Botanists are at variance with zoölogists, and with one another, in this particular; some taking as

been oftenest used before, irrespective of its original application, or of its applicability under the law of priority. But a much earlier protest against the strict law of priority, from an entomologist, is to be found in a tract published in 1872, the following title of which indicates the nature of its contents: —

1872. LEWIS, W. ARNOLD. A Discussion | of the | Law of Priority in Entomological | Nomenclature; | with Strictures on its Modern Application; | and | a Proposal for the Rejection of all | disused Names. | — | By | W. Arnold Lewis, | F. L. S., M. Entom. Soc. Lond., Barrister-at-Law. | — | Also containing | A Paper, by the same, read before the British Association | (Section D) on August 7, 1871; | And a Second, by the same, intended as a Contribution to the | Discussion in the 'Entomologist's Monthly Magazine.' | — | London: | Williams & Norgate, 14, Henrietta Street, | Covent Garden. | — | 1872. 1 vol. 8vo, paper cover, title, advt., and pp. 1–86.

(The first paper mentioned in the title is, 'A Proposal for a Modification of the strict Law of Priority in Zoological Nomenclature in Certain Cases,' pp. 69–82. The second is entitled, 'Synonymic Lists and Certainty in Nomenclature,' pp. 82–86.)

Another paper, also by an entomologist, may be consulted with profit. It is entitled as follows: —

1873. SHARP, DAVID. The | Object and Method | of | Zoological Nomenclature. | By | David Sharp. | — | " Nomina si nescis, perit et cognitio rerum." | — | London: | E. W. Janson, 28 Museum Street. | Williams & Norgate, Henrietta St. | — | November, 1873. Paper, sm. 8vo, cover-title backed by preface, and pp. 39.

(Well reviewed by A. R. Wallace, 'Nature,' Feb. 5, 1874, p. 258.)

[1] "In Mr. H. E. Strickland's original draft of these Rules and Recommendations the edition of Linnæus was left blank, and the XIIth was inserted by the Manchester Committee. This was done not as being the first in which the binomial nomenclature had been used, as it commenced with the Xth, but as being the last and most complete edition of Linnæus's works, and containing many species the Xth did not." — *Revised Rules of the B. A.*, p. 28, as printed in Rep. Brit. Ass. Adv. Sci., Birmingham Meeting, 1865. For evidence that Strickland himself was an advocate of Linnæus at 1758, see 'The Auk,' I., 1884, p. 400.

their starting-point the first edition of the 'Genera Plantarum' of Linnæus, published in 1737; others, his promulgation of rules in the 'Philosophia Botanica,' 1751; others, again, his 'Species Plantarum,' 1753. But, furthermore, as some zoölogists used the system methodically in works published prior to 1758,[1] and as generic names were employed in a strict sense by some writers of eminence in zoölogy as early as 1732,[2] the law of priority is restricted in time by neither one of two important codes recently promulgated, — that of the Société Zoologique de France, 1881,[3] and that of the Congrès Géologique International, 1882;[4] the only provisions for the inception of its operation being, that a given name, to be available, shall have been properly published and clearly defined, conformably with the rules of binomial nomenclature.

The Stricklandian Code was nevertheless taken by the International Geological Congress as its point of departure and basis of procedure in the formulation of the Rules it adopted. This code — first promulgated by the British Association for the Advancement of Science, at Manchester, in 1842, later adopted by the American Association of similar name and character, and reaffirmed and again adopted with little modification by the British Association, at Bath, in 1865[5] — has until recently been the principal code of zoölogical nomenclature; it is still recognized as the highest authority by most English-speaking zoölogists, and is followed with more or less reservation and evasion by naturalists at large. In most respects — excepting the rule which fixed the date of the

---

[1] As Artedi, Scopoli, Pallas, Clerck, etc.

[2] E. g. Breyn; to which may perhaps be added Link, 1722, Klein, 1731 and 1734, Linnæus, 1735, and Tournefort, 1742.

[3] Société Zoologique | de France | — | De la | Nomenclature | des | êtres organisés | — | Paris | Au Sièges de la Société | 7, rue des Grands-Augustins, 7 | — | 1881. Paper, 8vo, pp. 37.

[4] Règles à suivre pour établir la nomenclature des espèces. Rapport du Secrétaire de la Commission H. Douvillé. < Congrès Géologique International. Compte rendu de la 2me Session, Bologne, 1881, (pub. 1882,) pp. 592–608.

[5] See Notes on the modified Rules for Zoölogical Nomenclature, B. A., 1865, by A. E. Verrill, in Am. Jour. Sci. and Arts, 2d Series, Vol. XLVIII., July, 1869, pp. 92–110.

starting-point of nomenclature at 1766 — this honored code was admirably conceived at the time. It had great influence for good, and did much to bring zoölogical nomenclature from a loose and almost chaotic state to a fair degree of stability and orderly consistency. Its principal defects are those which could not then have been perceived and avoided, being inherent in the binomial system itself, as has become obvious in the subsequent forty-three years of progress in zoölogical science, during which time have arisen contingencies and complications which, being unforeseen in 1842, could not have been then provided for. In fine, the Stricklandian Code could not possibly have been made better than the radically faulty binomial scheme upon which it was based, and for the perpetuation of which in all its defects it sedulously provided. No one appears to have suspected, in 1842, that the Linnæan system was not the permanent heritage of science, or that in a few years a theory of evolution was to sap its very foundations, by radically changing men's conceptions of those things to which names were to be furnished. Nevertheless, the half-dozen emendations made to this code by the Bath Committee in 1865 were, with one exception, ill-advised, leaving the code less available and efficient than it had been before. The fact, however, that the Stricklandian Code has been from 1842 to the present year the recognized basis of nearly all attempts to improve the formal rules for zoölogical nomenclature, is ample evidence of its usefulness and general soundness, so long as we must continue to base our nomenclature upon the Linnæan binomial system. The wide-spread recognition of its weight and authority in nomenclature, and the almost universal currency of its leading provisions, which are in the main as satisfactory as any can well be which provide for a strictly binomial system, — in short, the strength of the Stricklandian Code, renders it still the natural and proper basis of any new code which may seek to provide for the comparatively few contingencies to meet which the former one has proven inadequate.[1]

[1] The Committee which drafted the original 'Stricklandian' Code, appointed at a meeting of the Council of the British Association for the Advancement of Science,

It has therefore seemed to your Committee advisable to take the original Stricklandian Code as the initial point of departure; to reaffirm and reproduce as many of its rules as may be desirable, without reference to the changes made in it in 1865, — changes which, with one exception, do not appear to your Committee to be available for adoption, although, for the sake of historical completeness, they may be duly noted in their

held in London, February 11, 1842, consisted of Mr. C. Darwin, Professor Henslow, Rev. L. Jenyns, Mr. W. Ogilby, Mr. J. Phillips, Dr. Richardson, Mr. J. O. Westwood, and Mr. H. E. Strickland (reporter); to whom were afterward added, W. J. Broderip, Professor Owen, W. E. Shuckard, G. R. Waterhouse, and W. Yarrell. The result of their labors appeared in a 'Series of Propositions for rendering the Nomenclature of Zoology uniform and permanent,' first printed in the Report of the Twelfth Meeting of the British Association, held at Manchester, June, 1842, p. 106 *et seq.* They also appeared in the 'Annals of Natural History,' and in the 'Philosophical Magazine.' C. L. Bonaparte submitted an Italian translation to the Scientific Congress held at Padua in 1843. A French translation also appeared in 'L'Institut' (11e Ann., No. 498, pp. 248–251, 13 Juil, 1843), and a review by Dr. A. A. Gould of the 'Propositions' was printed in the 'American Journal of Science and Arts' (Vol. XLV., 1843, pp. 1–12).

At the B. A. meeting at Oxford in 1860, it was "resolved, that the surviving members of the Committee appointed in 1842 — viz., Mr. C. Darwin, Rev. Professor Henslow, Rev. L. Jenyns, Mr. W. Ogilby, Professor Phillips, Sir John Richardson, Mr. J. O. Westwood, Professor Owen, Mr. W. E. Shuckard, and Mr. G. R. Waterhouse . . . . be reappointed, with Sir Wm. Jardine, Bart., and Mr. P. L. Sclater."

At the B. A. meeting at Newcastle, 1863, the Committee was reformed again, to consist of Sir Wm. Jardine, A. R. Wallace, J. E. Gray, C. C. Babington, Dr. Francis, P. L. Sclater, C. Spence Bate, P. P. Carpenter, Dr. J. D. Hooker, Professor Balfour, H. T. Stainton, J. Gwyn Jeffries, Prof. A. Newton, Prof. T. H. Huxley, Professor Allman, and G. Bentham, with power to add to its members. For the purpose of eliciting suggestions and recommendations, this Committee reprinted the original 'Series of Propositions,' etc., in a pamphlet entitled as follows: —

Rules | for | Zoological Nomenclature | by the late | Hugh E. Strickland, M. A., F. R. S. | Authorized by Section D of the | British Association | at Manchester, 1842. | — | Reprinted by Requisition of Section D at Newcastle, | 1863. | — | Edinburgh: | Printed by Neill and Company. | MDCCCLXIII. 8vo, pp. 25.

This is the original of the 'Stricklandian Code,' 1842, known also as the 'Rules of the British Association.' Upon this the Bath Committee, in 1865, engrafted its emendations, with the result of what is known as the 'Revised B. A. Rules,' entitled as follows: "Report of a Committee appointed to report on the Changes which they may consider desirable to make, if any, in the Rules of Zoological Nomenclature drawn up by Mr. H. E. Strickland, at the Instance of the British Association at their Meeting in Manchester in 1842." (Rep. 35th Meeting Brit. Assoc. Adv. Sci., held at Birmingham in Sept., 1865, (pub. 1866,) pp. 25–42.)

proper place in this Report; and then to build upon such a foundation with those additional recommendations and suggestions which in the judgment of the Committee are required to meet the demands of the present state of zoölogical science, and which seem most timely in view of its evident tendency, and probable progress in the future.

As is well known, Alphonse De Candolle provided botanists with a code of nomenclatural rules for the Vegetable Kingdom, the admirably sound character of which code caused it to receive the unanimous indorsement of the International Botanical Congress held in Paris in 1867. These rules are almost equally applicable to Zoölogy, the nomenclatural requirements of the Animal and Vegetable Kingdoms being nearly identical; and in general tenor and spirit they are much the same as those of the Stricklandian Code. In 1876, an American zoölogist, Mr. W. H. Dall, was appointed by Section B of the American Association for the Advancement of Science a committee of one, "to obtain an expression of opinion from the working naturalists of America, in regard to the nature of a set of rules for facilitating the decision of questions relating to nomenclature." In pursuance of this duty, Mr. Dall prepared a circular upon the subject, consisting of a series of questions relating to disputed points, which was widely distributed among the publishing naturalists of America, from whom a gratifyingly large number of responses were received. To Mr. Dall's report, as published,[1] embodying the purport of all their replies, was added an Appendix, consisting "of a *résumé* of all the principles and rules of nomenclature as hitherto set forth by the chief authorities on that subject, with the diverse views of different authors concerning each proposition appended to it and authenticated by their initials," the reporter further adding many comments of his own. These principles and rules were compiled equally in the interest of Zoölogy and of

---

[1] Nomenclature | in | Zoology and Botany. | A Report to the American Association for the Advancement of | Science at the Nashville Meeting, August 31, 1877. | — | By | W. H. Dall, | United States Coast Survey. | — | Salem: | Printed at the Salem Press. | December, 1877. 8vo, paper cover, title, and pp. 7-56.

Botany, and based largely upon the Zoölogical Code of Strickland and the Botanical Code of De Candolle. The Appendix, of thirty-three pages of mostly small type, giving a thorough and nearly complete *résumé* of the subject, forms a mine of information upon current usages and previous rulings in nomenclature. While its general character is that of a digest of what was at the time, or had before been, the laws of the subject, the reporter did not not fail to furnish much original matter, in the form of sound criticism and valuable suggestions on many important points; so that his codification of rules and principles may be consulted with profit by all who are interested in the subject of systematic nomenclature.[1]

In 1881, as already noted, the Zoölogical Society of France adopted a code of rules prepared by a commission specially appointed to consider the subject. These rules, only seventeen in

---

[1] Mr. Samuel H. Scudder had shortly before Mr. Dall's labors published a valuable paper entitled 'Canons of Systematic Nomenclature for the Higher Groups,' in the Amer. Jour. Sci. and Arts, 3d Series, III., May, 1872, pp. 348–351. (Separate, pp. 1–4.)

Entomology is by far the most extensive branch of Zoölogy, and much has been done by entomologists to promote the sound nomenclature of the department. Fabricius's 'Philosophia Entomologica,' 1778, is said to contain the first set of rules published for entomological nomenclature. Besides some papers already cited, we may in this connection note the following:—

'On some Changes in the Nomenclature of North American Coleoptera which have been recently proposed.' By John L. LeConte, M. D. Canad. Entom., October, 1874, pp. 185-197.

'On Entomological Nomenclature.' Canad. Entom., November, 1874, pp. 201-206; December, 1874, pp. 207-210. (Part I. is 'On the Law of Priority'; Part II. is 'On Generic Types.')

'Historical Sketch of the Generic Names proposed for Butterflies, a Contribution to Systematic Nomenclature.' By Samuel H. Scudder. Salem, 1875. 8vo, pp. 293.

'Observations on Nomenclature' constitute Part I. of Thorell's work on European Spiders, 4to, Upsala, 1869.

'Rules to be submitted to the Entomological Club of the A. A. A. S.,' 8vo, n. d., n. p., "ordered printed by resolution at the annual meeting for 1875," but never published, were drawn up by a portion of the Committee appointed by the Club, viz., J. L. LeConte, Wm. Saunders, and C. V. Riley. These proposed rules, twelve in number, were, like the questions propounded in the Dall circular, extensively circulated, chiefly among entomologists, to elicit responses. They were, however, never finally adopted by the Club.

number, and occupying less than three octavo pages, are likewise intended to apply to both Zoölogy and Botany. Their principal divergence from the Stricklandian Code is at the point of departure for the law of priority, as already stated. The rules are succeeded by a commentary of some thirty pages, prepared by M. Chaper, the reporter of the commission, one third of this matter relating to the starting-point for the action of the law of priority, which is discussed with special reference to pre-Linnæan authors, and favors the non-limitation of the law by the works of Linnæus.

The International Geological Congress, at its meeting held in 1882 at Bologna, also adopted a code of rules intended to apply equally to Zoölogy and Botany. They were proposed by a committee specially appointed for the purpose, who, after adopting certain general principles, took as its basis of departure the Stricklandian Code. These rules are even fewer than those of the code of the French Zoölogical Society, being only eleven in number, and occupying less than two octavo pages. They are followed by twenty-two pages of valuable commentary, offered to the Commission by its Secretary, M. H. Douvillé. This is largely historical, and, like M. Chaper's, argues for the non-limitation of the law of priority by the works of Linnæus, and for its restriction, as above said, only by the requirements of binomiality, proper publication, and clear definition. The only exceptions to the action of this law which the code recognizes as permissible are in the cases of preoccupation of a generic name in the same kingdom, and of a specific name in the same genus.

In 1883, M. A. De Candolle published his important 'Nouvelles Remarques sur la Nomenclature Botanique,' in which he reviews the discussions which were had during the sixteen years following the appearance of his Botanical Code of 1867,[1] and proposes a few changes which he considers that experience has shown to be necessary. These, following upon Dall's digest and upon the action respectively of the French Zoölogical So-

---

[1] 'Lois de la Nomenclature Botanique, rédigées et commentées par M. Alphonse De Candolle.' Paris, 1867. 8vo, pp. 60.

ciety and of the International Geological Congress, tend in the direction of securing the utmost attainable fixity of names and general stability in nomenclature, by giving the fullest scope possible to the operation of the law of priority.

De Candolle takes the first edition of the 'Species Plantarum,' 1753, as the starting-point of the binomial system in Botany, and therefore as the date of the beginning of the law of priority in respect to species, — a point substantially agreed upon by botanists. For generic names, however, he takes the first edition of the 'Genera Plantarum,' 1757; and his 'Article 15' provides that each natural group of plants must retain the most ancient name appended to it, if it be not inconsistent with the essential rules of nomenclature, whether adopted or given by Linnæus, or since his time; thus implying that the law of priority is not to extend to authors earlier than Linnæus. His provisions in regard to the emendation of names are very strict. His 'Article 60' is: 'A generic name should subsist just as it was made, though a purely typographical error may be corrected. The termination of a Latin specific name may be changed to bring it into agreement [in gender] with its generic name." This is a marked change from his previous code, in which Article 60 enjoined the suppression of hybrid names, or those formed by the combination of two languages.

It is evident, even from the foregoing brief and incomplete summary of some leading authorities upon nomenclature, that the general tendency at present is in the direction of the greatest attainable fixity of names, by the most rigid adherence to the law of priority under all practicable circumstances, and by the disregard as far as possible of all rules requiring the rejection of names for faulty construction, for barbarity, for being meaningless, and even for being literally false, — changes to be made only in cases of obvious typographical errors. The emendations proposed by your Committee to be made in the Stricklandian Code recognize this tendency, and are in harmony with it. Your Committee, however, does not agree to any of the dates which various codes take as their respective starting-points in nomenclature, and especially does not deem it expedient to take different dates for generic and specific names. The Committee, furthermore, in one or two cases, submits some decided innovations, positively at variance with the provisions of any previous nomenclatural code; believing that certain radical modifications are demanded by recent progress in science, and that these are a step in advance.

Referring now to the original Stricklandian Code of 1842, the principal changes which your Committee proposes and recommends for adoption by the Union may be summarized as follows: —

(1.) The adoption of the date of the Xth edition of the 'Systema Naturæ,' 1758, instead of that of the XIIth, 1766, as the starting-point of the law of priority for names of whatever groups; because this date, 1758, is in fact that of the establishment of the binomial system of nomenclature in Zoölogy, and of its first methodical application to the whole Animal Kingdom.

(2.) The rule that prior use of a name in Botany does not make that name unavailable in Zoölogy; with the injunction, however, that duplication of names in the Animal and Vegetable Kingdoms is to be sedulously avoided in future.

(3.) The principle of Trinomials: namely, departure from strict binomiality to the extent of using three words as the name of those subspecific forms which are sufficiently distinct to require recognition by name, yet which are known to intergrade with one another; the name of such forms to consist of three terms, — a generic, a specific, and a subspecific, — written consecutively and continuously, without the intervention of any mark of punctuation, any arbitrary character, any abbreviation, or any other sign or term whatsoever.

Furthermore, the Committee, while insisting strenuously upon the principle of an inflexible law of priority, has nevertheless sedulously attempted to guard, as far as may be possible, against needless or undue rejection of names in current usage in favor of obscure earlier ones which rest upon descriptions so vague or imperfect that their identification can be made out only by the process of exclusion, — by presuming that they can mean nothing else. The safeguard which the Committee proposes for these cases is, that a name to be valid must be identifiable by the means furnished by the original describer, or at least by such means taken in connection with sources of information contemporaneous with the original description. That is to say, the name of a species or other group, to be valid, must have been identifiable since the time it was proposed, and not have become so subsequently by the advance of the science.

The Committee has also attempted to define as clearly as possible the basis upon which generic, specific, and subspecific names may reasonably and properly rest.

While the Committee feels free to advise and recommend in respect to future practices and principles in systematic nomenclature, it is obvious that no suggestions or rules should be of a retroactive character, or partake of the nature of *ex post facto* laws. Yet, so multifarious and often conflicting have been the usages of publishing naturalists on many points of nomenclature, that in many cases no rule can be adopted which will not be to some extent retroactive. Thus, in seeking to attain a basis of uniformity and stability, it is always necessary to go back to the original forms of names, and consistently adhere to them, in entire disregard of the verbal innovations of purists or grammarians, who, aiming at classical correctness in names, have too often brought about instability and confusion. It seems out of the question to relax the law of priority, let the immediate inconvenient results of adherence to that law be what they may.

And, in respect of any temporary inconvenience, or of any seeming confusion which may be the immediate consequence of its action, the Committee feels able to give assurance that these are far lesser evils than some of those which it hopes to do away with. The case of an unstable and far from uniform system of nomenclature no more shows the need of improvement, than admits of those changes which are necessary; and though the evils inseparable from all states of transition may be obvious, they are themselves no less transitory, while the good results of the strict and consistent application of sound principles of nomenclature are likely long to endure.

The following series of twenty-one propositions and affirmations, abstracted and condensed from the minutes of the meetings of the Committee, will show at a glance the principal results reached. They are simply the gist of some of the resolutions passed by the Committee in session, the points involved being formally presented beyond, under 'Principles, Canons, and Recommendations.'

(*a*) The Stricklandian Code, B. A. Rules, 1842, 1865, the basis of zoölogical nomenclature: the whole subject to be considered therefrom.

(*b*) Trinomial nomenclature to be provided for.

(*c*) Botanical nomenclature not to be considered; use of names in Botany not to invalidate their subsequent use in Zoölogy.

(*d*) Linn. Syst. Nat., ed. X., 1758, to be the starting-point of zoölogical nomenclature, and of the operation of the law of priority, for *all* names.

(*e*) The law of priority to be inflexible; conditions of its proper application; its application to names of groups higher than genera.

(*f*) The maxim, 'Once a synonym always a synonym,' to be affirmed and extended to species and subspecies.

(*g*) Names to be Latin, or in Latin form.

(*h*) Names to be adopted on certain principles, without regard to persons.

(*i*) Absolute identification required to displace a modern current name by an older obscure one.

(*j*) Basis of a specific or subspecific name to be, either (1) an identifiable published description, or (2) a recognizable published plate or figure, or (3) the original named type specimen; diagnosis to be made upon the status of the name at the time it was proposed; identification of type specimens, to be valid, must be absolute.

(*k*) Basis of a generic or subgeneric name to be, either (1) a designated recognizably described species, or (2) a designated recognizable plate or figure, or (3) a published diagnosis; such names tenable upon (1) or (2), even if wanting (3).

(*l*) Type of a genus to be determined by the 'process of elimination,' if no type is originally mentioned.

(*m*) Generic names not to be invalidated by use of same name for a higher group (*e. g., Accipiter* tenable as a genus, though there is an order *Accipitres*). The same with specific names (*e. g., Pica pica*).

(*n*) Names differing like *Pica* and *Picus* both tenable; differing only like *Spermophila* and *Spermophilus*, the later one untenable.

(*o*) The maxim, "A name is only a name, and has no necessary meaning," affirmed; barbarous, hybrid, meaningless, or descriptively inappropriate names tenable.

(*p*) Original orthography of names to be preserved, unless a typographical error is evident.

(*q*) Transliteration of names, and terminations of personal names, to be provided for.

(*r*) Names raised in rank (as of a subspecies raised to a species, or of a subgenus raised to a genus) to be tenable in the new position.

(*s*) The authority for a name to be that of the original namer.

(*t*) When a generic name sinks into synonymy, any current family or subfamily name derived from such generic name to become untenable (*e. g.*, 'Sylvicolidæ' untenable, since *Sylvicola* is preoccupied).

(*u*) Rule thirteenth of the Stricklandian Code (rendering a specific name untenable when used for a genus) to be ignored.

With reference to the plan and form of the proposed American Ornithologists' Union 'List of North American Birds,' it was proposed and unanimously agreed:—

1. That the term 'North American,' as applied to the proposed List of Birds, be held to include the continent of North America north of the present United States and Mexican boundary, and Greenland; and the peninsula of Lower California, with the islands naturally belonging thereto.

2. That species be numbered consecutively, and that subspecies be enumerated by affixing the letters *a*, *b*, *c*, etc. to the number borne by their respective species; provided, that any subspecies of a species not included in the North American Fauna shall be separately numbered as if a species.

3. That stragglers or accidental visitors, not regarded as components of the North American Fauna, be distinguished by having their respective numbers in brackets.

4. That any subsequent additions to the list be interpolated in systematic order, and bear the number of the species immediately preceding, with the addition of a figure (1, 2, etc., as the case may require), separated from the original number by a period or decimal point, thus giving the interpolated number a decimal form (*e. g.*, 243.1, etc.), in order that the original numbers may be permanent.

5. That species or subspecies for any reason included in the List, in regard to the specific or subspecific validity of which any reasonable doubt exists, shall have their respective numbers followed by a note of interrogation.

6. That Giraud's at present unconfirmed species of Texan birds be included in the List on Giraud's authority.

7. That species and subspecies the zoölogical status of which cannot be satisfactorily determined, like, *e. g.*, *Regulus cuvieri* and *Spiza townsendi* of Audubon, be referred to a hypothetical list, in each case with a brief statement of the reasons for such allocation.

8. That a list of the fossil species of North American birds be added as an Appendix to the List proper.

9. That the names of subgeneric and supergeneric groups of North American birds be included in the List in systematic order, to the end that the List may represent a classification as well as a nomenclature of the birds.

10. That references be given to the original description of the species, and to the publication where the name as adopted in the List was first used; that the number borne by each species and subspecies in the Lists of Baird, 1858, of Coues, 1873, of Ridgway, 1880, and of Coues, 1882, be bracketed in chronological order after the synonymatic references.

11. That a summary statement of the habitat of each species and subspecies, with special reference to its North American range, be included in the List.

12. That the name of each bird shall consist of its generic without its subgeneric name, and of its specific with its subspecific name, if it have one, without the intervention of any other term.

13. That specific be typographically distinguished from subspecific names by the use of a smaller type for the latter.

14. That every technical name be followed by a vernacular name, selected with due regard to its desirability.

15. That the name of each species and subspecies be followed by the name of the original describer of the same, to be enclosed in parentheses when it is not also the authority for the name adopted.

16. That all specific and subspecific names shall begin with a lower-case letter.

17. That the sequence in classification followed in previous Lists be reversed, the List to begin with the lowest or most generalized type, and end with the highest or most specialized.

Although it is deemed by the Committee neither necessary nor desirable to embody in its Report the minutes of its meetings, a few further extracts may be presented in the present connection.

The subject of the formal introduction of trinomials into the binomial system — a matter upon which the Committee lays great stress — was brought up at the fourth meeting, December 15, 1883, in the form of the following resolution, which was unanimously adopted : —

"Whereas, the progress of Ornithology of late years has so greatly increased and perfected our knowledge of the exact morphological relations between allied forms of birds, and has so profoundly modified the conception of species held when the so-called binomial or Linnæan system of nomenclature was formulated and applied, that this system is no longer adequate to handle known facts, or a clear reflection of the modern conception of species based upon such facts, it becomes obviously proper and necessary to modify the system in so far as may be required to meet the new aspect of the case: it is therefore

"*Resolved*, That a trinomial system of nomenclature be adopted upon the basis and in the spirit of the binomial system ; such system allowing and providing for the use of names consisting of three terms — generic, specific, and subspecific — for those forms which, as a matter of fact, are known to intergrade in physical characters ; two terms — generic and specific — being employed as heretofore for those forms which are not known to so intergrade."

At the seventh meeting, December 19, 1883, the following resolution was unanimously adopted : —

"That the Committee resolve itself into two subcommittees, to one of which is referred the whole subject of specific and subspecific determinations of North American birds, and to the other the subject of formulating and codifying the nomenclatural results reached by the whole Committee ; the former subcommittee to consist of Mr. R. Ridgway, Mr. Wm. Brewster, and Mr. H. W. Henshaw ; the latter, to consist of Mr. J. A. Allen and Dr. E. Coues ; and that Dr. L. Stejneger be requested to co-operate with the former subcommittee in determining questions of synonymy."

INTRODUCTION.

At the eighth meeting (second session) of the Committee, held March 8, 1884, the subcommittee appointed to "formulate and codify the nomenclatural results reached by the Committee" presented its report; whereupon the following resolution prevailed: —

"That the report of the subcommittee on formulation and codification of nomenclatural rules be accepted and affirmed; and that the subcommittee be instructed to prepare a fair manuscript copy of the Code, to embody the Nomenclatural Rules which the Committee has adopted and proposes to recommend to the Union for adoption; taking the Stricklandian Code as the basis of departure, disencumbering that Code of whatever may be deemed superfluous or objectionable, and engrafting upon it the Rules and Recommendations which the whole Committee has approved."

II.

PRINCIPLES, CANONS, AND RECOMMENDATIONS.

"In venturing to propose these rules for the guidance of all classes of zoologists in all countries, we disclaim any intention of dictating to men of science the course which they may see fit to pursue. It must of course be always at the option of authors to adhere to or depart from these principles, but we offer them to the candid consideration of zoologists in the hope that they may lead to sufficient uniformity of method in future to rescue science from becoming a mere chaos of words." — H. E. STRICKLAND, 1842.

A. General Principles.

PRINCIPLE I. Zoölogical nomenclature is a means, not an end, of zoölogical science.

REMARKS. — It is to be deplored that it is apparently necessary to raise what is merely a trite truism to the dignity of a principle of nomenclature. But it seems proper to protest in this way against any misconception that the science of Zoölogy consists in the art of naming objects in that branch of science, and also against every wanton, capricious, arbitrary, or otherwise needless and undesirable change of names which have acquired current usage and definite signification in Zoölogy. It is undeniable that a "mere shuffling of names" (A. AGASSIZ) is the chief outcome of much study and much writing which is mistaken for scientific research and the advancement of science.

On this score and in the same tenor may be quoted several expressions from De Candolle,[1] relating to some of the general principles of nomenclature considered as a means to an end.

"Natural History cannot progress, nor can the study of its various branches be carried on and properly correlated, without a regular system in nomenclature which shall be recognized and employed by the majority of naturalists of all countries."

"The rules for nomenclature must be impartial, and founded on motives sufficiently clear and weighty to promote their general comprehension and acceptance."

[1] Quoted from Dall (Rep., p. 23), not from the original.

"The essential principles in everything which relates to nomenclature are, (1) the attainment of *fixity* in the designations for organized beings; (2) the avoidance of names or methods of applying names calculated to result in errors or to throw science into confusion; and lastly, (3) to avoid the unnecessary creation of names."

"No usage conflicting with the rules and liable to introduce error or confusion can be maintained. When no grave objections of this nature are liable to be raised, it may happen that an ancient usage may be conserved without opposition, but all should carefully guard against the imitation or extension of such practices. In the absence of a rule, or if the application of the rules be doubtful, an established usage may be taken as a proper guide."

PRINICIPLE II. Zoölogical nomenclature is the scientific language of systematic Zoölogy, and vernacular names are not properly within its scope.

REMARKS. — "In proposing a measure for the establishment of a permanent and universal zoological nomenclature, it must be premised that we refer solely to the Latin or systematic language of zoology. We have nothing to do with vernacular appellations. One great cause of the neglect and corruption which prevails in the scientific nomenclature of zoology has been the frequent and often exclusive use of vernacular names in lieu of the Latin binomial designations, which form the only legitimate language of systematic zoology. Let us then endeavor to render perfect the Latin or Linnæan method of nomenclature, which, being far removed from the scope of national vanities and modern antipathies, holds out the only hope of introducing into zoology that grand desideratum, an universal language." (*B. A. Code*, 1842.)

PRINCIPLE III. Scientific names are of the Latin form or language, and when derived from another language are to be Latinized in form; but names which have been used in zoölogical nomenclature as if they were Latin words cannot be changed or rejected, if they are otherwise unobjectionable.

REMARKS. — The above principle bears upon a large number of names, not only specific but also generic, and seems to require extended comment, especially as there is no uniformity of practice among zoölogists with regard to this class of names, which includes barbarisms of every kind.

"A pernicious practice, of very old date, exists, of applying to species names not only of barbarous origin, but without Latinization, and totally destitute of euphony. These are chiefly the local appellation of some savage tribe for the organism designated. Thus, we have *Hyperoodon butzkopf* Gray,

Balæna tschiekagliuk and *B. agamachtschik* Pallas, etc." (DALL, *Report*, p. 54.) Much as the infliction of such names upon science is to be regretted for the past, and sedulously as it should be avoided in the future, there appears to be no way by which such barbarisms can be changed or rejected, consistently with the rule requiring rigid adherence to the original orthography of names. Having been introduced in the science *as if they were* Latin words, that is to say, as a part of a Latin binomial designation, they are best treated simply as if misspelled or wrongly constructed : which fault, in the judgment of the Committee, does not require rejection, or even emendation.

The case is otherwise with a class of names of which *patelle viride*, cited by Dall, after Bourguignat, may be taken in illustration. This is not, nor is it intended to be, a Latin binomial introduced in zoölogical nomenclature at all, having no more standing than 'green limpet' could have in the language of science. It is simply a French vernacular name, however similar in sound and shape to *Patella viridis*, and is not properly within the scope of zoölogical nomenclature.

The examples of *Hyperoodon butzkopf* and *patelle viride* represent two large classes of cases of which they respectively furnish a criterion. Names of the former class are not to be modified or rejected ; names of the latter class form no part of zoölogical nomenclature, and are not to be considered at all. (See DALL, *Report*, p. 54.)

PRINCIPLE IV. Zoölogical nomenclature has no necessary connection with botanical nomenclature, and names given in one of these two systems cannot conflict with those of the other system ; use of a name in Botany, therefore, does not prevent its subsequent use in Zoölogy.

REMARKS — This has relation to one of the most mooted points among naturalists, and is intended to determine the question whether or not the use of a name in Botany shall prevent its subsequent employ in Zoölogy. The duplication of names in the two great branches of biology, though highly undesirable and to be sedulously avoided, is no sufficient reason for the rejection of a name which has once been introduced in either system of nomenclature. In this particular, Zoölogy may ignore botanical names without ill result. While it is quite true that "the principles and forms of nomenclature should be as similar as possible in Botany and Zoölogy" (DE CANDOLLE), it is no less true that "the manner in which Botany and the different branches of Zoölogy have reached their present state, being far from uniform, and the nature of the organisms treated of being dissimilar, an absolute identity in the application of nomenclature is impracticable, even if it were wholly desirable," though "the fundamental principles and the end to be attained are the same in both branches of study." (DALL, *Rep.*, p. 23.)

In the original Stricklandian Code the 'Rules' were restricted in their application to Zoölogy, and this restricted scope of the 'Rules' was explicitly reaffirmed in the 'Recommendations' prefixed to the Revised Code by the Bath Committee of the British Association in 1865, as follows : "I. That Botany should not be introduced in the Stricklandian Code and Recommendations."

The A. O. U. Committee reiterates this decision, and constructs its canons without reference to Botany, conformably with the usage of British zoölogists, though the rules adopted both by the Société Zoologique de France, in 1881, and the Congrès Géologique International, in 1882, are intended to apply alike to Zoölogy and Botany. Dall's essay also discusses both together.

Since botanists do not reject names because previously used in Zoölogy and indeed pay little regard to the duplication of names in the two kingdoms,[1] there is little reason for the rejection by zoölogists of names used in Zoölogy on account of their prior use in Botany. While there has been heretofore a lack of uniformity in the action of zoölogists in this matter, and an increasing tendency to ignore the B. A. rule requiring the rejection of names in Zoölogy preoccupied in Botany, — and as to make the rejection or adoption uniform would in either case require not far from an equal number of changes (in neither case many), — the adoption of this principle is urged without hesitation.

PRINCIPLE V. A name is only a name, having no meaning until invested with one by being used as the handle of a fact; and the meaning of a name so used, in zoölogical nomenclature, does not depend upon its signification in any other connection.

REMARKS. — The bearing of this principle upon the much desired *fixity* of names in Zoölogy, and its tendency to check those confusing changes which are too often made upon philological grounds, or for reasons of ease, elegance, or what not, may be best illustrated by the following quotation : —

"It being admitted on all hands that words are only the conventional signs of ideas, it is evident that language can only attain its end effectually by being permanently established and generally recognized. This consideration ought, it would seem, to have checked those who are continually attempting to subvert the established language of zoology by substituting terms of their own coinage. But, forgetting the true nature of language, they persist in confounding the *name* of a species or [other] group with its *definition;* and because the former often falls short of the fulness of expression found in the

---

[1] De Candolle advises botanists to "avoid making choice of names used in Zoölogy."

latter, they cancel it without hesitation, and introduce some new term which appears to them more characteristic, but which is utterly unknown to the science, and is therefore devoid of any authority.[1] If these persons were to object to such names of men as *Long, Little, Armstrong, Golightly*, etc., in cases where they fail to apply to the individuals who bear them, or should complain of the names *Gough, Lawrence*, or *Harvey*, that they were devoid of meaning, and should hence propose to change them for more characteristic appellations, they would not act more unphilosophically or inconsiderately than they do in the case before us; for, in truth, it matters not in the least by what conventional sound we agree to designate an individual object, provided the sign to be employed be stamped with such an authority as will suffice to make it pass current." (*B. A. Code*, 1842.)

These words, which in the original lead up to the consideration of the 'law of priority,' seem equally sound and pertinent in connection with the above principle of wider scope.

B. Canons of Zoölogical Nomenclature.

§ 1. *Of the Kinds of Names in Zoölogy.*

CANON I. Zoölogical nomenclature includes two kinds of names: (1) Common names definitive of the relative rank of groups in the scale of classification; (2) Proper names appellative of each group of organisms.

REMARKS. — *E. g., Familia Falconidæ.* Here the name *Familia* is definitive of the relative rank of *Falconidæ* in the scale of classification; and *Falconidæ* is appellative of that particular group of organisms, *i. e.*, of the family.

The vast majority of names in Zoölogy are of the second kind, or proper names, and it is to the correct use of these that nearly all rules and regulations of nomenclature solely apply. Common names are very few, being merely those of the score or more of taxonomic groups, successively subordinated in a certain manner, into which zoölogists have divided animal organisms from 'kingdom' to 'individual.' Proper names, on the other hand, number several hundred thousand.

The common names most firmly established among English-speaking zoölogists are the following: *Regnum, Classis, Ordo, Familia, Genus, Species, Varietas*, in regular descent from the most general or comprehensive to the

---

[1] "Linnæus says on this subject: 'Abstinendum ab hac innovatione quæ nunquam cessaret, quin indies aptiora detegerentur ad infinitum.'"

most particular or restricted. Between all these, however, intermediate groups are commonly recognized, and distinguished by the prefix *sub-* or *super-*; as, *sub-ordo*, *super-familia*. Among these common names those in most general employ are *Subordo*, *Subfamilia*, *Subgenus*, and *Subspecies*. Several other common names are in use, but to a limited extent, and without that definiteness of signification which attaches to the rest, since they are used for groups of very different relative rank by different authors, while the taxonomic subordination of the others is practically fixed. Such common names are *Phylum*, *Tribus*, *Legio*, *Cohors*, *Phalanx*, *Sectio*, etc.

"The above terms are more or less generally accepted; the relative values being more fully and generally recognized in Botany than in Zoölogy. In the literature of the latter branch some of the terms above mentioned are rarely found, though by no means unnecessary for careful discrimination. The term *Tribe* [and also *Cohort*, *Section*, etc.] in Zoölogy has been used with several different values. In this, as in other respects, the inchoate condition of zoölogical nomenclature as compared with that of Botany is clearly apparent." (DALL, *Rep.*, p. 24.)

Considering that fixity and precision are as desirable here as elsewhere in nomenclature, the following scale of common names is recommended as adequate to all practical requirements of even a refined system of classification : —

1. *Regnum:* Kingdom.
2. *Subregnum:* Subkingdom.
3. *Classis:* Class.
4. *Subclassis:* Subclass.
5. *Superordo:* Superorder.
6. *Ordo:* Order.
7. *Subordo:* Suborder.
8. *Superfamilia:* Superfamily.
9. *Familia:* Family.
10. *Subfamilia:* Subfamily.
11. *Genus:* Genus.
12. *Subgenus:* Subgenus.
13. *Species:* Species.
14. *Subspecies:* Subspecies.
15. *Varietas:* Variety.
16. *Animal:* Individual.

CANON II. All members of any one group in Zoölogy are included in and compose the next higher group, and no inversion of the relative rank of groups is admissible.

REMARKS. — Thus, all individuals belong to a species, all species to a genus, all genera to a family, all families to an order, all orders to a class; and so also of the other (intermediate) groups given under head of the preceding Canon.

"The definition of each of these terms or [common] names of groups varies, up to a certain point, according to the state of science or the views of the individual writer using them, but their relative rank, sanctioned by usage, cannot be inverted. No classification containing inversions, such as a division of a genus into families, or of a species into genera, can be admitted." (DE CANDOLLE, as rendered by DALL, *Rep.*, p. 25.)

CANON III. Proper names of groups above genera consist preferably of a single word, taken as a noun and in the nominative plural.

REMARKS. — It seems to the Committee highly desirable that the proper names of groups of whatever grade, down to (but not including) species, should be expressed in one word, to be considered as a nominative plural noun, standing alone, though grammatically, in fact, it may be an adjective or an adjectival form. This would do away with any change of termination according to gender, depending upon implied agreement with some unexpressed noun, as *Aves*, *Pisces*, etc., and bring all names of groups higher than genera into one grammatical category with single-word generic names, the latter being always in the singular, all the former plural.

The practice prevails to some extent of naming groups higher than genera in two or even three words; as, *Passeres acromyodi*, *Oscines scutelliplantares*. This usage is chiefly confined to intermediate groups, as superfamilies or suborders, or those groups of no fixed rank called 'tribes,' or 'sections.' While it is not highly objectionable, it is preferably avoided, a single nominative plural noun being considered adequate to meet all the reasonable requirements of such cases.

CANON IV. Proper names of families uniformly consist of a single word ending in *-idæ*; of subfamilies, of a single word ending in *-inæ*; of other groups, of one word or more of no fixed termination.

REMARKS. — The above Canon sets forth the now wellnigh universal usage of zoölogists as recommended in the following terms by the B. A. Code, 1842: —

"B. It is recommended that the assemblages of genera termed *families* should be uniformly named by adding the termination *-idæ* to the earliest known or most typically characterized genus in them; and that their subdivisions, termed *subfamilies*, should be similarly constructed, with the termination *-inæ*.

"These words are formed by changing the last syllable of the genitive case into *-idæ* or *-inæ*; as, *Strix*, *Strigis*, *Strigidæ*; *Buceros*, *Bucerotis*, *Bucerotidæ*, not *Strixidæ*, *Buceridæ*."

It is a frequent misconception, arising perhaps from some confounding of *-idæ* with *-oidæ*, — a mistake which at least one of the great dictionaries of the English language makes throughout, — that *-idæ* is derived from the Greek εἶδος, signifying likeness; but, like *-inæ*, *-idæ* is simply an adjectival patronymic termination.

The practical convenience of having a fixed termination of the family and subfamily name respectively is great and obvious. It were much to be desired, but it is idle to hope, and futile to attempt, the introduction of similar uniformity in the terminations of the names of other groups. Evidence of the desirableness and of the tendency are witnessed, for example, in those Cuvierian names of birds which end uniformly in *-rostres;* and of those Huxleian divisions terminating in *-morphæ*. Several zoölogists have used *-oidæ, -eæ*, etc., to characterize groups of a particular grade. But such usage is far from uniform or universal ; the reverse is current; and names of groups (excepting of families and subfamilies) ending indiscriminately are too thoroughly ingrained in the science to be eradicated without violence to the cardinal rules of nomenclature. It must suffice that names of supergeneric groups be held for nouns in the nominative plural.

CANON V. Proper names of families and subfamilies take the tenable name of some genus, preferably the leading one, which these groups respectively contain, with change of termination into *-idæ* or *-inæ*. When a generic name becomes a synonym, a current family or subfamily name based upon such generic name becomes untenable.

REMARKS. — A practice has prevailed, to some limited extent, of coining names of families and subfamilies without reference to any generic name. This is reprehensible ; and equally so is the practice of retaining for such groups a name derived from that of a genus which belongs to another family or subfamily, or which for any reason has lapsed into a synonym, or been found otherwise untenable : the genus *Sylvicola* being untenable in Ornithology, no group of birds can be named Sylvicolidæ or Sylvicolinæ.

CANON VI. Proper names of genera and subgenera are single words, preferably nouns, or to be taken as such, in the nominative singular, of no definite construction and no necessary signification.

REMARKS. — All that relates to the grammatical or philological proprieties, to elegance, euphony, appropriateness or the reverse, is not necessarily pertinent to zoölogical nomenclature. A generic name is not necessarily of classical origin, or even in Latin form, if only it be used as if it were a Latin word, conformably with rules of nomenclature.[1] (This results from Principle V.)

---

[1] But this concession must not be construed as giving admission to vernacular names formed from a classical root, like many generic names introduced by the Cuviers, Lesson, and notably other French writers of the early part of the present century. Such names have in many cases been later adopted into the science under a proper classical form, and should take date only from this later introduction.

"These names may be taken from any source whatever, or may be framed in an absolutely arbitrary manner. . . . .

"De Candolle justly remarks that it is with generic names as with our patronymics. Many surnames are inconvenient, or even absurd, from bearing an adjectival form, from having an inapplicable meaning, on account of being difficult to pronounce, or for some other reason. But, since they actually exist, why should they be changed? It is not the end of Science to make names: she avails herself of them to distinguish things. If a name is properly formed, and different from other names, the essential points are attained.

"Generic names may be taken from certain characters or appearances of the group, from the chief habitat, names of persons, common names, and even arbitrary combinations of letters. It is enough if they are properly constructed, and do not lead to confusion or error." (DALL, *Rep.*, p. 27.)

In heartily indorsing the tenor of the above extracts, we would nevertheless understand the expressions 'properly formed' and 'properly constructed' to mean rather 'contextually correct'; *i. e.*, the name to be a 'generic' word within the common meaning of that term in the binomial nomenclature, to be put in the place of a generic term, and to be used as a Latin word, whatever its actual 'form' or 'construction.'

CANON VII. Proper names of all groups in Zoölogy, from kingdom to subgenus, both inclusive, are written and printed with a capital initial letter.

REMARK. — The universal usage, and one of the ear-marks by which a professional zoölogist may be known from a literary person who uses zoölogical nomenclature occasionally.

CANON VIII. Proper names of species, and of subspecies or 'varieties,' are single words, simple or compound, preferably adjectival or genitival, or taken as such, when practicable agreeing in gender and number with any generic name with which they are associated in binomial or trinomial nomenclature, and written with a small initial letter.

REMARKS. — There is no inherent zoölogical difference between a 'generic' and a 'specific' name, — the *nomen genericum* and the *nomen triviale* of earlier zoölogists. Both alike designate a 'group' in Zoölogy, — the one a group of greater, the other a group of lesser classificatory value. Some necessary distinction, which has been misconceived to exist between these two names, is simply a fortuitous matter of the technique of nomenclature, apparently arising from the circumstance that the generic and the specific names form the contrasted though connected terms of a binomial designation. Recognition of the scientific fact, that a 'species,' so called, is not a fixed and special creation, as long supposed, but simply a group of the same intrinsic character as that called a 'genus,' though usually less extensive, and always of a lower taxonomic rank, has done more than any other single thing to advance the science of Zoölogy; for the whole theory of evolution turns, as it were, upon this point.

It is therefore obvious that nearly all that has been affirmed of generic names may be here reaffirmed of specific names. Points requiring further comment are comparatively trivial, and purely technical.

Specific and subspecific names (here conveniently treated together, as were generic and subgeneric names) differ from the names of higher groups chiefly in the fact, that as a rule they are adjectives, not nouns, or at least of such adjectival character as the genitive case of a noun implies. But even to this distinction the exceptions are many. Specific names, like Latin adjectives, unlike generic ones, are liable to change of termination to agree in gender with the generic names with which they may be coupled. Again, like Latin nouns, they are declinable, and may take a genitive case, singular or plural (but the plural is comparatively rare: *e. g., Icterus parisorum, Megalæma marshallorum, Passerculus sanctorum*). In many cases, no grammatical agreement with the associated generic name is possible. This occurs when the word is barbarous and not Latinized, and also when it is a Latin or Latinized noun in the nominative case.

Specific names have the peculiarity that, though they are always single words, in effect, they may be so loosely compounded as to take a hyphen, and therefore seem like two words. *E. g., Archibuteo sancti-johannis, Caloptenus femur-rubrum*. Among strict binomialists, in some departments of Zoölogy, especially Entomology, the propriety of the actual appearance of three words in a binomial designation has been questioned. "The usage of a third word, however, connected with the second by a hyphen, as is common and desirable in the case of gall-insects, *e. g., Cynips quercus-palustris*, is not to be considered an infraction of this [the binomial] rule." (C. V. RILEY.) Professor Riley says further, in the same connection: "In some cases, as in the names of gall-insects, it has become the custom to indicate the plant upon which the gall occurs, by combining the name of the plant with the specific name of the insect. Such indication is desirable and useful; . . . . and we are of opinion that the combined specific name, whether the botanical term be abbreviated or in full, should be looked upon as one [loosely compounded] word."

There being no necessary intrinsic difference between a generic and a specific name, zoölogists have sought to make an artificial distinction by using a small or 'lower-case' letter for the initial of every specific name, the capitals being confined to generic and higher names. The old practice was different, substantive specific names, especially those derived from names of persons or places, being written with a capital. The practice still prevails in

Botany, but zoölogists are about equally divided on this score. The case of "specific names to be written with a small initial," was formulated in the original B. A. Code as follows: —

"A convenient *memoria technica* may be effected by adopting our next proposition. It has been usual, when the titles of species are derived from proper names, to write them with a capital letter, and hence when the specific name is used alone it is liable to be accidentally mistaken for the name of a genus. But if the title of a *species* were *invariably* written with a *small* initial, and those of genera with a *capital*, the eye would at once distinguish the rank of the group referred to, and a possible source of error would be avoided. It should further be remembered that all species are equal [?] and should therefore be written all alike. We suggest then, that

"§ C. Specific names should *always* be written with a small initial letter, even when derived from persons or places, and generic names should always be written with a capital." (*B. A. Code*, 1842.)

This suggestion appears to have been very generally adopted, by British zoölogists especially, and of later years by many of those of America. But the framers of the Revised Code, in 1865, cancelled it, in the following terms: —

"VI. The recommendation, 'Specific names to be written with a small initial.' The Committee propose that this recommendation should be omitted. It is not of great importance, and may be safely left to naturalists to deal with as they think fit." (*Recommendations of the Bath Committee, B. A.*, 1865. [§ C. and its preamble, of the Original B. A. Code, are accordingly omitted in the Revised B. A. Code.])

The code of the French Zoölogical Society, and that of the International Zoölogical Congress, each leaves the writer free to follow his own preference in this matter.

Your Committee agrees that it is a trivial matter, hardly to enter into a canon of nomenclature. But its preference is decidedly in favor of the uniform use of the lower case, and, feeling called upon to express its view, it has embodied it in the above Canon, without in the least insisting upon its importance.

CANON IX. Proper names do not attach to individual organisms, nor to groups of lower grade than subspecies; names which may be applied to hybrids, to monstrosities or other individual peculiarities, or to artificial varieties, such as domestic breeds of animals, having no status in zoölogical nomenclature.

REMARK. — Such organisms, having no natural permanent existence, need no recognition by name in a zoölogical system.

§ 2. *Of the Binomial System as a Phase of Zoölogical Nomenclature.*

Few naturalists, whether botanists or zoölogists, appear to have considered the binomial system of naming objects as aught else than the permanent heritage of science, the entire superstructure of which should be built with the binomial nomenclature as the corner-stone, and the whole language of which should conform to the requirements of an inflexible binomial system. From this position your Committee recedes with emphasis.

The Committee considers that the rigidity and inelasticity of that system, which has been followed for more than a century, unfits it for the adequate expression of modern conceptions in Zoölogy, and that therefore a strict adherence to it is a hindrance rather than a help to the progress of science. It believes that strict binomialism in nomenclature has had its day of greatest usefulness and necessary existence; and that at present it can only be allowed equal place in nomenclature by the side of that more flexible, elastic, and adequate system of trinomials to which the Committee hopes that your action upon its Report will give formal place among the Canons of nomenclature.

The proper place and office of binomials may be formulated in the following Canon.

CANON X. Binomial nomenclature consists in applying to every individual organism, and to the aggregate of such organisms not known now to intergrade in physical characters with other organisms, two names, one of which expresses the specific distinctness of the organism from all others, the other its superspecific indistinctness from, or generic identity with, certain other organisms, actual or implied; the former name being the specific, the latter the generic designation; the two together constituting the technical name of any specifically distinct organism.

REMARKS. — The Committee finds little or nothing to cite in illustration or amplification of this Canon. The binomial nomenclature having been considered indispensable and all-sufficient, — in short as a foregone conclusion, — it has received abounding indiscriminate praise, but little searching and discriminating criticism. Your Committee is far from venturing to do away with it at present. It has attempted to define it with more strictness than has perhaps been done before, and by so doing to limit its operation to those cases in which it may still be found useful. The system is, moreover, so well understood, that what might be further said here may be best brought into the discussion, beyond, of the starting-point of nomenclature and of the law of priority.

§ 3. *Of the Trinomial System as a Phase of Zoölogical Nomenclature.*

CANON XI. Trinomial nomenclature consists in applying to every individual organism, and to the aggregate of such organisms known now to intergrade in physical characters, three names, one of which expresses the subspecific distinctness of the organism from all other organisms, and the other two of which express respectively its specific indistinctness from, or generic identity with, certain other organisms; the first of these names being the subspecific, the second the specific, and the third the generic designation; the three, written consecutively, without the intervention of any other word, term, or sign, constituting the technical name of any subspecifically distinct organism.

REMARKS. — This Canon, the Committee knows, directly contravenes the letter of the B. A. Code, and also, it believes, all previous codes of nomenclatural rules; but it feels prepared to maintain that it is not antagonistic to the B. A. or any other code, being conceived strictly in the whole spirit and tenor of the binomial system, though contrary to its letter. It evidently amplifies, increases the effective force of, and lends a new precision to, the old system. It is also plainly but a step in the direction of brevity, convenience, and explicitness, from the common but awkward practice of separating the third term, in the names of subspecies or varieties, from the second or specific term by the interpolation of 'var.,' which in several codes is formally provided for by special rules. The practice of indicating subspecies, as distinguished from species, by trinomials, has already come into nearly universal use with American ornithologists and mammalogists, and is employed to some extent by other American zoölogists. The system appears also to have found much favor among British and other foreign ornithologists of high standing, some of whom have already employed it in their publications. It seems likely to supply a present want, and subserve, at least for a time, a very useful purpose.

Your Committee's reasons for adopting the system for the class of cases to which it is adapted have already been formally enunciated in this Report (p. 16), in an extract from the minutes of its meetings.

The rules for the practical handling of trinomials, being not different from those for the use of binomials, will be given with the latter, beyond, under the appropriate heading.

A prevalent misapprehension respecting the meaning and office of the trinomial system may be here corrected. Trinomials are not necessarily to be used for those slightly distinct and scarcely stable forms which zoölogists are in the habit of calling 'varieties'; still less for sports, hybrids, artificial breeds, and the like; nor indeed to signalize some grade or degree of difference which it may be desired to note by name, but which is not deemed worthy of a specific designation. The system proceeds upon a sound scientific principle, underlying one of the most important zoölogical problems of the day, — no less a problem than that of the variation of animals under physical conditions of environment, and thus of the origin of species itself. The system is also intimately connected with the whole subject of the geographical distribution of animals; it being found, as a matter of experience, that the trinomial system is particularly pertinent and applicable to those geographical 'subspecies,' 'races,' or 'varieties,' which have become recognizable as such through their modification according to latitude, longitude, elevation, temperature, humidity, and other climatic conditions. Such local forms are often extremely different from one another; so different, in fact, that, were they not known to blend on the confines of their respective areas, they would commonly be rated as distinct species. This large and peculiarly interesting class of cases seems not to have hitherto been adequately provided for in the stringency of binomial nomenclature.

It is obvious, therefore, that the kind or quality, not the degree or quantity, of difference of one organism from another determines its fitness to be named trinomially rather than binomially. A difference, however little, that is reasonably constant, and therefore 'specific' in a proper sense, may be fully signalized by the binomial method. Another difference, however great in its extreme manifestation, that is found to lessen and disappear when specimens from large geographical areas, or from contiguous faunal regions, are compared, is therefore not 'specific,' and therefore is to be provided for by some other method than that which formally recognizes 'species' as the ultimate factors in zoölogical classification. In a word, *intergradation* is the touchstone of trinomialism.

It is also obvious, that, the larger the series of specimens handled, the more likely is intergradation between forms supposed to be distinct to be established, if it exists. This is perhaps one reason why trinomialism has been so tardy in entering nomenclature. For until the animals of large areas become well known, in all their phases, through extensive suites of specimens, neither the necessity of trinomialism, nor the possibility of putting it to the proper test, is apparent. It is gratifying evidence, therefore, of the progress of Ornithology, and of the position attained by that branch of science in America, that the members of an American Ornithological Association have it in their power first formally to enunciate the principles of the new method, the practicability of which they have already demonstrated to their fellow workers in Zoölogy.

§ 4. *Of the Beginning of Zoölogical Nomenclature proper, and of the Operation of the Law of Priority.*

CANON XII. The Law of Priority begins to be operative at the beginning of zoölogical nomenclature.

REMARK. — This Canon will be disputed by no one who observes the law of priority as a 'fundamental' maxim. The date to be assigned is quite another matter, on which great difference of opinion prevails.

CANON XIII. Zoölogical nomenclature begins at 1758, the date of the Xth edition of the 'Systema Naturæ' of Linnæus.

REMARKS. — With regard to this Canon, the utmost diversity of opinion has prevailed among botanists as well as zoölogists, and the Committee desires it to be subjected to searching criticism. It will first offer a brief historical *résumé*, mainly derived from Dall (*Rep.*, pp. 41-44) and other sources, covering the ground of Botany as well as Zoölogy.

Nomenclatural rules, foreshadowed by Linnæus in his 'Fundamenta Entomologica,' 1736, were first definitively proposed in the 'Philosophia Botanica,' 1751. These rules, however, related almost exclusively to the generic name. In 1745 he first employed for a few plants a specific name (*nomen triviale*), consisting of one word, in contradistinction from the polynomial description which had been as a rule the *nomen specificum* of naturalists. That which now seems the most happy and important of the Linnæan ideas, the restriction of the specific name as now understood, appears to have long been only a secondary matter with him, as he hardly mentions the *nomen triviale* in his works up to 1765. In 1753, in the 'Incrementa Botanices,' while dwelling upon his own reforms, he does not allude to binomial nomenclature. In the 'Systema Naturæ,' ed. x., 1758, the binomial system is for the first time consistently applied to all classes of organisms (though he had partially adopted it in 1745); whence many naturalists have regarded the tenth edition as the most natural starting-point. The system being of slow and intermittent growth, even with its originator, an arbitrary starting-point seems necessary. In the twelfth edition, 1766-68, numerous changes and reforms are instituted, and a number of his earlier names are arbitrarily changed. In fact, Linnæus never seems to have regarded specific names as subject to his rules.

It must be noted that an apparent rather than a real distinction has been observed, especially by botanists, between the citation of the authority for the names of genera, and that belonging to specific names. In the early part of the eighteenth century a few botanists, among whom Tournefort (Rei Herbar., 1749) may be especially mentioned, had progressed so far as to recognize and name, under the title of genera, groups answering essentially to the modern idea of genera. Linnæus himself adopted a number of these, using the names of Tournefort and others as authorities after the generic name adopted by himself. In this the great Swede has been almost unanimously followed by botanists, though such names take date only from the time of their adoption by Linnæus; very few authors, Bentham being the most prominent of them, having refused to cite any one excepting Linnæus as the authority for such genera.

Whether the course of the majority be considered judicious or not, it is now the accepted usage in Botany. As regards names in general, botanists appear to agree in adopting the date of the Linnæan 'Species Plantarum,' 1753, as the epoch from which their nomenclature must begin. This work contains the first instance of the consistent use of the *nomen triviale*, subsequent to the proposition of the rules in the 'Philosophia Botanica,' to which modern nomenclature is due.

Binomial designations cannot, of course, be reasonably claimed to antedate the period when binomial nomenclature, in a scientific sense, was invented; and, in spite of the solitary instance of 1745, no good reason appears for extending the range of scientific nomenclature to an earlier date than 1751.

(The above is quoted in substance from Dall.)

We have next to consider the action of the Manchester Committee of the British Association in 1842. The wording of the original B. A. Code is as follows: —

" As our subject matter is strictly confined to the *binomial system of nomenclature*, or that which indicates species by means of two Latin words, the one generic, the other spec'fic, and as this invaluable method originated solely with Linnæus, it is clear that, as far as species are concerned, we ought not to attempt to carry back the principle of priority beyond the date of the 12th edition of the 'Systema Naturæ.' Previous to that period, naturalists were wont to indicate species not by a *name* comprised in one word, but by a *definition* which occupied a sentence, the extreme verbosity of which method was productive of great inconvenience. It is true that one word sometimes sufficed for the definition of a species, but these rare cases were only binomial by accident and not by principle, and ought not therefore in any instance to supersede the binomial designations imposed by Linnæus.

" The same reasons apply also to generic names. Linnæus was the first to attach a definite value to genera, and to give them a systematic character by means of exact definitions; and therefore although the *names* used by previous authors may often be applied with propriety to modern genera, yet in such cases they acquire a new meaning, and should be quoted on the authority of the first person who used them in this secondary sense. It is true, that several old authors made occasional approaches to the Linnæan exactness of generic definition, but still these were but partial attempts; and it is certain that if in our rectification of the binomial nomenclature we once trace back our authorities into the obscurity which preceded the epoch of its foundation, we shall find no resting-place or fixed boundary for our researches. The nomenclature of Ray is chiefly derived from that of Gesner and Aldrovandus, and from these authors we might proceed backward to Ælian, Pliny, and Aristotle, till our zoological studies would be frittered away amid the refinements of classical learning."

So far the original B. A. Code, 1842; which, upon the foregoing considerations, recommended the following proposition: —

"§ 2. The binomial nomenclature having originated with Linnæus, the law of priority, in respect to that nomenclature, is not to extend to the writings of antecedent authors."

The exact date here implied is 1766; and this is explicitly reaffirmed by the Bath Committee in 1865,[1] who added to the foregoing § 2 the words, in brackets: "[and therefore the specific names published before 1766 cannot be used to the prejudice of names published since that date.]"

The action of both the B. A. Committees related, of course, only to Zoölogy. Commenting upon their action, Dall continues: —

"It is said that in the original draft of the report the number of the edition of the 'Systema Naturæ' was left blank, and afterwards filled up by the insertion of the 'twelfth.' This insertion renders the paragraph, otherwise judicious and accurate, glaringly incorrect. What motive resulted in the selection of the twelfth as opposed to the tenth, or of any special edition after

[1] "III. The Committee are of opinion, after much deliberation, that the XIIth edition of the 'Systema Naturæ' is that to which the limit of time should apply, viz. 1766. But as the works of Artedi and Scopoli have already been extensively used by ichthyologists and entomologists, it is recommended that names contained in or used from these authors should not be affected by this provision. This is particularly requisite as regards the generic names of Artedi afterwards used by Linnæus himself.

"In Mr. H. E. Strickland's original draft of these Rules and Recommendations the edition of Linnæus was left blank, and the XIIth was inserted by the Manchester Committee. This was done not as being the first in which the Binomial nomenclature had been used, as it commenced with the Xth, but as being the last and most complete edition of Linnæus's works, and containing many species the Xth did not. For these reasons it is now confirmed by this Committee, and also because these rules having been used and acted upon for twenty-three years, if the date were altered now, many changes of names would be required, and in consequence much confusion introduced." — *Recommendations of the Bath Committee, prefixed to the Revised Code,* 1865.

the adoption of the binomial form by Linnæus, has never been set forth in any satisfactory manner. If any special edition were chosen, the tenth has *prima facie* claims for first consideration. It is as clearly binomial as any, and it is as consistently so. . . . . To a considerable extent, in the works of the naturalists of Northern Europe, the tenth edition has been taken as the starting-point. . . . .

"It would appear that the Committee were 'plus saint que le Pape,' since they would reject names which Linnæus himself was ready to and did adopt. In this connection, Prof. Verrill (Am. Jour. Sci., July, 1869) has made some judicious remarks, calling attention to the works of Pallas, and Thorell has done the same for those of Clerck on the subject of spiders.

"An apologetic paragraph, following the remarks above quoted [see last foot-note] from the B. A. Committee report for 1865, inferentially admits the error of 1842, but goes on and reaffirms it on the ground that confusion would otherwise result.

"It is very doubtful if much confusion would be caused by leaving the question open, since half the naturalists of Europe and America have already adopted the tenth edition of their own motion, and the other half, or a large portion of them, may not unreasonably be believed to be only held back from joining the others by a desire to conform to the rules, even where injudiciously framed.

"In a large part of zoölogy the change would make no difference whatever, since the scientific study of such branches has begun since 1766."

Mr. Dall's own recommendation is as follows : —

"§ LVIII. The scientific study of different groups, having a value greater than or equal to that of a class (classis), having been begun at different epochs, and the inception of that study in each group respectively being usually due to some 'epoch-making' work, the students of each of the respective groups as above limited may properly unite in adopting the date of such work as the starting-point in nomenclature for the particular class to which it refers : *Provided*, — that (1), specific names shall in no case antedate the promulgation of the Linnæan rules (Philosophia Botanica, 1751); that (2), until formal notice by publication of the decision of such associated specialists (in such manner as may be by them determined upon) shall be decisively promulgated, the adoption of the epoch or starting-point recommended by the committee of the British Association in 1842, namely, the twelfth edition of the 'Systema Naturæ' of Linnæus (1766), shall be taken as the established epoch for all zoölogical nomenclature. Lastly, that (3), when the determination of the epoch for any particular group as above shall have been made, the decision shall be held to affect that group alone, the British Association date holding good for all other groups until the decision for each particular case shall have been made by the naturalists interested in it, upon its own merits."

(See also LeConte on this subject, Canad. Entom., November, 1874, pp. 203 *seq.*)

The principle embodied in the above recommendation of Dall is said by him to be "inferentially admitted to be valid by the B. A. Committee in their remarks on Artedi and Scopoli." Thorell, in his monograph of the Spiders, has adopted, so far as species are concerned, a similar plan, taking the binomial work of Clerck, 1757, on Swedish Spiders as his 'epoch-maker.' A. Agassiz, in Echinology, has brought the ancient names of Klein, Lang, Breyn, and others, into scientific nomenclature. G. R. Gray, in Ornithology, goes to the first edition of the 'Systema,' 1735, for genera, and to the tenth, 1758, for species, having many followers in different countries. In America, so far as Ornithology is concerned, the use of 1758 for the starting-point for species is practically universal, the tendency being to take genera from the same date also.

As to replies on this point to the circular issued by Mr. Dall, there are 18 for 1758, 17 for 1766, 1 for 1736, and two botanists for 1753; no answer, 7.

Your Committee, having duly weighed all the evidence before it, is compelled to dissent from the rulings of both the B. A. Committees, and from all others which do not make 1758 the starting-point for zoölogical nomenclature; and it is prepared to give reasons for the decision it has reached.

(1) The Xth edition is the one in which Linnæus first introduced the binomial nomenclature, and in which its use is uniform, consistent, and complete. (2) This date admits to recognition the works of Artedi, Scopoli, Clerck, Pallas, Brünnich, Brisson, in favor of the first-named two of whom, and of the last-named one, the B. A. Committees have had to make special exceptions,[1] thereby rendering the rule inconsistent in itself. (3) The Xth, rather than the XIIth, is already accepted as the starting-point by a majority of the naturalists of North America and of Northern Europe, with obviously a growing tendency to abandon the XIIth. The Commission de Nomenclature de la Société Zoologique de France (1881), and the Rules adopted by the Congrès Géologique International (1882), make no reference to any edition of the 'Systema Naturæ Linnæi,' nor do they place any limit of time for the beginning of the law of priority, but accept all generic and spe-

---

[1] For example, the paragraph immediately following § 2 in the original B. A. Code reads: "It should be here explained, that Brisson, who was a contemporary of Linnæus and acquainted with the 'Systema Naturæ,' defined and published certain genera of birds which are *additional* [and likewise prior] to those in the 12th edition of Linnæus's work, and which are therefore of perfectly good authority. But Brisson still adhered to the old mode of designating species by a sentence instead of a word, and therefore while we retain his defined genera we do not extend the same indulgence to the titles of his species, even when the latter are accidentally binomial in form." — *B. A. Code*, 1842.

For the exceptions made in 1865 by the B. A. Committee in favor of Artedi and Scopoli, see foot-note on p. 34.

cific names which conform to the rules of binomial nomenclature, even when they antedate the Xth edition of the 'Systema Naturæ.' They even advocate admission of Tournefort's generic names for Mollusks, published in a posthumous work edited by Gautieri in 1742; the genera of Lang, 1722; those of Klein, 1731 and 1734; and those of Breyn, 1732. (Botanists, though dating their departure in binomial nomenclature at 1737, the date of the first edition of Linnæus's 'Genera Plantarum,' adopt Tournefort's genera published in 1700.) The French Commission and that of the Geological Congress do not hesitate to say that the work of these authors is much better than that of Linnæus, who, through vanity or inability to appreciate so well the character of the work of his predecessors in Zoölogy as in Botany (he being pre-eminently a botanist rather than a zoölogist), systematically ignored his more scientific predecessors. (4) Besides admitting the works of other earlier binomialists which the adoption of the XIIth edition would exclude, the date 1758 clears up many questions of synonymy which arise from Linnæus's himself having arbitrarily changed in the XIIth edition many names introduced in the Xth, and in other cases used them in a different sense. (5) Furthermore, it is admitted that in the original Stricklandian draft the number of the edition was left blank, while the context clearly implies that the Xth was the one in mind; and there is nothing in § 2 of the original B. A. Rules which prohibits the adoption of the Xth. (6) Finally, the adoption of the Xth will necessitate very few changes in current names (in the younger departments of Zoölogy none), while it forms a rational and consistent starting-point towards which zoölogists at large are drifting. Therefore we have no hesitation in proposing as a substitute for § 2 of the B. A. Code the foregoing Canon, which, applied to § 2, would make it read as follows : —

" The starting-point of the binomial system of nomenclature in Zoölogy shall be the Xth (1758) edition of the 'Systema Naturæ' of Linnæus, and the law of priority in regard to specific (and generic) names is therefore not to extend to antecedent authors."

There is no question as to the fitness of this rule as regards specific names ; there may be in respect to generic names, since names were used for groups in what may be considered a generic sense by many pre-Linnæan writers, although the generic idea appears to have been essentially Linnæan. As a matter of convenience, it seems highly advisable to take the same starting-point for both generic and specific names, and to have the generic names adopted from pre-Linnæan authors date from their adoption by Linnæus or the first subsequent author who used them. Otherwise we endanger the stability in nomenclature which all so much desire to establish, by leaving open a mischievous loophole by means of which a well-established post-Linnæan generic name may be displaced in favor of a pre-Linnæan one. (See further on this point the second paragraph of the preamble to § 2 of the B. A. Code.) In limiting the action of the law of priority to the Xth edition of the 'Systema Naturæ,' the only objection met with is that of injustice to the pioneers in Zoölogy; but this lacks weight in view of remarks subsequently to be introduced (in reference to bibliography and synonymy), respecting due recognition of their labors. And here your Committee would emphatically urge that, the chief object of zoölogical nomenclature being to secure uniformity of practice in the bestowal and adoption of names, the rules to that end should be formed with reference to principles and without regard to personality, and that therefore the matter of justice or injustice is in this connection without pertinence.

The first rational application of the principles of classification in regard to the recognition of genera, as distinguished from species, is currently attributed to Tournefort in 1700, in his 'Institutiones Rei Herbariæ.' Later (1742), as already stated, he carried in a posthumous work the same practice into Conchology. Other pre-Linnæan zoölogists who recognized genera in a strictly scientific manner are Lang (1721), Klein (1731-1734), Breyn (1732),[1] Adanson (1757), and Clerck (1757). The latter was also a strict binomialist. There are possibly others, but in not fixing the starting-point at 1758 there is the disadvantage of having to admit the generic names of other pre-Linnæan writers the character of whose works gives them no proper scientific standing, as Link, Brown, Columa, etc.

Dr. Asa Gray makes the sensible proposition respecting Botany that " We have only to understand that genera adopted by Linnæus from Tournefort, etc., and so accredited, should continue to be thus cited ; that the date 1737 (Linn. Genera, ed. I.), is, indeed, the point of departure from which to reckon priority, yet that botanical genera began with Tournefort ; so that Tournefortian genera which are accepted date from the year 1700. That is the limit fixed by Linnæus, and it definitely excludes the herbalists and the ancients, whose writings may be consulted for historical elucidations, but not as authority for names."[2]

On the whole, it seems best that the origin of generic names in Zoölogy should date (as said above) only from 1758 ; that names adopted from earlier authors by Linnæus date only from their adoption by Linnæus ; and that in other cases pre-Linnæan names shall date from their first introduction by subsequent authors after 1758.

CANON XIV. The adoption of a 'statute of limitation,' in modification of the *lex prioritatis*, is impracticable and inadmissible.

[1] " Breynius as early as 1732 had, to some extent, adopted a binomial nomenclature, accurately (for his period) discriminated genera and species, many of which are readily recognized, but which had escaped the notice they deserved till a comparatively recent period."— A. AGASSIZ, *Revision of the Echini*, 1872, p. 12.

[2] Am. Jour. Sci., December, 1883, p. 423.

REMARKS. — In consequence of the frequent subversion of long-current and familiar names rendered necessary under the inflexible action of the *lex prioritatis*, through the discovery of some long-forgotten work in which occur names of earlier date than those currently in use for certain species, it has been repeatedly suggested by various writers that a 'statute of limitation,' in modification of the *lex prioritatis*, which should forever suppress and render ineligible names found in early and long-forgotten works, or names which for any reason have been for a considerable period overlooked, would prove a help towards securing stability in nomenclature. If such an end could be attained it would certainly prove a boon, and the importance of the proposition has led your Committee to give it attentive consideration. Having therefore considered the proposition in all its bearings, your Committee feels called upon in this connection to record its conviction that such a statute is inadmissible, for the following reasons. The proposition, as generally stated (see DALL, *Rep.*, p. 47), is to the effect that a name which has not been in use for a period of twenty-five years (or whatever period may be agreed upon) shall be thereafter excluded from use in that special connection, or, alternatively, that a name which has been universally, or even generally, adopted for a like period cannot be displaced for an earlier obscure name. The insuperable objection to any rule of this character is its vagueness and the uncertainty of its applicability, arising from the difficulty of absolutely determining that a name has not been in use for a given period, or whether another name has been universally used, or what shall be taken as 'current' or 'general,' in case anything short of 'universal' be allowed. Unless perfect agreement could be obtained, — and of this there is very little probability, — the proposed rule would tend to increase rather than lessen the confusion it would be the design to remove. As regards obsolete or forgotten works, others equally troublesome might be found to have escaped the operation of such a rule, in consequence of their date of publication falling just outside the period of limitation. Again, it might be difficult to decide whether or not a somewhat obsolete and more or less forgotten work was sufficiently obsolete to be set aside. Furthermore, it sometimes happens that certain names may be current among writers of one 'school' or nationality, which are rejected by those of other schools or nationalities; while in other cases it might be difficult to decide whether a more or less well known name had really sufficient currency to retain its place against an earlier less known but strictly tenable name. In some cases, of course, there would be no uncertainty as to the currency of a name under question, but in many such doubt would arise, and unanimity of opinion and practice in such case would be hopeless.

The 'statute of limitation' principle is akin to the *auctorum plurimorum* rule; both are Utopian, and both radically set at defiance the *lex prioritatis*.

CANON XV. The law of priority is to be rigidly enforced in respect to all generic, specific, and subspecific names.

REMARK. — In respect to subspecific names in relation to the law of priority, see beyond, under Canon XXIX.

CANON XVI. The law of priority is only partially operative in relation to names of groups higher than genera, and only where names are strictly synonymous.

REMARKS. — "While this generalization has not been formally enumerated in the B. A. Rules, it has become practically the general usage of naturalists. Thorell explicitly adopts it, and indeed it is impracticable to follow any other course, especially in relation to the more ancient names. A time will doubtless arrive when mutations in the names of the higher groups, parpicularly families, will be as unnecessary as they are undesirable; but in Zoölogy that time has not yet come.

"It should be clearly borne in mind that such changes are only allowable when by mutation of the characters, or through newly discovered facts, the name in question has become glaringly erroneous, or liable to introduce errors or confusion into science. In family names this occurs most often when a genus from whose name that of the family may have been taken is removed from association with the majority of the genera which that family has included, and that genus is inserted in another family which has already a well-established name. Also, when a large number of genera are redistributed into families, widely differing in their limits from those in which they had previously been known. In either of these cases the liability to error may be so great as to render a new name desirable. The answers to Query XXIII. of the circular [sent out by Mr. Dall] indicate that a majority of American naturalists concur in this conclusion." (DALL, *Rep.*, p. 27.)

A good instance of the soundness of this Canon is seen in the several ornithological groups named by Huxley, ending in *-gnathæ* and *-morphæ*. Many of them were already named groups, more or less exactly recognized; but the very different bases and definitions given them rendered it desirable that the names also should be different.

§ 5. *Of Names Published Simultaneously.*

CANON XVII. Preference between competitive specific names published simultaneously in the same work, or in two works of the same actual or ostensible date (no exact date being ascertainable), is to be decided as follows: —

1. Of names the equal pertinency of which may be in question, preference shall be given to that which is open to least doubt.

2. Of names of undoubtedly equal pertinency, (*a*) that founded upon the male is to be preferred to that founded upon the female, (*b*) that founded upon the adult to that on the young, and (*c*) that founded on the nuptial condition to that of the pre- or post-nuptial conditions.

3. Of names of undoubtedly equal pertinency, and founded upon the same condition of sex, age, or season, that is to be preferred which stands first in the book.

CANON XVIII. Preference between competitive generic names published simultaneously in the same work, or in two works of the same actual or ostensible date (no exact date being ascertainable), is to be decided as follows:—

1. A name accompanied by the specification of a type takes precedence over a name unaccompanied by such specification.

2. If all, or none, of the genera have types indicated, that generic name takes precedence the diagnosis of which is most pertinent.

§ 6. *Of the Retention of Names.*

CANON XIX. A generic name, when once established, is never to be cancelled in any subsequent subdivision of the group, but retained in a restricted sense for one of the constituent portions.

REMARKS. — This rule, adopted from the B. A. Code, has been generally accepted as sound in principle, but as difficult of application, especially in relation to what portion of the original genus, when subdivided, shall retain the original name; — in other words, what, in accordance with modern usage, shall be taken as the 'type' of the original genus, in cases where no type is specified.

In recommending this provision the B. A. Committee urged: "As the number of known species which form the groundwork of zoological science is always increasing, and our knowledge of their structure becomes more complete, fresh generalizations continually occur to the naturalist, and the number of genera and other groups requiring appellations is ever becoming more extensive. It thus becomes necessary to subdivide the contents of old groups and to make their definitions continually more restricted. In carrying out this process, it is an act of justice to the original author, that his generic name should never be lost sight of; and it is no less [even more] essential to the welfare of the science, that all which is sound in its nomenclature should remain unaltered amid the additions which are continually being made to it." (*B. A. Code*, 1842.)

CANON XX. When a genus is subdivided, the original name of the genus is to be retained for that portion of it which contained the original type of the genus, when this can be ascertained.

REMARK. — This principle is universally conceded, and requires no special comment.

CANON XXI. When no type is clearly indicated, the author who first subdivides a genus may restrict the original name to such part of it as he may judge advisable, and such assignment shall not be subject to subsequent modification.

REMARKS. — This in substance is the rule promulgated by the B. A. Committee in 1842, and it has been reiterated in most subsequent nomenclatural codes. Its propriety is perfectly apparent, and, as regards the future, no trouble need arise under it. It has happened, however, in the subdivision of comprehensive genera of Linnæus and other early authors, that most perplexing complications have arisen, successive authors having removed one species after another, as types or elements of new genera, till each of the species included in the original genus has received a new generic designation, while the old generic name, if not lost sight of, has come to be applied to species unknown to the author of the original genus! This of course is obviously and radically wrong.

The B. A. Committee suggests that, when authors omit to specify a type, "it may still in many cases be correctly inferred that the *first* species mentioned on their list, if found accurately to agree with their definition, was regarded by them as the type. A specific name or its synonyms will also often serve to point out the particular species which by implication must be regarded as the original type of a genus. In such cases we are justified in restoring the name of the old genus to its typical signification, even when later authors have done otherwise." De Candolle would restrict the old generic name, when no type is specified, to the oldest, best known, or most characteristic of the species originally included in the genus; or to that section of the old genus most numerously represented in species.

As Dall observes, "It would, manifestly, be liable to introduce errors and confusion, if it were insisted that the first species should invariably be taken as the type, or were it permitted to take species subsequently added to the group, and which the original author did not know when he established his genus. No arbitrary rule will suffice to determine, off-hand, questions of so much complication as is often the decision in regard to the type of an ancient genus which has been studied by a number of authors." (*Rep.*, pp. 39, 40.)

CANON XXII. In no case should the name be transferred to a group containing none of the species originally included in the genus.

REMARK. — This rule is in strict accordance with the B. A. Code and with current usage.

CANON XXIII. If, however, the genus contains both exotic and non-exotic species, — from the standpoint of the original author, — and the generic term is one originally applied by the ancient Greeks or Romans, the process of elimination is to be restricted to the non-exotic species.

REMARKS. — The purpose of this restriction in the application of the 'principle of elimination' is to prevent the palpable impropriety of the transference of an ancient Greek or Latin name to species unknown to the ancients. By the unrestricted action of the principle of elimination the genus *Tetrao*, for example, becomes transferred to an American species, viz., *Tetrao phasianellus* of Linnæus, the transference being in itself not only undesirable, but, as it happens, subversive of currently accepted names. The working of the proposed modification of the principle of elimination may be thus illustrated. The genus *Tetrao* Linn., 1758, contains the following

NON-EXOTIC SPECIES.	EXOTIC SPECIES.
1. *urogallus* (*Urogallus* Flem., 1822).	3. *canadensis*.
2. *tetrix*.	5. *phasianellus*.
4. *lagopus* (*Lagopus* Briss., 1760).	6. *cupido*.
7. *bonasia* (*Bonasia* Steph., 1819, + Bon., 1828).	

This leaves *tetrix* as the type of the genus *Tetrao*, since *Lyrurus* Sw. was not established for it till 1831.

On the other hand, the process of unrestricted elimination would result as follows : —

1. *urogallus* (*Urogallus* Flem., 1822);
2. *tetrix* (*Lyrurus* Sw., 1831);
3. *canadensis* (*Canace* Reich., 1852);
4. *lagopus* (*Lagopus* Briss., 1760);
5. *phasianellus* (*Pediocætes* Bd., 1858);

6. *cupido* (*Tympanuchus* Glog., 1842; *Cupidonia* Reich., 1850);
7. *bonasia* (*Bonasia* Steph., 1819, + Bon., 1828);

which would leave, as type for the genus *Tetrao*, *T. phasianellus*, which was the last species to be removed from the genus *Tetrao*, its removal being made by Baird in 1858, who made it the type of a genus *Pedioecetes*. No species being now left to bear the name *Tetrao*, it must be restored either to *T. phasianellus* (under the unrestricted action of the principle of elimination), or to *T. hyurus* (under the above-proposed restricted action of the principle of elimination). In the latter case, this ancient Greek name for a European species of Grouse would be still retained in nearly its original sense.

As in the case of *Tetrao*, so in the cases of many Linnæan and Brissonian genera, it has happened that, in the process of gradual elimination, exotic (or non-European) species only have been finally left in the original genus, while the European species have successively been made types of separate genera.

CANON XXIV. When no type is specified, the only available method of fixing the original name to some part of the genus to which it was originally applied is by the process of elimination, subject to the single modification provided for by Canon XXIII.

CANON XXV. A genus formed by the combination of two or more genera takes the name first given in a generic or subgeneric sense to either or any of its components. If both or all are of the same date, that one selected by the reviser is to be retained.

REMARKS.— The propriety of this rule is too obvious to require special comment. It therefore follows that a later name equivalent to several earlier ones must be cancelled, and that the earliest name applied to any of the previously established genera thus combined is to be taken as the designation of the new combination.

CANON XXVI. When the same genus has been defined and named by two authors, both giving it the same limits, the later name becomes a synonym of the earlier one; but in case these authors have specified types from different sections of the genus, and these sections be raised afterward to the rank of genera, then both names are to be retained in a restricted sense for the new genera.

CANON XXVII. When a subgenus is raised to full generic rank, its name is to be retained as that of the group thus raised. In like manner, names first proposed or used in a subspecific sense are tenable in case the subspecies be raised to full specific standing, and are to have priority over a new name for the subspecies so elevated.

REMARK. — This of course relates to names which are otherwise tenable, — in other words, have been duly published, and are not synonyms.

CANON XXVIII. When it becomes necessary to divide a composite species or subspecies, the old specific or subspecific name is to be retained for that form or portion of the group to which it was first applied, or to which it primarily related. If this cannot be positively ascertained, the name as fixed by the first reviser is to be retained.

REMARK. — This is simply the extension of the rules already provided for the determination of generic types to species which are composite in character, to which the general principles of elimination already set forth are equally applicable.

CANON XXIX. When a species is separated into subspecies, or when species previously supposed to be distinct are found to intergrade, the earliest name applied to any form of the group shall be the specific name of the whole group, and shall also be retained as the subspecific designation of the particular form to which it was originally applied. In other words, the rule of priority is to be strictly enforced in respect to subspecific names.

REMARKS. — While this principle is generally recognized, one ornithological writer of prominence[1] has introduced the practice of connecting the names of conspecies or subspecies in accordance with the supposed nearest affinities of such forms, regardless of priority of names. Such disregard of the law of priority, however, can lead only to instability and confusion, without any adequately compensating advantages. If we knew beyond question what was the original or stock-form of a group of conspecies, and the lines of evolution of the various imperfectly segregated forms, it would be possible to show the genetic relation of such forms in our nomenclature, and were nomenclature classification some gain might thus result. But since

[1] Mr. Henry Seebohm.

nomenclature is not classification, and since our knowledge of genetic relationships even within specific groups is egregiously imperfect, only change and confusion can result from any attempt to express genetic relationship in the collocation of subspecific designations.

In cases where obscurity might arise from designating the earliest-named form of a group of subspecies by simply a binomial name, the specific term may be repeated (*e. g.*, *Melospiza fasciata fasciata*), or it may be followed by the word *typica* (*e. g.*, *Melospiza fasciata typica*).

For the sake of brevity it may be even desirable, where the context makes the reference unequivocal, to abbreviate the second term of the trinomial, as is done with the generic part of binomial names (*e. g.*, *M. f. rufina* = *Melospiza fasciata rufina*).

Canon XXX. Specific names when adopted as generic are not to be changed.

Remarks. — This Canon is diametrically opposed to § 13 of the original B. A. Code, which declares that "specific names, when adopted as generic, must be changed." The Bath Committee, however, recommended that, when a specific name had been raised to a generic, "it is the *generic name* which must be thrown aside, not the old specific name." Both rulings were to the effect that the specific and generic names of a species should not be identical; the only objection thereto urged by the B. A. Committee being the "*inelegance* of this method." Many of these 'inelegances' had already crept into zoölogical nomenclature, and they have since greatly increased, although the majority of authors have avoided them. Yet all the later codes are at least constructively in favor of their admission, and they have recently received sanction in other high quarters. (*Cf.* Dall, *Report*, pp. 50, 51.) To rule against them would be clearly contrary to the principle of stability in names and the spirit of the present Code. While your Committee would strongly discourage the practice of elevating specific names to generic rank, those already thus instituted should be accepted.

"The practice," says Dall, "is objectionable on account of its producing tautological inelegance, and because it has resulted in the formation of a number of generic names of adjective form. On the other hand, in connection with certain of the Linnæan and other ancient and universally known species, it had several beneficial effects. It recalled the typical form for which the genus was constituted, and in many cases it might rightly be regarded rather as a change of rank than the creation of a new name. The ancient species . . . . often covered an assemblage of forms equivalent to a modern genus." Respecting the ruling of the Bath Committee, Mr. Dall continues: "This innovation, the sweeping character of which the Committee cannot have realized, if carried into effect would uproot hundreds of the generic names best known to science, and so familiar that the fact that they were originally specific names has been almost totally forgotten. Its spirit is opposed to the fundamental principles of nomenclature, and the end to be gained is of the most trivial character." (DALL, *Rep.*, pp. 50, 51.)

CANON XXXI. Neither generic nor specific names are to be rejected because of barbarous origin, for faulty construction, for inapplicability of meaning, or for erroneous signification.

REMARKS.— As already stated under Canon VI., of which this is the corollary, a name is merely a name, and should be treated as such, without regard to its construction or signification. This principle, while contrary to provisions of the B. A. Code and to the practice of many writers, has the sanction of modern authorities, and is in line with present tendencies in respect of fixity of names in nomenclature, as already explained.

CANON XXXII. A *nomen nudum*, generic or specific, may be adopted by a subsequent author, but the name takes both its date and authority from the time when, and from the author by whom, the name becomes clothed with significance by being properly defined and published.

§ 7. Of the Rejection of Names.

CANON XXXIII. A generic name is to be changed which has been previously used for some other genus in the same kingdom; a specific or subspecific name is to be changed when it has been applied to some other species of the same genus, or used previously in combination with the same generic name.

REMARKS. — In other words, a generic name cannot be tenable for more than one genus in the same kingdom, nor a specific or subspecific name for more than one species or subspecies of the same genus. This is in accordance with custom and all previous codes. In the present unsettled state of opinion regarding the status of forms considered by some writers as specific, and by others as subspecific, it seems best to place subspecific designations on the same basis in this respect as specific ones.

Therefore the maxim, "Once a synonym always a synonym," applies alike to generic, specific, and subspecific names.

A diversity of opinion prevails among naturalists in relation to whether a generic name which has lapsed from sufficient cause into synonymy should be entirely rejected, or whether it may be considered available for a new and valid genus. Usage seems strongly against the retention of such names; but a few writers have advocated their admissibility in some other class of the Animal Kingdom, or even the admissibility of the same name in different orders of the same class, as among insects. Inasmuch as a fixed rule is desirable, and as practice and precept are both on the whole favorable to the maxim quoted above, — names in one department of Zoölogy being continually changed when found to be preoccupied in another department, — and as most previous codes explicitly state that a generic name to be tenable must not be in double employ in the same kingdom, it seems to your Committee that the formal adoption of the maxim, " Once a synonym always a synonym," as regards generic names, must meet with general approval.

A 'synonym' is properly one of two or more different names for one and the same thing. A 'homonym' is one and the same name for two or more different things. But in the usage of naturalists this distinction of meaning is not generally recognized. Thus the examples about to be adduced in illustration of the operation of Canon XXXIII. are homonyms, not synonyms. It is therefore necessary to premise that your Committee includes homonyms in the maxim just cited.

The application of the maxim to specific and subspecific names has been less generally admitted, but can be shown to rest on a sound principle, since it aims at, and is calculated to promote, stability in names. The object of the rule, in its present application, is to make the use of the specific name altogether independent of the generic name; to oblige authors to use always the same specific name, even when they disagree as to the generic appellation. In many cases, it is true, the revival of a specific name which has lapsed into synonymy may lead to no confusion, but the cases where the reverse may occur are far more frequent. To illustrate: Gmelin, in 1788, described a Lark as *Alauda rufa*. Audubon, in 1843, also described a Lark as *Alauda rufa*. In the mean time, however, the *Alauda rufa* of Gmelin has been found to be a true *Anthus*, and being therefore transferred to that genus is called *Anthus rufus*. Now as these birds belong to widely separated families, it may be claimed that there is no possibility of confusing Audubon's name with the *Alauda rufa* of Gmelin, and that therefore the name *rufa* of Audubon is perfectly tenable. There are many parallel cases in zoölogical literature, and the tendency is to recognize both names as valid. But the case is not always so simple, being susceptible of several complications. For instance, to continue the above illustration hypothetically, let us suppose that, before the generic distinctness of the two species was discovered, the name of the Audubonian *Alauda rufa* had been found to be preoccupied and accordingly changed to *rufescens*, and that for many years the species was known as *Alauda rufescens*. Finally the original *Alauda rufa* is removed to *Anthus*, and some writers restore to Audubon's species its original name of *rufa*, while others prefer to retain the better known and later more current name *rufescens*.

Again: In 1804 a *Munia* was named *Loxia albiventris* by Hermann; in 1860 Swinhoe named a Crossbill *Loxia albiventris*. These birds certainly belong to different genera, and there is no fear of their being confounded. But it may be contended (indeed was long since so claimed by Lesson) that Hermann's *Loxia albiventris* (a *Munia*) is the true type of the genus *Loxia*, and that the Crossbills should be called *Crucirostra*. Others maintain that the latter are the true *Loxiæ*. Each view may have advocates, and we shall have two species bearing the name *Loxia albiventris*, whereas the rule, "Once a synonym," etc., at once debars the later name.

Again: Temminck, in 1828, named a bird *Procellaria tenuirostris* (Pl. Col., 587). In 1839 Audubon named a bird *Procellaria tenuirostris* (Orn. Biog., V., p. 333). By many authors these two species are referred to different genera, the former being regarded as a *Puffinus*. Schlegel, among others, considered them congeneric, and changed (Cat. Mus. P. B., Procellariæ, p. 22) the *tenuirostris* of Audubon to *smithi*. In doing this he was of course fully justified, from his view of the relationship of the two birds; while others, referring them to different genera, would, by current usage, be equally justified in retaining the same specific name for both species.

One further illustration: In 1788 Gmelin named a bird *Procellaria cinerea*. In 1820 Kuhl applied the same name to another species afterwards called *Procellaria kuhlii*. These two species are now commonly looked upon as belonging to different genera, the former being an *Adamastor*, the latter a *Puffinus*. They are not, however, called *Adamastor cinereus* and *Puffinus cinereus*, but *A. cinereus* and *P. kuhlii*.

These illustrations will serve as examples of the complications that arise and the instability which results from present methods in such cases, and show the lack of uniformity of usage now prevailing. Cases of this sort are in reality very numerous, and often egregiously misleading. Your Committee urges that the adoption of the maxim, "Once a synonym always a synonym," in relation to specific, as well as to generic names, will eradicate a prolific source of instability in nomenclature, and provide a consistent and uniform rule for a very troublesome class of cases. So long as naturalists differ in opinion respecting the limits of genera, the absence of such a rule leaves too many specific names open to personal arbitration and individual predilection.

CANON XXXIV. A *nomen nudum* is to be rejected as having no status in nomenclature.

REMARKS. — A name, generic or specific, which has been published without an accompanying diagnosis, or reference to an identifiable published figure or plate, or, in case of a generic name, to a recognizably described species, is not entitled to recognition, being merely a name, and therefore having no status in nomenclature. It may, however, be brought later into use, under the restrictions embodied in Canon XXXII.

CANON XXXV. An author has no right to change or reject names of his own proposing, except in accordance with rules of nomenclature governing all naturalists, he having only the same right as other naturalists over the names he has himself proposed.

REMARK. — This is so obvious, that it seems trite to dignify the matter by formulation as a Canon; yet not a few writers fail to recognize the fact, and claim the right, not only to emend the orthography of names proposed by themselves, but to change genera and subgenera by substituting for them new types, and to use the original type as the basis of another new genus.

CANON XXXVI. A name resting solely on an inadequate diagnosis is to be rejected, on the ground that it is indeterminable and therefore not properly defined.

CANON XXXVII. If an author describes a genus and does not refer to it any species, either then or previously described, the genus cannot be taken as established or properly defined, unless the characters given have an unmistakable significance.

CANON XXXVIII. A species cannot be considered as named unless both generic and specific names have been applied to it simultaneously, *i. e.*, unless the species has been definitely referred to some genus.

REMARKS. — *E. g.*, a West Indian Seal (*Monachus tropicalis* Gray) was once described by an author, who, because in doubt as to its generic affinities, simply gave, as he says, "the trivial name *Wilkianus* for the species," without referring it to any genus. Authorities, however, agree that a species thus designated cannot be considered as named.

CANON XXXIX. A name which has never been clearly defined in some published work is to be changed for the earliest name by which the object shall have been so defined, if such name exist; otherwise a new name is to be provided, or the old name may be properly defined and retained, its priority and authority to date from the time and author so defining it.

§ 8. *Of the Emendation of Names.*

CANON XL. The original orthography of a name is to be rigidly preserved, unless a typographical error is evident.

REMARKS. — In view of the fact that stability of names is one of the essential principles in nomenclature, and that the emendation of names, as shown by the recent history of zoölogical nomenclature, opens the door to a great evil, — being subject to abuse on the part of purists and classicists, who look with disfavor upon anything nomenclatural which is in the least degree unclassical in form, — it seems best that correctness of structure, or philological propriety, be held as of minor importance, and yield place to the two cardinal principles of priority and fixity. The permanence of a name is of far more importance than its signification or structure, as is freely admitted by the best authorities in both Botany and Zoölogy. Your Committee would therefore restrict the emendation of names to the correction of obvious or known typographical errors involving obscurity. They would therefore reject emendations of a purely philological character, and especially all such as involve a change of the initial letter of the name, as in cases where the Greek aspirate has been omitted by the original constructor. It therefore follows that hybrid names cannot be displaced; although it is to be hoped that they will be strenuously guarded against in future; and that, in general, word-coiners will pay the closest attention to philological proprieties.

"The tendency among working naturalists is to retain names in spite of faults." (A. GRAY.)

"A generic name should subsist just as it was made, although a purely typographical error may be corrected." (DE CANDOLLE.)

§ 9. *Of the Definition of Names.*

CANON XLI. A name to be tenable must have been defined and published.

REMARKS. — "Unless a species or group is intelligibly defined when the name is given, it cannot be recognized by others, and the signification of the name is consequently lost. .... Definition properly implies a distinct exposition of essential characters, and in all cases we conceive this to be indispensable, although some authors maintain that a mere enumeration of the component species, or even of a single type, is sufficient to authenticate a genus." (*B. A. Code*, 1842.)

Any tenable technical name is called the *onym*, as distinguished from an *anonym*, *nomen nudum*, or mere name unaccompanied by diagnosis; or from the *chironym*, an unpublished manuscript name; or from a *pseudonym*, a nickname or vernacular name. The *onym* is of two kinds; the *graphonym*, resting upon a published plate, diagnosis, or description, and the *typonym*, based upon indications of a type species or type specimen (see Canons XLII., XLIII.). *Onyms* are further named *mononyms*, *dionyms*, *trionyms*, or *polyonyms*, according to whether they consist of one, two, three, or more words. (*Cf.* COUES, *The Auk*, I., Oct. 1884, p. 321.)

CANON XLII. The basis of a generic or subgeneric name is either (1) a designated recognizably described species, or (2) a designated recognizable plate or figure, or (3) a published diagnosis.

REMARKS. — Some writers insist that a generic or subgeneric name in order to be tenable must be accompanied by a diagnosis. However proper such a requisition may seem theoretically, the principle is thoroughly impracticable, and if enforced would lead to hopeless confusion. The custom of naturalists has been quite otherwise, and the mere mention of a type has been found to be often a better index to an author's meaning than is frequently a diagnosis or even a long description. Either of the three alternatives given above may alone be accepted as a proper definition. In the case of a diagnosis, it must of course give some character or characters by which the organism it is intended to designate may be unmistakably recognized.

CANON XLIII. The basis of a specific or subspecific name is either (1) an identifiable published description, or (2) a recognizable published figure or plate, or (3) the original type specimen or specimens, absolutely identified as the type or types of the species or subspecies in question; but in no case is a type specimen to be accepted as the basis of a specific or subspecific name, when it radically disagrees with or is contradictory to the characters given in the diagnosis or description based upon it.

REMARKS. — It therefore follows that a specific or subspecific name resting on a description which was originally so vague as to render the name indeterminable, or which has become so through the later discovery of closely allied species, may be established by reference to an authentic type specimen, when such exists; but if the description proves to be so glaringly erroneous as to present characters contradictory to the type specimen, the type specimen is not to be taken as the basis of the name; the name in such case is to be ignored or treated just as it would have to be if no type specimen existed; and the species is to be reintroduced into science under a new name, as a new species, and with a proper description.

The authenticity of a type specimen is often a matter of the highest importance. The evidence will vary in different cases; it may be merely circumstantial, but of such a nature as to be positive in character; or the specimen may bear a label in the handwriting of the original describer signifying it to be his type; or the history of the specimen may be so well known to those having it in charge that there can be little reason for doubt in the matter. But tradition, in the general sense of the term, cannot be regarded as satisfactory evidence; and nothing short of the written statement of the author, securely attached to the specimen, affirming it to be the type, should in future be considered satisfactory evidence. Still, this requirement cannot be insisted upon for the past, since in few cases have types been heretofore thus designated, though their authenticity may be in many cases beyond cavil. Your Committee would recommend that in future authors should not only specify their types in their descriptions, and label them as their types, but should designate the collection in which they are deposited.

CANON XLIV. In determining the pertinence of a description or figure on which a genus, species, or subspecies may respectively rest, the consideration of pertinency is to be restricted to the species scientifically known at the time of publication of the description or figure in question, or to contemporaneous literature.

CANON XLV. Absolute identification is requisite in order to displace a modern current name by an older obscure one.

REMARKS. — The purpose of the foregoing rules (Canons XLIII.-XLV.) is to check the tendency to replace current names by earlier ones, the identification of which may be determined only by a process of elimination — on the ground that they can relate to nothing else — based on our present knowledge of Zoölogy, but which cannot be determined from the imperfect description given by the original describer, alone or supplemented by the contemporaneous literature of the subject; — in short, the identification of which rests on our present knowledge of the species inhabiting the assigned habitat of the form in question.

CANON XLVI. In describing an organism which is considered to represent a new genus as well as a new species, it is not necessary to formally separate the characters into two categories, generic and specific, in order to render tenable the names given to the organism in question, although such a distinction is desirable.

REMARKS. — In the case of fossil organisms, represented by a few fragments, the practice of giving a general description is especially common; but even here, as in all other cases, it would be far better to give a formal diagnosis or description of the generic characters as distinguished from the specific.

§ 10. *Of the Publication of Names.*

CANON XLVII. Publication consists in the public sale or distribution of printed matter, — books, pamphlets, or plates.

REMARKS. — In Botany the distribution, by sale or otherwise, of labelled specimens, bearing the date of their distribution, is likewise recognized as publication.

In respect to the matter of publication, the B. A. Committee wisely recommend as follows: "A large proportion of the complicated mass of synonyms which has now become the opprobrium of zoölogy, has originated either from the slovenly and imperfect manner in which species and groups have been originally defined, or from their definitions having been inserted in obscure local publications which have never obtained an extensive circulation. Therefore . . . . we would strongly advise the authors of new groups always to give, in the first instance, a full and accurate definition of their characters, and to insert the same in such periodicals or other works as are likely to obtain an immediate or extensive circulation."

Mr. Dall, on the same point, makes the following judicious and explicit recommendations.

"To avoid increasing the difficulties encountered in dealing with the already enormous mass of scientific names, authors are earnestly recommended to take the following precautions in publication: —

"1. To publish matter containing descriptions of new groups or species [or changes in nomenclature], in the regularly appearing proceedings of some well-established scientific society, or in some scientific serial of acknowledged standing and permanence.

"2. If a separate publication or independent work be issued by any author, copies should at once be sent to the principal learned societies, scientific libraries, and especially to those persons or associations known to be employed in the publication of bibliographical records or annual reviews of scientific progress.

"The work should also be placed at the disposition of the scientific world by an advertisement of copies placed in the hands of some firm, society, or individual for sale or distribution.

"3. To avoid most carefully the publication of new names or changes of nomenclature in newspapers; in serials not of a scientific nature or of limited circulation; in the occasional pamphlets issued by weak, torpid, or obscure associations which are distributed [only] to members or not at all; and in brief lists, catalogues [especially sale catalogues], or pamphlets independently issued, insufficiently distributed, or not to be found on sale." (*Rep.*, p. 46.)

The question of the restriction of the nature of the channels of publication through which new species and genera, and changes in nomenclature, should be made public, is considered by Mr. Dall, and was even included among the subjects covered by his circular, the replies to which were to the effect that, while such restriction would be very desirable, it seemed impracticable; an opinion reluctantly concurred in by Mr. Dall himself.

"It is clearly," Mr. Dall continues, "the duty of every publishing author to concur as far as possible in the suppression of methods leading to confusion," and to comply with recommendations "intended to lead toward this result."

CANON XLVIII. The reading of a paper before a scientific society or a public assembly does not constitute publication, and new genera and species first announced in this way date only from the time of their subsequent and irrevocable publication.

REMARKS. — It often happens that papers are read before a scientific body which are never printed. No one would claim publication in such cases. Often many months elapse between the reading of a paper before a society and its publication in the proceedings of the society. Credit for original discovery may be thus secured; but, in deference to the fundamental principle of fixity in nomenclature, new names or changes in nomenclature proposed in such papers obviously cannot be allowed to antedate actual publication.

CANON XLIX. The date borne by a publication is presumed to be correct till proved otherwise; although it is well known that in many instances, as in the proceedings or transactions of societies, and in works issued in parts, the date given is not that of actual publication; and when this fact can be substantiated, the actual date of publication, if it can be ascertained, is to be taken.

REMARKS. — It is notorious that the dates on the title-page of the completed volume of works issued in parts often antedate — sometimes postdate — the actual publication of the different parts, or are otherwise erroneous. Also, that the volumes of proceedings of learned societies not unfrequently bear simply the date of the period or year to which they relate, even when not published till months, and sometimes years, after the ostensible date;

and that serial publications, when not issued promptly, as not unfrequently happens, are sometimes antedated by several months. This state of things is happily less prevalent now than formerly, and is more frequently the result of inattention, or failure to appreciate the importance of precision in such matters, than from any motive of unfairness. At the present time authors in good standing are careful to make permanent record of the date of publication of each part of a work issued in successive brochures, or printer's 'signatures'; and societies not unfrequently give the exact date of the appearance of each signature or part of their various publications. This, it is needless to urge, is a practice which should become general.

Where doubt arises as to the priority of publication between a properly dated work and one improperly or dishonestly dated, it would hardly be unfair to throw the *onus probandi* on the publishers of the latter, or to favor the work the date of which is not open to question.

Finally, respecting the matter of publication, your Committee would submit the following.

Naturalists would do well (*a*) to indicate exactly the date of publication of their works, parts of works, or papers; (*b*) to avoid publishing a name without indicating the nature of the group (whether generic, subgeneric, or supergeneric) it is intended to distinguish; (*c*) to avoid including in their publications any unaccepted manuscript names, since such names only needlessly increase synonymy; (*d*) societies, government or other surveys, or other publishing boards, should indicate the date of issue of each part of works published serially or in instalments, as well as of all volumes and completed works.

Furthermore, the custodians of libraries, public or private, would do well to indicate, either in the work itself or in a proper book of record, the date of reception of all publications received, particularly in the case of those of a serial character, or which are issued in parts. (This, it may be observed, is a practice carefully adhered to in well-regulated libraries of the present time.)

§ 11. *Of the Authority for Names.*

CANON L. The authority for a specific or subspecific name is the first describer of the species or subspecies. When the first describer of the species or subspecies is not also the authority, it is to be enclosed in parentheses; *e. g., Turdus migratorius* L., or *Merula migratoria* (L.).

REMARK. — Ordinarily the use of authorities may be omitted, as in incidental reference to species of a well-known fauna in faunal lists, etc.; but, on the other hand, the use of authorities may be of the greatest importance in giving exact indication of the sènse in which a name is used; for instance, in check-lists, or monographic and revisionary works.

In writing the names of subspecies the authority for the specific or second element of the name may nearly always be omitted.

The relation of authorities may be otherwise indicated; as, *e.g.*, *Merula migratoria* L. sp.; or *Merula migratoria* Sw. & Rich. ex L.; or *Merula migratoria* Sw. & Rich. (L. sub *Turdus*), etc.; but the method first above mentioned has the merit of the greater simplicity and brevity.

Two very different practices have prevailed among naturalists in respect to authorities for names. The B. A. Code gave preference to the authority for the specific name, for the following reasons: "Of the three persons concerned with the construction of a binomial title . . . . we conceive that the author who *first* describes and names a species which forms the groundwork of later generalizations, possesses a higher claim to have his name recorded than he who afterwards defines a genus which is found to embrace that species, or who may be the mere accidental means of bringing the generic and specific names into contact. By giving the authority for the *specific* name in preference to all others, the inquirer is referred *directly* to the original description, habitat, etc., of the species, and is at the same time reminded of the date of its discovery." Agassiz and others opposed this practice, and gave preference to the referrer of the species to its proper genus, on the ground that it required greater knowledge of the structure and relationship of species to properly classify them than to simply name and describe them. By this school, the authority is considered as constituting part of the name. This method is also in accordance with the usage of the older zoölogists and botanists, from Linnæus down. But it often happens that the authority for the combination of names used is not that of the classifier, but of the author who has merely 'shuffled names,' or worked out the synonymy in accordance with nomenclatural rules, and has had nothing to do with the correct allocation of the species.

CANON LI. The authority for a name is not to be separated from it by any mark of punctuation (except as provided for under Canon L.).

REMARKS. — In respect to punctuation and typography, in relation to names and their authorities, usage varies; but it is quite generally conceded that no comma need be used between the name and its authority; "the authority," as Verrill has suggested, "being understood to be a noun in the genitive case, though written in the nominative form, or more frequently abbreviated." In printing the authority is usually and advisably distinguished by use of type differing from that of the name; if the latter be in Italic type the authority may be in Roman, or if in small capitals or in antique, the authority may be in Italic type, etc.

CANON LII. The name of the authority, unless short, is to be abbreviated, and the abbreviation is to be made in accordance with commonly recognized rules, and irregularly formed and non-distinctive abbreviations are to be avoided.

REMARKS. — In the case of a few well-known names usage may be considered to have established certain deviations from strict rule in the matter of abbreviation of authors' names, as the use of L. for Linnæus, DC. for De Candolle, Bd. for Baird, Scl. for Sclater, etc. In general, names of one syllable are short enough not to require abbreviation; when, however, it seems preferable to shorten them the first consonants are retained (as Br. for Brown), or the first consonant and the last, or last two when the name ends with a consonant or consonants (as Bd. for Baird, Gld. for Gould, Cs. for Coues, etc.). For names of more than one syllable, the first syllable and the first letter or letters of the second syllable should be retained (as Aud. for Audubon, Bon. for Bonaparte, Gorm. for Gorman; not Grm., which might stand for either Gorman, Garman, or Germar). To avoid confounding two names which begin with similar syllables, two syllables may be given, with one or two consonants of the third (as Bertol. for Bertolini, to distinguish it from Bertero), or the first syllable with the addition of a characteristic final consonant of the name (as Michx. for Michaux, as opposed to Micheli; or Lamx. for Lamouroux, as distinguished from Lamarck).

If several prominent authors in the same department of Zoölogy have the same name, they may be distinguished, if thought necessary, by prefixing their respective initials, or an abbreviation of the Christian name to the usual abbreviation; or if father and son, by affixing *fil.* or *f.* to the name of the younger.

In short, the points to be aimed at in abbreviating names of authorities are uniformity and distinctiveness. As Mr. Dall (whom in this matter we have closely followed) remarks, in some late works, only those familiar with the literature of the subject "can divine whether *Bth.* is the equivalent of Bentham, Beuth, or Booth, *Sz.* for Schultz, Steetz, or Szowitz; or what is the equivalent of *Htsch., Hk., H. Bn., Bn., Btl., Lm., Reich.,* or *Spng.*"

C. Recommendations for Zoölogical Nomenclature in the Future.

§ 12. *Of the Construction and Selection of Names.*

RECOMMENDATION I. As already provided under Canon II., the rules of Latin orthography are to be adhered to in the construction of scientific names.

REMARKS. — "In Latinizing Greek words there are certain rules of orthography known to classical scholars which must never be departed from. For instance, the names which modern authors have written *Aipunemia, Zenophasia, poiocephala,* must, according to the laws of etymology, be spelt *Æpycnemia, Xenophasia,* and *pæocephala.* In Latinizing modern words the rules of classic usage do not apply, and all that we can do is to give to such terms as classical an appearance as we can, consistently with the preservation of their etymology. In the case of European words whose orthography is fixed, it is best to retain the original form, even though it may include letters and combinations unknown in Latin. Such words, for instance, as *Woodwardi, Knighti, Bullocki, Eschscholtzi,* would be quite unintelligible if they were Latinized into *Vudvardi, Cnichti, Bullocci, Essolzi,* etc. But words of barbarous origin, having no fixed orthography, are more pliable, and hence, when adopted into the Latin, they should be rendered as classical in appearance as is consistent with the preservation of their original sound. Thus the words *Tockus, awsuree, argoondah, kundoo,* etc., should, when Latinized, have been written *Toccus, ausure, argunda, cundu,* etc. Such words ought, in all practicable cases, to have a Latin termination given them, especially if they are used generically." (*B. A. Code.*)

RECOMMENDATION II. In Latinizing personal names only the termination should be changed, except as in cases provided for under Recommendation IV.

REMARKS. — "In Latinizing proper names, the simplest rule appears to be to use the termination *-us,* genitive *-i,* when the name ends with a consonant; .... and *-ius,* gen. *-ii,* when it ends with a vowel, as *Latreille, Latreillii,* etc." (*B. A. Code.*) Since proper names for species, however, are used mainly — and we recommend that they be so used exclusively — in the possessive case, a still simpler and now generally adopted rule is to add an *i* to the name; as, *Latreille, Latreillei; Hale, Halei; Baird, Bairdi;* but euphony may in some instances require the fuller form, and here — as in many other instances — is a case where an author has the opportunity of displaying his good taste. It should be understood that this rule does not apply to names which are already Latin or Latinized in the nominative case. Thus *Linnæus* should become *Linnæi; Cygnæus, Cygnæi; Gunnerus, Gunneri; Nathusius, Nathusii; Nicolaus, Nicolai;* — not *Linnæusi, Cygnæusi, Gunnerusi, Nathusiusi, Nicolausi.* The same principle may also be safely followed in cases where the form of the name is perfectly Latin, though there may be some doubt whether it originally was Latinized or not; as, *Baldami* from *Baldamus, Blasii* from *Blasius;* not *Baldamusi, Blasiusi.* If the name were *Blase,* the genitive would be *Blasei,* as distinctive from *Blasii.* This recommendation of applying the regular Latin genitive whenever possible without obscuring the name, is particularly to be observed in many names ending in *a*, the genitive of which should be *æ;* as, *Molina, Molinæ; Cara, Caræ; Costa, Costæ; Orellana, Orellanæ; Lozana, Lozanæ; Marmora, Marmoræ; Botta, Bottæ;* and not *Molinai, Carai, Costai, Orellanai, Lozanai,* etc. A greater difficulty is experienced with some Italian and Spanish names, and similar ones of Roman origin, ending in *o* or *io*. Simply adding an *i* would in many cases give absolutely absurd results; as, *Antonio, Antonioi*. In such cases the only proper way seems to be to apply the regular Latin genitive, or to derive a genitive in the regular manner from a supposed regular Latin nominative form of the name: thus, *Antonii,* from *Antonio; Xamarri,* from *Xamarro; Naceyri,* from *Naceyro; Guirai,* from *Guirao; Durazzi,* from *Durazzo; Morozzi,* from *Morozzo*. A few names ending in *io,* the derivation of which from a true Latin nominative form is not obvious, may be treated in a similar manner; as, *Fatio, Fatii,* and not *Fatioi,* though we have seen *Fationis,* the propriety of which we have no means of determining. Analogous application may be made in case of similarly ending names not of Latin origin; as, for instance, *Kaleniczenki* seems preferable to *Kaleniczenkoi*.

The above suggestions apply to names of men. It has been the custom to add *æ* to the name, instead of *i,* to indicate that the person whose name was thus used is a woman, but *-iæ* will in many, perhaps most, cases be found preferable, on account of its greater euphony; for instance, *Maxwelliæ,* and not *Maxwellæ; Blackburniæ,* not *Blackburnæ*.

It is sometimes recommended that a personal specific name be put in the adjective form when it is not the name of the original collector or describer of the species. "Thus *Corvus corax,* Brun non Linnæus, or a new *Corvus* collected by Brun, would be *C. bruni.* A *Corvus* named after one's friend Brun, or an ornithologist Brun, would be *C. brunianus.*" This recommendation is impracticable, however, since *-ianus* is too long a termination to append to most names, as it might give us specific names like *Artzibascheffianus, Seidensacherianus, Olph-Galliardianus, Grandidierianus, Macgillivrayianus, Selys-Longschampsianus,* etc.

When Christian names which have a Latin or Latinized equivalent are adopted for species, the form should accord with the rules of Latin declination; *e. g., Alexandri, Caroli, Francisci, Hectoris, Ludovici, Guillielmi, Annæ, Margarethæ, Phœbes;* not *Alexanderi, Charlesi* or *Karli, Frantzi* or *Françoisi, Hectori, Louisi* or *Ludwigi, Williami;* much less *Annai, Margareti, Phœbei,* or the like. In many cases of women's Christian names, especially such as have no Latin or Latinized equivalent, the name may be left unaltered and uninflected, for instance, *Ingeborg, Gefion,* etc.; a practice which may be extended to names which in their present form are so altered that their derivation is not longer obvious, as *Fanny,* and the like. But in many cases the proper Latin form or equivalent is obvious; as, *Mariæ* from Mary, *Luciæ* from Lucy, *Gratiæ* from Grace, etc.

So much for specific appellations derived from personal proper names, the use of which, if practised with discretion, is not objectionable. But care should be exercised as to introducing names of persons who have not rendered some noteworthy service to science, either as investigators, collectors of materials, or promoters of zoölogical investigation. The same remark will apply with still greater force to generic names, in respect to which the Bath (1865) Committee of the British Association makes the following sound suggestion : —

"*Specific names* from persons have already been sufficiently prostituted, and personal *generic* names have increased to a large and undeserving extent. The handing down the name of a naturalist by a genus has always been considered as the highest honour that could be given, and should never be bestowed lightly.[1]"

The simplest rule for forming a generic appellation from a personal name seems to be to ascertain first the genitive of the name according to the above suggestions, and then to append an *a*. In this case, however, the silent *e* at the end of a name should be dropped ; *e. g.*, *Latreillia*, not *Latreilleia*. In some other cases the author will need to exercise his taste in forming the words when the genitive form does not end in *i*.

It has been suggested that the name be "disembarrassed from all titles and all preliminary particles" ; but it is evident that in many cases the "preliminary particle" is so important a part of the name that its exclusion would make the name unrecognizable. While, therefore, it is proper to omit the German *von*, for instance, in *Lanius homeyeri*, it would hardly be defensible to write *Busi* or *Mursii*, instead of *Dubusi* or *Desmursii*, when intending to honor Du Bus or Des Murs by naming a species after him. That 'particle' does not mean 'article' need hardly be mentioned, and names like La Fresnaye, etc., should not be dismembered, though in German names the article also has to be left out when the particle is dropped.

RECOMMENDATION III. The *best* zoölogical names are those which are derived from the Latin or Greek, and express some distinguishing characteristic of the object to which they are applied.

REMARKS. — This is Recommendation 'A.' of the B. A. 'Recommendations for the Improvement of Zoological Nomenclature in the Future,' under which the B. A. Committee considers 'Classes of objectionable names.' This subject has also since received detailed consideration from De Candolle in his 'Lois de la Nomenclature botanique,' and Mr. Dall has devoted several pages to it in his 'Report' (pp. 29-31), all of which may well be consulted in this connection. The principal of these recommendations may be summarized as follows : —

---

[1] " Hoc unicum et summum præmium laboris, sancte servandum, et caste dispensandum ad incitamentum et ornamentum Botanices. — *Phil. Botan.*, p. 171."

1. Avoid adjective generic names. "The names of genera are in all cases essentially substantive, and hence adjective terms cannot be employed for them without doing violence to grammar. The generic names *Hians, Criniger, Cursorius, Nitidula,* etc., are examples of this incorrect usage." (*B. A. Code.*)

2. Avoid generic names in the genitive case. Like adjective names, these can be used only in violation of both good taste and grammatical construction. (DALL.)

3. Avoid geographical names, which should never be used for genera, and only with discrimination for species. — Even for species, formerly some authors (Wagler, for instance) went so far as to substitute others whenever they occurred, while other authors (Swainson, for example) would tolerate them only when they applied *exclusively;* as, *Lepus hibernicus, Troglodytes europæus,* etc. The B. A. Committee were "by no means disposed to go to this length. It is not the less true that *Hirundo javanica* is a Javanese bird, even though it may occur in other countries also, and though other species of *Hirundo* may occur in Java. The utmost that can be urged against such words is, that they do not tell the *whole truth*." (*B. A. Code.*) The B. A. Committee advised restriction of such names to species confined to the countries whose names they bear.

4. Avoid barbarous names unless they are euphonious, easily modified to a Latin form, and are more or less well known in their original form as names of the species or genera to which they are to be applied; *e. g., Ajaja, Ara, Macao, Pompadora, Skua, Tijuca,* etc.

"Some authors protest strongly against the introduction of exotic words into our Latin nomenclature, others defend the practice with equal warmth. We may remark, first, that the practice is not contrary to classical usage, for the Greeks and Romans did occasionally, though with reluctance, introduce barbarous words in a modified form into their respective languages. Secondly, the preservation of the trivial names which animals bear in their native countries is often of great use to the traveller in aiding him to discover and identify the species. We do not therefore consider, if such words have a Latin termination given to them, that the occasional and judicious use of them as scientific terms can be justly objected to." (*B. A. Code.*)

5. "Technical names. — All words expressive of trades and professions have been by some writers excluded from zoology, but without sufficient reason. Words of this class, *when carefully chosen,* often express the peculiar characters and habits of animals in a metaphorical manner, which is highly elegant. We may cite the generic terms *Arvicola, Lanius, Pastor, Tyrannus, Regulus, Mimus, Ploceus,* etc., as favourable examples of this class of names." (*B. A. Code.*)

6. Mythological names should be applied with great care, and only when they have some perceptible reference or allusion to the object on which they are conferred. They may sometimes be used as generic names "with

the same propriety as technical ones, in cases where a direct allusion can be traced between the narrated actions of a personage and the observed habits or structure of an animal. Thus when the name *Progne* is given to a Swallow, *Clotho* to a Spider, *Hydra* to a Polyp, *Athene* to an Owl, *Nestor* to a gray-headed Parrot, etc., a pleasing and beneficial connexion is established between classical literature and physical science." (*B. A. Code.*)

7. Avoid hybrid names. — "Compound words, whose components are taken from two different languages, are great deformities in nomenclature, and naturalists should be especially guarded not to introduce any more such terms into zoology, which furnishes too many examples of them already. We have them compounded of Greek and Latin, as *Dendrofalco, Gymnocorvus, Monoculus, Arborophila, flavigaster;* Greek and French, as *Jacamaralcyon, Jacamerops;* Greek and English, as *Bullockoides, Gilbertsocrinites.*" (*B. A. Code.*)

8. Avoid generic names closely resembling others already in existence, even when the etymology may be different; as, *Pica* and *Picus, Otostomia* and *Odostomia, Tachyphonus* and *Trachyphonus,* etc. The danger of confusion in such cases is evident, and should be guarded against.

9. "Corrupted words. — In the construction of compound Latin words, there are certain grammatical rules which have been known and acted on for two thousand years, and which a naturalist is bound to acquaint himself with before he tries his skill in coining zoological terms. One of the chief of these rules is, that in compounding words all the radical or essential parts of the constituent members must be retained, and no change made except in the variable terminations. . . . . A name made up of the first half of one word and the last half of another, is as deformed a monster in nomenclature as a Mermaid or a Centaur would be in zoology; yet we find examples in the names *Corcorax* (from *Corvus* and *Pyrrhocorax*), *Cypsnagra* (from *Cypselus* and *Tanagra*), *Merulaxis* (from *Merula* and *Synallaxis*), *Loxigilla* (from *Loxia* and *Fringilla*), etc. In other cases, where the *commencement* of both the simple words is retained in the compound, a fault is still committed by cutting off too much of the radical and vital portions, as is the case in *Bucorvus* (from *Buceros* and *Corvus*), *Ninox* (from *Nisus* and *Noctua*), etc." (*B. A. Code.*)

10. "Nonsense names. — Some authors having found difficulty in selecting generic names which have not been used before, have adopted the plan of coining words at random without any derivation or meaning whatever. The following are examples: *Viralva, Xema, Azeca, Assiminia, Quedius, Spisula.* To the same class we may refer *anagrams* of other generic names, as *Dacelo* and *Cedola* of *Alcedo, Zapornia* of *Porzana,* etc. Such verbal trifling as this is in very bad taste, and is especially calculated to bring the science into contempt. . . . . It is contrary to the genius of all languages, which appear never to produce new words by spontaneous generation, but always to derive them from some other source, however distant or obscure. And it

is peculiarly annoying to the etymologist, who after seeking in vain through the vast storehouses of human language for the parentage of such words, discovers at last that he has been pursuing an *ignis fatuus.*" (*B. A. Code.*)

11. Indicate the etymology of each name proposed. — While it is not now intended that names erroneously constructed shall be subject to emendation (see above, Canon XL. and Remarks), it is highly desirable that the etymology of all generic names newly proposed should be clearly indicated.

12. Avoid names of great length, or of harsh and inelegant pronunciation. Words of more than five syllables should as far as possible be avoided. In the construction of names it is obvious that euphony should be regarded. Thus such names as *Eschscholtzi, Sylviorthorhynchus, Strigymnhemipus, Synthliborhamphus, Xiphidiorhynchus, Wurmizusume,* etc., are decidedly objectionable.

13. Avoid comparative names. — Specific names expressive of comparative size, as *minor, minimus, maximus,* should be avoided, as they may be rendered inaccurate by the later discovery of additional species. Names denoting resemblance to another species or genus should be also avoided, as *Picoides, Emberizoides, Pseudoluscinia, rubeculoides,* etc. (*B. A. Code.*)

14. Generic names compounded from those of other genera, if not too long, and properly formed (not made corrupt by trying to render them shorter), may sometimes be adopted with advantage, since they serve to express the position of a genus intermediate between, or allied with, two other genera. (*B. A. Code.*)

15. Avoid making a wrong application of the ancient names of animals. Names of animals found in classic authors have in numerous cases been applied at random to exotic genera or species wholly unknown to the ancients. This practice should be discouraged. The use, however, of ancient names, *when correctly applied,* is most desirable, for it is better in framing scientific terms to select old words than to form new ones. (*B. A. Code.*)

16. In modifying existing names — as, for instance, of genera in naming subgenera or sections, or of species in designating allied species — by means of prefixes and suffixes, the following precautions should receive attention. Before a Greek derivative *eu-* and *pseudo-* may be used, the former especially in modifying generic names; after a Greek derivative, *-astrum, -oides,* or *-opsis.* Before a Latin derivative, *sub-* may be used; after it, *-ella, -una, -ina, -ites,* etc. The prefix *eu-* may be used before generic names; the prefixes *sub-* and *pseudo-* should be restricted to specific names; the suffixes are applicable to either generic or specific names. Usage has justified to some extent the application of these modifications to words of uncertain etymology or arbitrary formation, in connection with which Greek syllables should be entirely avoided. So far as specific names are concerned, *pseudo-* may be employed when it is desired to connect the name of a species with another with which it has been confounded. The suffixes *-ella, -una, -ina,* are used in

modifying a Latin generic name, to indicate that a new genus thus named is in some way related to the one whose name is thus modified. They are also used in reforming a name which is inadmissible for any reason, in order to preserve a suggestive and convenient similarity. For instance, *Cæcilia*, if employed for a shell, but which was found to be preoccupied in some other class, might be modified to *Cæcilianella*, in order that convenience in consulting indices might be conserved for the new name in connection with the old one. (DALL, *Rep.*, p. 30.)

17. Geographical specific names are formed by adding the suffixes *-us*, *-ius*, *-icus*, *-inus*, *-itus*, (or their feminine or neuter equivalents, as the case may require,) and *-ensis*, the name itself suffering no modification except in its termination.

18. Manuscript names used by collectors in their notes or on labels, if well chosen, may be adopted, the adopter of the name of course supplying a description; and he should further state that the name has not previously been formally introduced. Without this precaution the use of manuscript names is highly objectionable, and has been the source of great confusion and annoyance. The manuscript names of Beck, Solander, Leach, and others, have long been stumbling-blocks, from having been quoted by naturalists with no reference to the fact that they were unaccompanied by descriptions, and therefore without standing. (DALL, *Rep.*, p. 33.)

19. In subdividing an old genus it would be better to make the subdivisions agree in gender with that of the original group, in order that specific names may be preserved unaltered.

§ 13. *Of the Transliteration of Names.*

RECOMMENDATION IV. Names adopted from languages written in other than Roman characters, as the Greek, Russian, Arabic, Japanese, etc., or from languages containing characters not represented in the Roman alphabet, as the Spanish, French, German, Scandinavian, Western Slavonian, etc., should be rendered by the corresponding Roman letters or combinations of letters.

REMARKS. — The transliteration of letters not Roman into those of the Latin alphabet is a matter of some difficulty and uncertainty, as philologists are not yet in agreement as to the rules. The only alphabet in regard to which scholars nearly agree being the Greek one, the commonly adopted system should be followed, and also in case of names derived from the modern Greek language. In regard to the other alphabets, it is to be recommended that in transliterating the spelling be as nearly phonetic as possible, and in accordance with the sound indicated by the letters of the Latin alphabet. This is to prevent such transliterations as *yessoensis* for *jessoensis*, *Chernik* for *Tschernik*, *y* and *ch* having sounds in the Latin alphabet different from those which they are intended to indicate in the above words. There are two methods of transliterating the Russian alphabet. One is by rendering the letters by the corresponding Latin letters, which method should always be followed in geographical names, with the proviso, however, that where the Russian name in the nominative case ends with the letter ъ the ending Latinizing the word is to be appended to the soft consonant preceding the ъ: *e. g.*, nom. *Orloff* (ending in Russian въ), gen. *Orlovi*, adject. *Orlovianus*, and not *Orloffi*, *Orloffianus*, this being in conformity with the spirit of the Russian language, which has gen. *Orlova*. The other method of transliterating the Russian letters, much used by Russians themselves, is to render them by the corresponding letters of the Polish language. The alphabet of the latter is only quasi-Roman, however, though most of the letters have the same value as the Roman letters. This method of transliteration should only be resorted to when a Russian author is in the habit of so transliterating his own name, and it is known to the scientific world in that form: for instance, *Severzowi*, and not *Severzovi*, he himself invariably spelling his name Severzow when writing it in Roman letters.

In regard to names derived from the Japanese language, it is to be remarked that the Japanese have now officially adopted a system of transliteration according to the "Italian pronunciation," which should be followed.

In most modern alphabets which are based upon the Roman one occur a few peculiar letters which have to be transliterated, as the Spanish *ñ*; the French *é*, *è*, *â*, and *ç*; the German *ä*, *ö*, *ü*; the Scandinavian *å*, *ø*; the Slavonian *č*, etc. The Spanish *ñ* may be rendered by doubling the consonant so marked, or by *ni*, according to circumstances; the French *é*, *è*, and *â*, simply by omitting the marks of accent, and *ç* by *s*; the German *ä*, *ö*, and *ü*, by *æ*, *œ*, and *ue*; the Scandinavian *å* and *ø*, by *ao* and *œ*; the Slavonian *č* or *cz*, by *tsch*. However, if a name has a different but settled transliteration, this should be employed, as, for instance, *Taczanowskii*, and not *Tatschanovskii*, as the person using such transliteration must be content to have his name mispronounced, as in the case quoted, the usual pronunciation being *Takzanowski* (and we have seen it Latinized by French authors into *Tackzanowskia!*). But what about names like *Tetrao mlokosiewiczii*, named after an obscure forester somewhere in Russia? The best recommendation we can make is to avoid them altogether. Do not burden our nomenclature with names of persons whom science does not know, or with names which civilized people cannot read at sight, nor pronounce when read, nor remember when read and pronounced.

§ 14. *Of the Description of Zoölogical Objects.*

RECOMMENDATION V. When naming a new species or subspecies, always give a diagnosis, as short as possible, but still containing all the essential features by which the species or subspecies may be distinguished from the other known members of the genus to which it is referred. Base the diagnosis on the type specimen, and indicate the museum where the type is deposited, and the catalogue number by which it may be identified. Give a comparison with the nearest allied forms, and tabulate, if possible, the characters of the new form in a 'key' to the genus, or a section of it.

RECOMMENDATION VI. When establishing a new genus, always mention at least the family to which it is considered to belong, and a single typical species; give then the diagnostic characters by which the members of the genus may be distinguished from those of the allied genera.

§ 15. *Of the Bibliography of Names.*

RECOMMENDATION VII. In preparing tables of bibliographical references in works of a revisionary or monographic character, all published works which throw light upon the history of the organisms in question are subject to citation.

REMARKS. — The object of such citation is twofold; — (1) to afford a guide to the literature of the subject; (2) to show what name or combination of names is tenable for the organism under consideration, and the authorities for such names.

RECOMMENDATION VIII. Citations are to be made in chronological order, the earliest name given to the organism standing first, and the other designations following in due sequence; then under each designation are to be arranged, also in chronological order, the several works or papers which treat of the organism under such designation. The date of publication is always to be made a part of the citation.

REMARKS. — The pre-Linnæan or early historical references are thus separated from the nomenclatural or synonymatic, on which, however, the latter often depend, and are therefore historically important. All bibliographical references are in a measure historical, but a distinction has been made between such as are strictly historical and those mainly biological. While it may be impracticable to separate them into distinct series, it will greatly facilitate the labor of later students of the group if authors will indicate the character of the knowledge conveyed in the work cited by a brief parenthetical statement following the citation, as biographical, descriptive, embryological, monographic, geographical distribution, etc., as the case may be, — a practice already adopted by some writers. The extent to which bibliographical references may be profitably cited will vary with the nature of the work in hand, but in works of a monographic character, they should include all essential works, whether relating to the status of names, or to the development, relationship, habits, or distribution of the organism under consideration.

Since pre-Linnæan authors are necessarily subject to citation, although their names of groups are untenable (unless later adopted by binomial writers), the relation of their work to the science becomes duly recognized, and they acquire such credit as the character of their work may entitle them to receive. Much has been said on the score of justice in relation to the early authors; and it has been claimed that to ignore their names of groups in our nomenclature is to do them great injustice. Your Committee, however, begs leave to submit, as already stated under Canon XIV., that the matter of justice or injustice in relation to authors is not to be considered in matters of nomenclature, which should be based exclusively on certain general principles of utility, convenience, and practicability. In every historical *résumé* of our knowledge of particular groups or species, every author who has contributed to our knowledge, whether pre-Linnæan or modern, polynomial or binomial, receives his due modicum of recognition, meted in proportion to the merit of his endeavors. So that he is not only recognized in bibliographical citation, but in every sketch of the progress of our knowledge of the organisms about which he may have written.

RECOMMENDATION IX. When the diagnostic characters or the limits of a group have been changed, such change should be shown by an abridged indication of the character of the change, as 'mut. char.,' 'pro parte,' to follow the citation.

§ 16. *Of the Selection of Vernacular Names.*

RECOMMENDATION X. Vernacular names, though having no standing in scientific nomenclature, and being not strictly subject to the law of priority, have still an importance that demands the due exercise of care in their selection, especially with reference to their fitness and desirability.

REMARKS. — It not infrequently happens that well-known, abundant, and familiar species have several nearly equally familiar vernacular designations, in which case the most euphonious and otherwise most fitting should be selected and given prominence. In the case of two equally unobjectionable names, the earliest should be given preference. In general, vernacular names may well be selected on the *auctorum plurimorum* principle.

Since many species known to science are without vernacular names, otherwise than unknown barbarous ones, and since it is necessary, or at least desirable, sooner or later to supply them with vernacular designations, these should be as far as possible formed by translating, or in part adopting, the technical names of science; and authors of monographic works, like, for example, the British Museum 'Catalogue of Birds,' or faunal works, like many which might be named, (but which unfortunately in too many cases ignore vernacular names,) would do their fellow naturalists, and through them the public, a favor by considerately supplying vernacular designations to species, particularly in such departments of Zoölogy as Mammalogy and Ornithology, and indeed Vertebrates generally, together with the better known or more exemplary forms among Invertebrates.

CHECK-LIST

OF

NORTH AMERICAN BIRDS,

ACCORDING TO THE CANONS OF NOMENCLATURE

OF THE

AMERICAN ORNITHOLOGISTS' UNION.

CHECK-LIST.[1]

Order PYGOPODES. Diving Birds.

Suborder PODICIPEDES. Grebes.

Family PODICIPIDÆ. Grebes.

Genus ÆCHMOPHORUS Coues.

Æchmophorus Coues, Pr. Ac. Nat. Sci. Phila. April, 1862, 229. Type, *Podiceps occidentalis* Lawr.

1. **Æchmophorus occidentalis** (Lawr.).
    Western Grebe.

    Podiceps occidentalis Lawr. in Baird's B. N. Am. 1858, 894.
    Æchmophorus occidentalis Coues, Pr. Ac. Nat. Sci. Phila. 1862, 229.

    [B 704, C 608, R 729, C 845.]

    Habitat. Western North America, eastward to Manitoba.

Genus COLYMBUS Linnæus.

Colymbus Linn. S. N. ed. 10, I. 1758, 135. Type, by elimination, *Colymbus cristatus* Linn.

Subgenus COLYMBUS.

2. **Colymbus holbœllii** (Reinh.).
    Holbœll's Grebe.

    Podiceps holbœllii Reinh. Vid. Med. 1853, 76.
    Colymbus holbœllii Ridgw. Water B. N. Am. II. 1884, 428.

---

[1] For a detailed statement of the scope and plan of the present Check-List of North-American Birds, see *anteà*, pp. 14, 15.

[B 702, C 610, R 731, C 847.]

HAB. North America at large, including Greenland. Also Eastern Siberia, and southward to Japan. Breeds in high latitudes, migrating south in winter.

SUBGENUS **DYTES** KAUP.

Dytes KAUP, Sk. Ent. Eur. Thierw. 1829, 49. Type, *Colymbus auritus* LINN.

3. **Colymbus auritus** LINN.
   Horned Grebe.

Colymbus auritus LINN. S. N. ed. 10, I. 1758, 135.

[B 706, C 611, R 732, C 848.]

HAB. Northern Hemisphere. Breeds from the Northern United States northward.

4. **Colymbus nigricollis californicus** (HEERM.).
   American Eared Grebe.

Podiceps californicus HEERM. Pr. Ac. Nat. Sci. Phila. 1854, 179.
Colymbus nigricollis californicus RIDGW. Pr. U. S. Nat. Mus. VIII. 1885, 356.

[B 707, C 612, R 733 a, C 850.]

HAB. Northern and Western North America, from the Mississippi Valley westward.

SUBGENUS **PODICEPS** LATHAM.

Podiceps LATH. Ind. Orn. II. 1790, 780. Type, by elimination, *Colymbus fluviatilis* TUNST.

5. **Colymbus dominicus** LINN.
   St. Domingo Grebe.

Colymbus dominicus LINN. S. N. ed. 12, I. 1766, 223.

[B 708 a, C 613, R 734, C 851.]

HAB. Texas and Southern California southward through Tropical America to Paraguay, including the West Indies.

ORDER PYGOPODES.

Genus **PODILYMBUS** Lesson.

Podilymbus Less. Traité, I. 1831, 595. Type, *Colymbus podiceps* Linn.

6. Podilymbus podiceps (Linn.).
Pied-billed Grebe.

Colymbus podiceps Linn. S. N. ed. 10, I. 1758, 136.
Podilymbus podiceps Lawr. in Baird's B. N. Am. 1858, 898.

[B 709, C 614, R 735, C 852.]

Hab. British Provinces southward to Brazil, Buenos Ayres, and Chili, including the West Indies and the Bermudas, breeding nearly throughout its range.

Suborder CEPPHI. Loons and Auks.

Family URINATORIDÆ. Loons.

Genus **URINATOR** Cuvier.

Urinator Cuv. Anat. Comp. I. 1799, tabl. ii. Type, *Colymbus imber* Gunn.

7. Urinator imber (Gunn.).
Loon.

Colymbus imber Gunnerus, Trondh. Selsk. Skr. I. 1761, pl. iii.
Urinator imber Stejn. Orn. Expl. Kamtschat. 1885, 313.

[B 698, C 605, R 736, C 840.]

Hab. Northern part of Northern Hemisphere. In North America breeds from the northern tier of States northward; ranges in winter south to the Gulf of Mexico.

8. Urinator adamsii (Gray).
Yellow-billed Loon.

Colymbus adamsii Gray, P. Z. S. 1859, 167.
Urinator adamsii Stejn. Pr. U. S. Nat. Mus. V. 1882, 43.

[B —, C 605 *a*, R 737, C 841.]

HAB. Arctic America, west of Hudson's Bay. Casual in Northern Europe and Asia.

9. **Urinator arcticus** (LINN.).
Black-throated Loon.

Colymbus arcticus LINN. S. N. ed. 10, I. 1758, 135.
Urinator arcticus STEJN. Pr. U. S. Nat. Mus. V. 1882, 43.

[B 699, C 606, R 738, C 842.]

HAB. Northern part of the Northern Hemisphere. In North America migrating south in winter to the Northern United States.

10. **Urinator pacificus** (LAWR.).
Pacific Loon.

Colymbus pacificus LAWR. in BAIRD'S B. N. Am. 1858, 889.
Urinator pacificus STEJN. Pr. U. S. Nat. Mus. V. 1882, 43.

[B 700, C 606 *a*, R 739, C 843.]

HAB. Pacific coast of North America, south in winter to Cape St. Lucas and Guadalupe Island.

11. **Urinator lumme** (GUNN.).
Red-throated Loon.

Colymbus lumme GUNN. Trond. Selsk. Skr. I. 1761, pl. ii. fig. 2.
Urinator lumme STEJN. Pr. U. S. Nat. Mus. V. 1882, 43.

[B 701, C 607, R 740, C 844.]

HAB. Northern part of Northern Hemisphere, migrating southward in winter nearly across the United States.

FAMILY **ALCIDÆ**. AUKS, MURRES, AND PUFFINS.

SUBFAMILY **FRATERCULINÆ**. PUFFINS.

GENUS **LUNDA** PALLAS.

Lunda PALL. Zoog. Rosso-As. II. 1826, 363. Type, *Alca cirrhata* PALL.

12. Lunda cirrhata PALL.
Tufted Puffin.

Alca cirrhata PALL. Spic. Zool. V. 1769, 7, pl. i., pl. ii. figs. 1, 2, 3.
Lunda cirrhata PALL. Zoog. Rosso-As. II. 1826, 363, pl. 82.

[B 712, 716, C 619, R 745, C 856.]

HAB. Coasts and islands of the North Pacific from California to Alaska, and from Japan to Bering's Strait. Accidental on the coast of Maine.

GENUS **FRATERCULA** BRISSON.

Fratercula BRISS. Orn. VI. 1760, 81. Type, *Alca arctica* LINN.

13. Fratercula arctica (LINN.).
Puffin.

Alca arctica LINN. S. N. ed. 10, I. 1758, 13.
Fratercula arctica SCHÄFFER, Mus. Orn. 1789, 61.

[B 715, C 618, R 743, C 854.]

HAB. Coasts and islands of the North Atlantic, breeding on the North American coast from the Bay of Fundy northward. South in winter to Long Island, and casually further.

13 a. Fratercula arctica glacialis (TEMM.).
Large-billed Puffin.

Mormon glacialis "LEACH," TEMM. Man. d'Orn. 2d ed. II. 1820, 933.
Fratercula arctica β glacialis BLASIUS, List B. Europ. 1862, 24.

[B 714, C 618 a, R 743 a, C 855.]

HAB. Coasts and islands of the Arctic Ocean, from Spitzbergen to Baffin's Bay.

14. Fratercula corniculata (NAUM.).
Horned Puffin.

Mormon corniculata NAUM. Isis, 1821, 782, pl. vii. figs. 3, 4.
Fratercula corniculata BRANDT, Bull. Ac. St. Pétersb. II. 1837, 348.

[B 713, C 617, R 744, C 853.]

HAB. Coasts and islands of the North Pacific, from the Kurile Islands to Sitka.

SUBFAMILY **PHALERINÆ**. AUKLETS, MURRELETS, GUILLEMOTS.

GENUS **CERORHINCA** BONAPARTE.

Cerorhinca BONAP. Ann. Lyc. N. Y. 1828, 427. Type, *C. occidentalis* BP. = *Alca monocerata* PALL.

15. Cerorhinca monocerata (PALL.).
Rhinoceros Auklet.

Alca monocerata PALL. Zoog. Rosso-As. II. 1826, 362.
Cerorhina monocerata CASS. in BAIRD'S B. N. Am. 1858, 905.

[B 717, 718, C 620, R 746, C 857.]

HAB. Coasts and islands of the North Pacific, breeding southward to California and Japan; in winter, southward to Lower California.

GENUS **PTYCHORAMPHUS** BRANDT.

Ptychoramphus BRANDT, Bull. Ac. St. Pétersb. II. 1837, 347. Type, *Uria aleutica* PALL.

16. Ptychoramphus aleuticus (PALL.).
Cassin's Auklet.

Uria aleutica PALL. Zoog. Rosso-As. II. 1726, 370.
Ptychoramphus aleuticus BRANDT, Bull. Ac. St. Pétersb. II. 1837, 347.

[B 724, C 625, R 751, C 862.]

HAB. Pacific coast of North America, from the Aleutian Islands to San Diego, breeding southward to the Farallones.

GENUS **CYCLORRHYNCHUS** KAUP.

Cyclorrhynchus KAUP, Sk. Ent. Eur. Thierw. 1829, 15. Type, *Alca psittacula* PALL.

17. Cyclorrhynchus psittaculus (PALL.).
Paroquet Auklet.

Alca psittacula PALL. Spic. Zool. V. 1760, 13, pl. ii., pl. v. figs. 4-6.
Cyclorhynchus psittaculus STEJN. Pr. U. S. Nat. Mus. VII. Aug. 5, 1884, 216.

[B 725, C 621, R 747, C 858.]

HAB. Coasts and islands of the North Pacific, from the Aleutian and Kurile Islands northward.

Genus **SIMORHYNCHUS** MERREM.

Subgenus **SIMORHYNCHUS**.

Simorhynchus MERREM, in ERSCH & GRUBER'S Encycl. I sect. II. 1819, 405. Type, *Alca cristatella* PALL.

18. **Simorhynchus cristatellus** (PALL.).
    Crested Auklet.

Alca cristatella PALL. Spic. Zool. V. 1769, 20, pl. iii., pl. v. figs. 7–9.
Simorhynchus cristatellus BONAP. Compt. Rend. XLII. 1856, 774.

[B 719, 720, C 622, R 748, C 859.]

HAB. Coasts and islands of the North Pacific, from Kadiak and Japan northward.

Subgenus **PHALERIS** TEMMINCK.

Phaleris TEMM. Man. Orn. 1820, p. cxii. Type, by elimination, *Alca pygmæa* GMEL.

19. **Simorhynchus pygmæus** (GMEL.).
    Whiskered Auklet.

Alca pygmæa GMEL. S. N. I. ii. 1788, 555.
Simorhynchus pygmæus BRANDT, Mél. Biol. VII. 1869, 222.

[B 721, C 623, R 749, C 860.]

HAB. Coasts and islands of the North Pacific, from Unalashka through the Aleutian chain to Kamtschatka.

Subgenus **CICERONIA** REICHENBACH

Ciceronia REICH. Syst. Av. 1852, p. iii. Type, *Phaleris microceros* BRANDT = *Uria pusilla* PALL.

20. **Simorhynchus pusillus** (PALL.).
    Least Auklet.

Uria pusilla PALL. Zoog. Rosso-As. II. 1826, 373, pl. 70.
Simorhynchus pusillus COUES, Pr. Ac. Nat. Sci. Phila. 1862, 324.

[B 722, 723, C 624, R 750, C 861.]

HAB. Coasts and islands of the North Pacific, from Sitka and Japan northward to Bering's Strait.

GENUS **SYNTHLIBORAMPHUS** BRANDT.

Synthliboramphus BRANDT, Bull. Ac. St. Pétersb. II. 1837, 347. Type, *Alca antiqua* GMEL.

21. **Synthliboramphus antiquus** (GMEL.).
    Ancient Murrelet.

Alca antiqua GMEL. S. N. I. ii. 1788, 554.
Synthliboramphus antiquus BRANDT, Bull. Ac. St. Pétersb. II. 1837, 347.

[B 734, 736, C 627, R 753, 759, C 864, 870.]

HAB. Coasts and islands of the North Pacific, from Sitka and Japan northward. Accidental in Wisconsin.

22. **Synthliboramphus wumizusume** (TEMM.).
    Temminck's Murrelet.

Uria wumizusume TEMM. Pl. Col. 1838, 579.
Synthliborhamphus wumizusume REICH. Vollst. Naturg. Vög. Natatores, 1845, pl. iv. fig. 31.

[B 737, C 628, R 754, C 865.]

HAB. Coasts and islands of the North Pacific, from Washington Territory northward, and Japan.

GENUS **BRACHYRAMPHUS** BRANDT.

Brachyramphus BRANDT, Bull. Ac. St. Pétersb. II. 1837, 346. Type, *Colymbus marmoratus* GMEL.

23. **Brachyramphus marmoratus** (GMEL.).
    Marbled Murrelet.

Colymbus marmoratus GMEL. S. N. I. ii. 1788, 583.
Brachyramphus marmoratus BRANDT, Bull. Ac. St. Pétersb. II. 1837, 346.

[B 732, 733, C 629, R 755, C 866.]

Hab. Coasts and islands of the North Pacific; on the American coast from San Diego northward, and breeding as far south as Vancouver Island.

24. Brachyramphus kittlitzii Brandt.
Kittlitz's Murrelet.

Brachyramphus kittlitzii Brandt, Bull. Ac. St. Pétersb. II. 1837, 346.

[B 735, C 630, R 756, C 867.]

Hab. Kamtschatka and Aleutian Islands, east to Unalashka.

25. Brachyramphus hypoleucus Xantus.
Xantus's Murrelet.

Brachyrhamphus hypoleucus Xantus, Pr. Ac. Nat. Sci. Phila., Nov. 1859, 299.

[B —, C —, R 757, C 868.]

Hab. Coast of Southern California, from San Diego to Cape St. Lucas.

26. Brachyramphus craveri (Salvad.).
Craveri's Murrelet.

Uria craveri Salvad. Atti Soc. It. Sc. Nat. VIII. 1866, Estr. p. 17.
Brachyrhamphus craverii Coues, Pr. Ac. Nat. Sci. Phila. 1868, 66.

[B —, C —, R 758, C 869.]

Hab. Island of Natividad, Gulf of California.

Genus CEPPHUS Pallas.

Cepphus Pall. Spic. Zool. V. 1769, 33. Type, *C. lacteolus* Pall. = *C. grylle*, albino.

27. Cepphus grylle (Linn.).
Black Guillemot.

Alca grylle Linn. S. N. ed. 10, I. 1758, 130.
Cepphus grylle Brehm, Handb. Vög. Deutschl. 1831, 987.

[B 726, *part*, C 631, *part*, R 760, *part*, C 871, *part*.]

Hab. Coasts of Northern Europe, south to Denmark and the British Islands. Coast of Maine, south in winter to Philadelphia; Newfoundland (?).

28. **Cepphus mandtii** (LICHT.).
Mandt's Guillemot.

Uria mandtii LICHT. in MANDT'S Obs. Itin. Dissert. 1822, 30.
Cepphus mandtii BP. Cat. Parzud. 1856, 12.

[B 726, *part*, C 631, *part*, R 760, *part*, C 871, *part*.]

HAB. Arctic regions of both continents; south on the Atlantic coast of North America in winter to New Jersey, breeding to Hudson's Bay and Labrador; Alaskan coast, south, in winter, to Norton Sound.

29. **Cepphus columba** PALL.
Pigeon Guillemot.

Cepphus columba PALL. Zoog. Rosso-As. II. 1826, 348.

[B 727, C 632, R 761, C 872.]

HAB. Coasts and islands of the North Pacific, southward from Bering's Strait to Northern Japan and Southern California.

SUBFAMILY ALCINÆ. AUKS AND MURRES.

GENUS **URIA** BRISSON.

Uria BRISS. Orn. VI. 1760, 70. Type, by elimination, *Colymbus troile* LINN.

30. **Uria troile** (LINN.).
Murre.

Colymbus troile LINN. Faun. Suec. ed. 1761, 52; S. N. ed. 12, I. 1766, 220.
Uria troile LATH. Ind. Orn. II. 1790, 796.

[B 729, 730, C 634, R 763, C 874.]

HAB. Coasts and islands of the North Atlantic, southward on the coast of North America, in winter, to Southern New England; breeding from Nova Scotia northward.

30 *a*. **Uria troile californica** (BRYANT).
California Murre.

Catarractes californicus BRYANT, Pr. Bost. Soc. 1861, 11, figs. 3, 5.
Uria troile californica RIDGW. Water B. N. Am. II. 1884, 483.

[B —, C —, R 763 *a*, C 875.]

HAB. Coasts and islands of the North Pacific, breeding from California north to the Prybilof Islands.

31. Uria lomvia (LINN.).
Brünnich's Murre.

Alca lomvia LINN. S. N. ed. 10, I. 1758, 130.
Uria lomvia BRYANT, Proc. Bost. Soc. N. H. VIII. May, 1861, 75.

[B 731, C 635, R 764 *a*, C 876.]

HAB. Coasts and islands of the North Atlantic and Eastern Arctic Oceans; south on the Atlantic coast of North America to New Jersey, breeding from the Gulf of St. Lawrence northward.

31 *a*. Uria lomvia arra (PALL.).
Pallas's Murre.

Cepphus arra PALL. Zoog. Rosso-As. II. 1826, 347.
Uria lomvia arra RIDGW. Water B. N. Am. II. Sept. 1884, 485.

[B —, C —, R 764, C —.]

HAB. Coasts and islands of the North Pacific and Western Arctic Oceans.

GENUS **ALCA** LINNÆUS.

Alca LINN. S. N. ed. 10, I. 1758, 130. Type, by elimination, *Alca torda* LINN.

32. Alca torda LINN.
Razor-billed Auk.

Alca torda LINN. S. N. ed. 10, I. 1758, 130.

[B 711, C 616, R 742, C 877.]

HAB. Coasts and islands of the North Atlantic, south in winter on the North American coast to Southern New England.

GENUS **PLAUTUS** BRÜNNICH.

Plautus BRÜNN. Zool. Fund. 1772, 78. Type, *Alca impennis* LINN.

33. **Plautus impennis** (Linn.).
    Great Auk.

Alca impennis Linn. S. N. ed. 10, I. 1758, 130.
Plautus impennis Steenstr. Vid. Med. Nat. For. Kjøb. 1855, 114.

[B 710, C 615, R 741, C 878.]

Hab. Formerly the coasts and islands of the North Atlantic, from Massachusetts and Ireland northward nearly to the Arctic Circle. Believed to be now extinct.

Subfamily **ALLINÆ**. Dovekies.

Genus **ALLE** Link.

Alle Link, Beschr. Nat. Samml. Univ. Rostock, I. 1806, 17. Type, *Alca alle* Linn.

34. **Alle alle** (Linn.).
    Dovekie.

Alca alle Linn. S. N. ed. 10, I. 1758, 131.
Alle alle Stejneger, Stand. Nat. Hist. IV. 1885, 69.

[B 738, C 626, R 752, C 863.]

Hab. Coasts and islands of the North Atlantic and Eastern Arctic Oceans; in North America south in winter to New Jersey; breeds in high northern latitudes.

Order LONGIPENNES. Long-winged Swimmers.

Family **STERCORARIIDÆ**. Skuas and Jaegers.

Genus **MEGALESTRIS** Bonaparte.

Megalestris Bonap. Cat. Parzudaki, 1856, 11. Type, *Catharacta skua* Brünn.

ORDER LONGIPENNES. 85

35. Megalestris skua (Brünn.).
Skua.

Catharacta skua Brünn. Orn. Bor. 1764, 33.
Megalestris skua Ridgw. Pr. U. S. Nat. Mus. III. Sept. 4, 1880, 208.

[B 652, C 539, R 696, C 764.]

Hab. Coasts and islands of the North Atlantic, chiefly northward. South to Spain and Massachusetts. Apparently rare on the coast of North America.

Genus **STERCORARIUS** Brisson.

Stercorarius Briss. Orn. V. 1760, 149. Type, *Larus parasiticus* Linn.

36. Stercorarius pomarinus (Temm.).
Pomarine Jaeger.

Larus pomarinus Temm. Man. d'Orn. 1815, 514.
Stercorarius pomarinus Vieill. Nouv. Dict. XXXII. 1819, 158.

[B 653, C 540, R 697, C 765.]

Hab. Seas and inland waters of northern portions of the Northern Hemisphere, south in winter to Africa and Australia, and probably South America. Not known to occur in winter on the Atlantic coast of North America north of Long Island.

37. Stercorarius parasiticus (Linn.).
Parasitic Jaeger.

Larus parasiticus Linn. S. N. ed. 10, I. 1758, 136.
Stercorarius parasiticus Schäff. Mus. Orn. 1789, 62, pl. 37.

[B 654, C 541, R 698, C 766.]

Hab. Northern part of Northern Hemisphere, southward in winter to South Africa and South America. Breeds in high northern districts, and winters from the Middle States and California southward to Brazil and Chili.

38. Stercorarius longicaudus Vieill.
Long-tailed Jaeger.

Stercorarius longicaudus Vieill. Nouv. Dict. XXXII. 1819, 157.

[B 655, C 542, R 699, C 767.]

HAB. Northern part of Northern Hemisphere, breeding in high northern districts; south in winter to the Gulf of Mexico.

FAMILY LARIDÆ. GULLS AND TERNS.

SUBFAMILY LARINÆ. GULLS.

GENUS **GAVIA** BOIE.

Gavia BOIE, Isis, 1822, 563. Type, *Larus eburneus* PHIPPS = *Larus albus* GUNN.

39. Gavia alba (GUNN.).
Ivory Gull.

Larus albus GUNN. in LEEM's Beskr. Finm. Lapp. 1767, 285.
Gavia alba STEJN. Pr. U. S. Nat. Mus. V. 1882, 39.

[B 676, 677, C 550, R 657, C 785.]

HAB. Arctic Seas, south in winter on the Atlantic coast of North America to Labrador and Newfoundland, casually to New Brunswick, and on the Pacific side to Bering's Sea.

GENUS **RISSA** STEPHENS.

Rissa "LEACH," STEPH. Gen. Zool. XIII. 1825, 180. Type, *Larus tridactylus* LINN.

40. Rissa tridactyla (LINN.).
Kittiwake.

Larus tridactylus LINN. S. N. ed. 10, I. 1758, 136.
Rissa tridactyla BONAP. Comp. List, 1838, 62.

[B 672, C 552, R 658, C 782.]

HAB. Arctic regions, south in Eastern North America in winter to the Great Lakes and the Middle States.

40 *a*. Rissa tridactyla pollicaris RIDGW.
Pacific Kittiwake.

Rissa tridactyla pollicaris "STEJN. MS." RIDGW. Water B. N. Am. II. 1884, 202.

[B —, C 552 *a*, R 658 *a*, C 783.]

HAB. Coasts of North Pacific and Bering's Sea.

41. Rissa brevirostris (BRUCH).
Red-legged Kittiwake.

Larus brevirostris BRUCH, J. f. O. 1853, 103.
Rissa brevirostris LAWR. in BAIRD's B. N. Am. 1858, 855.

[B 674, 675, C 553, R 659, C 784.]

HAB. Coast and islands of Bering's Sea.

GENUS **LARUS** LINNÆUS.

Larus LINN. S. N. ed. 10, I. 1758, 136. Type, by elimination, *L. canus* LINN.

42. Larus glaucus BRÜNN.
Glaucous Gull.

Larus glaucus BRÜNN. Orn. Bor. 1764, 44.

[B 656, C 543, R 660, C 768.]

HAB. Arctic regions, south in winter in North America to the Great Lakes and Long Island. North Pacific.

43. Larus leucopterus FABER.
Iceland Gull.

Larus leucopterus FABER, Prodr. Isl. Orn. 1822, 91.

[B 658, C 544, R 661, C 769.]

HAB. Arctic regions, south in winter in North America to Massachusetts, occasionally much further south.

44. Larus glaucescens NAUM.
Glaucous-winged Gull.

Larus glaucescens NAUM. Naturg. Vög. Deutschl. X. 1840, 351.

[B 657, 659, C 545, R 662, C 770.]

HAB. Pacific coast of North America, from Alaska south to California; on the Asiatic side south to Japan.

45. **Larus kumlieni** BREWST.
Kumlien's Gull.

Larus kumlieni BREWST. Bull. Nutt. Orn. Club, VIII. 1883, 216.

[B —, C —, R —, C —.]

HAB. North Atlantic coast of North America, breeding in Cumberland Gulf; south in winter to the coast of the Middle States.

46. **Larus nelsoni** HENSH.
Nelson's Gull.

Larus nelsoni HENSH. Auk, I. July, 1884, 250.

[B —, C —, R —, C —.]

HAB. Coast of Norton Sound, Alaska.

47. **Larus marinus** LINN.
Great Black-backed Gull.

Larus marinus LINN. S. N. ed. 10, I. 1758, 136.

[B 660, C 546, R 663, C 771.]

HAB. Coasts of the North Atlantic; south in winter to Long Island and Italy.

48. **Larus schistisagus** STEJN.
Slaty-backed Gull.

Larus schistisagus STEJN. Auk, I. July, 1884, 231.

[B —, C —, R —, C —.]

HAB. North Pacific, chiefly on the Asiatic side; Herald Island, Arctic Ocean, and Alaska.

49. **Larus occidentalis** AUD.
Western Gull.

Larus occidentalis AUD. Orn. Biog. V. 1839, 320.

[B 662, C 547 *b*, R 664, C 774.]

HAB. Pacific coast of North America, breeding from Southern California northward.

[50.] **Larus affinis** REINH.
      Siberian Gull.

Larus affinis REINH. Vid. Med. 1853, 78.
$$[B\ —,\ C\ —,\ R\ 665,\ C\ 776.]$$
HAB. Greenland; Asia and Europe, southward in winter to North Africa.

51. **Larus argentatus** BRÜNN.
      Herring Gull.

Larus argentatus BRÜNN. Orn. Bor. 1764, 44.
$$[B\ —,\ C\ 547,\ R\ 666,\ C\ 772.]$$
HAB. Old World, south to the Azores; Cumberland Sound; occasional on the eastern coast of the United States.

51 *a*. **Larus argentatus smithsonianus** COUES.
      American Herring Gull.

Larus smithsonianus COUES, Pr. Ac. Nat. Sci. Phila. 1862, 296.
Larus argentatus var. *smithsonianus* COUES, Check List, 1873, no. 547 *a*.
$$[B\ 661,\ C\ 547\,a,\ R\ 666\,a,\ C\ 773.]$$
HAB. North America generally, breeding on the Atlantic coast from Maine northward; in winter south to Cuba and Lower California.

52. **Larus cachinnans** PALL.
      Pallas's Gull.

Larus cachinnans PALL. Zoog. Rosso-As. II. 1826, 318.
$$[B\ —,\ C\ —,\ R\ 667,\ C\ 775.]$$
HAB. Asia, from the Red Sea to the Pacific and Arctic Oceans; coast of Alaska, south in winter to California.

53. **Larus californicus** LAWR.
      California Gull.

Larus californicus LAWR. Ann. Lyc. N. Y. VI. 1854, 79.
$$[B\ 663,\ C\ 548\,a,\ R\ 668,\ C\ 777.]$$
HAB. Western Province of North America, from Alaska to Mexico.

54. Larus delawarensis ORD.
Ring-billed Gull.

Larus delawarensis ORD, GUTHRIE'S Geog. 2d Am. ed. 1815, 319.

[B 664, C 548, R 669, C 778.]

HAB. North America at large; south in winter to Cuba and Mexico.

55. Larus brachyrhynchus RICH.
Short-billed Gull.

Larus brachyrhynchus RICH. F. B. A. II. 1831, 421.

[B 665, 673, C 549, R 670, C 780.]

HAB. Arctic America and Pacific coast, south in winter to Southern California.

[56.] Larus canus LINN.
Mew Gull.

Larus canus LINN. S. N. ed. 10, I. 1758, 136.

[B —, C —, R 671, C 779.]

HAB. Europe and Asia; accidental in Labrador.

57. Larus heermanni CASS.
Heermann's Gull.

Larus heermanni CASS. Pr. Ac. Nat. Sci. Phila. VI. 1852, 187.

[B 666, C 551, R 672, C 781.]

HAB. Pacific coast of North America, from British Columbia to Panama.

58. Larus atricilla LINN.
Laughing Gull.

Larus atricilla LINN. S. N. ed. 10, I. 1758, 136.

[B 667, C 554, R 673, C 786.]

HAB. Eastern tropical and warm temperate America, chiefly along the sea-coast, from Maine to Brazil; Pacific coast of Middle America.

59. Larus franklinii Sw. & Rich.
Franklin's Gull.

Larus franklinii Sw. & Rich. F. B. A. II. 1831, 424, pl. 71.

[B 668, 669, C 555, R 674, C 787.]

Hab. Interior of North America, breeding chiefly north of the United States; south in winter to Central and South America.

60. Larus philadelphia (Ord).
Bonaparte's Gull.

Sterna philadelphia Ord, Guthrie's Geog. 2d Am. ed. II. 1815, 319.
Larus philadelphia Gray, List Brit. B. 1863, 235.

[B 670, C 556, R 675, C 788.]

Hab. Whole of North America, breeding mostly north of the United States; south in winter to Mexico and Central America.

Genus RHODOSTETHIA Macgillivray.

Rhodostethia Macgil. Man. Brit. Orn. II. 1842, 253. Type, *Larus roseus* Macgil.

61. Rhodostethia rosea (Macgil.).
Ross's Gull.

Larus roseus Macgil. Mem. Wern. Soc. V. 1824, 249.
Rhodostethia rosea Bonap. Rev. Crit. Orn. Eur. Degland, 1850, 201.

[B 678, C 557, R 676, C 789.]

Hab. Arctic regions; Point Barrow, Alaska; Melville Peninsula; England, Faroes, Heligoland, etc.

Genus XEMA Leach.

Xema "Leach," Ross's Voy. App. 1819, p. lvii. Type, *Larus sabinii* Sab.

62. Xema sabinii (Sab.).
Sabine's Gull.

Larus sabinii J. Sab. Trans. Linn. Soc. XII. 1818, 520, pl. 29.
Xema sabini Edw. & Beverl. App. Ross's Voy. Baff. Bay, 4to ed. 1819, lvii.

[B 680, C 558, R 677, C 790.]

HAB. Arctic regions; in North America south in winter to New York, the Great Lakes, and Great Salt Lake; casual south to Peru.

SUBFAMILY **STERNINÆ.** TERNS.

GENUS **GELOCHELIDON** BREHM.

Gelochelidon BREHM, Naturg. Vög. Deutschl. 1831, 774. Type, *G. meridionalis* BREHM = *Sterna nilotica* HASSELQ.

63. Gelochelidon nilotica (HASSELQ.).
Gull-billed Tern.

Sterna nilotica HASSELQ. Reise nach Pal. Deutsche Ausg. 1762, 325. *Gelochelidon nilotica* STEJN. Auk, I. Oct. 1884, 366.

[B 681, C 560, R 679, C 792.]

HAB. Nearly cosmopolitan; in North America chiefly along the Atlantic and Gulf coasts of the United States.

GENUS **STERNA** LINNÆUS.

SUBGENUS **THALASSEUS** BOIE.

Thalasseus BOIE, Isis, 1822, 563. Type, *Sterna caspia* PALL. = *S. tschegrava* LEPECH.

64. Sterna tschegrava LEPECH.
Caspian Tern.

Sterna tschegrava LEPECH. Nov. Comm. Petrop. XIV. 1770, 500, pl. 13, fig. 2.

[B 682, C 561, R 680, C 793.]

HAB. Nearly cosmopolitan; in North America breeding southward to Virginia, Lake Michigan, Texas, Nevada, and California.

SUBGENUS **ACTOCHELIDON** KAUP.

Actochelidon KAUP, Sk. Ent. Eur. Thierw. 1829, 31. Type, *Sterna cantiaca* GMEL. = *S. sandvicensis* GMEL.

65. **Sterna maxima** BODD.
Royal Tern.

Sterna maxima BODD. Tabl. P. E. 1783, 58.

[B 683, C 562, R 681, C 794.]

HAB. Tropical America, and warmer parts of North America, northward to Massachusetts, the Great Lakes, and California. West coast of Africa, north to Tangiers.

66. **Sterna elegans** GAMB.
Elegant Tern.

Sterna elegans GAMB. Pr. Ac. Nat. Sci. Phila. IV. 1848, 129.

[B 684, C 563, R 682, C 795.]

HAB. Pacific coast of America, from California to Chili.

67. **Sterna sandvicensis acuflavida** (CABOT).
Cabot's Tern.

Sterna acuflavida CABOT, Pr. Boston Soc. N. H. II. 1847, 257.
Sterna sandvicensis acuflavida RIDGW. Water B. N. Am. II. 1884, 288.

[B 685, C 564, R 683, C 796.]

HAB. Tropical America, northward along the Atlantic coast, irregularly, to Southern New England.

SUBGENUS **STERNA**

Sterna LINN. S. N. ed. 10, I. 1758, 137. Type, by elimination, *S. hirundo* LINN.

[68.] **Sterna trudeaui** AUD.
Trudeau's Tern.

Sterna trudeaui AUD. Orn. Biog. V. 1839, 125, pl. 409.

[B 687, C 571, R 684, C 802.]

HAB. Southern South America. Casual, or accidental, on the Atlantic coast of the United States (New Jersey, Long Island).

69. Sterna forsteri NUTT.
Forster's Tern.

Sterna forsteri NUTT. Man. II. 1834, 274.

[B 691, 686, C 566, R 685, C 798.]

HAB. North America generally, breeding from Manitoba southward to Virginia, Illinois, Texas, and California; in winter southward to Brazil.

70. Sterna hirundo LINN.
Common Tern.

Sterna hirundo LINN. S. N. ed. 10, I. 1758, 137.

[B 689, C 565, R 686, C 797.]

HAB. Greater part of the Northern Hemisphere and Africa. In North America chiefly confined to the Eastern Province, breeding from the Arctic coast, somewhat irregularly, to Florida and Texas, and wintering northward to Virginia. Apparently not occurring in the Pacific.

71. Sterna paradisæa BRÜNN.
Arctic Tern.

Sterna paradisæa BRÜNN. Orn. Bor. 1764, 46.

[B 690, 693, C 567, 568, R 687, C 799.]

HAB. Northern Hemisphere; in North America breeding from Massachusetts to the Arctic regions, and wintering southward to Virginia and California.

72. Sterna dougalli MONTAG.
Roseate Tern.

Sterna dougalli MONTAG. Orn. Dict. Suppl. 1813, —.

[B 692, C 569, R 688, C 800.]

HAB. Temperate and tropical regions; north on the Atlantic coast of North America to Massachusetts, and casually to Maine.

73. Sterna aleutica BAIRD.
Aleutian Tern.

Sterna aleutica BAIRD, Tr. Chicago Ac. Nat. Sci. I. 1869, 321, pl. 31, fig. 1.

[B —, C 572, R 689, C 803.]

HAB. Coast of Alaska from Kadiak to Norton Sound.

SUBGENUS **STERNULA** BOIE.

Sternula BOIE, Isis, 1822, 563. Type, *Sterna minuta* LINN.

74. **Sterna antillarum** (LESS.).
Least Tern.

Sternula antillarum LESS. Descr. Mam. et Ois. 1847, 256.
Sterna antillarum COUES, Pr. Ac. Nat. Sci. Phila. 1862, 552.

[B 694, C 570, R 690, C 801.]

HAB. Northern South America, northward to California and New England, and casually to Labrador, breeding nearly throughout its range.

SUBGENUS **HALIPLANA** WAGLER.

Haliplana WAGL. Isis, 1832, 1224. Type, *Sterna fuliginosa* GMEL.

75. **Sterna fuliginosa** GMEL.
Sooty Tern.

Sterna fuliginosa GMEL. S. N. I. ii. 1788, 605.

[B 688, C 573, R 691, C 804.]

HAB. Tropical and subtropical coasts of the globe. In America from Chili to Western Mexico and the Carolinas, and casually to New England.

[76.] **Sterna anæthetus** SCOP.
Bridled Tern.

Sterna anæthetus SCOP. Del. Faun. et Flor. Ins. II. 1786, no. 72, 92.

[B —, C 574, R 692, C 805.]

HAB. Tropical regions generally. Casual in Florida.

GENUS **HYDROCHELIDON** BOIE.

Hydrochelidon BOIE, Isis, 1822, 563. Type, *Sterna nigra* LINN.

77. Hydrochelidon nigra surinamensis (GMEL.).
Black Tern.

Sterna surinamensis GMEL. S. N. I. ii. 1788, 604.
Hydrochelidon nigra surinamensis STEJN. Pr. U. S. Nat. Mus. 1882, 40.

[B 695, C 575, R 693, C 806.]

HAB. Temperate and tropical America. From Alaska and the Fur Countries to Chili, breeding from the Middle United States northward.

[78.] **Hydrochelidon leucoptera** (MEISN. & SCHINZ).
White-winged Black Tern.

Sterna leucoptera MEISN. & SCHINZ, Vög. Schweiz, 1815, 264.
Hydrochelidon leucoptera BOIE, Isis, 1822, 563.

[B —, C 575 *bis*, R 694, C 807.]

HAB. Eastern Hemisphere, accidental in North America (Wisconsin).

GENUS **ANOUS** STEPHENS.

Anous STEPH. Gen. Zool. XIII. pt. i. 1826, 139. Type, *Sterna stolida* LINN.

79. Anous stolidus (LINN.).
Noddy.

Sterna stolida LINN. S. N. ed. 10, I. 1758, 137.
Anous stolidus GRAY, List Gen. B. 1841, 100.

[B 696, C 576, R 695, C 808.]

HAB. Tropical and subtropical regions; in America from Brazil and Chili north to the Gulf and South Atlantic States.

FAMILY **RYNCHOPIDÆ**. SKIMMERS.

GENUS **RYNCHOPS** LINN.

Rynchops LINN. S. N. ed. 10, I. 1758, 138. Type, *R. nigra* LINN.

80. **Rynchops nigra** LINN.
    Black Skimmer.

Rynchops nigra LINN. S. N. ed. 10, I. 1758, 228.

[B 697, C 577, R 656, C 809.]

HAB. Warmer parts of America, north on the Atlantic coast to New Jersey, and casually to the Bay of Fundy.

ORDER TUBINARES. TUBE-NOSED SWIMMERS.

FAMILY DIOMEDEIDÆ. ALBATROSSES.

GENUS **DIOMEDEA** LINNÆUS.

Diomedea LINN. S. N. ed. 10, I. 1758, 132. Type, *D. exulans* LINN.

81. **Diomedea nigripes** AUD.
    Black-footed Albatross.

Diomedea nigripes AUD. Orn. Biog. V. 1839, 327.

[B —, C 579, R 700, C 811.]

HAB. North Pacific, including west coast of North America.

82. **Diomedea albatrus** PALL.
    Short-tailed Albatross.

Diomedea albatrus PALL. Spic. Zool. V. 1769, 28.

[B 631, C 578, R 701, C 810.]

HAB. Pacific Ocean, including western coast of America, northward to Bering's Sea.

GENUS **THALASSOGERON** RIDGWAY.

Thalassogeron RIDGW. Water B. N. Am. II. 1884, 357. Type, *Diomedea culminata* GOULD.

[83.] **Thalassogeron culminatus** (GOULD).
Yellow-nosed Albatross.

Diomedea culminata GOULD, P. Z. S. 1843, 107.
Thalassogeron culminatus RIDGW. Water B. N. Am. II. 1884, 358.

[B 632, C —, R 702, C —.]

HAB. Indian and South Pacific Oceans: casual off the coast of Oregon.

GENUS **PHŒBETRIA** REICHENBACH.

Phœbetria REICH. Syst. Av. 1852, p. v. Type, *Diomedea fuliginosa* GMEL.

84. **Phœbetria fuliginosa** (GM.).
Sooty Albatross.

Diomedea fuliginosa GMEL. S N. I. ii. 1788, 568.
Phœbetria fuliginosa REICH. Syst. Av. 1852, p. v.

[B 633, C 580, R 703, C 812.]

HAB. Oceans of the Southern Hemisphere, northward to the coast of Oregon.

FAMILY **PROCELLARIIDÆ**. FULMARS AND SHEARWATERS.

SUBFAMILY **PROCELLARIINÆ**. FULMARS.

GENUS **OSSIFRAGA** HOMBRON & JACQUINOT.

Ossifraga HOMB. & JACQ. Compt. Rend XVIII. 1844, 356. Type, *Procellaria gigantea* GMEL.

[85.] **Ossifraga gigantea** (GM.).
Giant Fulmar.

Procellaria gigantea GMEL. S. N. I. ii. 1788, 563.
Ossifraga gigantea REICH. Syst. Av. 1852, p. iv.

[B 634, C 581, R 704, C 813.]

HAB. Southern Oceans; casual off the coast of Oregon.

ORDER TUBINARES. 99

Genus **FULMARUS** Stephens.

Subgenus **FULMARUS**.

Fulmarus Stephens, Gen. Zool. XIII. pt. i. 1826, 233. Type, *Procellaria glacialis* Linn.

86. Fulmarus glacialis (Linn.).
Fulmar.

Procellaria glacialis Linn. Faun. Suec. 2d ed. 1761, 51; S. N. ed. 12, I. 1766, 213.
Fulmarus glacialis Steph. Gen. Zool. XIII. pt. i. 1826, 234, pl. 27.

[B 635, C 582, R 705, C 814.]

Hab. North Atlantic, south on the American coast to Massachusetts.

86 a. Fulmarus glacialis minor Kjærbœlling.
Lesser Fulmar.

Procellaria minor Kjærb. Danm. Fugle, 1852, 324.
Fulmarus glacialis b. *minor* Bonap. Consp. II. 1856, 187.

[B —, C —, R —, C —.]

Hab. North Atlantic.

86 b. Fulmarus glacialis glupischa Stejn.
Pacific Fulmar.

Fulmarus glacialis glupischa Stejn. Auk, I. July, 1884, 234.

[B 636, C 582 a, R 705 a, C 815.]

Hab. North Pacific, south on the American coast to Mexico.

86 c. Fulmarus glacialis rodgersii (Cass.).
Rodgers's Fulmar.

Fulmarus rodgersii Cass. Pr. Ac. Nat. Sci. Phila. 1862, 290.
Fulmarus glacialis var. *rodgersi* Coues, Key, 1872, 327.

[B —, C 582 b, R 705 b, C 816.]

Hab. Bering's Sea.

SUBGENUS **PRIOCELLA**. HOMBRON & JACQUINOT.

Priocella HOMB. & JACQ. Compt. Rend. XVIII. 1844, 357. Type, *P. garnoti* HOMB. & JACQ. = *Procellaria glacialoides* SMITH.

87. **Fulmarus glacialoides** (SMITH).
Slender-billed Fulmar.

Procellaria glacialoides SMITH, Illustr. S. Afr. B. 1849 (?), t. 51.
Fulmarus glacialoides STEJN. Auk, 1884, p. 233.

[B 637, C 583, R 706, C 817.]

HAB. Seas of the Southern Hemisphere, and northward along Pacific coast of North America.

GENUS **PUFFINUS** BRISSON.

Puffinus BRISS. Orn. VI. 1760, 131. Type, *Procellaria puffinus* BRÜNN.

88. **Puffinus borealis** CORY.
Cory's Shearwater.

Puffinus borealis CORY, Bull. Nutt. Orn. Club, VI. April, 1881, 84.

[B —, C —, R —, C 888.]

HAB. Off the coast of Massachusetts.

89. **Puffinus major** FABER.
Greater Shearwater.

Puffinus major FABER, Prodr. Isl. Orn. 1822, 56.

[B 647, C 597, R 709, C 832.]

HAB. Atlantic Ocean; south to Cape Horn and Cape of Good Hope.

[90.] **Puffinus puffinus** (BRÜNN.).
Manx Shearwater.

Procellaria puffinus BRÜNN. Orn. Bor. 1764, 29.
Puffinus puffinus LICHT. Nomencl. Mus. Berol. 1854, 100.

[B 649, C 599, R 711, C 834.]

HAB. North Atlantic, chiefly on the eastern side; accidental in Greenland, and rare or casual off the North American coast (?).

ORDER TUBINARES.

91. **Puffinus creatopus** COUES.
    Pink-footed Shearwater.

   Puffinus creatopus " COOPER, MS.," COUES, Pr. Ac. Nat. Sci. Phila. April, 1864, 131.

   [B —, C 598, R 710, C 833.]

   HAB. Pacific Ocean; on the American coast from Lower California to Juan Fernandez Islands.

92. **Puffinus auduboni** FINSCH.
    Audubon's Shearwater.

   Puffinus auduboni FINSCH, P. Z. S. 1872, 111.

   [B 650, C 600, R 712, C 835.]

   HAB. Warmer parts of the Atlantic, north casually to New Jersey.

93. **Puffinus gavia** (FORST.).
    Black-vented Shearwater.

   Procellaria gavia FORST. Descr. An. 1844, 148.
   Puffinus gavia FINSCH, J. f. O. 1872, 256.

   [B —, C 601, R 713, C 836.]

   HAB. Pacific Ocean, chiefly southward; coast of Lower California.

94. **Puffinus stricklandi** RIDGW.
    Sooty Shearwater.

   Puffinus stricklandi RIDGW. Water B. N. Am. II. 1884, 390.

   [B 648, C 602, R 714, C 837.]

   HAB. North Atlantic, south on the American coast to South Carolina.

95. **Puffinus griseus** (GMEL.).
    Dark-bodied Shearwater.

   Procellaria grisea GMEL. S. N. I. ii. 1788, 564.
   Puffinus griseus FINSCH, J. f. O. 1874, 209.

   [B —, C 603, R 715, C 838.]

   HAB. South Pacific, north on the American coast to Lower California.

96. Puffinus tenuirostris (TEMM.).
Slender-billed Shearwater.

Procellaria tenuirostris TEMM. Pl. Col. 1828, 587.
Puffinus tenuirostris TEMM. & SCHLEG. Faun. Jap. Aves, 1849, 131, pl. 86.

[B —, C 604, R 716, C 839.]

HAB. North Pacific; from Sitka to Kotzebue Sound on the American coast.

SUBGENUS **PRIOFINUS** HOMBRON & JACQUINOT.

Priofinus HOMBR. & JACQ. Compt. Rend. XVIII. 1844, 355. Type, *Procellaria cinerea* GMEL.

[97.] Puffinus cinereus (GMEL.).
Black-tailed Shearwater.

Procellaria cinerea GMEL. S. N. I. ii. 1788, 563.
Puffinus cinereus LAWR. in BAIRD'S B. N. Am. 1858, 835.

[B 651, C 595, R 707, C 830.]

HAB. South Pacific; accidental off the coast of California.

GENUS **ÆSTRELATA** BONAPARTE.

Æstrelata BONAP. Consp. II. 1856, 188. Type, *Procellaria hasitata* KUHL.

[98.] Æstrelata hasitata (KUHL).
Black-capped Petrel.

Procellaria hasitata KUHL, Mon. Proc. Beitr. Zool. 1 Abt. 1820, 142.
Æstrelata hæsitata COUES, Pr. Ac. Nat. Sci. Phila. 1866, 139.

[B 638, C 585, R 717, C 819.]

HAB. Warmer parts of the Atlantic Ocean, straying to Florida, Long Island, England, and France.

[99.] Æstrelata gularis (PEALE).
Peale's Petrel.

Procellaria gularis PEALE, Zool. U. S. Expl. Exp. 1848, 299.
Œstrelata gularis BREWST. Bull. Nutt. Orn. Club, IV. 1881, 94.

[B —, C —, R —, C 887.]

HAB. Antarctic Ocean; accidental in Western New York.

100. **Æstrelata fisheri** RIDGW.
Fisher's Petrel.

Œstrelata fisheri RIDGW. Pr. U. S. Nat. Mus. V. June 26, 1883, 656.
[B —, C —, R —, C —.]

HAB. Coast of Alaska (Kadiak).

GENUS **BULWERIA** BONAPARTE.

Bulweria BONAP. Cat. Met. Ucc. Eur. 1842, 81. Type, *Procellaria bulweri* JARD. & SELBY.

[101.] **Bulweria bulweri** (JARD. & SELBY).
Bulwer's Petrel.

Procellaria bulweri JARD. & SELBY, Illustr. Orn. ——, pl. 65.
Bulweria bulweri BOUCARD, Cat. Av. 1876, 69.
[B —, C —, R 718, C 820.]

HAB. Eastern Atlantic, including coasts of Europe and Africa. Accidental in Greenland.

GENUS **DAPTION** STEPHENS.

Daption STEPH. Gen. Zool. XIII. 1825, 239. Type, *Procellaria capensis* LINN.

[102.] **Daption capensis** (LINN.).
Pintado Petrel.

Procellaria capensis LINN. S. N. ed. 10, I. 1758, 132.
Daption capensis STEPH Gen. Zool. XIII. pt. i. 1825, 241.
[B 639, C 584, R 719, C 818.]

HAB. Oceans of the Southern Hemisphere, north to about latitude 25°. Accidental on the coasts of California and England.

GENUS **HALOCYPTENA** COUES.

Halocyptena COUES, Pr. Ac. Nat. Sci. Phila. March, 1864, 78. Type, *H. microsoma* COUES.

103. Halocyptena microsoma Coues.
Least Petrel.

Halocyptena microsoma Coues, Pr. Ac. Nat. Sci. Phila. 1864, 79.

[B —, C 586, R 720, C 821.]

HAB. Coast of Lower California.

Genus **PROCELLARIA** Linnæus.

Procellaria Linn. S. N. ed. 10, I. 1758, 131. Type, by elimination, *P. pelagica* Linn.

104. Procellaria pelagica Linn.
Stormy Petrel.

Procellaria pelagica Linn. S. N. ed. 10, I. 1758, 131.

[B 645, C 587, R 721, C 822.]

HAB. Atlantic Ocean, south on the American side to the Newfoundland Banks. West coast of Africa and coast of Europe.

Genus **OCEANODROMA** Reichenbach.

Oceanodroma Reich. Syst. Av. 1852, p. iv. Type, *Procellaria furcata* Gmel.

105. Oceanodroma furcata (Gmel.).
Fork-tailed Petrel.

Procellaria furcata Gmel. S. N. I. ii. 1788, 561.
Oceanodroma furcata Reich. Syst. Av 1852, p. iv.

[B 640, C 591, R 726, C 826.]

HAB. North Pacific, south on the American coast to Oregon.

106. Oceanodroma leucorhoa (Vieill.).
Leach's Petrel.

Procellaria leucorhoa Vieill. N. Dict. d'Hist. Nat. XXV. 1817, 422.
Oceanodroma leucorhoa Stejn. Orn. Expl. Kamtsch. 1885, 97.

[B 642, C 588, R 723, C 823.]

HAB. North Atlantic and North Pacific Oceans; south on the coast of the United States to Virginia and California; breeds from Maine and the Hebrides northward on the coasts of the Atlantic.

107. Oceanodroma melania (BONAP.).
Black Petrel.

Procellaria melania BONAP. Compt. Rend. XXVIII. 1854, 662.
Oceanodroma melania STEJN. Orn. Expl. Kamtsch. 1885, 371.

[B —, C 589, R 724, C 824.]

HAB. South Pacific, northward to Lower California.

108. Oceanodroma homochroa (COUES).
Ashy Petrel.

Cymochorea homochroa COUES, Pr. Ac. Nat. Sci. Phila. 1864, 77.
Oceanodroma homochroa RIDGW. Pr. U. S. Nat. Mus. VIII. 1885, 356.

[B 643, C 590, R 725, C 825.]

HAB. Coast of California.

SUBFAMILY **OCEANITINÆ**.

GENUS **OCEANITES** KEYSERLING & BLASIUS.

Oceanites KEYS. & BLAS. Wirb. Eur. I. 1840, xciii. Type, *Procellaria oceanica* KUHL.

109. Oceanites oceanicus (KUHL).
Wilson's Petrel.

Procellaria oceanica KUHL, Beitr. Zool. Mon. Proc. 1820, 136, pl. 10, fig. 1.
Oceanites oceanica LICHT. Nomencl. Mus. Berol. 1854, 99.

[B 644, C 593, R 722, C 828.]

HAB. North and South Atlantic and Southern Oceans.

GENUS **CYMODROMA** RIDGWAY.

Cymodroma RIDGW. Water B. N. Am. II. 1884, 418. Type, *Procellaria grallaria* VIEILL.

[110.] **Cymodroma grallaria** (VIEILL.).
    White-bellied Petrel.

Procellaria grallaria VIEILL. Nouv. Dict. XXVI. 1817, 418.
Cymodroma grallaria RIDGW. Water B. N. Am. II. 1884, 419.

[B 646, C 594, R 728, C 829.]

HAB. Tropical oceans generally; accidental on the coast of Florida.

GENUS **PELAGODROMA** REICHENBACH.

Pelagodroma REICH. Syst. Av. 1852, p. iv. Type, *Procellaria marina* LATH.

[111.] **Pelagodroma marina** (LATH.).
    White-faced Petrel.

Procellaria marina LATH. Ind. Orn. II. ii. 1790, 826.
Pelagodroma marina REICH. Syst. Av. 1852, p. iv.

[B —, C —, R —, C —.]

HAB. South Atlantic, and Southern Seas. Casual off the coast of Massachusetts.

ORDER STEGANOPODES. TOTIPALMATE SWIMMERS.

FAMILY **PHAËTHONTIDÆ**. TROPIC BIRDS.

GENUS **PHAËTHON** LINNÆUS.

Phaëthon LINN. S. N. ed. 10, I. 1758, 134. Type, *P. æthereus* LINN.

112. **Phaëthon flavirostris** BRANDT.
    Yellow-billed Tropic Bird.

Phaëthon flavirostris BRANDT, Bull. Ac. St. Pétersb. II. 1837, 349.

ORDER STEGANOPODES. 107

[B 629, C 538, R 654, C 763.]

HAB. West Indies and Atlantic coast of Central America, north to Florida; accidental in Western New York. Samoan Islands.

113. **Phaëthon æthereus** LINN.
   Red-billed Tropic Bird.

Phaëthon æthereus LINN. S. N. ed. 10, I. 1758, 134.

[B —, C —, R 655, C 762.]

HAB. Coasts of tropical America, north on the Pacific coast to Lower California; accidental on the Newfoundland Banks.

FAMILY **SULIDÆ**. GANNETS.

GENUS **SULA** BRISSON.

SUBGENUS **SULA**.

Sula BRISS. Orn. VI. 1760, 495. Type, by elimination, *Pelecanus sula* LINN.

[114.] **Sula cyanops** SUND.
   Blue-faced Booby.

Dysporus cyanops SUND. Phys. Tidskr. Lund, 1837, pt. 5.
Sula cyanops SUND. Isis, 1842, 858.

[B —, C —, R 651, C —.]

HAB. South Pacific, West Indies, and northward to Southern Florida.

115. **Sula sula** (LINN.).
   Booby.

Pelecanus sula LINN. Syst. Nat. 12 ed. I. 1766, 218.
Sula sula RIDGW. Pr. U. S. Nat. Mus. VIII. 1885, 356.

[B 618, C 525, R 652, C 747.]

HAB. Coasts of tropical and subtropical America, north to Georgia.

[116.] **Sula piscator** (LINN.).
   Red-footed Booby.

   Pelecanus piscator LINN. S. N. ed. 10, I. 1758, 134.
   Sula piscator BONAP. Consp. II. 1857, 166.

   [B —, C —, R 653, C —.]

HAB. Coast and islands of tropical and subtropical seas, north to Western Mexico and Florida.

SUBGENUS **DYSPORUS** ILLIGER.

   Dysporus ILLIG. Prodr. 1811, 279. Type, by elimination, *Pelecanus bassanus* LINN.

117. **Sula bassana** (LINN.).
   Gannet.

   Pelecanus bassanus LINN. S. N. ed. 10, I. 1758, 133.
   Sula bassana BOIE, Isis, 1822, p. 563.

   [B 617, C 524, R 650, C 746.]

HAB. Coasts of the North Atlantic, south in winter to the Gulf of Mexico and Africa; breeds from Nova Scotia and the British Islands northward.

FAMILY **ANHINGIDÆ**. DARTERS.

GENUS **ANHINGA** BRISSON.

   Anhinga BRISSON, Orn. VI. 1760, 476. Type, *Anhinga* MARCGR. = *Plotus anhinga* LINN.

118. **Anhinga anhinga** (LINN.).
   Anhinga.

   Plotus anhinga LINN. S. N. ed. 12, I. 1766, 218.
   Anhinga anhinga STEJN. Stand. Nat. Hist. IV. 1885, 193.

   [B 628, C 536, R 649, C 760.]

HAB. Tropical and subtropical America, north to the Carolinas and the mouth of the Ohio River.

ORDER STEGANOPODES.

FAMILY **PHALACROCORACIDÆ.** CORMORANTS.

GENUS **PHALACROCORAX** BRISSON.

SUBGENUS **PHALACROCORAX**

Phalacrocorax BRISS. Orn. VI. 1760, 511. Type, *Pelecanus carbo* LINN.

119. Phalacrocorax carbo (LINN.).
Cormorant.

Pelecanus carbo LINN. S. N. ed. 10, I. 1758, 133.
Phalacrocorax carbo CUVIER, Règne Animal, I. 1817, 524.

[B 620, C 528, R 642, C 750.]

HAB. Coasts of the North Atlantic, south in winter on the coast of the United States, casually, to the Carolinas; breeding (formerly) from Massachusetts northward.

120. Phalacrocorax dilophus (SW. & RICH.).
Double-crested Cormorant.

Pelecanus (*Carbo*) *dilophus* SW. & RICH. F. B. A. II. 1831, 473.
Phalacrocorax dilophus NUTT. Man. II. 1834, 483.

[B 623, C 530, R 643, C 751.]

HAB. Eastern coast of North America, breeding from the Bay of Fundy northward; southward in the interior to the Great Lakes and Wisconsin.

120 a. Phalacrocorax dilophus floridanus (AUD.).
Florida Cormorant.

Phalacrocorax floridanus AUD. Orn. Biog. III. 1835, 387.
Phalacrocorax dilophus floridanus RIDGW. Pr. U. S. Nat. Mus. III. Aug. 24, 1880, 205.

[B 624, C 530 a, R 643 a, C 753.]

HAB. Coast of the South Atlantic and Gulf States, northward in the Mississippi Valley to Southern Illinois.

120 *b*. Phalacrocorax dilophus cincinatus (Brandt).
White-crested Cormorant.

Carbo cincinatus Brandt, Bull. Sc. Ac. St. Pétersb. III. 1838, 55.
Phalacrocorax dilophus cincinnatus Ridgw. Pr. U. S. Nat. Mus. III. Aug. 24, 1880, 205.

[B 622, C 529, R 643 *b*, C 752.]

Hab. West coast of North America, south in winter to California.

120 *c*. Phalacrocorax dilophus albociliatus Ridgw.
Farallone Cormorant.

Phalacrocorax dilophus albociliatus Ridgw. Proc. Biol. Soc. Wash. II. Apr. 10, 1884, 94.

[B —, C —, R —, C —.]

Hab. Coast of California, south to Cape St. Lucas and Revilla-Gigedo Islands.

121. Phalacrocorax mexicanus (Brandt).
Mexican Cormorant.

Carbo mexicanus Brandt, Bull. Sc. Ac. St. Pétersb. III. 1838, 55.
Phalacrocorax mexicanus Scl. & Salv. Nom. Neotr. 1873, 124.

[B 625, C 531, R 644, C 754.]

Hab. West Indies, South and Central America to Southern United States ; north in the interior to Kansas and Southern Illinois.

Subgenus **COMPSOHALIEUS** Ridgway.

Compsohalieus Ridgw. Water B. N. Am. II. 1884, 145. Type, *Carbo penicillatus* Brandt.

122. Phalacrocorax penicillatus (Brandt).
Brandt's Cormorant.

Carbo penicillatus Brandt, Bull. Sc. Ac. St. Pétersb III. 1838, 55.
Phalacrocorax penicillatus Heerm. Pr. Ac. Nat. Sci. Phila. VII. 1854, 178.

[B 626, C 532, R 645, C 755.]

ORDER STEGANOPODES.

HAB. Pacific coast of North America, from Cape St. Lucas to Washington Territory.

SUBGENUS **URILE** BONAPARTE.

Urile BONAP. Consp. II. 1856, 175. Type, *Pelecanus urile* GMEL.

123. **Phalacrocorax pelagicus** PALL.
Pelagic Cormorant.

Phalacrocorax pelagicus PALL. Zoog. Rosso-As. II. 1826, 303.

[B —, C —, R —, C —.]

HAB. Aleutian and Kurile Islands, and Kamtschatka, south to Japan.

123 *a*. **Phalacrocorax pelagicus robustus** RIDGW.
Violet-green Cormorant.

Phalacrocorax pelagicus robustus RIDGW. Water B. N. Am. II. 1884, 160.

[B 627, C 535, R 646, C 758.]

HAB. Coast of Alaska, from Norton Sound to Sitka.

123 *b*. **Phalacrocorax pelagicus resplendens** (AUD.).
Baird's Cormorant.

Phalacrocorax resplendens AUD. Orn. Biog. V. 1839, 148.
Phalacrocorax pelagicus resplendens RIDGW. Water B. N. Am. I. 1884, 160.

[B —, C —, R 646 *a*, C 759.]

HAB. Pacific coast of North America, from Washington Territory south to Cape St. Lucas and Mazatlan.

124. **Phalacrocorax urile** (GMEL.).
Red-faced Cormorant.

Pelecanus urile GMEL. S. N. I. ii. 1788, 575.
Phalacrocorax urile RIDGW. Water B. N. Am. II. 1884, 162.

[B —, C 534, R 647, C 757.]

HAB. Prybilof and Aleutian Islands, and coast of Kamtschatka.

FAMILY **PELECANIDÆ**. PELICANS.

GENUS **PELECANUS** LINNÆUS.

Pelecanus LINN. S. N. ed. 10, I. 1758, 132.   Type, by elimination, *P. onocrotalus* LINN.

SUBGENUS **CYRTOPELICANUS** REICHENBACH.

Cyrtopelicanus REICH. Syst. Av. 1852, p. vii. Type, *Pelecanus erythrorhynchos* GMEL.

125. Pelecanus erythrorhynchos GMEL.
American White Pelican.

Pelecanus erythrorhynchos GMEL. S. N. I. ii. 1788, 571.

[B 615, C 526, R 640, C 748.]

HAB. Temperate North America, north in the interior to about Lat. 61°, south to Central America; now rare or accidental in the Northeastern States; abundant in the Middle Province and along the Gulf coast; common on the coast of California and Western Mexico.

SUBGENUS **LEPTOPELICANUS** REICHENBACH.

Leptopelicanus REICH. Syst. Av. 1852, p. vii. Type, *Pelecanus fuscus* LINN.

126. Pelecanus fuscus LINN.
Brown Pelican.

Pelecanus fuscus LINN. S. N. ed. 12, I. 1766, 215.

[B 616, C 527, R 641, C 749.]

HAB. Atlantic coast of tropical and subtropical America, north on the Atlantic coast to North Carolina; accidental in Illinois.

127. Pelecanus californicus RIDGW.
California Brown Pelican.

Pelecanus (fuscus?) californicus RIDGW. Water B. N. Am. II. 1884, 143.
P[elecanus] californicus RIDGW. l. c.

[B —, C —, R —, C —.]

HAB. Pacific coast, from San Francisco to Cape St. Lucas, and probably to Mexico and Central America.

FAMILY **FREGATIDÆ.** MAN-O'-WAR BIRDS.

GENUS **FREGATA** CUVIER.

Fregata CUV. Leç. d'Anat. Comp. I. 1799–1800, tab. ii. Type, *Pelecanus aquilus* LINN.

128. **Fregata aquila** (LINN.).
   Man-o'-War Bird.

Pelecanus aquilus LINN. S. N. ed. 10, I. 1758, 133.
Fregata aquila REICH. Syst. Av. 1852, p. vi.

[B 619, C 537, R 639, C 761.]

HAB. Tropical and subtropical coasts generally; in America, north to Florida, Texas, and California, and casually on the Atlantic coast to Nova Scotia.

ORDER ANSERES. LAMELLIROSTRAL SWIMMERS.

FAMILY **ANATIDÆ.** DUCKS, GEESE, AND SWANS.

SUBFAMILY **MERGINÆ.** MERGANSERS.

GENUS **MERGANSER** BRISSON.

Merganser BRISS. Orn. VI. 1760, 230. Type, *Mergus merganser* LINN.

129. **Merganser americanus** (CASS.).
   American Merganser.

Mergus americanus CASSIN, Pr. Ac. Nat. Sci. Phila. VI. 1853, 187.
Merganser americanus STEJN. Orn. Expl. Kamtsch. 1885, 177.

[B 611, C 521, R 636, C 743.]

HAB. North America generally, breeding south to the Northern United States.

130. **Merganser serrator** (LINN.).
Red-breasted Merganser.

Mergus serrator LINN. S. N. ed. 10, I. 1758, 129.
Merganser serrator SCHÄFFER, Mus. Orn. 1789, 66.

[B 612, C 522, R 637, C 744.]

HAB. Northern portions of Northern Hemisphere; south, in winter, throughout the United States.

GENUS **LOPHODYTES** REICHENBACH.

Lophodytes REICHENBACH, Syst. Av. 1852, p. ix. Type, *Mergus cucullatus* LINN.

131. **Lophodytes cucullatus** (LINN.).
Hooded Merganser.

Mergus cucullatus LINN. S. N. ed. 10, I. 1758, 129.
Lophodytes cucullatus REICHENBACH, Syst. Av. 1852, p. ix.

[B 613, C 523, R 638, C 745.]

HAB. North America generally, south to Mexico and Cuba, breeding nearly throughout its range.

SUBFAMILY **ANATINÆ**. RIVER DUCKS.

GENUS **ANAS** LINNÆUS.

Anas LINN. S. N. ed. 10, I. 1758, 122. Type, *A. boschas* LINN.

132. **Anas boschas** LINN.
Mallard.

Anas boschas LINN. S. N. ed. 10, I. 1758, 127.

[B 576, C 488, R 601, C 707.]

HAB. Northern parts of Northern Hemisphere; in America south to Panama and Cuba, breeding southward to the Northern United States.

133. **Anas obscura** GMEL.
   Black Duck.

   Anas obscura GMEL. S. N. I. 1788, 541.

   [B 577, C 489, R 602, C 708.]

   HAB. Eastern North America, west to Utah and Texas, north to Labrador, breeding southward to the Northern United States.

134. **Anas fulvigula** RIDGW.
   Florida Duck.

   Anas obscura var. *fulvigula* RIDGW. Am. Nat. VIII. Feb. 1874, 111.
   Anas fulvigula RIDGW. Pr. U. S. Nat. Mus. III. Aug. 24, 1880, 203.

   [B —, C 489 *a*, R 603, C 709.]

   HAB. Florida; Kansas.

   SUBGENUS **CHAULELASMUS** BONAPARTE.

   Chaulelasmus BONAP. Comp. List, 1838, 56. Type, *Anas strepera* LINN.

135. **Anas strepera** LINN.
   Gadwall.

   Anas strepera LINN. S. N. ed. 10, I. 1758, 125.

   [B 584, C 491, R 604, C 711.]

   HAB. Nearly cosmopolitan. In North America breeds chiefly within the United States.

   SUBGENUS **MARECA** STEPHENS.

   Mareca STEPHENS, Gen. Zool. XII. pt. ii. 1824, 130. Type, *Anas penelope* LINN.

136. **Anas penelope** LINN.
   Widgeon.

   Anas penelope LINN. S. N. ed. 10, I. 1758, 126.

   [B 586, C 492, R 606, C 712.]

   HAB. Northern parts of the Old World. In North America breeds in the Aleutian Islands, and occurs occasionally in the Eastern United States.

137. **Anas americana** GMEL.
Baldpate.

Anas americana GMELIN, S. N. I. 1788, 526.

[B 585, C 493, R 607, C 713.]

HAB. North America, from the Arctic Ocean south to Guatemala and Cuba.

SUBGENUS **NETTION** KAUP.

Nettion KAUP, Sk. Ent. Europ. Thierw. 1829, 95. Type, *Anas crecca* LINN.

[138.] **Anas crecca** LINN.
European Teal.

Anas crecca LINN. S. N. ed. 10, I. 1758, 126.

[B 580, C 494, R 611, C 714.]

HAB. Northern parts of the Old World. Casual in Eastern North America and the Aleutian Islands.

139. **Anas carolinensis** GMELIN.
Green-winged Teal.

Anas carolinensis GMEL. S. N. I. 1788, 533.

[B 579, C 495, R 612, C 715.]

HAB. North America, breeding chiefly north of the United States, and migrating south to Honduras and Cuba.

SUBGENUS **QUERQUEDULA** STEPHENS.

Querquedula STEPHENS, Gen. Zool. XII. pt. ii. 1824, 142. Type, *Anas querquedula* LINN.

140. **Anas discors** LINN.
Blue-winged Teal.

Anas discors LINN. S. N. ed. 12, I. 1766, 205.

[B 581, C 496, R 609, C 716.]

HAB. North America in general, but chiefly the Eastern Province; north to Alaska, and south to the West Indies and Northern South America; breeds from the Northern United States northward.

141. Anas cyanoptera VIEILL.
Cinnamon Teal.

Anas cyanoptera VIEILLOT, Nouv. Dict. d'Hist. Nat. V. 1816, 104.

[B 582, C 497, R 610, C 717.]

HAB. Western America from Columbia River south to Chili, Patagonia, and Falkland Islands; east in North America to the Rocky Mountains; casual in the Mississippi Valley.

GENUS **SPATULA** BOIE.

Spatula BOIE, Isis, 1822, 564. Type, *Anas clypeata* LINN.

142. Spatula clypeata (LINN.).
Shoveller.

Anas clypeata LINN. S. N. ed. 10, I. 1758, 124.
Spatula clypeata BOIE, Isis, 1822, 564.

[B 583, C 498, R 608, C 718.]

HAB. Northern Hemisphere. In North America breeding from Alaska to Texas; not abundant on the Atlantic coast.

GENUS **DAFILA** STEPHENS.

Dafila STEPHENS, Gen. Zool. XII. pt. ii. 1824, 126.

143. Dafila acuta (LINN.).
Pintail.

Anas acuta LINN. S. N. ed. 10, I. 1758, 126.
Dafila acuta BONAP. Comp. List, 1838, 56.

[B 578, C 490, R 605, C 710.]

HAB. Northern Hemisphere. In North America breeds from the northern parts of the United States northward, and migrates south to Panama and Cuba.

GENUS **AIX** BOIE.

Aix BOIE, Isis, 1828, 329. Type, *Anas sponsa* LINN.

144. Aix sponsa (LINN.).
Wood Duck.

Anas sponsa LINN. S. N. ed. 10, I. 1758, 128.
Aix sponsa BONAP. Comp. List, 1838, 57.

[B 587, C 499, R 613, C 719.]

HAB. Temperate North America, breeding throughout its range.

GENUS NETTA KAUP.

Netta KAUP, Sk. Ent. Europ. Thierw. 1829, 102. Type, *Anas rufina* PALL.

[145.] Netta rufina (PALL.).
Rufous-crested Duck.

Anas rufina PALL. It. II. App. 1773, 731.
Netta rufina RIDGW. Pr. U. S. Nat. Mus. VIII. 1885, 355.

[B —, C —, R —, C 886.]

HAB. Eastern Hemisphere; accidental in Eastern United States.

GENUS AYTHYA BOIE.

Aythya BOIE, Isis, 1822, 564. Type, by elimination, *Anas ferina* LINN.

146. Aythya americana (EYT.).
Redhead.

Fuligula americana EYTON, Monogr. Anat. 1838, 155.
Aythya americana BAIRD, B. N. Am. 1858, 793.

[B 591, C 503, R 618, C 723.]

HAB. North America, breeding from California and Maine northward.

147. Aythya vallisneria (WILS.).
Canvas-back.

Anas vallisneria WILSON, Am. Orn. VIII. 1814, 103.
Aythya valisneria BOIE, Isis, 1826, 980.

[B 592, C 504, R 617, C 724.]

HAB. Nearly all of North America, breeding from the Northwestern States northward to Alaska.

SUBGENUS **FULIGULA** STEPHENS.

Fuligula STEPHENS, Gen. Zool. XII. pt. ii. 1824, 187. Type, by elimination, *Anas fuligula* LINN.

148. **Aythya marila nearctica** STEJN.
American Scaup Duck.

Aythya marila nearctica STEJN. Orn. Expl. Kamtsch. 1885, 161.

[B 588, C 500, R 614, C 720.]

HAB. North America, breeding far north.

149. **Aythya affinis** (EYT.).
Lesser Scaup Duck.

Fuligula affinis EYT. Mon. Anat. 1838, 157.
Aythya affinis STEJN. Orn. Expl. Kamtsch. 1885, 161.

[B 589, C 501, R 615, C 721.]

HAB. North America in general, breeding chiefly north of the United States, migrating south to Guatemala and the West Indies.

150. **Aythya collaris** (DONOV.).
Ring-necked Duck.

Anas collaris DONOV. Br. Birds, VI. 1809, pl. 147.
Aythya collaris RIDGW. Pr. U. S. Nat. Mus. VIII. 1885, 356.

[B 590, C 502, R 616, C 722.]

HAB. North America, breeding far north and migrating south to Guatemala and the West Indies.

GENUS **GLAUCIONETTA** STEJNEGER.

Glaucionetta STEJN. Pr. U. S. Nat. Mus. VIII. 1885, 409. Type, *Anas clangula* LINN.

151. Glaucionetta clangula americana (BONAP.).
American Golden-eye.

Clangula americana BONAP. Comp. List, 1838, 58.
Glaucionetta clangula americana STEJN. Pr. U. S. Nat. Mus. VIII. 1885, 409.

[B 593, C 505, R 620, C 725.]

HAB. North America, breeding from Maine and the British Provinces northward; in winter, south to Cuba.

152. Glaucionetta islandica (GMEL.).
Barrow's Golden-eye.

Anas islandica GMEL. S. N. I. 1788, 541.
Glaucionetta islandica STEJN. Pr. U. S. Nat. Mus. VIII. 1885, 409.

[B 594, C 506, R 619, C 726.]

HAB. Northern North America, south in winter to New York, Illinois, and Utah; breeding from the Gulf of St. Lawrence northward, and south in the Rocky Mountains to Colorado; Greenland; Iceland.

GENUS **CHARITONETTA** STEJNEGER.

Charitonetta STEJN. Orn. Expl. Kamtsch. 1885, 163. Type, *Anas albeola* LINN.

153. Charitonetta albeola (LINN.).
Buffle-head.

Anas albeola LINN. Syst. Nat. ed. 10, I. 1758, 124.
Charitonetta albeola STEJN. Orn. Expl. Kamtsch. 1885, 166.

[B 595, C 507, R 621, C 727.]

HAB. North America; south in winter to Cuba and Mexico. Breeds from Maine northward, through the Fur Countries and Alaska.

GENUS **CLANGULA** LEACH.

Clangula LEACH, in Ross's Voy. Disc. 1819, App. p. xlviii. Type, *Anas glacialis* LINN.

154. Clangula hyemalis (LINN.).
Old-squaw.

Anas hyemalis LINN. S. N. ed. 10, I. 1758, 126.
Clangula hiemalis BREHM, Handb. Vög. Deutschl. 1831, 933.

[B 597, C 508, R 623, C 728.]

HAB. Northern Hemisphere; in North America south to the Potomac and the Ohio; breeds far northward.

GENUS **HISTRIONICUS** LESSON.

Histrionicus LESSON, Man. d'Orn. II. 1828, 415. Type, *Anas histrionica* LINN.

155. **Histrionicus histrionicus** (LINN.).
Harlequin Duck.

Anas histrionica LINN. S. N. ed. 10, I. 1758, 127.
Histrionicus histrionicus BOUCARD, Cat. Av. 1876, 60.

[B 596, C 510, R 622, C 730.]

HAB. Northern North America, breeding from Newfoundland, the Northern Rocky Mountains, and the Sierra Nevada, northward; south in winter to the Middle States and California; Eastern Asia; Iceland.

GENUS **CAMPTOLAIMUS** GRAY.

Camptolaimus GRAY, List Gen. 1841, 95. Type, *Anas labradoria* GM.

156. **Camptolaimus labradorius** (GMEL.).
Labrador Duck.

Anas labradoria GMEL. S. N. I. 1788, 537.
Camptolaimus labradorus GRAY, List Gen. 1841, 95.

[B 600, C 510, R 624, C 730.]

HAB. Formerly Northern Atlantic coast, from New Jersey (in winter) northward, breeding from Labrador northward. Now extremely rare, and perhaps extinct.

GENUS **ENICONETTA** GRAY.

Eniconetta GRAY, List Gen. 1840, 75. Type, *Anas stelleri* PALL.

157. **Eniconetta stelleri** (PALL.).
Steller's Duck.

Anas stelleri PALL. Spicil. Zool. VI. 1769, 35.
Eniconetta stelleri GRAY, List Gen. 1840, 75.

[B 598, C 511, R 625, C 731.]

HAB. Arctic and subarctic coasts of the Northern Hemisphere.

Genus **ARCTONETTA** GRAY.

Arctonetta GRAY, P. Z. S. 1855, 12. Type, *Fuligula fischeri* BRANDT.

158. Arctonetta fischeri (BRANDT).
Spectacled Eider.

Fuligula fischeri BRANDT, Mém. Acad. St. Pétersb. VI. 1849, 6, 10.
Arctonetta fischeri BLAKISTON, Ibis, 1863, 150.

[B 599, C 512, R 626, C 732.]

HAB. Coast of Alaska, north to Point Barrow.

Genus **SOMATERIA** LEACH.

Subgenus **SOMATERIA**.

Somateria LEACH, in Ross's Voy. Disc. 1819, App. p. xlviii. Type, *Anas mollissima* LINN.

159. Somateria mollissima (LINN.).
Eider.

Anas mollissima LINN. S. N. ed. 10, I. 1758, 124.
Somateria mollissima BOIE, Isis, 1822, 564.

[B 606, *part*, C 513, *part*, R 627, C 733.]

HAB. Northern Europe and Northeastern North America, including Greenland and Northern Labrador; south in winter on the Atlantic coast to Maine.

160. Somateria dresseri SHARPE.
American Eider.

Somateria dresseri SHARPE, Ann. Mag. Nat. Hist. July, 1871, 51.

[B 606, *part*, C 513, *part*, R 627 a, C 734.]

HAB. Atlantic coast of North America, from Maine to Labrador; south in winter to the Delaware.

161. **Somateria v-nigra** GRAY.
Pacific Eider.

Somateria v-nigra GRAY, P. Z. S. 1855, 212.

[B 607, C 514, R 628, C 735.]

HAB. Coasts of the North Pacific; in the interior to the Great Slave Lake district, and in Eastern Siberia.

SUBGENUS **ERIONETTA** COUES.

Erionetta COUES, Key N. A. Birds, ed. 2, 1884, 709. Type, *Anas spectabilis* LINN.

162. **Somateria spectabilis** (LINN.).
King Eider.

Anas spectabilis LINN. S. N. ed. 10, I. 1758, 123.
Somateria spectabilis LEACH, in Ross's Voy. Disc. 1819, App. p. xlviii.

[B 608, C 515, R 629, C 736.]

HAB. Northern part of Northern Hemisphere, breeding in the Arctic regions; in North America south casually in winter to New Jersey and the Great Lakes.

GENUS **OIDEMIA** FLEMING.

SUBGENUS **OIDEMIA**.

Oidemia FLEMING, Philos. Zool. II. 1822, 260. Type, by elimination, *Anas nigra* LINN.

163. **Oidemia americana** SW. & RICH.
American Scoter.

Oidemia americana SW. & RICH. Faun. Bor. Amer. II. 1831, 450.

[B 604, C 516, R 630, C 737.]

HAB. Coasts and larger lakes of Northern North America; breeds in Labrador and the northern interior; south in winter to New Jersey, the Great Lakes, and California.

SUBGENUS **MELANITTA** BOIE.

Melanitta BOIE, Isis, 1822, 564. Type, by elimination, *Anas fusca* LINN.

[164.] **Oidemia fusca** (Linn.).
Velvet Scoter.

Anas fusca Linn. S. N. ed. 10, I. 1758, 123.
Oidemia fusca Stephens, Gen. Zool. XII. pt. ii. 1824, 216.

[B —, C —, R 631, C —.]

Hab. Northern Old World; accidental (?) in Alaska and Greenland.

165. **Oidemia deglandi** Bonap.
White-winged Scoter.

Oidemia deglandi Bonap. Rev. Crit. de l'Orn. Europ. de Dr. Degl., 1850, 108.

[B 601, C 517, R 632, C 738.]

Hab. Northern North America, breeding in Labrador and the Fur Countries; south in winter to the Middle States, Southern Illinois, and Southern California.

Subgenus **PELIONETTA** Kaup.

Pelionetta Kaup, Sk. Ent. Eur. Thierw. 1829, 107. Type, *Anas perspicillatus* Linn.

166. **Oidemia perspicillata** (Linn.).
Surf Scoter.

Anas perspicillata Linn. S. N. ed. 10, I. 1758, 125.
Oidemia perspicillata Stephens, Gen. Zool. XII. pt. ii. 1824, 219.

[B 602, 603, C 518, 518 a, R 633, C 739, 740.]

Hab. Coasts and larger inland waters of Northern North America; in winter south to the Carolinas, the Ohio River, and Lower California.

Genus **ERISMATURA** Bonaparte.

Erismatura Bonap. Saggio Distr. Meth. 1832, 143. Type, *Anas rubidus* Wils.

167. **Erismatura rubida** (Wils.).
Ruddy Duck.

Anas rubidus Wilson, Am. Orn. VIII. 1814, 128.
Erismatura rubida Bonap. Comp. List, 1838, 59.

[B 609, C 519, R 634, C 741.]

HAB. North America in general, south to Cuba, Guatemala, and Northern South America, breeding throughout most of its North American range.

GENUS **NOMONYX** RIDGWAY.

Nomonyx RIDGW. Pr. U. S. Nat. Mus. II. 1880, 15. Type, *Anas dominica* LINN.

[168.] **Nomonyx dominicus** (LINN.).
    Masked Duck.

Anas dominica LINN. S. N. ed. 12, 1766, 201.
Nomonyx dominicus RIDGW. Pr. U. S. Nat. Mus. II. 1880, 15.

[B 610, C 520, R 635, C 742.]

HAB. Tropical America; accidental in Eastern North America (Wisconsin; Lake Champlain).

SUBFAMILY ANSERINÆ. GEESE.

GENUS **CHEN** BOIE.

Chen BOIE, Isis, 1822, 563. Type, *Anser hyperboreus* PALL.

169. **Chen hyperborea** (PALL.).
    Lesser Snow Goose.

Anser hyperboreus PALL. Spicil. Zool. VI. 1769, 25.
Chen hyperborea BOIE, Isis, 1822, 563.

[B —, C 480 a, R 591 a, C 696.]

HAB. Pacific coast to the Mississippi Valley, breeding in Alaska; south in winter to Southern Illinois and Southern California.

169 a. **Chen hyperborea nivalis** (FORST.).
    Greater Snow Goose.

Anas nivalis FORSTER, Philos. Trans. LXII. 1772, 413.
Chen hyperboreus nivalis RIDGW. Pr. Biol. Soc. Wash. II. 1884, 107.

[B 563, C 480, R 591, C 695.]

HAB. North America, breeding far north, and migrating south in winter, chiefly along the Atlantic coast, reaching Cuba.

170. **Chen rossii** (BAIRD).
 Ross's Snow Goose.

Anser rossii "BAIRD MSS.," CASS. Pr. Ac. Nat. Sci. Phila. 1861, 73.
Chen rossii RIDGW. Pr. U. S. Nat. Mus. III. Aug. 24, 1880, 203.

[B —, C 481, R 592, C 697.]

HAB. Arctic America in summer, Pacific coast to Southern California in winter.

GENUS **ANSER** BRISSON.

Anser BRISSON, Orn. VI. 1760, 261. Type, *Anas anser* LINN.

[171.] **Anser albifrons** (GM.).
 White-fronted Goose.

Anas albifrons GMEL. S. N. I. 1788, 509.
Anser albifrons BECHST. Gem. Naturg. Deutschl. IV. 1809, 898.

[B —, C —, R 593, C 692.]

HAB. Northern parts of Eastern Hemisphere and Greenland.

171 *a*. **Anser albifrons gambeli** (HARTL.).
 American White-fronted Goose.

Anser gambeli HARTLAUB, Rev. Mag. Zool. 1852, 7.
Anser albifrons var. *gambeli* COUES, Key, 1872, 282.

[B 565, 566, C 478, R 593 *a*, C 693.]

HAB. North America, breeding far northward; in winter south to Mexico and Cuba.

GENUS **BRANTA** SCOPOLI.

Branta SCOPOLI, Ann. I. Hist. Nat. 1769, 67. Type, *Anas bernicla* LINN.

172. **Branta canadensis** (LINN.).
 Canada Goose.

Anas canadensis LINN. S. N. ed. 10, I. 1758, 123.
Branta canadensis BANNISTER, Pr. Ac. Nat. Sci. Phila. 1870, 131.

[B 567, C 485, R 594, C 702.]

HAB. Temperate North America, breeding in the Northern United States and British Provinces; south in winter to Mexico.

172 a. **Branta canadensis hutchinsii** (Sw. & RICH.).
Hutchins's Goose.

Anser hutchinsii Sw. & RICH. Faun. Bor. Am. II. 1831, 470.
Branta canadensis var. *hutchinsii* COUES, Key, 1872, 284.

[B 569, C 485 b, R 594 a, C 704.]

HAB. North America, breeding in the Arctic regions, and migrating south in winter, chiefly through the Western United States and Mississippi Valley; Eastern Asia.

172 b. **Branta canadensis occidentalis** (BAIRD).
White-cheeked Goose.

Bernicla occidentalis BAIRD, B. N. Am. 1858, 766.
Branta canadensis occidentalis RIDGW. Pr. U. S. Nat. Mus. VIII. 1885, 355.

[B 567 a, C —, R 594 c, C —.]

HAB. Pacific coast region, from Sitka south, in winter, to California.

172 c. **Branta canadensis minima** RIDGW.
Cackling Goose.

Branta minima RIDGW. Pr. U. S. Nat. Mus. VIII. No. 2, April 20, 1885, 23.
Branta canadensis minima RIDGW. Pr. U. S. Nat. Mus. VIII. 1885, 355.

[B 568, C 485 a, R 594 b, C 703, *part.*]

HAB. Coast of Alaska, migrating southward into the Western United States, east to Wisconsin.

173. **Branta bernicla** (LINN.).
Brant.

Anas bernicla LINN. S. N. ed. 10, I. 1758, 124.
Branta bernicla SCOPOLI, Ann. I. Hist. Nat. 1769, 67.

[B 570, C 484, R 595, C 700.]

HAB. Northern parts of the Northern Hemisphere; in North America chiefly on the Atlantic coast; rare in the interior, or away from salt water.

174. **Branta nigricans** (LAWR.).
Black Brant.

Anser nigricans LAWRENCE, Ann. Lyc. N. Y. IV. 1846, 171.
Branta nigricans BANNISTER, Pr. Ac. Nat. Sci. Phila. 1870, 131.

[B 571, C —, R 596, C 701.]

HAB. Arctic and Western North America; rare or casual in the Atlantic States.

[175.] **Branta leucopsis** (BECHST.).
Barnacle Goose.

Anas leucopsis BECHSTEIN, Orn. Taschb. Deutschl. 1803, 424.
Branta leucopsis BANNISTER, Pr. Ac. Nat. Sci. Phila. 1870, 131.

[B 572, C 483, R 597, C 699.]

HAB. Northern parts of the Old World; casual in Eastern North America.

GENUS **PHILACTE** BANNISTER.

Philacte BANNISTER, Pr. Ac. Nat. Sci. Phila. 1870, 131. Type, *Anas canagica* SEVAST.

176. **Philacte canagica** (SEVAST.).
Emperor Goose.

Anas canagica SEVASTIANOFF, N. Act. Petrop. XIII. 1800, 346.
Philacte canagica BANNISTER, Pr. Ac. Nat. Sci. Phila. 1870, 131.

[B 573, C 482, R 598, C 698.]

HAB. Coast and islands of Alaska.

GENUS **DENDROCYGNA** SWAINSON.

Dendrocygna SWAINSON, Classif. Birds, II. 1837, 365. Type, *Anas arcuata* CUV.

177. **Dendrocygna autumnalis** (LINN.).
     Black-bellied Tree-duck.

   Anas autumnalis LINN. S. N. ed. 10, I. 1758, 127.
   Dendrocygna autumnalis EYTON, Monogr. Anat. 1838, 109.

   [B 574, C 487, R 599, C 7c6.]

   HAB. Southwestern border of the United States and southward (Mexico, West Indies, etc.).

178. **Dendrocygna fulva** (GMEL.).
     Fulvous Tree-duck.

   Anas fulva GMEL. S. N. I. 1788, 530.
   Dendrocygna fulva BURMEISTER, Reise durch die La Plata Staaten, 1856, 515.

   [B 575, C 486, R 600, C 705.]

   HAB. Southern border of the United States (Louisiana, Texas, Nevada, California) and southward.

SUBFAMILY **CYGNINÆ.** SWANS.

GENUS **OLOR** WAGLER.

Olor WAGLER, Isis, 1832, 1234. Type, *Anas cygnus* LINN.

[179.] **Olor cygnus** (LINN.).
     Whooping Swan.

   Anas cygnus LINN. S. N. ed. 10, I. 1758, 122.
   Olor cygnus BONAPARTE, Catal. Parzudaki, 1856, 15.

   [B —, C —, R 586, C 690.]

   HAB. Europe and Asia; Greenland.

180. **Olor columbianus** (ORD).
     Whistling Swan.

   Anas columbianus ORD, in GUTHRIE'S Geogr. 2d Am. ed. 1815, 319.
   Olor columbianus STEJN. Pr. U. S. Nat. Mus. V. 1882, 210.

   [B 561 *bis*, C 477, R 588, C 689.]

   HAB. The whole of North America, breeding far north.

181. Olor buccinator (Rich.).
　　Trumpeter Swan.

Cygnus buccinator Richards. Fauna Bor. Am. I. 1831, 464.
Olor buccinator Wagler, Isis, 1832, 1234.

[B 562, C 476, R 589, C 688.]

Hab. Chiefly the interior of North America, from the Gulf coast to the Fur Countries, breeding from Iowa and Dakota northward; west to the Pacific coast, but rare or casual on the Atlantic.

Order ODONTOGLOSSÆ. Lamellirostral Grallatores.

Family PHŒNICOPTERIDÆ. Flamingoes.

Genus PHŒNICOPTERUS Linn.

Phœnicopterus Linn. S. N. ed. 10, I. 1758, 139. Type, *P. ruber* Linn.

182. Phœnicopterus ruber Linn.
　　American Flamingo

Phœnicopterus ruber Linn. S. N. ed. 10, I. 1758, 139.

[B 502, C 475, R 585, C 687.]

Hab. Atlantic coasts of subtropical and tropical America; Florida Keys.

Order HERODIONES. Herons, Storks, Ibises, etc.

Suborder IBIDES. Spoonbills and Ibises.

Family PLATALEIDÆ. Spoonbills.

Genus AJAJA Reich.

Ajaja Reich. Handb. 1852, p. xvi. Type, *Platalea ajaja* Linn.

183. **Ajaja ajaja** (Linn.).
  Roseate Spoonbill.

  Platalea ajaja Linn. S. N. ed. 10, I. 1758, 140.
  Ajaja ajaja Boucard, Cat. Av. 1876, 54.

  (B 501, C 488, R 505, C 653.)

Hab. Southern United States southward to the Falkland Islands and Patagonia.

Family IBIDIDÆ. Ibises.

Genus GUARA Reichenbach.

Guara Reich. Syst. Av. 1852, p. xiv. Type, *Tantalus ruber* Linn.

184. **Guara alba** (Linn.).
  White Ibis.

  Scolopax alba Linn. S. N. ed. 10, I. 1758, 145.
  Guara alba Stejn. Stand. Nat. Hist. IV. 1885, 9.

  [B 499, C 446, R 501, C 651.]

Hab. South Atlantic and Gulf States southward to the West Indies and Northern South America; casually on the Atlantic coast to

Long Island; in the interior to the Lower Ohio Valley and Great Salt Lake.

[185.] Guara rubra (LINN.).
Scarlet Ibis.

Tantalus ruber LINN. S. N. ed. 12, I. 1766, 241.
Guara rubra REICH. Syst. Av. 1852, p. xiv.

[B 498, C 447, R 502, C 652.]

HAB. Florida, Louisiana (?), and Texas, southward to the West Indies and Northern South America. No record of its recent occurrence in the United States.

GENUS **PLEGADIS** KAUP.

Plegadis KAUP, Skizz. Entw. Gesch. 1829, 82. Type, *Tantalus falcinellus* LINN. = *Tringa autumnalis* HASSELQ.

186. Plegadis autumnalis (HASSELQ.).
Glossy Ibis.

Tringa autumnalis HASSELQUIST, Reise nach Paläst. Deutsche Ausg. 1762, 306.
Plegadis autumnalis STEJN. Stand. Nat. Hist. IV. 1885, 160.

[B 500, C 445, R 503, C 649.]

HAB. Northern Old World, West Indies, and Eastern United States. Only locally abundant, and of irregular distribution in America.

187. Plegadis guarauna (LINN.).
White-faced Glossy Ibis.

Scolopax guarauna LINN. S. N. ed. 12, I. 1766, 242.
Plegadis guarauna RIDGW. Pr. U. S. Nat. Mus. I. Oct. 2, 1878, 163.

[B —, C 445 *bis*, 445 *ter*, R 504, C 650.]

HAB. Western United States (Texas, Utah, Nevada, Oregon, California, etc.), southward to Mexico, West Indies, and Central and South America.

Suborder CICONIÆ. Storks, etc.

Family CICONIIDÆ. Storks and Wood Ibises.

Subfamily TANTALINÆ. Wood Ibises.

Genus **TANTALUS** Linnæus.

Tantalus Linn. S. N. ed. 10, I. 1758, 140. Type, *T. loculator* Linn.

188. Tantalus loculator Linn.
Wood Ibis.

Tantalus loculator Linn. S. N. ed. 10, I. 1758, 140.

[B 497, C 444, R 500, C 648.]

Hab. Southern United States, from the Ohio Valley, Colorado, Utah, California, etc., south to Buenos Ayres; casually northward to Pennsylvania and New York.

Subfamily CICONIINÆ. Storks.

Genus **MYCTERIA** Linnæus.

Mycteria Linn. S. N. ed. 10, I. 1758, 140. Type, *M. americana* Linn.

[189.] Mycteria americana Linn.
Jabiru.

Mycteria americana Linn. S. N. ed. 10, I. 1758, 140.

[B —, C 448 *bis*, R 499, C 654.]

Hab. Tropical America, north casually to Southern Texas.

Suborder HERODII. Herons, Egrets, Bitterns, etc.

Family ARDEIDÆ. Herons, Bitterns, etc.

Subfamily BOTAURINÆ. Bitterns.

Genus **BOTAURUS** Hermann.

Subgenus **BOTAURUS**.

Botaurus Hermann, Tabl. Affin. Anim. 1783, 135. Type, *Ardea stellaris* Linn.

190. Botaurus lentiginosus (Montag.).
American Bittern.

Ardea lentiginosa Montag. Orn. Dict. Suppl. 1813, —.
Botaurus lentiginosus Steph. Gen. Zool. XI. ii. 1819, 592.

[B 492, C 460, R 497, C 666.]

Hab. Temperate North America, south to Guatemala and the West Indies.

Subgenus **ARDETTA** Gray.

Ardetta Gray, List Gen. B. App. 1842, 13. Type, *Ardea minuta* Linn.

191. Botaurus exilis (Gmel.).
Least Bittern.

Ardea exilis Gmel. S. N. I. ii. 1788, 645.
Botaurus exilis Reichenow, J. f. O. 1877, 244.

[B 491, C 461, R 498, C 667.]

Hab. Temperate North America, from the British Provinces to the West Indies and Brazil.

SUBFAMILY **ARDEINÆ**. HERONS AND EGRETS.

GENUS **ARDEA** LINN.

SUBGENUS **ARDEA**.

Ardea LINN. S. N. ed. 10, I. 1758, 141. Type, by elimination, *A. cinerea* LINN.

192. **Ardea occidentalis** AUD.
Great White Heron.

Ardea occidentalis AUD. Orn. Biog. III. 1835, 542.

[B 489, C 451, R 486, C 656, *part.*]

HAB. Florida; Jamaica; accidental in Southern Illinois.

193. **Ardea wardi** RIDGW.
Ward's Heron

Ardea wardi RIDGW. Bull. Nutt. Orn. Club, VII. Jan 1882, 5.

[B —, C —, R —, C —.]

HAB. Florida.

194. **Ardea herodias** LINN.
Great Blue Heron.

Ardea herodias LINN. S. N. ed. 10, I. 1758, 143.

[B 437, C 449, R 487, C 655.]

HAB. North America, from the Arctic regions southward to the West Indies and Northern South America.

[195.] **Ardea cinerea** LINN.
European Blue Heron.

Ardea cinerea LINN. S. N. ed. 10, I. 1758, 143.

[B —, C —, R 488, C 657.]

HAB. Most of the Eastern Hemisphere; accidental in Southern Greenland.

SUBGENUS **HERODIAS** BOIE.

Herodias BOIE, Isis, 1822, 559. Type, by elimination, *Ardea egretta* GMEL.

196. **Ardea egretta** GMEL.
American Egret.

Ardea egretta GMEL. S. N. I. ii. 1788, 629.

[B 486, 486*, C 452, R 489, C 658.]

HAB. Temperate and tropical America, from New Jersey, Minnesota, and Oregon south to Patagonia; casually on the Atlantic coast to Nova Scotia.

SUBGENUS **GARZETTA** KAUP.

Garzetta KAUP, Skizz. Entw. Gesch. 1829, 76. Type, *Ardea garzetta* LINN.

197. **Ardea candidissima** GMEL.
Snowy Heron.

Ardea candidissima GMEL. S. N. I. ii. 1788, 633.

[B 485, C 453, R 490, C 659.]

HAB. Temperate and tropical America, from Long Island and Oregon south to Buenos Ayres; casual on the Atlantic coast to Nova Scotia.

SUBGENUS **DICHROMANASSA** RIDGWAY.

Dichromanassa RIDGW. Bull. U. S. Geol. & Geog. Surv. Terr. IV. Feb. 5, 1878, 246. Type, *Ardea rufa* BODD.

198. **Ardea rufa** BODD.
Reddish Egret.

Ardea rufa BODD. Tabl. P. E. 1783, 54.

[B 483, 482, C 455, R 491, C 661.]

HAB. Gulf States and Mexico south to Guatemala, Jamaica, and Cuba; north to Southern Illinois.

SUBGENUS **HYDRANASSA** BAIRD.

Hydranassa BAIRD, B. N. Am. 1858, 660 (in text). Type, *Ardea ludoviciana* WILS. = *A. tricolor* MÜLL.

199. **Ardea tricolor ruficollis** (GOSSE).
Louisiana Heron.

Egretta ruficollis GOSSE, B. Jamaica, 1847, 338.
Ardea tricolor ruficollis RIDGW. Pr. U. S. Nat. Mus. VIII. 1885, 355.

[B 484, C 454, R 492, C 660.]

HAB. Gulf States, Mexico, Central America, and West Indies, casually northward to New Jersey and Indiana.

SUBGENUS **FLORIDA** BAIRD.

Florida BAIRD, B. N. Am. 1858, 671. Type, *Ardea cærulea* LINN.

200. **Ardea cœrulea** LINN.
Little Blue Heron.

Ardea cærulea LINN. S. N. ed. 10, I. 1758, 143.

[B 490, C 456, R 493, C 662.]

HAB. New Jersey, Illinois, and Kansas, southward through Central America and the West Indies to Guiana and New Grenada; casually north on the Atlantic coast to Massachusetts and Maine.

SUBGENUS **BUTORIDES** BLYTH.

Butorides "BLYTH, 1849," BONAP. Consp. II. 1855, 128. Type, *Ardea javanica* HORSF.

201. **Ardea virescens** LINN.
Green Heron.

Ardea virescens LINN. S. N. ed. 10, I. 1758, 144.

[B 493, C 457, R 494, C 663.]

HAB. Canada and Oregon, southward to Northern South America and the West Indies; rare or absent in the Middle Province.

GENUS **NYCTICORAX** STEPHENS.

SUBGENUS **NYCTICORAX**.

Nycticorax STEPH. Gen. Zool. XI. ii. 1819, 608. Type, *Ardea nycticorax* LINN.

202. **Nycticorax nycticorax nævius** (BODD.).
   Black-crowned Night Heron.

> *Ardea nævia* BODD. Tabl. Pl. Enl. 1783, 56.
> *Nycticorax nycticorax nævius* ZELEDON, Pr. U. S. Nat. Mus. VIII. 1885, 113.

[B 495, C 458, R 495, C 664.]

HAB. America, from the British Possessions southward to the Falkland Islands, including part of the West Indies.

SUBGENUS **NYCTHERODIUS** REICHENBACH.

> *Nyctherodius* REICH. Syst. Av. 1852, p. xvi. Type, *Ardea violacea* LINN.

203. **Nycticorax violaceus** (LINN.).
   Yellow-crowned Night Heron.

> *Ardea violacea* LINN. S. N. ed. 10, I. 1758, 143.
> *Nycticorax violacea* VIGORS, Zool. Journ. III. 1827, 446.

[B 496, C 459, R 496, C 665.]

HAB. Warm-temperate Eastern North America, from the Carolinas and the Lower Ohio Valley south to Brazil; casually north to Massachusetts and west to Colorado.

ORDER PALUDICOLÆ CRANES, RAILS, ETC.

SUBORDER GRUES. CRANES.

FAMILY GRUIDÆ. CRANES.

GENUS GRUS PALLAS.

> *Grus* PALL. Misc. Zool. 1766, 66. Type, *Ardea grus* LINN.

204. **Grus americana** (LINN.).
   Whooping Crane.

   Ardea americana LINN. S. N. ed. 10, I. 1758, 142.
   Grus americana SW. & RICH. Faun. Bor. Am. II. 1831, 372.

   [B 478, C 462, R 582, C 668.]

HAB. Interior of North America, from the Fur Countries to Florida, Texas, and Mexico, and from Ohio to Colorado. Formerly on the Atlantic coast, at least casually, to New England.

205. **Grus canadensis** (LINN.).
   Little Brown Crane.

   Ardea canadensis LINN. S. N. ed. 10, I. 1758, 141.
   Grus canadensis TEMM. Man. I. 1820, p. c.

   [B 480, C 463, R 584, C 669.]

HAB. Arctic and subarctic America, breeding from the Fur Countries and Alaska to the Arctic coast, migrating south in winter into the Western United States.

206. **Grus mexicana** (MÜLL.).
   Sandhill Crane.

   Ardea (grus) mexicana MÜLL. S. N. Suppl. 1776, 110.
   Grus mexicana RIDGW. Pr. U. S. Nat. Mus. VIII. 1885, 356.

   [B 479, C —, R 583, C 670.]

HAB. Southern half of North America; now rare near the Atlantic coast, except in Georgia and Florida.

SUBORDER RALLI. RAILS, GALLINULES, COOTS, ETC.

FAMILY ARAMIDÆ. COURLANS.

GENUS **ARAMUS** VIEILLOT.

Aramus VIEILL. Analyse, 1816, 58. Type, *Ardea scolopacea* GMEL.

207. Aramus giganteus (Bonap.).
Limpkin.

Rallus giganteus Bonap. Jour. Ac. Nat. Sci. Phila. V. 1825, 31.
Aramus giganteus Baird, B. N. Am. 1858, 657.

[B 481, C 464, R 581, C 671.]

Hab. Florida, West Indies, and Atlantic coast of Central America.

Family **RALLIDÆ**. Rails, Gallinules, and Coots.

Subfamily **RALLINÆ**. Rails.

Genus **RALLUS** Linnæus.

Rallus Linn. S. N. ed. 10, I. 1758, 153. Type, *R. aquaticus* Linn.

208. Rallus elegans Aud.
King Rail.

Rallus elegans Aud. Orn. Biog. III. 1835, 27, pl. 203.

[B 552, C 466, R 569, C 676.]

Hab. Fresh-water marshes of the Eastern Province of the United States, from the Middle States, Northern Illinois, Wisconsin, and Kansas southward. Casually north to Massachusetts, Maine, and Ontario.

209. Rallus beldingi Ridgw.
Belding's Rail.

Rallus beldingi Ridgw. Pr. U. S. Nat. Mus. V. 1882, 345.

[B —, C —, R —, C —.]

Hab. Espiritu Santo Islands, Gulf of California.

210. Rallus obsoletus Ridgw.
California Clapper Rail.

Rallus elegans var. *obsoletus* Ridgw. Am. Nat. VIII. 1871, 111.
Rallus obsoletus Ridgw. Bull. Nutt. Orn. Club, V. July, 1880, 139.

[B —, C 466 *a*, R 570, C 674.]

HAB. Salt marshes of the Pacific coast, from Washington Territory (?) to Lower California.

211. Rallus longirostris crepitans (GMEL.).
Clapper Rail.

Rallus crepitans GMEL. S. N. I. ii. 1788, 713.
Rallus longirostris crepitans RIDGW. Bull. Nutt. Orn. Club, V. July, 1880, 140.

[B 553, C 465, R 571, C 673.]

HAB. Salt marshes of the Atlantic coast of the United States, from New Jersey southward; resident from the Potomac southward. Casual north to Massachusetts.

211 *a*. Rallus longirostris saturatus HENSH.
Louisiana Clapper Rail.

Rallus longirostris saturatus "HENSHAW MS." RIDGW. Bull. Nutt. Orn. Club, V. July, 1880, 140.

[B —, C —, R 571 *a*, C 675.]

HAB. Salt marshes of the Gulf States, from Florida to Louisiana.

212. Rallus virginianus LINN.
Virginia Rail.

Rallus virginianus LINN. S. N. ed. 12, I. 1766, 263.

[B 554, C 467, R 572, C 677.]

HAB. North America, from the British Provinces south to Guatemala and Cuba.

GENUS **PORZANA** VIEILLOT.
SUBGENUS **PORZANA**.

Porzana VIEILL. Analyse, 1816, 61. Type, *Rallus porzana* LINN.

[213.] Porzana porzana (LINN.).
Spotted Crake.

Rallus porzana LINN. S. N. ed. 12, I. 1766, 262.
Porzana porzana BOUCARD, Cat. Av. 1876, 7.

[B —, C —, R 573, C 678.]

HAB. Northern parts of the Old World; occasional in Greenland.

214. **Porzana carolina** (LINN.).
Sora.

Rallus carolinus LINN. S. N. ed. 10, I. 1758, 153.
Porzana carolina BAIRD, Lit. Rec. & Jour. Linn. Assoc. Penn. Coll. Oct. 1845, 255.

[B 555, C 648, R 574, C 679.]

HAB. Temperate North America, but most common in the Eastern Province, breeding chiefly northward. South to the West Indies and Northern South America.

SUBGENUS **COTURNICOPS** BONAPARTE.

Coturnicops BONAP. Compt. Rend. XLIII. 1856, 599. Type, *Fulica noveboracensis* GMEL.

215. **Porzana noveboracensis** (GMEL.).
Yellow Rail.

Fulica noveboracensis GMEL. S. N. I. ii. 1788, 701.
Porzana noveboracensis BAIRD, Lit. Rec. & Jour. Linn. Assoc. Penn. Coll. Oct. 1845, 255.

[B 557, C 469, R 575, C 680.]

HAB. Eastern North America, from Nova Scotia and Hudson's Bay west to Utah and Nevada. No extralimital record except Cuba and the Bermudas.

SUBGENUS **CRECISCUS** CABANIS.

Creciscus CAB. J. f. O. 1856, 428. Type, *Rallus jamaicensis* LINN.

216. **Porzana jamaicensis** (GMEL.).
Black Rail.

Rallus jamaicensis GMEL. S. N. I. ii. 1788, 718.
Porzana jamaicensis BAIRD, Lit. Rec. & Jour. Linn. Assoc. Penn. Coll. Oct. 1845, 257.

[B 556, C 470, R 576, C 681.]

HAB. Temperate North America, north to Massachusetts, Northern Illinois, and Oregon; south to West Indies and in Western South America to Chili.

216 *a*. Porzana jamaicensis coturniculus BAIRD.
Farallone Rail.

Porzana jamaicensis var. *coturniculus* "BAIRD, MS." RIDGW. Am. Nat. VIII. Feb. 1874, 111.

[B —, C 470 *a*, R 576 *a*, C 682.]

HAB. Farallone Islands, California.

GENUS CREX BECHSTEIN.

Crex BECHST. Orn. Taschb. Deutschl. 1802, 336. Type, *Rallus crex* LINN.

[217.] Crex crex (LINN.).
Corn Crake.

Rallus crex LINN. S. N. ed. 10, I. 1758, 153.
Crex crex STEJN. Stand. Nat. Hist. IV. 1885, 128.

[B 558, C 471, R 577, C 683.]

HAB. Europe and Northern Asia; casual in Greenland, Bermudas, and Eastern North America.

SUBFAMILY GALLINULINÆ. GALLINULES.

GENUS IONORNIS REICHENBACH.

Ionornis REICH. Syst. Av. 1852, p. xxi. Type, *Fulica martinica* LINN.

218. Ionornis martinica (LINN.).
Purple Gallinule.

Fulica martinica LINN. S. N. ed. 12, I. 1766, 259.
Ionornis martinica REICH. Syst. Av. 1852, p. xxi.

[B 561, C 473, R 578, C 685.]

HAB. South Atlantic and Gulf States, casually northward to Maine, New York, Wisconsin, etc.; south throughout the West Indies to Brazil.

GENUS **GALLINULA** BRISSON.

Gallinula BRISS. Orn. VI. 1760, 2. Type, *Fulica chloropus* LINN.

219. **Gallinula galeata** (LICHT.).
Florida Gallinule.

Crex galeata LICHT. Verz. Doubl. 1823, 80.
Gallinula galeata BONAP. Am. Orn. IV. 1832, 128.

[B 560, C 472, R 579, C 685.]

HAB. Temperate and tropical America, from Canada to Brazil and Chili.

SUBFAMILY **FULICINÆ**. COOTS.

GENUS **FULICA** LINNÆUS.

Fulica LINN. S. N. ed. 10, I. 1758, 152. Type, *F. atra* LINN.

[220.] **Fulica atra** LINN.
European Coot.

Fulica atra LINN. S. N. ed. 10, I. 1758, 152.

[B —, C —, R —, C 885.]

HAB. Northern parts of the Eastern Hemisphere in general; accidental in Greenland.

221. **Fulica americana** GMEL.
American Coot.

Fulica americana GMEL. S. N. I. ii. 1788, 704.

[B 559, C 474, R 580, C 686.]

HAB. North America, from Greenland and Alaska southward to the West Indies and Central America.

Order LIMICOLÆ. Shore Birds.

Family PHALAROPODIDÆ. Phalaropes.

Genus CRYMOPHILUS Vieillot.

Crymophilus Vieill. Anal. 1816, 62. Type, *Tringa fulicarius* Linn.

222. Crymophilus fulicarius (Linn.).
Red Phalarope.

Tringa fulicaria Linn. S. N. ed. 10, I. 1758, 148.
Crymophilus fulicarius Stejn. Auk, II. 1885, 183.

[B 521, C 411, R 563, C 604.]

Hab. North parts of Northern Hemisphere, breeding in the Arctic regions and migrating south in winter; in the United States south to the Middle States, Ohio Valley, and Cape St. Lucas; chiefly maritime.

Genus PHALAROPUS Brisson.

Subgenus PHALAROPUS.

Phalaropus Briss. Orn. VI. 1760, 12. Type, by elimination, *Tringa lobata* Linn.

223. Phalaropus lobatus (Linn.).
Northern Phalarope.

Tringa lobata Linn. S. N. ed. 10, I. 1758, 148, 824.
Phalaropus lobatus Stejn. Auk, II. 1885, 183 (nec Latham qui *Crymophilus fulicarius*, nec Wilson qui *Ph. tricolor*).

[B 520, C 410, R 564, C 603.]

Hab. Northern portions of Northern Hemisphere, breeding in arctic latitudes; south in winter to the tropics.

Subgenus STEGANOPUS Vieillot.

Steganopus Vieill. N. Dict. d'Hist. Nat. XXXII. 1819, 136. Type, *S. tricolor* Vieill.

224. Phalaropus tricolor (VIEILL.).
Wilson's Phalarope.

Steganopus tricolor VIEILL. N. Dict. d'Hist. Nat. XXXII. 1819, 136.
Phalaropus tricolor STEJN. Auk, II. 1885, 183.

[B 519, C 409, R 565, C 602.]

HAB. Temperate North America, chiefly the interior, breeding from Northern Illinois and Utah northward to the Saskatchewan region; south in winter to Brazil and Patagonia.

FAMILY RECURVIROSTRIDÆ. AVOCETS AND STILTS.

GENUS RECURVIROSTRA LINNÆUS.

Recurvirostra LINN. S. N. ed. 10, I. 1758, 151. Type, *R. avosetta* LINN.

225. Recurvirostra americana GM.
American Avocet.

Recurvirostra americana GMEL. S. N. I. ii. 1788, 693.

[B 517, C 407, R 566, C 600.]

HAB. Temperate North America, from the Saskatchewan and Great Slave Lake southward; in winter, south to Guatemala and the West Indies. Rare in the Eastern Province.

GENUS HIMANTOPUS BRISSON.

Himantopus BRISS. Orn. VI. 1760, 33. Type, *Charadrius himantopus* LINN.

226. Himantopus mexicanus (MÜLL.).
Black-necked Stilt.

Charadrius mexicanus MÜLL. S. N. Suppl. 1776, 117.
Himantopus mexicanus ORD, WILS. Orn. VII. 1824, 52.

[B 518, C 408, R 567, C 601.]

HAB. Temperate North America, from the Northern United States southward to the West Indies, Brazil, and Peru. Rare in the Eastern Province, except in Florida.

Family SCOLOPACIDÆ. Snipes, Sandpipers, etc.

Genus SCOLOPAX Linnæus.

Scolopax Linn. S. N. ed. 10, I. 1758, 145. Type, *S. rusticola* Linn.

[227.] **Scolopax rusticola** Linn.
    European Woodcock.

Scolopax rusticola Linn. S. N. ed. 10, I. 1758, 146.

[B —, C 413, R 524, C 606.]

Hab. Northern parts of the Old World; occasional in Eastern North America.

Genus PHILOHELA Gray.

Philohela Gray, List Gen. B. 1841, 90. Type, *Scolopax minor* Gm.

228. **Philohela minor** (Gmel.).
    American Woodcock.

Scolopax minor Gmel. S. N. I. ii. 1788, 661.
Philohela minor Gray, List Gen. B. 1841, 90.

[B 522, C 412, R 525, C 606.]

Hab. Eastern Province of North America, north to the British Provinces, west to Dakota, Kansas, etc.; breeding throughout its range. No extralimital records.

Genus GALLINAGO Leach.

Gallinago Leach, Syst. Cat. Brit. Mam. & Birds, 1816, 31. Type, *Scolopax major* Linn.

[229.] **Gallinago gallinago** (Linn.).
    European Snipe.

Scolopax gallinago Linn. S. N. ed. 10, I. 1758, 147.
Gallinago gallinago Licht. Nom. Mus. Berol. 1854, 93.

[B —, C —, R 526, C 607.]

Hab. Northern parts of the Old World; frequent in Greenland, accidental in the Bermudas.

230. Gallinago delicata (ORD).
Wilson's Snipe.

Scolopax delicata ORD, WILS. Orn. IX. 1825, p. ccxviii.
Gallinago delicata RIDGW. MS.

[B 523, C 414, R 526 *a*, C 608.]

HAB. North and Middle America, breeding from the Northern United States northward; south in winter to the West Indies and Northern South America.

GENUS **MACRORHAMPHUS** LEACH.

Macrorhamphus LEACH, Syst. Cat. Brit. Mam. & B. 1816, 31. Type *Scolopax grisea* GMEL.

231. Macrorhamphus griseus (GMEL.).
Dowitcher.

Scolopax grisea GMEL. S. N. I. ii. 1788, 658.
Macrorhamphus griseus LEACH, Syst. Cat. Brit. Mam. & B. 1816, 31.

[B 524, C 415, R 527, C 609.]

HAB. Eastern North America, breeding far north.

232. Macrorhamphus scolopaceus (SAY).
Long-billed Dowitcher.

Limosa scolopacea SAY, LONG'S Exp. II. 1823, 170.
Macrorhamphus scolopaceus LAWR. Ann. Lyc. N. Y. V. 1852, 4, pl. 1.

[B 525, C 415 *a*, R 527 *a*, C 610.]

HAB. Mississippi Valley and Western Province of North America, from Mexico to Alaska. Less common but of regular occurrence along the Atlantic coast of the United States.

GENUS **MICROPALAMA** BAIRD.

Micropalama BAIRD, B. N. Am. 1858, 726. Type, *Tringa himantopus* BONAP.

233. Micropalama himantopus (BONAP.).
Stilt Sandpiper.

Tringa himantopus BONAP. Ann. Lyc. N. Y. II. 1826, 157.
Micropalama himantopus BAIRD, B. N. Am. 1858, 726.

[B 536, C 416, R 528, C 611.]

HAB. Eastern Province of North America, breeding north of the United States, and migrating in winter to the West Indies and Central and South America.

GENUS **TRINGA** LINNÆUS.

SUBGENUS **TRINGA**.

Tringa LINN. S. N. ed. 10, I. 1758, 148. Type, by elimination, *T. canutus* LINN.

234. Tringa canutus LINN.
Knot.

Tringa canutus LINN. S. N. ed. 10, I. 1758, 149.

[B 526, C 426, R 529, C 626.]

HAB. Nearly cosmopolitan. Breeds in high northern latitudes, but visits the Southern Hemisphere during its migrations.

SUBGENUS **ARQUATELLA** BAIRD.

Arquatella BAIRD, B. N. Am. 1858, 714. Type, *Tringa maritima* BRÜNN.

235. Tringa maritima BRÜNN.
Purple Sandpiper.

Tringa maritima BRÜNN. Orn. Bor. 1764, 54.

[B 528, C 423, R 530, C 620.]

HAB. Northern portions of the Northern Hemisphere; in North America chiefly the northeastern portions, breeding in the high north, migrating in winter to the Eastern and Middle States, the Great Lakes, and the shores of the larger streams in the Mississippi Valley.

236. **Tringa couesi** (RIDGW.).
   Aleutian Sandpiper.

   Arquatella couesi RIDGW. Bull. Nutt. Orn. Club, V. July, 1880, 160.
   Tringa couesi HARTLAUB, Journ. f. Orn. 1883, 280.

   [B —, C —, R 531, C 621.]

   HAB. Aleutian Islands and coast of Alaska, north to St. Michael's.

237. **Tringa ptilocnemis** COUES.
   Prybilof Sandpiper.

   Tringa ptilocnemis COUES, ELLIOTT'S Alaska, 1873 (not paged).

   [B —, C 426 bis, R 532, C 622.]

   HAB. Prybilof Islands, Alaska.

SUBGENUS **ACTODROMAS** KAUP.

   Actodromas KAUP, Sk. Ent. Eur. Thierw. 1829, 37. Type, *Tringa minuta* LEISL.

238. **Tringa acuminata** (HORSF.).
   Sharp-tailed Sandpiper.

   Totanus acuminatus HORSF. Linn. Trans. XIII. 1821, 192.
   Tringa acuminata SWINH. P. Z. S. 1863, 315.

   [B —, C —, R 533, C 619.]

   HAB. Eastern Asia, and coast of Alaska, migrating south to Australia.

239. **Tringa maculata** VIEILL.
   Pectoral Sandpiper.

   Tringa maculata VIEILL. Nouv. Dict. XXXIV. 1819, 465.

   [B 531, C 420, R 534, C 616.]

   HAB. The whole of North America, the West Indies, and the greater part of South America. Breeds in the Arctic regions. Of frequent occurrence in Europe.

240. **Tringa fuscicollis** Vieill.
    White-rumped Sandpiper.

   Tringa fuscicollis Vieill. Nouv. Dict. XXXIV. 1819, 461.

   [B 533, C 421, R 536, C 617.]

   Hab. Eastern Province of North America, breeding in the high north. In winter, the West Indies, Central and South America, south to the Falkland Islands. Occasional in Europe.

241. **Tringa bairdii** (Coues).
    Baird's Sandpiper.

   Actodromas bairdii Coues, Pr. Ac. Nat. Sci. Phila. 1861, 194.
   Tringa bairdii Scl. P. Z. S. 1867, 332.

   [B —, C 419, R 537, C 615.]

   Hab. The whole of North and South America, but chiefly the interior of North and the western portions of South America. Rare along the Atlantic coast, and not yet recorded from the Pacific coast.

242. **Tringa minutilla** Vieill.
    Least Sandpiper.

   Tringa minutilla Vieill. Nouv. Dict. XXXIV. 1819, 452.

   [B 532, C 418, R 538, C 614.]

   Hab. The whole of North and South America, breeding north of the United States. Accidental in Europe.

   Subgenus **PELIDNA** Cuvier.

   Pelidna Cuv. Règne An. 1817, 490. Type, *Tringa alpina* Linn.

[243.] **Tringa alpina** Linn.
    Dunlin.

   Tringa alpina Linn. S. N. ed. 10, I. 1758, 149.

   [B —, C —, R 539, C 623.]

   Hab. Northern parts of the Old World; accidental in North America.

243 a. Tringa alpina pacifica (Coues).
Red-backed Sandpiper.

Pelidna pacifica Coues, Pr. Ac. Nat. Sci. Phila. 1861, 189.
Tringa alpina pacifica Ridgw. MS.

[B 530, C 424, R 539 a, C 624.]

Hab. North America in general, breeding far north. Eastern Asia.

Subgenus **ANCYLOCHEILUS** Kaup.

Ancylocheilus Kaup, Sk. Ent. Eur. Thierw. 1829, 50. Type, *Tringa subarquata* Temm. = *T. ferruginea* Brünn.

244. Tringa ferruginea Brünn.
Curlew Sandpiper.

Tringa ferruginea Brünn. Orn. Bor. 1764, 53.

[B 529, C 425, R 540, C 625.]

Hab. Old World in general; occasional in Eastern North America.

Genus **EURYNORHYNCHUS** Nilsson.

Eurynorhynchus Nilss. Orn. Suec. II. 1821, 29. Type, *Platalea pygmæa* Linn.

[**245.**] **Eurynorhynchus pygmæus** (Linn.).
Spoon-bill Sandpiper.

Platalea pygmæa Linn. S. N. ed. 10, I. 1758, 140.
Eurynorhynchus pygmæus Pearson, Jour. As. Soc. Beng. V. 1836, 127.

[B —, C —, R 542*, C 884.]

Hab. Asia; in summer along the Arctic coast, in winter Southern and Southeastern Asia. Accidental on the coast of Alaska.

Genus **EREUNETES** Illiger.

Ereunetes Illig. Prodr. 1811, 262. Type, *E. petrificatus* Illig. = *Tringa pusilla* Linn.

ORDER LIMICOLÆ.

246. **Ereunetes pusillus** (Linn.).
    Semipalmated Sandpiper.

   Tringa pusilla Linn. S. N. ed. 12, I. 1766, 252.
   Ereunetes pusillus Cass. Pr. Ac. Nat. Sci. Phila. 1860, 195.

   [B 535, C 417, R 541, C 612.]

   Hab. Eastern Province of North America, breeding north of the United States; south in winter to the West Indies and South America.

247. **Ereunetes occidentalis** Lawr.
    Western Sandpiper.

   Ereunetes occidentalis Lawr. Pr. Ac. Nat. Sci. Phila. 1864, 107.

   [B —, C 417 a, R 541 a, C 613.]

   Hab. Chiefly Western Province of the United States, occasional eastward to the Atlantic coast; breeding far north and migrating in winter to Central and South America.

Genus **CALIDRIS** Cuvier.

Calidris Cuv. Leç. Anat. Comp. I. 1799–1800, tabl. ii. Type, *Tringa arenaria* Linn.

248. **Calidris arenaria** (Linn.).
    Sanderling.

   Tringa arenaria Linn. S. N. ed. 12, I. 1766, 251.
   Calidris arenaria Leach, Syst. Cat. Brit. Mam. & B. 1816, 28.

   [B 534, C 427, R 542, C 627.]

   Hab. Nearly cosmopolitan, breeding in the Arctic and Subarctic regions, migrating, in America, south to Chili and Patagonia.

Genus **LIMOSA** Brisson.

Limosa Briss. Orn. V. 1760, 261. Type, *Scolopax limosa* Linn.

249. **Limosa fedoa** (Linn.).
    Marbled Godwit.

   Scolopax fedoa Linn. S. N. ed. 10, I. 1758, 146.
   Limosa fedoa Ord, Wils. Orn. VII. 1824, 30.

[B 547, C 428, R 543, C 628.]

HAB. North America; breeding in the interior (Missouri region and northward), migrating in winter southward to Central America and Cuba.

250. Limosa lapponica baueri (NAUM.).
Pacific Godwit.

Limosa baueri NAUMANN, Vög Deutschl. VIII. 1834, 429.
Limosa lapponica baueri STEJN. Orn. Expl. Kamtsch. 1885, 122.

[B —, C 430, R 544, C 631.]

HAB. Shores and islands of the Pacific Ocean, from Australia to Alaska. On the American coast recorded south of Alaska only from Lower California.

251. Limosa hæmastica (LINN.).
Hudsonian Godwit.

Scolopax hæmastica LINN. S. N. ed. 10, I. 1758, 147.
Limosa hæmastica COUES, Birds Northwest, 1874, 760.

[B 548, C 429, R 545, C 629.]

HAB. Eastern North America and the whole of Middle and South America. Breeds only in the high north.

[252.] Limosa limosa (LINN.).
Black-tailed Godwit.

Scolopax limosa LINN. S. N. ed. 10, I. 1758, 147.
Limosa limosa RIDGW. Pr. U. S. Nat. Mus. VIII. 1885, 356.

[B —, C —, R 546, C 630.]

HAB. Northern parts of the Old World; accidental in Greenland.

GENUS **TOTANUS** BECHSTEIN.

Totanus BECH. Orn. Tasch. Deutschl. 1803, 282. Type, *Scolopax totanus* LINN.

SUBGENUS **GLOTTIS** KOCH.

Glottis KOCH, Baier. Zool. 1816, 304. Type, *Totanus glottis* BECHST.
= *Scolopax nebularius* GUNNER.

[253.] **Totanus nebularius** (GUNN.).
Green-shank.

Scolopax nebularius GUNNER. in LEEM, Lapp. Beskr. 1767, 251.
Totanus nebularius STEJN. Pr. U. S. Nat. Mus. V. 1882, 37.

[B 538, C 434, R 547, C 635.]

HAB. Eastern Hemisphere; accidental in Florida.

254. **Totanus melanoleucus** (GMEL.).
Greater Yellow-legs.

Scolopax melanoleuca GMEL. S. N. I. ii. 1788, 659.
Totanus melanoleucus VIEILL. Nouv. Dict. VI. 1816, 398.

[B 539, C 432, R 548, C 633.]

HAB. America in general, breeding in the cold temperate and sub-arctic portions of North America, and migrating south to Chili and Buenos Ayres.

255. **Totanus flavipes** (GMEL.).
Yellow-legs.

Scolopax flavipes GMEL. S. N. I. ii. 1788, 659.
Totanus flavipes VIEILL. Nouv. Dict. VI. 1816, 410.

[B 540, C 433, R 549, C 634.]

HAB. America in general, breeding in the cold temperate and sub-arctic districts, and migrating south in winter to Southern South America. Less common in the Western than in the Eastern Province of North America.

SUBGENUS **RHYACOPHILUS** KAUP.

Rhyacophilus KAUP, Sk. Ent. Eur. Thierw. 1829, 140. Type, *Tringa glareola* LINN.

256. Totanus solitarius (WILS.).
    Solitary Sandpiper.

Tringa solitaria WILS. Am. Orn. VII. 1813, 53, pl. 58, fig. 3.
Totanus solitarius BONAP. Journ. Ac. Nat. Sci. Phila. V. 1825, 86.

[B 541, C 435, R 550, C 637.]

HAB. North America, breeding occasionally in the Northern United States, more commonly northward, and migrating southward as far as Brazil and Peru.

[**257.**] **Totanus ochropus** (LINN.).
    Green Sandpiper.

Tringa ochrophus (err. typ.) LINN. S. N. ed. 10, I. 1758, 149.
Totanus ochropus TEMM. Man. 1815, 420.

[B —, C —, R 551, C 636.]

HAB. Northern parts of the Old World. Accidental in Nova Scotia.

GENUS **SYMPHEMIA** RAFINESQUE.

Symphemia RAFINESQUE, Jour. de Phys. VII. 1819, 418. Type, *Scolopax semipalmata* GMEL.

258. Symphemia semipalmata (GMEL.).
    Willet.

Scolopax semipalmata GMEL. S. N. I. ii. 1788, 659.
Symphemia semipalmata HARTL. Rev. Zool. 1845, 342.

[B 537, C 431, R 552, C 632.]

HAB. Temperate North America, south to the West Indies and Brazil.

GENUS **HETERACTITIS** STEJNEGER.

Heteractitis STEJN. Auk, I. July, 1884, 236. Type, *Scolopax incanus* GMEL.

259. Heteractitis incanus (GMEL.).
    Wandering Tatler.

Scolopax incanus GMEL. S. N. I. ii. 1788, 658.
Heteractitis incanus STEJN. Auk, I. July, 1884, 236.

[B 542, C 440, R 553, C 642.]

Hab. Eastern islands and shores of the Pacific Ocean; frequent during migrations on the coast of Alaska.

Genus **PAVONCELLA** Leach.

Pavoncella Leach, Syst. Cat. Brit. Mam. & B. 1816, 29. Type, *Tringa pugnax* Linn.

[260.] **Pavoncella pugnax** (Linn.).
Ruff.

Tringa pugnax Linn. S. N. ed. 10, I. 1758, 148.
Pavoncella pugnax Leach, Syst. Cat. Brit. Mam. & B. 1816, 29.

[B 544, C 437, R 554, C 639.]

Hab. Northern parts of the Old World, straying occasionally to Eastern North America.

Genus **BARTRAMIA** Lesson.

Bartramia Less. Traité, 1831, 553. Type, *B. laticauda* Less. = *Tringa longicauda* Bechst.

261. **Bartramia longicauda** (Bechst.).
Bartramian Sandpiper.

Tringa longicauda Bechst. Uebers. Lath. Ind. Orn. II. 1812, 453.
Bartramius longicaudus Bonap. Rev. et Mag. Zool. XX. 1857, 59.

[B 545, C 438, R 555, C 640.]

Hab. Eastern North America, north to Nova Scotia and Alaska, breeding throughout its North American range; migrating in winter southward, as far even as Southern South America. Occasional in Europe.

Genus **TRYNGITES** Cabanis.

Tryngites Cab. Jour. für Orn. 1856, 418. Type, *Tringa rufescens* Vieill. = *T. subruficollis* Vieill.

262. **Tryngites subruficollis** (VIEILL.).
Buff-breasted Sandpiper.

Tringa subruficollis VIEILL. Nouv. Dict. XXXIV. 1819, 465.
Tryngites subruficollis RIDGW. Pr. U. S. Nat. Mus. VIII. 1885, 356.

[B 546, C 439, R 556, C 641.]

HAB. North America, especially in the interior; breeds in the Yukon district and the interior of British America, northward to the Arctic coast; South America in winter. Of frequent occurrence in Europe.

GENUS **ACTITIS** ILLIGER.

Actitis ILLIG. Prodr. 1811, 262.   Type, *Tringa hypoleucos* LINN.

263. **Actitis macularia** (LINN.).
Spotted Sandpiper.

Tringa macularia LINN. S. N. ed. 12, I. 1766, 249.
Actitis macularia NAUMANN, Vög. Deutschl. VIII. 1836, 34.

[B 543, C 436, R 557, C 638.]

HAB. North and South America, south to Brazil. Breeds throughout temperate North America. Occasional in Europe.

GENUS **NUMENIUS** BRISSON.

Numenius BRISS. Orn. VI. 1760, 311.   Type, *Scolopax arquata* LINN.

264. **Numenius longirostris** WILS.
Long-billed Curlew.

Numenius longirostris WILS. Am. Orn. VIII. 1814, 24, pl. 64, fig. 4.

[B 549, C 441, R 558, C 643.]

HAB. Temperate North America, migrating south to Guatemala and the West Indies. Breeds in the South Atlantic States, and in the interior through most of its North American range.

265. **Numenius hudsonicus** LATH.
   Hudsonian Curlew.

   Numenius hudsonicus LATH. Ind. Orn. II. 1790, 712.

   [B 550, C 442, R 559, C 645.]

HAB. All of North and South America, including the West Indies; breeds in the high north, and winters chiefly south of the United States.

266. **Numenius borealis** (FORST.).
   Eskimo Curlew.

   Scolopax borealis FORST. Phil. Trans. LXII. 1772, 411, 431.
   Numenius borealis LATH. Ind. Orn. II. 1790, 712.

   [B 551, C 443, R 560, C 646.]

HAB. Eastern Province of North America, breeding in the Arctic regions, and migrating south to the southern extremity of South America.

[267.] **Numenius phæopus** (LINN.).
   Whimbrel.

   Scolopax phæopus LINN. S. N. ed. 10, I. 1758, 146.
   Numenius phæopus LATH. Ind. Orn. II. 1790, 711.

   [B —, C —, R 561, C 644.]

HAB. Northern parts of the Old World; occasional in Greenland.

[268.] **Numenius tahitiensis** (GMEL.).
   Bristle-thighed Curlew.

   Scolopax tahitiensis GMEL. S. N. I. ii. 1788, 656.
   Numenius tahitiensis RIDGW. Pr. U. S. Nat. Mus. III. Aug. 24, 1880, 201.

   [B —, C 442 *bis*, R 562, C 647.]

HAB. Islands of the Pacific Ocean. Occasional on the coast of Alaska.

Family CHARADRIIDÆ. Plovers.

Genus VANELLUS Brisson.

Vanellus Briss. Orn. V. 1760, 94. Type, *Tringa vanellus* Linn.

[269.] Vanellus vanellus (Linn.).
Lapwing.

Tringa vanellus Linn. S. N. ed. 10, I. 1758, 148.
Vanellus vanellus Licht. Nom. Mus. Berol. 1854, 95.

[B —, C —, R 512, C 593.]

Hab. Northern parts of Eastern Hemisphere. In North America, occasional in Greenland and the islands in Norton Sound, Alaska.

Genus CHARADRIUS Linnæus.

Subgenus SQUATAROLA Cuvier.

Squatarola Cuv. Règ. An. I. 1817, 467. Type, *Tringa squatarola* Linn.

270. Charadrius squatarola (Linn.).
Black-bellied Plover.

Tringa squatarola Linn. S. N. ed. 10, I. 1758, 149.
Charadrius squatarola Naum. Vög. Deutschl. VII. 1834, 250.

[B 510, C 395, R 513, C 580.]

Hab. Nearly cosmopolitan, but chiefly in the Northern Hemisphere, breeding far north, and migrating south in winter; in America, to the West Indies, Brazil, and New Grenada.

Subgenus CHARADRIUS Linnæus.

Charadrius Linn. S. N. ed. 10, I. 1758, 150. Type, *C. apricarius* Linn.

[271.] Charadrius apricarius Linn.
Golden Plover.

Charadrius apricarius Linn. S. N. ed. 10, I. 1758, 150.

[B —, C —, R 514, C 583.]

HAB. Europe, south to Africa in winter; Greenland.

272. Charadrius dominicus MÜLL.
American Golden Plover.

Charadrius dominicus MÜLL. S. N. Suppl. 1776, 116.

[B 503, C 396, R 515, C 581.]

HAB. Arctic America, migrating southward throughout North and South America to Patagonia.

272 a. Charadrius dominicus fulvus (GMEL.).
Pacific Golden Plover.

Charadrius fulvus GMEL. S. N. I. ii. 1788, 687.
Charadrius dominicus fulvus RIDGW. Pr. U. S. Nat. Mus. III. 1880, 198.

[B —, C —, R 515 a, C 582.]

HAB. Asia, and islands of the Pacific Ocean; in North America, Prybilof Islands and coast of Alaska.

GENUS ÆGIALITIS BOIE.

SUBGENUS OXYECHUS REICHENBACH.

Oxyechus REICH. Syst. Av. 1853, p. xviii. Type, *Charadrius vociferus* LINN.

273. Ægialitis vocifera (LINN.).
Killdeer.

Charadrius vociferus LINN. S. N. ed. 10, I. 1758, 150.
Ægialites vociferus BONAP. Geog. & Comp. List, 1838, 45.

[B 504, C 397, R 516, C 584.]

HAB. Temperate North America, migrating in winter to the West Indies, and Central and Northern South America.

SUBGENUS **ÆGIALITIS** BOIE.

Ægialitis BOIE, Isis, 1822, 558. Type, by elimination, *Charadrius hiaticula* LINN.

274. Ægialitis semipalmata BONAP.
Semipalmated Plover.

Ægialites semipalmatus BONAP. Geog. & Comp. List, 1838, 45.

[B 507, C 399, R 517, C 586.]

HAB. Arctic and subarctic America, migrating south throughout tropical America, as far as Brazil and Peru.

275. Ægialitis hiaticula (LINN.).
Ring Plover.

Charadrius hiaticula LINN. S. N. ed. 10, I. 1758, 150.
Ægialitis hiaticula BOIE, Isis, 1822, 558.

[B —, C —, R 518, C 589.]

HAB. Northern parts of the Old World and portions of Arctic America, breeding on the west shore of Cumberland Gulf.

[276.] Ægialitis dubia (SCOP.).
Little Ring Plover.

Charadrius dubius SCOPOLI, Delic. F. et Fl. Insubr. II. 1786, 93.
Ægialites dubius WALDEN, Trans. Zool. Soc. VIII. ii. 1872, 89.

[B —, C 400 *bis*, R 519, C 590.]

HAB. Most of the Eastern Hemisphere, breeding northward. Accidental on the coast of California and in Alaska.

277. Ægialitis meloda (ORD).
Piping Plover.

Charadrius melodus ORD. ed. WILS. VII. 1824, 71.
Ægialites melodus BONAP. Geog. & Comp. List, 1838, 45.

[B 508, C 400, R 520, C 587.]

HAB. Eastern Province of North America, breeding from the coast of Virginia (at least formerly) northward; in winter, West Indies.

277 a. **Ægialitis meloda circumcincta** RIDGW.
   Belted Piping Plover.

   Ægialitis melodus var. *circumcinctus* RIDGW. Am. Nat. VIII. 1874, 109.

   [B —, C 400 a, R 520 a, C 588.]

   HAB. Missouri River region; occasional eastward to Atlantic coast.

278. **Ægialitis nivosa** CASS.
   Snowy Plover.

   Ægialitis nivosa CASS. in BAIRD, B. N. Am. 1858, 696.

   [B 509, C 401, R 521, C 591.]

   HAB. Western Province of North America; in winter, both coasts of Central America, and Western South America to Chili.

[279.] **Ægialitis mongola** (PALL.).
   Mongolian Plover.

   Charadrius mongolus PALL. Reise Russ. Reich. III. 1776, 700.
   Ægialites mongolus SWINH. P. Z. S. 1870, 140.

   [B —, C —, R —, C —.]

   HAB. Northern Asia, southward to Northeastern Africa, India, Malay Archipelago, and Australia. Choris Peninsula, Alaska; accidental.

   SUBGENUS **OCHTHODROMUS** REICHENBACH.

   Ochthodromus REICH. Syst. Av. 1852, p. xviii. Type, *Charadrius wilsonius* ORD.

280. **Ægialitis wilsonia** (ORD).
   Wilson's Plover.

   Charadrius wilsonia ORD, WILS. Orn. IX. 1814, 77, pl. 73, fig. 5.
   Ægialites wilsonius BONAP. Geog. & Comp. List, 1838, 45.

   [B 506, C 398, R 522, C 585.]

   HAB. Coasts of North and South America, from Long Island and Lower California southward to Brazil and Peru, including the West Indies. Casual north to Nova Scotia.

Subgenus **PODASOCYS** Coues.

Podasocys Coues, Pr. Ac. Nat. Sci. Phila. 1866, 96. Type, *Charadrius montanus* Towns.

281. **Ægialitis montana** (Towns.).
  Mountain Plover.

Charadrius montanus Towns. Jour. Ac. Nat. Sci. Phila. VII. 1837, 192.
Ægialitis montanus Cass. in Baird, B. N. Am. 1858, 693.

[B 505, C 402, R 523, C 592.]

Hab. Temperate North America, from the Great Plains westward; accidental in Florida.

Family **APHRIZIDÆ**. Surf Birds and Turnstones.

Subfamily **APHRIZINÆ**. Surf Birds.

Genus **APHRIZA** Audubon.

Aphriza Aud. Orn. Biog. V. 1839, 249. Type, *A. townsendii* Aud. = *Tringa virgata* Gmel.

282. **Aphriza virgata** (Gmel.).
  Surf Bird.

Tringa virgata Gmel. S. N. I. ii. 1788, 674.
Aphriza virgata Gray, Gen. B. III. 1847, pl. cxlvii.

[B 511, C 403, R 511, C 594.]

Hab. Pacific coast of America, from Alaska to Chili; Sandwich Islands.

Subfamily **ARENARIINÆ**. Turnstones.

Genus **ARENARIA** Brisson.

Arenaria Briss. Orn. V. 1760, 132. Type, *Tringa interpres* Linn.

283. Arenaria interpres (LINN.).
Turnstone.

Tringa interpres LINN. S. N. ed. 10, I. 1758, 148.
Arenaria interpres VIEILL. Gal. Ois. II. 1834, 102.

[B 515, C 406, R 509, C 598.]

HAB. Nearly cosmopolitan. In America from Greenland and Alaska to the Straits of Magellan; more or less common in the interior of North America, on the shores of the Great Lakes and the larger rivers. Breeds in high northern latitudes.

284. Arenaria melanocephala (VIG.).
Black Turnstone.

Strepsilas melanocephalus VIG. Zool. Jour. IV. Jan. 1829, 356.
Arenaria melanocephala STEJN. Auk, I. July, 1884, 229.

[B 516, C 406*a*, R 510, C 599.]

HAB. Pacific coast of North America, from Alaska to Monterey, California; breeding in Alaska.

FAMILY HÆMATOPODIDÆ. OYSTER CATCHERS.

GENUS HÆMATOPUS LINNÆUS.

Hæmatopus LINN. S. N. ed. 10, I. 1758, 152. Type, *H. ostralegus* LINN.

[285.] Hæmatopus ostralegus LINN.
Oyster-catcher.

Hæmatopus ostralegus LINN. S. N. ed. 10, I. 1758, 152.

[B —, C —, R 506, C 595.]

HAB. Sea-coasts of the Eastern Hemisphere; occasional in Greenland.

286. Hæmatopus palliatus TEMM.
American Oyster-catcher.

Hæmatopus palliatus TEMM. Man. II. 1820, 532.

[B 512, C 404, R 507, C 596.]

HAB. Sea-coasts of temperate and tropical America, from New Jersey and Lower California to Patagonia; occasional or accidental on the Atlantic coast north to Massachusetts and Grand Menan.

287. **Hæmatopus bachmani** AUD.
Black Oyster-catcher.

Hæmatopus bachmani AUD. Orn. Biog. V. 1839, 245, pl. 427.

[B 513, C 405, R 508, C 597.]

HAB. Pacific coast of North America, from Alaska to Lower California.

FAMILY **JACANIDÆ**, JACANAS.

GENUS **JACANA** BRISSON.

Jacana BRISS. Orn. V. 1760, 121. Type, by elimination, *Fulica spinosa* LINN.

[288.] **Jacana gymnostoma** (WAGL.).
Mexican Jaçana.

Parra gymnostoma WAGLER, Isis, 1831, 517.
Jacana gymnostoma ZELEDON, Pr. U. S. Nat. Mus. VIII. 1885, 114.

[B —, C —, R 568, C 672.]

HAB. Lower Rio Grande Valley, Texas, south to Central America; Cuba.

Order GALLINÆ. Gallinaceous Birds.

Suborder PHASIANI. Pheasants, Grouse, Partridges, Quails, etc.

Family TETRAONIDÆ. Grouse, Partridges, etc.

Subfamily PERDICINÆ. Partridges.

Genus COLINUS Lesson.

Colinus Less. Man. d'Orn. II. 1828, 190. Type, *Tetrao virginianus* Linn.

289. Colinus virginianus (Linn.).
Bob-white.

Tetrao virginianus Linn. S. N. ed. 10, I. 1758, 161.
Colinus virginianus Stejn. Auk, II. Jan. 1885, 45.

[B 471, C 389, R 480, C 571.]

Hab. Eastern United States and Southern Canada, from Southern Maine to the South Atlantic and Gulf States; west to Dakota, Eastern Kansas, and Eastern Texas.

289 a. Colinus virginianus floridanus (Coues).
Florida Bob-white.

Ortyx virginianus var. *floridanus* Coues, Key, 1872, 237.
Colinus virginianus floridanus Stejn. Auk, II. Jan. 1885, 45.

[B —, C 389 a, R 480 a, C 572.]

Hab. Florida.

289 b. Colinus virginianus texanus (Lawr.).
Texan Bob-white.

Ortyx texanus Lawr. Ann. Lyc. N. Y. VI. April, 1853, 1.
Colinus virginianus texanus Stejn. Auk, II. Jan. 1885, 45.

[B 472, C 389 *b*, R 480 *b*, C 573.]

HAB. Southern and Western Texas, north to Western Kansas.

290. **Colinus graysoni** (LAWR.).
Grayson's Bob-white.

Ortyx graysoni LAWR. Ann. Lyc. N. Y. VIII. May, 1867, 476.
Colinus graysoni STEJN. Auk, II. Jan. 1885, 45.

[B —, C —, R —, C —.]

HAB. Mexico, north into Southern Arizona.

291. **Colinus ridgwayi** BREWST.
Masked Bob-white.

Colinus ridgwayi BREWST. Auk, II. April, 1885, 199.

[B —, C —, R —, C —.]

HAB. Mexican border of Arizona and southward.

GENUS **OREORTYX** BAIRD.

Oreortyx BAIRD, B. N. Am. 1858, 642. Type, *Ortyx picta* DOUGL.

292. **Oreortyx pictus** (DOUGL.).
Mountain Partridge.

Ortyx picta DOUGL. Trans. Linn. Soc. XVI. 1829, 143.
Oreortyx pictus BAIRD, B. N. Am. 1858, 642.

[B 473, C 390, R 481, C 574.]

HAB. Washington Territory, Oregon, and northern coast region of California.

292 *a*. **Oreortyx pictus plumiferus** (GOULD).
Plumed Partridge.

Ortyx plumifera GOULD, P. Z. S. 1837, 42.
Oreortyx pictus var. *plumiferus* RIDGW. in Hist. N. Am. B. III. 1874, 476.

[B —, C —, R 481 *a*, C —.]

HAB. Sierra Nevada, and southern coast ranges of California to Cape St. Lucas.

Genus CALLIPEPLA Wagler.

Subgenus CALLIPEPLA.

Callipepla Wagler, Isis, 1832, 277. Type, *C. strenua* Wagl. = *Ortyx squamatus* Vig.

293. Callipepla squamata (Vig.).
Scaled Partridge.

Ortyx squamatus Vig. Zool. Jour. V. 1830, 275.
Callipepla squamata Gray, Gen. III. 1846, 514.

[B 476, C 393, R 484, C 577.]

Hab. Table-lands of Mexico, into Western Texas, New Mexico, and Arizona.

293 a. Callipepla squamata castanogastris Brewst.
Chestnut-bellied Scaled Partridge.

Callipepla squamata castanogastris Brewst. Bull. Nutt. Orn. Club, VIII. Jan. 1883, 34.

[B —, C —, R —, C —.]

Hab. Eastern Mexico and Lower Rio Grande Valley in Texas.

Subgenus LOPHORTYX Bonaparte.

Lophortyx Bonap. Geog. & Comp. List, 1838, 42. Type, *Tetrao californicus* Shaw.

294. Callipepla californica (Shaw).
California Partridge.

Tetrao californicus Shaw, Nat. Misc. 1797 (?), pl. cccxlv.
Callipepla californica Gould, Mon. Odont. 1850, pl. xvi.

[B 474, C 391, R 482, C 575.]

Hab. Coast region of California and Oregon.

294 a. Callipepla californica vallicola Ridgway.
Valley Partridge.

Callipepla californica vallicola Ridgw. Pr. U. S. Nat. Mus. VIII. 1885, 355.

[B —, C —, R —, C —.]

HAB. Interior valleys and foot-hills of the Pacific Province, south to Cape St. Lucas.

295. **Callipepla gambeli** (NUTTALL).
Gambel's Partridge.

Lophortyx gambeli "NUTTALL," GAMB. Pr. Ac. Nat. Sci. Phila. 1843, 260.
Callipepla gambeli GOULD, Mon. Odont. 1850, pl. xvii.

[B 475, C 392, R 483, C 576.]

HAB. Western Texas, New Mexico, Southern Utah, Arizona, Lower Colorado Valley, and southward into Western Mexico.

GENUS **CYRTONYX** GOULD.

Cyrtonyx GOULD, Mon. Odont. 1850, 14. Type, *Ortyx massena* LESS. = *O. montezumæ* VIG.

296. **Cyrtonyx montezumæ** (VIG.).
Massena Partridge.

Ortyx montezumæ VIGORS, Zool. Journ. V. 1830, 275.
Cyrtonyx montezumæ STEJN. Auk, II. Jan. 1885, 46.

[B 477, C 394, R 485, C 578.]

HAB. Northwestern Texas, New Mexico, Arizona, and Northwestern Mexico.

SUBFAMILY **TETRAONINÆ**. GROUSE.

GENUS **DENDRAGAPUS** ELLIOT.

SUBGENUS **DENDRAGAPUS**.

Dendragapus ELLIOT, Pr. Ac. Nat. Sci. Phila. 1864, 23. Type, *Tetrao obscurus* SAY.

297. **Dendragapus obscurus** (SAY).
Dusky Grouse.

Tetrao obscurus SAY, LONG'S Exp. II. 1823, 14.
Dendragapus obscurus ELLIOT, Pr. Ac. Nat. Sci. Phila. 1864, 23.

[B 459, C 381, R 471, C 557.]

HAB. Rocky Mountains, from Central Montana to New Mexico and Arizona.

297 *a*. **Dendragapus obscurus fuliginosus** RIDGW.
Sooty Grouse.

Canace obscura var. *fuliginosa* RIDGW. Bull. Essex Inst. V. Dec. 1873, 199.
Dendragapus obscurus fuliginosus RIDGW. Pr. U. S. Nat. Mus. VIII. 1885, 355.

[B —, C 381 *b*, R 471 *a*, C 559.]

HAB. Northwest coast mountains, from California to Sitka.

297 *b*. **Dendragapus obscurus richardsonii** (SAB.).
Richardson's Grouse.

Tetrao richardsonii "SAB. MS." DOUGL. Linn. Trans. XVI. iii. 1829, 141.
Dendragapus obscurus richardsoni RIDGW. Pr. U. S. Nat. Mus. VIII. 1885, 355.

[B —, C 381 *a*, R 471 *b*, C 558.]

HAB. Rocky Mountains, from Central Montana northward into British America.

SUBGENUS **CANACHITES** STEJNEGER.

Canachites STEJN. Pr. U. S. Nat. Mus. VIII. 1885, 410. Type, *Tetrao canadensis* LINN.

298. **Dendragapus canadensis** (LINN.).
Canada Grouse.

Tetrao canadensis LINN. S. N. ed. 10, I. 1758, 159.
Dendragapus canadensis RIDGW. Pr. U. S. Nat. Mus. VIII. 1885, 355.

[B 460, C 380, R 472, C 555.]

HAB. British America, east of the Rocky Mountains, from Alaska south to Northern Michigan, Northern New York, and Northern New England.

299. Dendragapus franklinii (DOUGL.).
   Franklin's Grouse.

   Tetrao franklinii DOUGL. Trans. Linn. Soc. XVI. iii. 1829, 139.
   Dendragapus franklinii RIDGW. Pr. U. S. Nat. Mus. VIII. 1885, 355.

   [B 461, C 380 *a*, R 472 *a*, C 556.]

HAB. Northern Rocky Mountains (chiefly north of the United States) to the Pacific coast.

GENUS **BONASA** STEPHENS.

Bonasa STEPH. Gen. Zool. XI. 1819, 298. Type, *Tetrao umbellus* LINN.

300. Bonasa umbellus (LINN.).
   Ruffed Grouse.

   Tetrao umbellus LINN. S. N. ed. 12, I. 1766, 275.
   Bonasa umbellus STEPH. Gen. Zool. XI. 1819, 300.

   [B 465, C 385, R 473, C 565.]

HAB. Eastern United States, south to North Carolina, Georgia, Mississippi, and Arkansas.

300 *a*. Bonasa umbellus togata (LINN.).
   Canadian Ruffed Grouse.

   Tetrao togatus LINN. S. N. ed. 12, 1766, 275.
   Bonasa umbellus togata RIDGW. Pr. U. S. Nat. Mus. VIII. 1885, 355.

   [B —, C —, R —, C —.]

HAB. The densely timbered portions of Northern Maine and the British Provinces, west to Eastern Oregon and Washington Territory.

300 *b*. Bonasa umbellus umbelloides (DOUGL.).
   Gray Ruffed Grouse.

   Tetrao umbelloides DOUGL. Trans. Linn. Soc. XVI. 1829, 148.
   Bonasa umbellus var. *umbelloides* BAIRD, B. N. Am. 1858, 925.

   [B 465*, C 385 *a*, R 473 *a*, C 566.]

HAB. Rocky Mountain region of the United States and British America, north to Alaska.

ORDER GALLINÆ.   173

300 c. **Bonasa umbellus sabini** (Dougl.).
   Oregon Ruffed Grouse.

   Tetrao sabini Dougl. Trans. Linn. Soc. XVI. iii. 1829, 137.
   Bonasa umbellus var. *sabinei* Coues, Key, 1872, 235.

   [B 466, C 385 *b*, R 473 *b*, C 567.]

Hab. Coast mountains of Oregon, Washington Territory, and British Columbia.

Genus **LAGOPUS** Brisson.

Lagopus Briss. Ornith. I. 1760, 181.   Type, *Tetrao lagopus* Linn.

301. **Lagopus lagopus** (Linn.).
   Willow Ptarmigan.

   Tetrao lagopus Linn. S. N. ed. 10, I. 1758, 159.
   Lagopus lagopus Stejn. Pr. U. S. Nat. Mus. VIII. 1885, 20.

   [B 467, 470, C 386, R 474, C 568.]

Hab. Arctic regions; in America, south to Sitka, British Provinces, and Northern New York.

301 *a*. **Lagopus lagopus alleni** Stejn.
   Allen's Ptarmigan.

   Lagopus alba alleni Stejn. Auk, I. 1884, 369.
   Lagopus lagopus alleni Stejn. Pr. U. S. Nat. Mus. VIII. 1885, 20.

   [B —, C —, R —, C —.]

Hab. Newfoundland.

302. **Lagopus rupestris** (Gmel.).
   Rock Ptarmigan.

   Tetrao rupestris Gmel. S. N. I. ii. 1788, 751.
   Lagopus rupestris Leach, Zool. Misc. II. 1817, 290.

   [B 468, C 387, R 475, C 569.]

Hab. Arctic America, from Alaska to Labrador.

302 a. Lagopus rupestris reinhardti (BREHM).
Reinhardt's Ptarmigan.

Lagopus reinhardi (err. typ.) BREHM, Lehrb. Eur. Vög. 1823, 440.
Lagopus rupestris reinhardti BLASIUS, List Eur. B. 1862, 16.

[B —, C —, R —, C —.]

HAB. Greenland, and western shores of Cumberland Gulf.

302 b. Lagopus rupestris nelsoni STEJN.
Nelson's Ptarmigan.

Lagopus rupestris nelsoni STEJN. Auk, I. 1884, 226.

[B —, C —, R —, C —.]

HAB. Island of Unalashka.

302 c. Lagopus rupestris atkhensis (TURNER).
Turner's Ptarmigan.

Lagopus mutus atkhensis TURNER, Pr. U. S. Nat. Mus. V. July 29, 1882, 227, 230.
Lagopus rupestris atkhensis NELSON, Cruise Corwin, 1883, 56 e + 82.

[B —, C —, R —, C —.]

HAB. Atkha Island, Aleutian Islands.

303. Lagopus welchi BREWST.
Welch's Ptarmigan.

Lagopus welchi BREWST. Auk, II. April, 1885, 194.

[B —, C —, R —, C —.]

HAB. Newfoundland.

304. Lagopus leucurus SWAINS.
White-tailed Ptarmigan.

Lagopus leucurus SWAINS. Fauna Bor. Amer. II. 1831, pl. 63.

[B 469, C 388, R 476, C 570.]

HAB. Alpine summits of the mountains of Western North America, from New Mexico north into British America.

ORDER GALLINÆ.

Genus **TYMPANUCHUS** Gloger.

Tympanuchus "Gloger, 1842," fide Sundev. Met. Nat. Av. Disp. 1874, 114. Type, *Tetrao cupido* Linn.

305. Tympanuchus americanus (Reich.).
Prairie Hen.

Cupidonia americanus Reich. Syst. Av. 1852, p. xxix.; based on Vollst. Naturg. Hühnen., pl. 217, figs. 1896-1898.
Tympanuchus cupido americanus Ridgw. MS.

[B 464, C 384, R 477, C 563.]

Hab. Prairies of the Mississippi Valley, south to Louisiana, east to Kentucky and Indiana.

306. Tympanuchus cupido (Linn.).
Heath Hen.

Tetrao cupido Linn. S. N. ed. 10, I. 1758, 160.
Tympanuchus cupido Ridgw. Pr. U. S. Nat. Mus. VIII. 1885, 355.

[B 464, *part*, C 384, *part*, R 477, *part*, C 563, *part*.]

Hab. Island of Martha's Vineyard, Mass.

307. Tympanuchus pallidicinctus (Ridgw.).
Lesser Prairie Hen.

Cupidonia cupido var. *pallidicincta* Ridgw. Bull. Essex Inst. V. Dec. 1873, 199.
Tympanuchus pallidicinctus Ridgw. Pr. U. S. Nat. Mus. VIII. 1885, 355.

[B —, C 384 *a*, R 477 *a*, C 564.]

Hab. Eastern edge of the Great Plains, from Texas northward.

Genus **PEDIOCÆTES** Baird.

Pediocætes Baird, B. N. Am. 1858, 625. Type, *Tetrao phasianellus* Linn

308. **Pediocætes phasianellus** (LINN.).
Sharp-tailed Grouse.

Tetrao phasianellus LINN. S. N. ed. 10, I. 1758, 160.
Pediocætes phasianellus ELLIOT, Pr. Ac. Nat. Sci. Phila. 1862, 403 (nec BAIRD, 1858, qui subsp. *columbianus*).

[B —, C 383, R 478, C 561.]

HAB. British America, from the northern shore of Lake Superior and British Columbia to Hudson's Bay Territory and Alaska.

308 *a*. **Pediocætes phasianellus columbianus** (ORD).
Columbian Sharp-tailed Grouse.

Phasianus columbianus ORD, GUTHRIE'S Geog. 2d Am. ed. II. 1815, 317.
Pediæcetes phasianellus var. *columbianus* COUES, Key, 1872, 234.

[B 463, C 383 *a*, R 478 *a*, C 562.]

HAB. Plains of the Northwestern United States.

308 *b*. **Pediocætes phasianellus campestris** RIDGW.
Prairie Sharp-tailed Grouse.

Pediæcetes phasianellus campestris RIDGW. Proc. Biol. Soc. Wash. II. April 10, 1884, 93.

[B —, C —, R —, C —.]

HAB. Plains and prairies of the United States east of the Rocky Mountains, south to New Mexico.

GENUS **CENTROCERCUS** SWAINSON.

Centrocercus SWAINS. Fauna Bor. Am. II. 1831, 358, 496. Type, *Tetrao urophasianus* BONAP.

309. **Centrocercus urophasianus** (BONAP.).
Sage Grouse.

Tetrao urophasianus BONAP. Zool. Journ. III. 1827, 213.
Centrocercus urophasianus SWAINS. Fauna Bor. Am. II. 1831, 497, pl. 58.

[B 462, C 382, R 479, C 560.]

HAB. The sage plains of the Rocky Mountain plateau and westward, from Dakota, Colorado, and New Mexico, to Nevada, Eastern California, Oregon, and Washington Territory.

FAMILY **PHASIANIDÆ**. PHEASANTS, ETC.

SUBFAMILY **MELEAGRINÆ**. TURKEYS.

GENUS **MELEAGRIS** LINNÆUS.

Meleagris LINN. S. N. ed. 10, I. 1758, 156. Type, *M. gallopavo* LINN.

310. **Meleagris gallopavo** LINN.
Wild Turkey.

Meleagris gallopavo LINN. S. N. ed. 10, I. 1758, 156.

[B 457, C 379 a, R 470 a, C 554.]

HAB. United States, from Southern Canada to the Gulf coast, and west to the Plains, along the timbered river valleys; formerly along the Atlantic coast to Southern Maine.

310 a. **Meleagris gallopavo mexicana** (GOULD).
Mexican Turkey.

Meleagris mexicana GOULD, P. Z. S. 1856, 61.
Meleagris gallopavo var. *mexicana* BAIRD, Hist. N. Am. B. III. 1874, 410.

[B 458, C 379, R 470, C 553.]

HAB. Southwestern United States, from Texas to Arizona, south over the table-lands of Mexico.

Suborder PENELOPES. Curassows and Guans.

Family CRACIDÆ. Curassows and Guans.

Subfamily PENELOPINÆ. Guans.

Genus **ORTALIS** Merrem.

Ortalis Merr. Av. Rar. Icones et Desc. II. 1786, 40. Type, *Phasianus motmot* Linn.

311. Ortalis vetula maccalli Baird.
   Chachalaca.

Ortalida maccalli Baird, B. N. Am. 1858, 611.
Ortalida vetula var. *maccalli* Baird, Hist. N. Am. B. III. 1874, 398.

[B 456, C 378, R 469, C 552.]

Hab. Valley of the Rio Grande, and southward into Mexico.

Order COLUMBÆ. Pigeons.

Family COLUMBIDÆ. Pigeons.

Genus **COLUMBA** Linnæus.

Columba Linn. S. N. ed. 10, I. 1758, 162. Type, by elimination, *C. œnas* Linn.

312. Columba fasciata Say.
   Band-tailed Pigeon.

Columba fasciata Say, Long's Exp. II. 1823, 10.

[B 445, C 367, R 456, C 539.]

HAB. Western United States, from Washington Territory and New Mexico south to Guatemala.

313. Columba flavirostris WAGL.
Red-billed Pigeon.

Columba flavirostris WAGL. Isis, 1831, 519.

[B 446, C 368, R 457, C 540.]

HAB. Southern border of the United States, from Arizona and the Rio Grande Valley south to Costa Rica.

314. Columba leucocephala LINN.
White-crowned Pigeon.

Columba leucocephala LINN. S. N. ed. 10, I. 1758, 164.

[B 447, C 369, R 458, C 541.]

HAB. Southern Keys of Florida, Greater Antilles, and coast of Honduras.

GENUS **ECTOPISTES** SWAINSON.

Ectopistes SWAINS. Zool Jour. III. 1827, 362. Type, *Columba migratoria* LINN.

315. Ectopistes migratorius (LINN.).
Passenger Pigeon.

Columba migratoria LINN. S. N. ed. 12, I. 1766, 285 (♂).
Ectopistes migratoria SWAINS. Zool. Journ. III. 1827, 362.

[B 448, C 370, R 459, C 543.]

HAB. Eastern North America, from Hudson's Bay southward, and west to the Great Plains, straggling westward to Nevada and Washington Territory.

GENUS **ZENAIDURA** BONAPARTE.

Zenaidura BONAP. Consp. Av. II. Dec. 1854, 84. Type, *Columba carolinensis* LINN. = *C. macroura* LINN.

316. Zenaidura macroura (LINN.).
   Mourning Dove.

   Columba macroura LINN. S. N. ed. 10, 1758, 164 (part).
   Zenaidura macroura RIDGW. Pr. U. S. Nat. Mus. VIII. 1885, 355.

   [B 451, C 371, R 460, C 544.]

HAB. North America, from Southern Maine, Southern Canada, and Oregon, south to Panama and the West Indies.

GENUS **ZENAIDA** BONAPARTE.

   Zenaida BONAP. Geog. & Comp. List, 1838, 41. Type, *Columba zenaida* BONAP.

317. Zenaida zenaida (BONAP.).
   Zenaida Dove.

   Columba zenaida BONAP. Jour. Ac. Nat. Sci. Phila. V. 1825, 30.
   Zenaida zenaida RIDGW. Pr. U. S. Nat. Mus. VIII. 1885, 355.

   [B 449, C 372, R 462, C 545.]

HAB. Florida Keys, Greater Antilles, and coast of Yucatan.

GENUS **ENGYPTILA** SUNDEVALL.

   Engyptila SUNDEV. Met. Nat. Av. Disp. 1872, 156. Type, *Columba rufaxilla* RICH. & BERN.

318. Engyptila albifrons (BONAP.).
   White-fronted Dove.

   Leptoptila albifrons BONAP. Consp. Av. II. Dec. 1854, 74.
   Engyptila albifrons COUES, Bull. Nutt. Orn. Club, V. April, 1880, 100.

   [B —, C —, R 463, C 542.]

HAB. Valley of the Lower Rio Grande in Texas, and southward to Guatemala.

GENUS **MELOPELIA** BONAPARTE.

   Melopelia BONAP. Consp. Av. II. Dec. 1854, 81. Type, *Columba leucoptera* LINN.

319. Melopelia leucoptera (LINN.).
White-winged Dove.

Columba leucoptera LINN. S. N. ed. 10, I. 1758, 164.
Melopelia leucoptera BONAP. Consp. Av. II. Dec. 1854, 81.

[B 450, C 373, R 464, C 546.]

HAB. Southern border of the United States, from Texas, New Mexico, Arizona, and Lower California, southward to Costa Rica and the West Indies.

GENUS **COLUMBIGALLINA** BOIE.

Columbigallina BOIE, Isis, 1826, 977. Type, *Columba passerina* LINN.

320. Columbigallina passerina (LINN.).
Ground Dove.

Columba passerina LINN. Syst. Nat. ed. 10, I. 1758, 165.
Columbigallina passerina ZELEDON, Pr. U. S. Nat. Mus. VIII. 1885, 112.

[B 453, C 374, R 465, C 547.]

HAB. South Atlantic and Gulf States, Texas, New Mexico, Arizona, and California, south to the West Indies and Northern South America.

GENUS **SCARDAFELLA** BONAPARTE.

Scardafella BONAP. Consp. Av. II. Dec. 1854, 85. Type, *Columba squamosa* TEMM.

321. Scardafella inca (LESS.).
Inca Dove.

Chamæpelia inca LESSON, Descr. Quadr. etc. Buffon, 1850, 211.
Scardafella inca BONAP. Consp. Av. II. Dec. 1854, 85.

[B 452, C 375, R 466, C 549.]

HAB. Rio Grande Valley, Arizona, and Lower California, south to Guatemala.

GENUS **GEOTRYGON** GOSSE.

Geotrygon GOSSE, B. Jam. 1847, 316, foot-note. Type, *G. sylvatica* GOSSE = *Columba cristata* TEMM.

[322.] **Geotrygon martinica** (GMEL.).
　　Key West Quail-dove.

Columba martinica GMEL. S. N. I. ii. 1788, 78 L.
Geotrygon martinica BONAP. Consp. Av. II. Dec. 1854, 74.

[B 454, C 376, R 467, C 550.]

HAB. Key West, Florida, and West Indies.

GENUS **STARNŒNAS** BONAPARTE.

Starnœnas BONAP. Geog. & Comp. List, 1838, 41. Type, *Columba cyanocephala* LINN.

[323.] **Starnœnas cyanocephala** (LINN.).
　　Blue-headed Quail-dove.

Columba cyanocephala LINN. S. N. ed. 10, I. 1758, 163.
Starnœnas cyanocephala BONAP. Geog. & Comp. List, 1838, 41.

[B 455, C 377, R 468, C 551.]

HAB. Florida Keys and Cuba.

ORDER RAPTORES. BIRDS OF PREY.

SUBORDER SARCORHAMPHI. AMERICAN VULTURES.

FAMILY **CATHARTIDÆ**. AMERICAN VULTURES.

GENUS **PSEUDOGRYPHUS** RIDGWAY.

Pseudogryphus RIDGW. Hist. N. Am. B. III. Jan. 1874, 337, 338. Type, *Vultur californianus* SHAW.

324. Pseudogryphus californianus (SHAW).
California Vulture.

Vultur californianus SHAW, Nat. Misc. IV. 1797, pl. ccci.
Pseudogryphus californianus RIDGW. Hist. N. Am. B. III. 1874, 338.

[B 2, C 364, R 453, C 536.]

HAB. Pacific coast region of the United States, from Oregon southward, and in the interior to Southern Utah.

GENUS **CATHARTES** ILLIGER.

Cathartes ILLIG. Prodr. 1811, 236. Type, by elimination, *Vultur aura* LINN.

325. Cathartes aura (LINN.).
Turkey Vulture.

Vultur aura LINN. S. N. ed. 10, I. 1758, 86.
Cathartes aura SPIX, Aves Bras. I. 1825, 2.

[B 1, C 365, R 454, C 537.]

HAB. Temperate North America, from New Jersey, Ohio Valley, Saskatchewan region, and Washington Territory southward to Patagonia. Casual northward on the Atlantic coast to Maine.

GENUS **CATHARISTA** VIEILLOT.

Catharista VIEILL. Analyse, 1816, 21. Type, by elimination, *Vultur atratus* BARTR.

326. Catharista atrata (BARTR.).
Black Vulture.

Vultur atratus BARTR. Trav. Car. 1792, 285.
Catharista atrata GRAY, Handl. I. 1869, 3.

[B 3, C 366, R 455, C 538.]

HAB. South Atlantic and Gulf States, north to North Carolina and the Lower Ohio Valley, west to the Great Plains, and south through Mexico and Central America, the West Indies, and most of South America. Straggling north to New York and Maine.

Suborder FALCONES. Vultures, Falcons, Hawks, Buzzards, Eagles, Kites, Harriers, etc.

Family FALCONIDÆ. Vultures, Falcons, Hawks, Eagles, etc.

Subfamily ACCIPITRINÆ. Kites, Buzzards, Hawks, Goshawks, Eagles, etc.

Genus ELANOIDES Vieillot.

Elanoides Vieill. Nouv. Dict. XXIV. 1818, 101. Type, *Falco furcatus* = *F. forficatus* Linn.

327. Elanoides forficatus (Linn.).
Swallow-tailed Kite.

Falco forficatus Linn. S. N. ed. 10, I. 1758, 89.
Elanoides forficatus Coues, Pr. Ac. Nat. Sci. Phila. 1875, 345.

[B 34, C 337, R 426, C 493.]

Hab. Southern United States, especially in the interior, from Pennsylvania and Minnesota southward, throughout Central and South America; westward to the Great Plains. Casual eastward to Southern New England. Accidental in England.

Genus ELANUS Savigny.

Elanus Savig. Descr. de l'Égypte, 1809, 97. Type, *E. cæsius* = *Falco melanopterus* Daud.

328. Elanus leucurus (Vieill.).
White-tailed Kite.

Milvus leucurus Vieill. Nouv. Dict. XX. 1818, 563 (errore 556).
Elanus leucurus Bonap. Geog. & Comp. List, 1838, 4.

[B 35, C 336, R 427, C 492.]

Hab. Southern United States, from South Carolina, Southern Illinois, and California, southward to Chili and Buenos Ayres.

ORDER RAPTORES.   185

Genus **ICTINIA** Vieillot.

Ictinia Vieill. Analyse, 1816, 24.   Type, *Falco mississippiensis* Wils.

329. **Ictinia mississippiensis** (Wils.).
   Mississippi Kite.

   Falco mississippiensis Wils. Am. Orn. III. 1811, 80, pl. 25, fig. 1.
   Ictinia mississippiensis Gray, Gen. B. I. 1845, 26.

   [B 36, C 335, R 428, C 491.]

   Hab.   Southern United States, southward from South Carolina on the coast, and Wisconsin and Iowa in the interior, to Mexico.

Genus **ROSTRHAMUS** Lesson.

Rostrhamus Less. Traité, 1831, 55.   Type, *Falco hamatus* Illig.

330. **Rostrhamus sociabilis** (Vieill.).
   Everglade Kite.

   Herpetotheres sociabilis Vieill. Nouv. Dict. XVIII. 1818, 318.
   Rostrhamus sociabilis D'Orb. Voy. Ois. II. 1847, 73.

   [B 37, C 334, R 429, C 490.]

   Hab.   Florida, Cuba, Eastern Mexico, Central America, and Eastern South America, to the Argentine Republic.

Genus **CIRCUS** Lacépède.

Circus Lacép. Mem. de l'Inst. III. 1801, 506.   Type, *Falco cyaneus* Linn.

331. **Circus hudsonius** (Linn.).
   Marsh Hawk.

   Falco hudsonius Linn. S. N. ed. 12, I. 1766, 128.
   Circus hudsonius Vieill. Ois. Am. Sept. I. 1807, pl. 9.

   [B 38, C 333, R 430, C 489.]

   Hab.   North America in general, south to Panama.

Genus **ACCIPITER** Brisson.

Subgenus **ACCIPITER.**

Accipiter Briss. Orn. I. 1760, 310.   Type, by elimination, *Falco nisus* Linn.

332. Accipiter velox (Wils.).
Sharp-shinned Hawk.

Falco velox Wils. Am. Orn. V. 1812, 116, pl. 45, fig. 1.
Accipiter velox Vigors, Zool. Journ. I. 1824, 338.

[B 17, C 338, R 432, C 494.]

Hab.   North America in general, south to Panama.

333. Accipiter cooperi (Bonap.).
Cooper's Hawk.

Falco cooperi Bonap. Am. Orn. II. 1828, 1, pl. x. fig. 1.
Accipiter cooperi Gray, List B. Brit. Mus. Accipitres, 1844, 38.

[B 15, 16, C 339, R 431, C 495.]

Hab.   North America in general, south to Southern Mexico.

Subgenus **ASTUR** Lacépède.

Astur Lacép. Mem. de l'Inst. III. 1801, 505.   Type, *Falco palumbarius* Linn.

334. Accipiter atricapillus (Wils.).
American Goshawk.

Falco atricapillus Wils. Am. Orn. VI. 1812, 80, pl. 52, fig. 3.
Accipiter atricapillus Seebohm, Brit. Birds, I. 1883, iv.

[B 14, C 340, R 433, C 496.]

Hab.   Northern and Eastern North America, breeding mostly north of the United States, south in winter to the Middle States.   Accidental in England.

334 a. Accipiter atricapillus striatulus Ridgw.
Western Goshawk.

Astur atricapillus var. *striatulus* Ridgw. in Hist. N. Am. B. III. 1874, 240.
Accipiter atricapillus striatulus Ridgw. Pr. U. S. Nat. Mus. VIII. 1885, 355.

ORDER RAPTORES.   187

[B —, C —, R 433 *a*, C 497.]

HAB. Western North America.

GENUS **PARABUTEO** RIDGWAY.

Parabuteo RIDGW. in Hist. N. Am. B. III. Jan. 1874, 250.   Type, *Falco harrisi* AUD.

335. Parabuteo unicinctus harrisi (AUD.).
   Harris's Hawk.

Falco harrisi AUD. B. Am. V. 1839, 30, pl. 392.
Parabuteo unicinctus var. *harrisi* RIDGW. in Hist. N. Am. B. III. Jan. 1874, 254.

[B 46, C 348, R 434, C 512.]

HAB. Mississippi, Texas, and Arizona, southward to Panama.

GENUS **BUTEO** CUVIER.

Buteo CUV. Leç. Anat. Comp. I. tabl. ii. Ois. 1779–1800.   Type, *Falco buteo* LINN.

[336.] Buteo buteo (LINN.).
   European Buzzard.

Falco buteo LINN. S. N. ed. 10, I. 1758, 90.
Buteo buteo LICHT. Nomencl. Mus. Berol. 1854, 3.

[B —, C —, R 435, C —.]

HAB. Europe and Western Asia. Accidental in North America (Michigan?).

337. Buteo borealis (GMEL.).
   Red-tailed Hawk.

Falco borealis GMEL. S. N. I. ii. 1788, 266.
Buteo borealis VIEILL. Nouv. Dict. IV. 1816, 478.

[B 23, C 351, R 436, C 516.]

HAB. Eastern North America, west to the Great Plains.

337 a. **Buteo borealis kriderii** Hoopes.
Krider's Hawk.

Buteo borealis var. *kriderii* Hoopes, Pr. Ac. Nat. Sci. Phila. 1873, 238, pl. 5.

[B —, C 351 c, R 436 a, C 519.]

Hab. Plains of the United States, from Minnesota to Texas.

337 b. **Buteo borealis calurus** (Cass.).
Western Red-tail.

Buteo calurus Cass. Pr. Ac. Nat. Sci. Phila. VII. 1855, 281.
Buteo borealis var. *calurus* Ridgw. Bull. Essex Inst. V. Nov. 1873, 186.

[B 20, 24, C 351 a, R 436 b, C 517.]

Hab. Western North America, from the Rocky Mountains to the Pacific, south into Mexico; casual east to Illinois.

337 c. **Buteo borealis lucasanus** Ridgw.
Saint Lucas Red-tail.

Buteo borealis var. *lucasanus* Ridgw. in Coues's Key, 1872, 216 (under *B. borealis*).

[B —, C 351 b, R 436 c, C 518.]

Hab. Peninsula of Lower California.

338. **Buteo harlani** (Aud.).
Harlan's Hawk.

Falco harlani Aud. B. Am. I. 1830, 441, pl. 86.
Buteo harlani Bonap. Geog. & Comp. List, 1838, 3.

[B 22, C 350, R 438, C 515.]

Hab. Kansas, Louisiana, and Texas, south to Central America. Casual in Southern Illinois and Pennsylvania.

339. **Buteo lineatus** (Gmel.).
Red-shouldered Hawk.

Falco lineatus Gmel. S. N. I. ii. 1788, 268.
Buteo lineatus Jard. ed. Wils. Am. Orn. II. 1832, 290.

[B 25, C 352, R 439, C 520.]

HAB. Eastern North America, west to Texas and the Plains, south to the Gulf coast and Mexico.

339 *a*. **Buteo lineatus alleni** RIDGW.
Florida Red-shouldered Hawk.

Buteo lineatus alleni RIDGW. Pr. U. S. Nat. Mus. VII. Jan. 19, 1884, 514.

[B —, C —, R —, C —.]

HAB. Florida.

339 *b*. **Buteo lineatus elegans** (CASS.).
Red-bellied Hawk.

Buteo elegans CASS. Pr. Ac. Nat. Sci. Phila. 1855, 281.
Buteo lineatus var. *elegans* RIDGW. in Hist. N. Am. B. III. Jan. 1874, 257, 277.

[B 26, C 352 *a*, R 439 *a*, C 521.]

HAB. Western United States, from Western Texas to California, and south into Mexico.

340. **Buteo abbreviatus** CABAN.
Zone-tailed Hawk.

Buteo abbreviatus CAB. in SCHOMB. Reise Brit. Guian. III. 1848, 739.

[B —, C 353, R 440, C 522.]

HAB. Texas, Arizona, and Southern California, south to Northern South America.

341. **Buteo albicaudatus** VIEILL.
White-tailed Hawk.

Buteo albicaudatus VIEILL. Nouv. Dict. IV. 1816, 477.

[B —, C —, R 441, C 513.]

HAB. Rio Grande Valley, Texas, and southward through Mexico and Central America, and most of South America.

342. **Buteo swainsoni** BONAP.
Swainson's Hawk.

Buteo swainsoni BONAP. Geog. & Comp. List, 1838, 3.

[B 18, 19, 21, 28, C 354, R 442, C 523.]

HAB. Western North America, from Wisconsin, Illinois, Arkansas, and Texas to the Pacific coast; north to the arctic regions, and south to Buenos Ayres. Casual east to Massachusetts.

343. **Buteo latissimus** (WILS.).
Broad-winged Hawk.

Falco latissimus WILS. Am. Orn. VI. 1812, 92, pl. 54, fig. 1.
Buteo latissimus SHARPE, Cat. B. Brit. Mus. I. Accip. 1874, 193.

[B 27, C 355, R 443, C 524.]

HAB. Eastern North America, from New Brunswick and the Saskatchewan region to Texas and Mexico, and thence southward to Central America, Northern South America, and the West Indies.

SUBGENUS **BUTEOLA** BONAPARTE.

Buteola BONAP. Compt. Rend. XLI. 1855, 651. Type, *Buteo brachyurus* VIEILL.

[344.] **Buteo brachyurus** VIEILL.
Short-tailed Hawk.

Buteo brachyurus VIEILL. Nouv. Dict. IV. 1816, 477.

[B —, C —, R —, C —.]

HAB. Mexico, Central America, and most of South America. Florida (accidental?).

GENUS **URUBITINGA** LESSON.

Urubitinga LESS. Rev. Zool. 1839, 132. (*Cf.* Compl. Buff. VII. 1837, 64.) Type, *Falco urubitinga* GMEL.

345. **Urubitinga anthracina** (LICHT.).
Mexican Black Hawk.

Falco anthracinus LICHT. Preis-Verz 1830, 3.
Urubitinga anthracina LAFR. Rev. Zool. 1848, 241.

[B —, C —, R 444, C 528.]

HAB. Arizona, southward to Northern South America.

Genus ASTURINA Vieillot.

Asturina Vieill. Analyse, 1816, 24. Type, *Falco nitidus* Gmel.

346. Asturina plagiata Schlegel.
Mexican Goshawk.

Asturina plagiata "Licht." Schlegel, Mus. P. B. Asturinæ, 1862, 1.

[B 33, C 358, R 445, C 527.]

Hab. Southwestern border of the United States, southward to Panama. Southern Illinois (accidental?).

Genus ARCHIBUTEO Brehm.

Archibuteo Brehm, Isis, 1828, 1269. Type, *Falco lagopus* Gmel.

[347.] Archibuteo lagopus (Brünn.).
Rough-legged Hawk.

Falco lagopus Brünn. Orn. Bor. 1764, 4.
Archibuteo lagopus Gray, List Gen. B. ed. 2, 1841, 3.

[B —, C —, R —, C —.]

Hab. Northern parts of the Old World; Alaska.

347 a. Archibuteo lagopus sancti-johannis (Gmel.).
American Rough-legged Hawk.

Falco sancti-johannis Gmel. S. N. I. ii. 1788, 273
Archibuteo lagopus var. *sancti-johannis* Ridgw. in Coues's Key, 1872, 218.

[B 30, 31, C 356, R 447, C 525.]

Hab. Whole of North America north of Mexico, breeding chiefly north of the United States.

348. Archibuteo ferrugineus (Licht.).
Ferruginous Rough-leg.

Falco ferrugineus Licht. Abh. K. Akad. Berl. 1838, 428.
Archibuteo ferrugineus Gray, Gen. B. fol. ed. 1849, 12.

[B 32, C 357, R 448, C 526.]

HAB. Western North America, from the Plains (Iowa to Texas) westward to the Pacific, and from the Saskatchewan region south into Mexico.

Genus **AQUILA** Brisson.

Aquila Briss. Orn. I. 1760, 419. Type, *Falco chrysaëtos* Linn.

349. **Aquila chrysaëtos** (Linn.).
Golden Eagle.

Falco chrysaëtos Linn. S. N. ed. 10, I. 1758, 88.
Aquila chrysaëtus Dumont, Dict. Sci. Nat. I. 1816, 339.

[B 39, C 361, R 449, C 532.]

HAB. North America south to Mexico, and northern parts of the Old World.

Genus **THRASAËTUS** Gray.

Thrasaëtus Gray, P. Z. S. 1837, 108. Type, *Vultur harpyia* Linn.

[350.] **Thrasaëtus harpyia** (Linn.).
Harpy Eagle.

Vultur harpyia Linn. S. N. ed. 10, I. 1758, 86.
Thrasaëtus harpyia Gray, P. Z. S. 1837, 108.

[B —, C —, R 450, C 631.]

HAB. Lower Rio Grande Valley, casual, south to Paraguay.

Genus **HALIÆETUS** Savigny.

Haliæetus Savigny, Descr. de l'Égypte, 1809, 35. Type, *Falco albicilla* Linn.

[351.] **Haliæetus albicilla** (Linn.).
Gray Sea Eagle.

Falco albicilla Linn. S. N. ed. 10, I. 1758, 89.
Haliæetus albicilla Leach, Syst. Cat. M. B. Br. Mus. 1816, 9.

[B 42, C —, R 452, C 533.]

HAB. Northern Europe and Asia; Greenland.

ORDER RAPTORES.

352. **Haliæetus leucocephalus** (LINN.).
    Bald Eagle.

   Falco leucocephalus LINN. S. N. ed. 12, I. 1766, 124.
   Haliætus leucocephalus BOIE, Isis, 1822, 548.

   [B 41, 43, C 362, R 451, C 534.]

   HAB. North America at large, south to Mexico.

SUBFAMILY **FALCONINÆ**. FALCONS.

GENUS **FALCO** LINNÆUS.

   Falco LINN. S. N. ed. 10, I. 1758, 88. Type, by elimination, *F. subbuteo* LINN.

SUBGENUS **HIEROFALCO** CUVIER.

   Hierofalco CUV. Règ. An. I. 1817, 312. Type, *Falco candicans* GMEL. = *F. islandus* BRÜNN.

353. **Falco islandus** BRÜNN.
    White Gyrfalcon.

   Falco islandus BRÜNN. Orn. Bor. 1764, 2.

   [B 11, C 341 *a*, R 412, C 501.]

   HAB. Arctic regions, including Arctic America and Greenland.

354. **Falco rusticolus** LINN.
    Gray Gyrfalcon.

   Falco rusticolus LINN. S. N. ed. 10, I. 1758, 88.

   [B 12, C —, R 412 *a*, C 500.]

   HAB. Iceland, Southern Greenland, and Northeastern North America, straggling southward in winter to Southern New England.

354 *a*. **Falco rusticolus gyrfalco** (LINN.).
    Gyrfalcon.

   Falco gyrfalco LINN. S. N. ed. 10, I. 1758, 91.
   Falco rusticolus gyrfalco STEJN. Auk, II. 1885, 187.

[B —, C 341, R 412 *b*, C 498.]

HAB. Interior of Arctic America, from Hudson's Bay to Alaska.

354 *b*. Falco rusticolus obsoletus (GMEL.).
Black Gyrfalcon.

Falco obsoletus GMEL. S. N. I. i. 1788, 268.
Falco rusticolus obsoletus STEJN. Auk, II. 1885, 187.

[B —, C —, R 412 *c*, C 499.]

HAB. Labrador, south in winter to Maine and New York.

355. Falco mexicanus SCHLEG.
Prairie Falcon.

Falco mexicanus SCHLEG. Abh. Geb. Zool. 1841, 15.

[B 10, C 342, R 413, C 502.]

HAB. United States, from the eastern border of the Plains to the Pacific, south into Mexico; casual eastward to Illinois.

SUBGENUS **RHYNCHODON** NITZSCH.

Rhynchodon NITZSCH, Pterylog. 1840, 78. Type, by elimination, *Falco peregrinus* LATH.

356. Falco peregrinus anatum (BONAP.).
Duck Hawk.

Falco anatum BONAP. Geog. & Comp. List, 1838, 4.
Falco peregrinus β. *anatum* BLASIUS, List B. Eur. 1862, 3.

[B 5, 6, C 343, R 414, C 503.]

HAB. North America at large.

356 *a*. Falco peregrinus pealei RIDGW.
Peale's Falcon.

Falco communis var. *pealei* RIDGW. Bull. Essex Inst. V. Dec. 1873, 201.
Falco peregrinus pealei RIDGW. Pr. U. S. Nat. Mus. III. Aug. 24, 1880, 192.

[B —, C 343 *a*, R 414 *a*, C 504.]

HAB. Pacific coast region of North America, from Oregon to the Aleutian and Commander Islands.

ORDER RAPTORES. 195

SUBGENUS **ÆSALON** KAUP.

Æsalon KAUP, Sk. Ent. Eur. Thierw. 1829, 40. Type, *Falco æsalon* GMEL. = *F. regulus* PALL.

357. Falco columbarius LINN.
Pigeon Hawk.

Falco columbarius LINN. S. N. ed. 10, I. 1758, 90.

[B 7, C 344, R 417, C 505.]

HAB. The whole of North America, south to the West Indies and Northern South America.

357 a. Falco columbarius suckleyi RIDGW.
Black Merlin.

Falco columbarius var. *suckleyi* RIDGW. Bull. Essex Inst. V. Dec. 1873, 201.

[B —, C 344 a, R 417 a, C 506.]

HAB. Northwest coast region of North America, from California to Sitka.

358. Falco richardsonii RIDGW.
Richardson's Merlin.

Falco (*Hypotriorchis*) *richardsonii* RIDGW. Pr. Ac. Nat. Sci. Phila. Dec. 1870, 145.

[B —, C 345, R 418, C 507.]

HAB. Interior and western plains of North America, from the Mississippi River to the Pacific coast, and from the Arctic regions to Texas.

SUBGENUS **RHYNCHOFALCO** RIDGWAY.

Rhynchofalco RIDGW. Pr. Boston Soc. Nat. Hist. 1873, 46. Type, *Falco femoralis* TEMM. = *F. fusco-cærulescens* VIEILL.

359. Falco fusco-cœrulescens VIEILL.
Aplomado Falcon.

Falco fusco-cærulescens VIEILL. Nouv. Dict. XI. 1817, 90.

[B 9, C 347, R 419, C 511.]

HAB. Texas and New Mexico, south to Patagonia.

SUBGENUS **TINNUNCULUS** VIEILLOT.

Tinnunculus VIEILL. Ois. Am. Sept. I. 1807, 39.

360. Falco sparverius LINN.
American Sparrow Hawk.

Falco sparverius LINN. S. N. ed. 10, I. 1758, 90.

[B 13, C 346, 346 *a*, R 420, 420 *a*, C 508, 509.]

HAB. Whole of North America, south to Northern South America.

[361.] Falco sparverioides VIG.
Cuban Sparrow Hawk.

Falco sparverioides VIG. Zool. Jour. III. Aug.-Nov. 1827, 436.

[B —, C —, R 421, C 510.]

HAB. Cuba. Accidental in Florida.

GENUS **POLYBORUS** VIEILLOT.

Polyborus VIEILL. Analyse, 1816, 22. Type, *Falco tharus* MOL.

362. Polyborus cheriway (JACQ.).
Audubon's Caracara.

Falco cheriway JACQ. Beitr. 1784, 17, tab. 4.
Polyborus cheriway CAB. in SCHOMB. Guiana, III. 1848, 741.

[B 45, C 363, R 423, C 535.]

HAB. Southern border of the United States (Florida, Texas, Arizona), and Lower California, south to Ecuador and Guiana.

363. Polyborus lutosus RIDGW.
Guadalupe Caracara.

Polyborus lutosus RIDGW. Bull. U. S. Geog. & Geol. Surv. Terr. No. 6, 2d ser. Feb. 8, 1876, 459.

[B —, C —, R 424, C —.]

HAB. Guadalupe Island, Lower California.

SUBFAMILY **PANDIONINÆ**. OSPREYS.

GENUS **PANDION** SAVIGNY.

Pandion SAVIGN. Descr. de l'Égypte, Ois. 1809, 95. Type, *Falco haliaëtus* LINN.

364. **Pandion haliaëtus carolinensis** (GMEL.).
American Osprey.

Falco carolinensis GMEL. S. N. I. i. 1788, 263.
Pandion haliaëtus var. *carolinensis* RIDGW. Pr. Ac. Nat. Sci. Phila. Dec. 1870, 143.

[B 44, C 360, R 425, C 530.]

HAB. North America, from Hudson's Bay and Alaska south to the West Indies and Northern South America.

SUBORDER STRIGES. OWLS.

FAMILY **STRIGIDÆ**. BARN OWLS.

GENUS **STRIX** LINNÆUS.

Strix LINN. S. N. ed. 10, I. 1758, 92. Type, *S. aluco* LINN. ed. 10.

365. **Strix pratincola** BONAP.
American Barn Owl.

Strix pratincola BONAP. Geog. & Comp. List, 1838, 7.

[B 47, C 316, R 394, C 461.]

HAB. Warmer parts of North America, from the Middle States, Ohio Valley, and California southward through Mexico.

FAMILY BUBONIDÆ. HORNED OWLS, ETC.

GENUS ASIO BRISSON.

Asio BRISS. Orn. I. 1760, 28.   Type, *Strix otus* LINN.

366. Asio wilsonianus (LESS.).
American Long-eared Owl.

Otus wilsonianus LESS. Traité, 1831, 110.
Asio wilsonianus COUES, Check List, ed. 2, 1882, 81, No. 472.

[B 51, C 320, R 395, C 472.]

HAB. Temperate North America.

367. Asio accipitrinus (PALL.).
Short-eared Owl.

Strix accipitrina PALL. Reise Russ. Reichs. I. 1771, 455.
Asio accipitrinus NEWT. YARR. Brit. B. ed. 4, I. 1872, 163.

[B 52, C 321, R 396, C 473.]

HAB. Throughout North America; nearly cosmopolitan.

GENUS SYRNIUM SAVIGNY.

Syrnium SAVIGN. Descr. de l'Égypte, Ois. 1809, 298. Type, *Strix stridula* LINN.

368. Syrnium nebulosum (FORST.).
Barred Owl.

Strix nebulosa FORST. Philos. Trans. XXII. 1772, 386.
Syrnium nebulosum BOIE, Isis, 1828, 315.

[B 54, C 323, R 397, C 476.]

ORDER RAPTORES.

HAB. Eastern United States, west to Minnesota and Texas, north to Nova Scotia and Quebec.

368 *a*. **Syrnium nebulosum alleni** RIDGW.
Florida Barred Owl.

Strix nebulosa alleni RIDGW. Pr. U. S. Nat. Mus. III. March 27, 1880, 8.

[B —, C —, R 397 *a*, C 477.]

HAB. Florida.

369. **Syrnium occidentale** XANTUS.
Spotted Owl.

Syrnium occidentale XANTUS, Pr. Ac. Nat. Sci. Phila. 1859, 193.

[B —, C 324, R 398, C 478.]

HAB. Southwestern United States (New Mexico, Arizona, California), and Lower California and Mexico.

GENUS **ULULA** CUVIER.

Ulula CUV. Règ. An. I. 1817, 329. Type, *Strix uralensis* PALL.

370. **Ulula cinerea** (GMEL.).
Great Gray Owl.

Strix cinerea GMEL. S. N. I. i. 1788, 291.
Ulula cinerea BONAP. Consp. Av. I. 1850, 53.

[B 53, C 322, R 399, C 474.]

HAB. Arctic America, straggling southward, in winter, to the northern border of the United States.

[370 *a*.] **Ulula cinerea lapponica** (RETZ.).
Lapp Owl.

Strix lapponica RETZ. Faun. Suec. 1800, 79.
Ulula cinerea lapponica RIDGW. Pr. U. S. Nat. Mus. III. Aug. 24, 1880, 191.

[B —, C —, R 399 *a*, C 475.]

HAB. Arctic portions of the Old World; accidental in Alaska.

Genus **NYCTALA** Brehm.

Nyctala Brehm, Isis, 1828, 1271. Type, *Strix tengmalmi* Gmel.

371. **Nyctala tengmalmi richardsoni** (Bonap.).
Richardson's Owl.

Nyctale richardsoni Bonap. Geog. & Comp. List, 1838, 7.
Nyctale tengmalmi var. *richardsoni* Ridgw. Am. Nat. VI. 1872, 283.

[B 55, C 327, R 400, C 482.]

Hab. Arctic America, south occasionally in winter into the Northern United States.

372. **Nyctala acadica** (Gmel.).
Saw-whet Owl.

Strix acadica Gmel. S. N. I. 1788, 296.
Nyctale acadica Bonap. Geog. & Comp. List, 1838, 7.

[B 56, 57, C 328, R 401, C 483.]

Hab. North America at large, breeding from the Middle States northward.

Genus **MEGASCOPS** Kaup.

Megascops Kaup, Isis, 1848, 765. Type, *Strix asio* Linn.

373. **Megascops asio** (Linn.).
Screech Owl.

Strix asio Linn. Syst. Nat. ed. 10, I. 1758, 92.
Megascops asio Stejn. Auk, II. April, 1885, 184.

[B 49. *part,* C 318, R 402, C 465.]

Hab. Temperate Eastern North America, south to Georgia, and west to the Plains. Accidental in England.

373 *a*. **Megascops asio floridanus** (Ridgw.).
Florida Screech Owl.

Scops asio var. *floridanus* Ridgw. Bull. Essex Inst. Dec. 1873, 200.
Megascops asio floridanus Stejn. Auk, II. April, 1885, 184.

[B —, C 318 c, R 402 a, C 469.]

HAB. Southern Georgia and Florida.

373 b. **Megascops asio mccallii** (CASS.).
   Texan Screech Owl.

   Scops mccallii CASS. Illust. B. Cal. Tex. etc. July, 1854, 184.
   Megascops asio maccalli STEJN. Auk, II. April, 1885, 184.

   [B 50, C 318 b, R 402 b, C 468.]

HAB. Valley of the Lower Rio Grande in Texas, south to Guatemala.

373 c. **Megascops asio bendirei** (BREWST.).
   California Screech Owl.

   Scops asio bendirei BREWST. Bull. Nutt. Orn. Club, VII. Jan. 1882, 31.
   Megascops asio bendirei STEJN. Auk, II. April, 1885, 184.

   [B —, C —, R —, C —.]

HAB. Coast region of California.

373 d. **Megascops asio kennicottii** (ELLIOT).
   Kennicott's Screech Owl.

   Scops kennicottii ELLIOT, Pr. Ac. Nat. Sci. Phila. 1867, 69.
   Megascops asio kennicotti STEJN. Auk, II. April, 1885, 184.

   [B —, C 318 a, R 402 d, C 466.]

HAB. Northwest coast region, from Sitka to Oregon, and eastward to Idaho and Montana.

373 e. **Megascops asio maxwelliæ** (RIDGW.).
   Rocky Mountain Screech Owl.

   Scops asio var. *maxwelliæ* RIDGW. Field & Forest, June, 1877, 210, 213.
   Megascops asio maxwelliæ STEJN. Auk, II. April, 1885, 184.

   [B —, C —, R 402 c, C 467.]

HAB. Rocky Mountains, from Colorado to Montana.

373 *f*. Megascops asio trichopsis (WAGL.).
   Mexican Screech Owl.

   Scops trichopsis WAGL. Isis, 1832, 276.
   Megascops asio trichopsis RIDGW. Pr. U. S. Nat. Mus. VIII. 1885, 355.

   [B —, C —, R 403, C 470.]

HAB. New Mexico, Arizona, Lower California, and Western Mexico.

374. Megascops flammeolus (KAUP).
   Flammulated Screech Owl.

   Scops flammeola KAUP. Trans. Zool. Soc. Lond. IV. 1862, 226.
   Megascops flammeolus STEJN. Auk, II. April, 1885, 184.

   [B —, C 319, R 404, C 471.]

HAB. Guatemala and Central Mexico, north to Colorado and California.

GENUS **BUBO** CUVIER.

Bubo CUV. Règ. An. 1817, 351. Type, *Strix bubo* LINN.

375. Bubo virginianus (GMEL.).
   Great Horned Owl.

   Strix virginiana GMEL. S. N. I. i. 1788, 287.
   Bubo virginianus BONAP. Geog. & Comp. List, 1838, 6.

   [B 48, C 317, R 405, C 462.]

HAB. Eastern North America, west to the Mississippi Valley, and from Labrador south to Costa Rica.

375 *a*. Bubo virginianus subarcticus (HOY).
   Western Horned Owl.

   Bubo subarcticus HOY, Pr. Ac. Nat. Sci. Phila. VI. 1852, 211.
   Bubo virginianus β. *subarcticus* RIDGW. Orn. 40th Par. 1877, 572.

   [B 48, *part*, C 317 *a*, *part*, R 405 *a*, *part*, C 463, *part*.]

HAB. Western United States from the Great Plains westward; southward to the Mexican table-lands. East, casually, to Wisconsin and Illinois.

375 *b*. **Bubo virginianus arcticus** (SWAINS.).
    Arctic Horned Owl.

    Strix (Bubo) arctica SWAINS. Fauna Bor. Am. ii. 1831, 86, pl. 30.
    Bubo virginianus var. *arcticus* CASS. Illust. B. Cal. etc. 1854, 178.

    [B 48, *part*, C 317 *a*, *part*, R 405 *b*, C 463, *part*.]

    HAB. Interior of Arctic America (Fur Countries), south, in winter, to Dakota, Montana, and Wyoming.

375 *c*. **Bubo virginianus saturatus** RIDGW.
    Dusky Horned Owl.

    Bubo virginianus saturatus RIDGW. Orn. 40th Par. 1877, 572, foot-note.

    [B 48, *part*, C 317 *b*, R 405 *c*, C 464.]

    HAB. Northwest coast region, from the Columbia River northward; Labrador.

GENUS **NYCTEA** STEPHENS.

    Nyctea STEPH. Gen. Zool. XIII. ii. 1826, 63. Type, *Strix nyctea* LINN.

376. **Nyctea nyctea** (LINN.).
    Snowy Owl.

    Strix nyctea LINN. S. N. ed. 10, I. 1758, 93.
    Nyctea nyctea LICHT. Nomen. Mus. Berol. 1854, 7.

    [B 61, C 325, R 406, C 479.]

    HAB. Northern portions of the Northern Hemisphere. In North America breeding mostly north of the United States; in winter migrating south to the Middle States, straggling to South Carolina, Texas, and the Bermudas.

GENUS **SURNIA** DUMÉRIL.

    Surnia DUMÉR. Zool. Anal. 1806, 34. Type, *Strix ulula* LINN.

[377.] **Surnia ulula** (LINN.).
    Hawk Owl.

    Strix ulula LINN. S. N. ed. 10, I. 1758, 93.
    Surnia ulula BONAP. Cat. Met. Ucc. Eur. 1842, 22.

[B —, C —, R 407 *a*, C 481.]

HAB. Arctic portions of the Old World. Casual in Alaska.

377 *a*. **Surnia ulula caparoch** (MÜLL.).
    American Hawk Owl.

Strix caparoch MÜLL. S. N. Suppl. 1776, 69.
Surnia ulula caparoch STEJN. Auk, I. Oct. 1884, 363.

[B 62, C 326, R 407, C 480.]

HAB. Arctic America, migrating in winter to the northern border of the United States. Occasional in England.

GENUS **SPEOTYTO** GLOGER.

Speotyto GLOG. Handb. Naturg. 1842, 226. Type, *Strix cunicularia* MOL.

378. **Speotyto cunicularia hypogæa** (BONAP.).
    Burrowing Owl.

Strix hypogæa BONAP. Am. Orn. I. 1825, 72.
Spheotyto cunicularia var. *hypogæa* RIDGW. in COUES's Key, 1872, 208.

[B 58, 59, C 332, R 408, C 487.]

HAB. United States, from the Pacific coast to the Great Plains, south to Central America. Accidental in Massachusetts.

378 *a*. **Speotyto cunicularia floridana** RIDGW.
    Florida Burrowing Owl.

Speotyto cunicularia var. *floridana* RIDGW. Am. Sportsm. V. July 4, 1874, 216.

[B —, C —, R 408 *a*, C 488.]

HAB. Florida.

GENUS **GLAUCIDIUM** BOIE.

Glaucidium BOIE, Isis, 1826, 970. Type, *Strix nana* KING.

379. **Glaucidium gnoma** WAGL.
    Pygmy Owl.

Glaucidium gnoma WAGL. Isis, 1832, 275.

[B 60, C 329, R 409, C 484.]

HAB. Western United States, from the Pacific coast to Colorado, and from British Columbia south to the table-lands of Mexico.

380. **Glaucidium phalænoides** (DAUD.).
    Ferruginous Pygmy Owl.

Strix phalænoides DAUD. Traité Orn. II. 1800, 206.
Glaucidium phalænoides CAB. J. f. O. 1869, 208.

[B —, C 330, R 410, C 485.]

HAB. Southern border of the United States (Texas to Arizona), south to Southern Brazil.

GENUS **MICRATHENE** COUES.

Micrathene COUES, Pr. Ac. Nat. Sci. Phila. 1866, 51. Type, *Athene whitneyi* COOPER.

381. **Micrathene whitneyi** (COOPER).
    Elf Owl.

Athene whitneyi COOPER, Pr. Cal. Ac. Sci. 1861, 118.
Micrathene whitneyi COUES, Pr. Ac. Nat. Sci. Phila. 1866, 51.

[B —, C 331, R 411, C 486.]

HAB. Southern and Lower California and Arizona, south into Mexico.

ORDER PSITTACI. PARROTS, MACAWS, PAROQUETS, ETC.

FAMILY **PSITTACIDÆ**.

GENUS **CONURUS** KUHL.

Conurus KUHL, Consp. Psitt. 1820, 4. Type, *Psittacus carolinensis* GMEL.

382. Conurus carolinensis (Linn.).
Carolina Paroquet.

Psittacus carolinensis Linn. S. N. ed. 10, I. 1758, 97.
Conurus carolinensis Less. Traité, 1831, 211.

[B 63, C 315, R 392, C 460.]

Hab. Formerly Florida and the Gulf States north to Maryland, the Great Lakes, Iowa, and Nebraska, west to Colorado, the Indian Territory, and Texas, and straggling northeastward to Pennsylvania and New York. Now restricted to the Gulf States and the Lower Mississippi Valley, and of local occurrence only.

Order COCCYGES. Cuckoos, etc.

Suborder CUCULI. Cuckoos, etc.

Family CUCULIDÆ. Cuckoos, Anis, etc.

Subfamily CROTOPHAGINÆ. Anis.

Genus **CROTOPHAGA** Linnæus.

Crotophaga Linn. S. N. ed. 10, I. 1758, 105. Type, *C. ani* Linn.

[383.] **Crotophaga ani** Linn.
Ani.

Crotophaga ani Linn. S. N. ed. 10, I. 1758, 105.

[B 66, 67, C 288, R 389, C 425.]

Hab. West Indies, and Eastern South America. Rare or casual in Southern Florida, and accidental near Philadelphia.

384. Crotophaga sulcirostris SWAINS.
Groove-billed Ani.

Crotophaga sulcirostris SWAINS. Philos. Mag. I. 1827, 440.

[B —, C —, R 390, C 426.]

HAB. Lower California, and valley of the Lower Rio Grande in Texas, south to Northern South America.

SUBFAMILY **COCCYGINÆ**. AMERICAN CUCKOOS.

GENUS **GEOCOCCYX** WAGLER.

Geococcyx WAGLER, Isis, 1831, 524. Type, *G. variegata* WAGL. = *Saurothera californiana* LESS.

385. Geococcyx californianus (LESS.).
Road-runner.

Saurothera californiana LESSON, Compl. Buff. VI. 1829 (?), 420.
Geococcyx californianus BAIRD, B. N. Am. 1858, 73.

[B 68, C 289, R 385, C 427.]

HAB. Texas, New Mexico, Southern Colorado, and westward to California; south into Mexico.

GENUS **COCCYZUS** VIEILLOT.

Coccyzus VIELL. Analyse, 1816, 28. Type, *Cuculus americanus* LINN.

386. Coccyzus minor (GMEL.).
Mangrove Cuckoo.

Cuculus minor GMEL. S. N. I. i. 1788, 411.
Coccyzus minor CAB. J. f. O. 1856, 104.

[B 71, C 292, R 386, C 429.]

HAB. Southern Florida, Louisiana, the West Indies, and Central America to Northern and Eastern South America.

387. Coccyzus americanus (LINN.).
Yellow-billed Cuckoo.

Cuculus americanus LINN. S. N. ed. 10, I. 1758, 111.
Coccyzus americanus BONAP. Journ. Ac. Nat. Sci. Phila. III. ii. 1824, 367.

[B 69, C 291, R 387, C 429.]

HAB. Temperate North America, from New Brunswick, Canada, Minnesota, Nevada, and Oregon south to Costa Rica and the West Indies. Less common from the eastern border of the Plains westward.

388. Coccyzus erythrophthalmus (WILS.).
Black-billed Cuckoo.

Cuculus erythrophthalmus WILS. Am. Orn. IV. 1811, 16, pl. 28.
Coccyzus erythrophthalmus BONAP. Journ. Ac. Nat. Sci. Phila. III. ii. 1824, 367.

[B 70, C 290, R 388, C 428.]

HAB. Eastern North America, from Labrador and Manitoba south to the West Indies and the valley of the Amazon; west to the Rocky Mountains. Accidental in the British Islands and Italy.

SUBORDER **TROGONES.** TROGONS.

FAMILY **TROGONIDÆ.** TROGONS.

GENUS **TROGON** LINNÆUS.

Trogon LINN. S. N. ed. 12, I. 1766, 167. Type, *T. viridis* LINN.

[389.] **Trogon ambiguus** GOULD.
Coppery-tailed Trogon.

Trogon ambiguus GOULD, P. Z. S. 1835, 30.

[B 65, C 284, R 384, C 422.]

HAB. Mexico, north to the valley of the Lower Rio Grande in Texas.

Suborder ALCYONES. Kingfishers.

Family ALCEDINIDÆ. Kingfishers.

Genus **CERYLE** Boie.

Ceryle BOIE, Isis, 1828, 316. Type, *Alcedo rudis* LINN.

Subgenus **STREPTOCERYLE** Bonaparte.

Streptoceryle BONAP. Consp. Vol. Anisod. 1854, 10. Type, *Alcedo torquata* LINN.

390. **Ceryle alcyon** (LINN.).
 Belted Kingfisher.

Alcedo alcyon LINN. S. N. ed. 10, I. 1758, 115.
Ceryle alcyon BONAP. P. Z. S. 1837, 108.

[B 117, C 286, R 382, C 423.]

HAB. North America, south to Panama and the West Indies.

Subgenus **CHLOROCERYLE** Kaup.

Chloroceryle KAUP, Fam. Eisv. 1848, 8. Type, *Alcedo superciliosa* LINN.

391. **Ceryle cabanisi** (TSCHUDI).
 Texan Kingfisher.

Alcedo cabanisi TSCHUDI, Faun. Per. Orn. 1844, 253.
Ceryle cabanisi BONAP. Consp. Av. I. 1850, 160.

[B 118, C 287, R 383, C 424.]

HAB. Valley of the Lower Rio Grande, Texas, and Lower Colorado River, Arizona, south to Ecuador and Western Peru.

ORDER PICI. WOODPECKERS, WRYNECKS, ETC.

FAMILY PICIDÆ. WOODPECKERS.

GENUS **CAMPEPHILUS** GRAY.

Campephilus GRAY, List Gen. B. 1840, 54. Type, *Picus principalis* LINN.

392. Campephilus principalis (LINN.).
   Ivory-billed Woodpecker.

Picus principalis LINN. S. N. ed. 10, I. 1758, 113.
Campephilus principalis GRAY, List Gen. B. 1840, 54.

[B 72, C 293, R 359, C 431.]

HAB. Formerly South Atlantic and Gulf States, from North Carolina to Texas, north in the Mississippi Valley to Missouri, Southern Illinois, and Southern Indiana. Now restricted to the Gulf States and the Lower Mississippi Valley, where only locally distributed.

GENUS **DRYOBATES** BOIE.

Dryobates BOIE, Isis, 1826, 977. Type, *Picus pubescens* LINN.

393. Dryobates villosus (LINN.).
   Hairy Woodpecker.

Picus villosus LINN. S. N. ed. 12, I. 1766, 175.
D[ryobates] villosus CABANIS, Mus. Hein. IV. June 15, 1863, 66.

[B 74, *part*, C 298, *part*, R 360, C 438, *part.*]

HAB. Middle portion of the Eastern United States, from the Atlantic coast to the Great Plains.

393 *a*. Dryobates villosus leucomelas (BODD.).
   Northern Hairy Woodpecker.

Picus leucomelas BODDAERT, Tabl. Pl. Enl. 1783, 21.
Dryobates villosus leucomelas RIDGW. Pr. U. S. Nat. Mus. VIII. 1885, 355.

[B 74, *part*, C 298, *part*, R 360 *a*, C 438, *part*.]

HAB. Northern North America, south to about the northern border of the United States.

393 *b*. Dryobates villosus audubonii (SWAINS.).
Southern Hairy Woodpecker.

Picus audubonii SWAINS. & RICH. Fauna Bor. Am. II. 1831, 306.
Dryobates villosus audubonii RIDGW. Pr U. S. Nat. Mus VIII. 1885, 355.

[B 74, *part*, C 298, *part*, R 360, *part*, C 438, *part*.]

HAB. Southern portions of the United States, east of the Plains.

393 *c*. Dryobates villosus harrisii (AUD.).
Harris's Woodpecker.

Picus harrisii AUD. Orn. Biog. V. 1839, 191.
Dryobates villosus harrisii RIDGW. Pr. U. S. Nat. Mus. VIII. 1885, 355.

[B 75, C 298 *a*, R 360 *b*, C 439.]

HAB. Western United States, from the Rocky Mountains to the Pacific coast, south into Mexico and Central America.

394. Dryobates pubescens (LINN.).
Downy Woodpecker.

Picus pubescens LINN. S. N. ed. 12, I. 1766, 175.
D[ryobates] pubescens CABANIS, Mus. Hein. IV. June 15, 1863, 62.

[B 76, C 299, R 361, C 440.]

HAB. Northern and Eastern North America, from British Columbia and the eastern edge of the Plains northward and eastward.

394 *a*. Dryobates pubescens gairdnerii (AUD.).
Gairdner's Woodpecker.

Picus gairdnerii AUD. Orn. Biog. V. 1839, 317.
Dryobates pubescens gairdnerii RIDGW. Pr. U. S. Nat. Mus. VIII. 1885, 355.

[B 77, C 299 *a*, R 361 *a*, C 441.]

HAB. Western United States, from the Rocky Mountains westward.

395. **Dryobates borealis** (VIEILL.).
Red-cockaded Woodpecker.

Picus borealis VIEILL. Ois. Am. Sept. II. 1807, 66.
Dryobates borealis RIDGW. Pr. U. S. Nat. Mus. VIII. 1885, 355.

[B 80, C 296, R 362, C 433.]

HAB. Southeastern United States, from New Jersey (at least formerly), Tennessee, and Indian Territory south to Eastern Texas and the Gulf coast.

396. **Dryobates scalaris** (WAGL.).
Texan Woodpecker

Picus scalaris WAGLER, Isis, 1829, 511.
Dryobates scalaris RIDGW. Pr. U. S. Nat. Mus. VIII. 1885, 355.

[B 79, C 297, R 363, C 434.]

HAB. Southern border of the United States, from Texas to California, south into Mexico.

396 *a*. **Dryobates scalaris lucasanus** (XANTUS).
Saint Lucas Woodpecker.

Picus lucasanus XANTUS, Pr. Ac. Nat. Sci. Phila. 1859, 298.
Dryobates scalaris lucasanus RIDGW. Pr. U. S. Nat. Mus. VIII. 1885, 355.

[B —, C 297 *b*, R 363 *a*, C 436.]

HAB. Lower California.

397. **Dryobates nuttallii** (GAMB.).
Nuttall's Woodpecker.

Picus nuttallii GAMBEL, Pr. Ac. Nat. Sci. Phila. April, 1843, 259.
Dryobates nuttallii RIDGW. Pr. U. S. Nat. Mus. VIII. 1885, 355.

[B 78, C 297 *a*, R 364, C 435.]

HAB. California.

398. **Dryobates stricklandi** (MALH.).
   Strickland's Woodpecker.

   Picus stricklandi MALHERBE, Rev. Zool. 1845, 373.
   Dryobates stricklandi RIDGW. Pr. U. S. Nat. Mus. VIII. 1885, 355.

   [B —, C —, R 365, C 437.]

   HAB. Southern Arizona, south into Western Mexico.

   GENUS **XENOPICUS** BAIRD.

   Xenopicus BAIRD, B. N. Am. 1858, 83. Type, *Leuconerpes albolarvatus* CASS.

399. **Xenopicus albolarvatus** (CASS.).
   White-headed Woodpecker.

   Leuconerpes albolarvatus CASSIN, Pr. Ac. Nat. Sci. Phila. Oct. 1850, 106.
   Xenopicus albolarvatus MALHERBE, Monogr. Pic. II. 1862, 221.

   [B 81, C 295, R 366, C 442.]

   HAB. Pacific coast region, from Washington Territory south to Southern California, east to the eastern slope of the Sierra Nevada.

   GENUS **PICOIDES** LACÉPÈDE.

   Picoides LACÉPÈDE, Mém. de l'Inst. III. 1801, 509. Type, *Picus tridactylus* LINN.

400. **Picoides arcticus** (SWAINS.).
   Arctic Three-toed Woodpecker.

   Picus (Apternus) arcticus SWAINS. Fauna Bor. Am. II. 1831, 313.
   Picoides arcticus GRAY, Gen. B. I. 1845, 434.

   [B 82, C 300, R 367, C 443.]

   HAB. Northern North America, from the arctic regions south to the northern border of the United States; much further south in the western part of the United States (Nevada, California), along the mountain ranges.

401. Picoides americanus BREHM.
American Three-toed Woodpecker.

Picoides americanus BREHM, Handb. Vög. Deutschl. 1831, 195.

[B 83, C 301, R 368, C 444.]

HAB. Northern North America, from the arctic regions southward, in winter, to the Northern United States.

401 a. Picoides americanus alascensis (NELS.).
Alaskan Three-toed Woodpecker.

Picoides tridactylus alascensis NELSON, Auk, I. April, 1884, 165.
Picoides americanus alascensis RIDGW. Pr. U. S. Nat. Mus. VIII. 1885, 355.

[B —, C —, R —, C —.]

HAB. Alaska.

401 b. Picoides americanus dorsalis BAIRD.
Alpine Three-toed Woodpecker.

Picoides dorsalis BAIRD, B. N. Am. 1858, 100.
Picoides americanus dorsalis BAIRD, Orn. Calif. I. 1870, 386.

[B 84, C 301 a, R 368 a, C 445.]

HAB. Rocky Mountain region of the United States, south into New Mexico.

GENUS **SPHYRAPICUS** BAIRD.

Sphyrapicus BAIRD, B. N. Am. 1858, 101. Type, *Picus varius* LINN.

402. Sphyrapicus varius (LINN.).
Yellow-bellied Sapsucker.

Picus varius LINN. S. N. ed. 12, I. 1766, 176.
Sphyrapicus varius BAIRD, B. N. Am. 1858, 103.

[B 85, C 302, R 369, C 446.]

HAB. North America north and east of the Great Plains, south to the West Indies, Mexico, and Guatemala.

402 *a*. **Sphyrapicus varius nuchalis** BAIRD.
    Red-naped Sapsucker.

Sphyrapicus varius var. *nuchalis* BAIRD, B. N. Am. 1858, 103.

[B 86, C 302 *a*, R 369 *a*, C 447.]

HAB. Rocky Mountain region of the United States, south into Mexico.

403. **Sphyrapicus ruber** (GMEL.).
    Red-breasted Sapsucker.

Picus ruber GMEL. S. N. I. 1788, 429.
Sphyrapicus ruber BAIRD, B. N. Am. 1858, 104.

[B 87, C 302 *b*, 303? R 369 *b*, C 448.]

HAB. Pacific coast region of the United States.

404. **Sphyrapicus thyroideus** (CASS.).
    Williamson's Sapsucker.

Picus thyroideus CASSIN, Pr. Ac. Nat. Sci. Phila. 1850-1851, 349.
Sphyrapicus thyroideus BAIRD, B. N. Am. 1858, 106.

[B 88, 89, C 304, 305, R 370, C 449.]

HAB. Rocky Mountain region of the United States, west to the Pacific coast.

GENUS **CEOPHLŒUS** CABANIS.

Ceophlœus CABANIS, Journ. f. Orn. 1862, 176. Type, *Picus pileatus* LINN.

405. **Ceophlœus pileatus** (LINN.).
    Pileated Woodpecker.

Picus pileatus LINN. S. N. ed. 10, I. 1758, 113.
C[eophlœus] pileatus CABANIS, J. f. O. 1862, 176.

[B 90, C 294, R 371, C 432.]

HAB. Formerly whole wooded region of North America; now rare or extirpated in the more thickly settled parts of the Eastern States.

Genus **MELANERPES** Swainson.

Subgenus **MELANERPES**.

Melanerpes Swains. Fauna Bor. Am. II. 1831, 316. Type, *Picus erythrocephalus* Linn.

406. Melanerpes erythrocephalus (Linn.).
Red-headed Woodpecker.

Picus erythrocephalus Linn. S. N. ed. 10, I. 1758, 113.
Melanerpes erythrocephalus Swains. Fauna Bor. Am. II. 1831, 316.

[B 94, C 309, R 375, C 453.]

Hab. United States, west to the Rocky Mountains, straggling westward to Salt Lake Valley; rare or local east of the Hudson River.

407. Melanerpes formicivorus bairdi Ridgw.
Californian Woodpecker.

Melanerpes formicivorus bairdi Ridgw. Bull. No. 21 U. S. Nat. Mus. 1881, 34, 85.

[B 95, C 310, R 377, C 454.]

Hab. Pacific coast region of the United States, east into Arizona, south into Mexico.

407 a. Melanerpes formicivorus angustifrons Baird.
Narrow-fronted Woodpecker.

Melanerpes formicivorus var. *angustifrons* Baird, Orn. Cal. I. 1870, 405.

[B —, C 310 a, R 377 a, C 455.]

Hab. Lower California.

Subgenus **ASYNDESMUS** Coues.

Asyndesmus Coues, Pr. Ac. Nat. Sci. Phila. 1866, 55. Type, *Picus torquatus* Wils.

408. Melanerpes torquatus (Wils.).
Lewis's Woodpecker.

Picus torquatus Wilson, Am. Orn. III. 1811, 31, pl. xx. fig. 3.
Melanerpes torquatus Bonap. Geog. & Comp. List, 1838, 40.

[B 96, C 311, R 376, C 456.]

ORDER PICI.

Hab. Western United States, from the Black Hills and the Rocky Mountains to the Pacific.

Subgenus **CENTURUS** Swainson.

Centurus Swains. Classif. B. II. 1837, 310. Type, *Picus carolinus* Linn.

409. **Melanerpes carolinus** (Linn.).
    Red-bellied Woodpecker.

Picus carolinus Linn. S. N. ed. 10, I. 1758, 113.
Melanerpes carolinus Ridgw. Ann. Lyc. N. Y. X. Jan. 1874, 378.

[B 91, C 306, R 372, C 450.]

Hab. Eastern United States, to the Rocky Mountains; rare or accidental east of the Hudson River.

410. **Melanerpes aurifrons** (Wagl.).
    Golden-fronted Woodpecker.

Picus aurifrons Wagler, Isis, 1829, 512.
Melanerpes aurifrons Ridgw. Pr. U. S. Nat. Mus. VIII. 1885, 355.

[B 92, C 307, R 373, C 451.]

Hab. Southern Texas and Eastern Mexico.

411. **Melanerpes uropygialis** (Baird).
    Gila Woodpecker.

Centurus uropygialis Baird, Pr. Ac. Nat. Sci. Phila. June, 1854, 120.
Melanerpes uropygialis Ridgw. Pr. U. S. Nat. Mus. VIII. 1885, 355.

[B 93, C 308, R 374, C 452.]

Hab. Southern Arizona, Southeastern California, Lower California, and Western Mexico.

Genus **COLAPTES** Swainson.

Colaptes Swains. Zool. Journ. III. Dec. 1827, 353. Type, *Cuculus auratus* Linn.

412. **Colaptes auratus** (Linn.).
    Flicker.

Cuculus auratus Linn. S. N. ed. 10, I. 1758, 112.
Colaptes auratus Vigors, Zool. Journ. III. 1827, 444.

[B 97, C 312, R 378, C 457.]

HAB. Northern and Eastern North America, west to the eastern slope of the Rocky Mountains and Alaska. Occasional on the Pacific slope, from California northward. Accidental in Europe.

413. Colaptes cafer (GMEL.).
Red-shafted Flicker.

Picus cafer GMEL. S. N. I. 1788, 431.
Colaptes cafer STEJN. Stand. Nat. Hist. IV. 1885, 428.

[B 98, C 314, R 378 *b*, C 459.]

HAB. Rocky Mountain region of the United States, to the Pacific coast; north to Sitka, south to Southern Mexico.

413 *a*. Colaptes cafer saturatior RIDGW.
Northwestern Flicker.

Colaptes mexicanus saturatior RIDGW. Pr. Biol. Soc. Wash. II. April 10, 1884, 90.
Colaptes cafer saturatior RIDGW. MS.

[B —, C —, R —, C —.]

HAB. Northwest coast, from Columbia River to Sitka.

414. Colaptes chrysoides (MALH.).
Gilded Flicker.

Geopicus chrysoides MALH. Rev. et Mag. Zool. IV. 1852, 553.
Colaptes chrysoides REICH. Handb. Spec. Ornith. Scansoriæ, 1854, 413.

[B 99, C 313, R 379, C 458.]

HAB. Southern Arizona and Southern California, south to Cape St. Lucas.

415. Colaptes rufipileus RIDGW.
Guadalupe Flicker.

Colaptes mexicanus rufipileus RIDGW. Bull. U. S. Geol. & Geog. Surv. Terr. II. No. 2, April 1, 1876, 191.
Colaptes rufipileus RIDGW. Bull. Nutt. Orn. Club, II. July, 1877, 60.

[B —, C —, R 380, C —.]

HAB. Guadalupe Island, Lower California.

Order MACROCHIRES. Goatsuckers, Swifts, etc.

Suborder CAPRIMULGI. Goatsuckers, etc.

Family CAPRIMULGIDÆ. Goatsuckers, etc.

Genus ANTROSTOMUS Gould.

Antrostomus Gould, Icones Avium, 1838. Type, *Caprimulgus carolinensis* Gmel.

416. Antrostomus carolinensis (Gmel.).
Chuck-will's-widow.

Caprimulgus carolinensis Gmel. S. N. I. ii. 1788, 1028.
Antrostomus carolinensis Gould, Icones Avium, 1838.

[B 111, C 264, R 353, C 396.]

Hab. South Atlantic and Gulf States, south through Eastern Mexico to Central America; Cuba. North, in the interior, to Southern Illinois.

417. Antrostomus vociferus (Wils.).
Whip-poor-will.

Caprimulgus vociferus Wils. Am. Orn. V. 1812, 71, pl. 41, figs. 1–3.
Antrostomus vociferus Bonap. Geog. & Comp. List, 1838, 8.

[B 112, C 265, R 354, C 397.]

Hab. Eastern United States to the Plains, south to Guatemala.

417 a. Antrostomus vociferus arizonæ Brewst.
Stephens's Whip-poor-will.

Antrostomus vociferus arizonæ Brewst. Bull. Nutt. Orn. Club, VII. Oct. 1882, 211.

[B —, C —, R —, C 881.]

Hab. Arizona, and table-lands of Mexico.

Genus **PHALÆNOPTILUS** Ridgway.

Phalænoptilus Ridgw. Pr. U. S. Nat. Mus. III. March 27, 1880, 5. Type, *Caprimulgus nuttalli* Aud.

418. **Phalænoptilus nuttalli** (Aud.).
Poor-will.

Caprimulgus nuttalli Aud. B. Am. VII. 1843, 350, pl. 495.
Phalænoptilus nuttalli Ridgw. Pr. U. S. Nat. Mus. III. 1880, 5.

[B 113, C 266, R 355, C 398.]

Hab. Western United States, from the Pacific coast eastward to Eastern Nebraska and Eastern Kansas, south to Southern Mexico.

Genus **NYCTIDROMUS** Gould.

Nyctidromus Gould, Icones Avium, II. 1838, pl. ii. Type, *N. derbyanus* Gould = *Caprimulgus albicollis* Gmel.

419. **Nyctidromus albicollis** (Gmel.).
Parauque.

Caprimulgus albicollis Gmel. S. N. I. ii. 1788, 1030.
Nyctidromus albicollis Burm. Th. Bras. II. 1856, 389.

[B —, C —, R 356, C 395.]

Hab. Valley of the Lower Rio Grande, south through Central and most of South America.

Genus **CHORDEILES** Swainson.

Chordeiles Swains. Fauna Bor. Am. II. 1831, 496. Type, *Caprimulgus virginianus* Gmel.

420. **Chordeiles virginianus** (Gmel.).
Nighthawk.

Caprimulgus virginianus Gmel. S. N. I. ii. 1788, 1028.
Chordeiles virginianus Swains. Fauna Bor. Am. II. 1831, 496.

[B 114, C 267, R 357, C 399.]

Hab. Northern and Eastern North America, east of the Great Plains, south through tropical America to Buenos Ayres.

420 *a*. **Chordeiles virginianus henryi** (Cass.).
    Western Nighthawk.

> *Chordeiles henryi* Cass. Illustr. B. Cal. Tex. etc. I. 1855, 233.
> *Chordeiles virginianus* var. *henryi* Coues, Key, 1872, 181.

[B 115, C 267 *a*, R 357 *a*, C 400.]

Hab Western United States, from the Plains to the Pacific coast, south into Mexico.

[420 *b*.] **Chordeiles virginianus minor** (Cab.).
    Cuban Nighthawk.

> *Chordeiles minor* Cab. J. f. O. 1856, 5.
> *Chordeiles virginianus* c. *minor* Coues, Birds Northwest, 1874, 264.

[B —, C —, R 357 *b*, C 401.]

Hab. Cuba and Southern Florida.

421. **Chordeiles texensis** Lawr.
    Texan Nighthawk.

> *Chordeiles texensis* Lawr. Ann. Lyc. N. Y. VI. Dec 1856, 167.

[B 116, C 268, R 358, C 402.]

Hab. Southern border of the United States, from Texas to California; south to Central America.

Suborder CYPSELI Swifts.

Family MICROPODIDÆ. Swifts.

Subfamily CHÆTURINÆ. Spine-tailed Swifts.

Genus CYPSELOIDES Streubel.

Cypseloides Streubel, Isis, 1848, 366. Type, *Hemichelidon fumigata* Nutt.

422. Cypseloides niger (GMEL.).
Black Swift.

Hirundo nigra GMEL. S. N. I. ii. 1788, 1025.
Cypseloides niger SCL. P. Z. S. June 27, 1865, 615.

[B 108, C 270, R 350, C 404.]

HAB. Rocky Mountain region (Colorado), west to the Pacific coast; north to British Columbia, and south to Mexico and the West Indies.

GENUS **CHÆTURA** STEPHENS.

Chætura STEPH. Gen. Zool. XIII. pt. ii. 1825, 76. Type, *Hirundo pelagica* LINN.

423. Chætura pelagica (LINN.).
Chimney Swift.

Hirundo pelagica LINN. S. N. ed. 10, I. 1758, 192.
Chætura pelasgia STEPH. Gen. Zool. XIII. pt. ii. 1825, 76.

[B 109, C 271, R 351, C 405.]

HAB. Eastern North America, north to Labrador and the Fur Countries, west to the Plains, and passing south of the United States in winter.

424. Chætura vauxii (TOWNS.).
Vaux's Swift.

Cypselus vauxii TOWNS. Journ. Ac. Nat. Sci. Phila. VIII. 1839, 148.
Chætura vauxii DEKAY, Zool. N. Y. II. 1844, 36.

[B 110, C 272, R 352, C 406.]

HAB. Pacific slope, from British Columbia south into Mexico.

SUBFAMILY **MICROPODINÆ**.

GENUS **MICROPUS** MEYER & WOLF.

Micropus MEYER & WOLF, Taschb. Deutsch. Vög. I. 1810, 280. Type, *Hirundo apus* LINN.

425. **Micropus melanoleucus** (BAIRD).
    White-throated Swift.

    Cypselus melanoleucus BAIRD, Pr. Ac. Nat. Sci. Phila. June, 1854, 118.
    Micropus melanoleucus RIDGW. Auk, I. July, 1884, 230.

    [B 107, C 269, R 349, C 403.]

HAB. Western United States, from the Rocky Mountains to the Pacific, and south to Central America.

SUBORDER **TROCHILI**. HUMMINGBIRDS.

FAMILY **TROCHILIDÆ**. HUMMINGBIRDS.

GENUS **EUGENES** GOULD.

    Eugenes GOULD, Mon. Troch. pt. xii. 1856. Type, *Trochilus fulgens* SWAINS.

426. **Eugenes fulgens** (SWAINS.).
    Rivoli Hummingbird.

    Trochilus fulgens SWAINS. Phil. Mag. 1827, 441.
    Eugenes fulgens GOULD, Mon. Troch. II. 1856, pl. 59.

    [B —, C 274 *bis*, R 334, C 408.]

HAB. Southern Arizona, through Mexico to Guatemala.

GENUS **CŒLIGENA** LESSON.

    Cæligena LESS. Ind. & Synop. Gen. Troch. 1832, p. xviii. Type, *Ornismya clemenciæ* LESS.

427. **Cœligena clemenciæ** LESS.
    Blue-throated Hummingbird.

    Ornismya clemenciæ LESS. Ois. Mouch. 1829, 216, pl. 80.
    Cæligena clemenciæ LESS. Ind. & Synop. Gen. Troch. 1832, p. xviii.

[B —, C —, R —, C —.]

HAB. Mexico and Southern Arizona.

GENUS **TROCHILUS** LINNÆUS.

SUBGENUS **TROCHILUS**.

Trochilus LINN. S. N. ed. 10, I. 1758, 119. Type, by elimination, *T. colubris* LINN.

428. Trochilus colubris LINN.
Ruby-throated Hummingbird.

Trochilus colubris LINN. S. N. ed. 10, I. 1758, 120.

[B 101, C 275, R 335, C 409.]

HAB. Eastern North America to the Plains, north to the Fur Countries, and south, in winter, to Cuba and Veragua.

429. Trochilus alexandri BOURC. & MULS.
Black-chinned Hummingbird.

Trochilus alexandri BOURC. & MULS. Ann. Soc. Agric. Lyons, IX. 1846, 330.

[B 102, C 276, R 336, C 410.]

HAB. Pacific coast region, from California east to Utah and Arizona, and southward.

SUBGENUS **CALYPTE** GOULD.

Calypte GOULD, Introd. Troch. 1861, 87. Type, *Ornismya costæ* BOURC.

430. Trochilus costæ (BOURC.).
Costa's Hummingbird.

Ornismya costæ BOURC Rev. Zool. 1839, 294.
Trochilus costæ GRAY, Handl. I. 1869, 145.

[B 106, C 280, R 337, C 415.]

HAB. Southern California, Arizona, and Western Mexico.

431. **Trochilus anna** (Less.).
   Anna's Hummingbird.

   Ornismya anna Less. Suppl. Ois. Mouch. 1831, 115, pl. vii.
   Trochilus anna Jardine, Nat. Lib. Orn. I. 1833, 93.

   [B 105, C 279, R 338, C 415.]

   Hab. Southern California, Southern Arizona, and Mexico.

   Subgenus **SELASPHORUS** Swainson.

   Selasphorus Swains. Fauna Bor. Am. II. 1831, 324. Type, *Trochilus rufus* Gmel.

432. **Trochilus platycercus** Swains.
   Broad-tailed Hummingbird.

   Trochilus platycercus Swains. Phil. Mag. I. 1827, 441.

   [B 104, C 278, R 339, C 413.]

   Hab. Rocky Mountain plateau region, south to Guatemala.

433. **Trochilus rufus** Gmel.
   Rufous Hummingbird.

   Trochilus rufus Gmel. S. N. I. i. 1788, 497.

   [B 103, C 277, R 340, C 411.]

   Hab. Rocky Mountains to the Pacific, north to Sitka, south into Mexico.

434. **Trochilus alleni** (Hensh.).
   Allen's Hummingbird.

   Selasphorus alleni Hensh. Bull. Nutt. Orn. Club, II. 1877, 54.
   Trochilus alleni Ridgw. Pr. U. S. Nat. Mus. VIII. 1885, 355.

   [B —, C —, R 341, C 412.]

   Hab. Pacific coast, north to British Columbia, east to Southern Arizona.

SUBGENUS **ATTHIS** REICHENBACH.

Atthis REICH. Aufz. der Colib. 1853, 12. Type, *Ornysmia heloisa* LESS. & DELATT.

435. Trochilus heloisa (LESS. & DELATT.).
Heloise's Hummingbird.

Ornysmia heloisa LESS. & DELATT. Rev. Zool. 1839, 15.
Trochilus heloisa GRAY, Handl. I. 1869, 145.

[B —, C 281, R 342, C 416.]

HAB. Southern Texas and Eastern Mexico.

SUBGENUS **STELLULA** GOULD.

Stellula GOULD, Introd. Troch. 1861, 90. Type, *Trochilus calliope* GOULD.

436. Trochilus calliope GOULD.
Calliope Hummingbird.

Trochilus (Calothorax) calliope GOULD, P. Z. S. 1847, 11.

[B —, C 282, R 343, C 417.]

HAB. Mountains of the Pacific slope, from British Columbia south to Lower California, and east to Montana, Nevada, and New Mexico.

SUBGENUS **CALOTHORAX** GRAY.

Calothorax GRAY, Gen. B. 1840, 13. Type, *Cynanthus lucifer* SWAINS.

437. Trochilus lucifer (SWAINS.).
Lucifer Hummingbird.

Cynanthus lucifer SWAINS. Phil. Mag. 1827, 442.
Trochilus lucifer GIEBEL, Thes. Orn. III. 1877, 683.

[B —, C —, R 344, C 418.]

HAB. Mexico and Southern Arizona.

GENUS **AMAZILIA** REICHENBACH.

Amazilia REICH. Syst. Av. 1849, pl. 39. Type, *Orthorhynchus amazili* LESS.

438. **Amazilia fuscicaudata** (Fraser).
 Rieffer's Hummingbird.

Trochilus fuscicaudatus Fras. P. Z. S. 1840, 17.
Amazilia fuscicaudata Ridgw. Pr. U. S. Nat. Mus. I. Oct. 2, 1878, 147.

[B —, C —, R 345, C 419.]

Hab. Lower Rio Grande Valley in Texas, south through Eastern Mexico to Central America and Northern South America.

439. **Amazilia cerviniventris** Gould.
 Buff-bellied Hummingbird.

Amazilius cerviniventris Gould, P. Z. S. 1856, 150.

[B —, C —, R 346, C 420.]

Hab. Valley of the Lower Rio Grande south into Eastern Mexico.

Genus **BASILINNA** Boie.

Basilinna Boie, Isis, 1831, 546. Type, *Trochilus leucotis* Vieill.

440. **Basilinna xantusi** (Lawr.).
 Xantus's Hummingbird.

Amazilia xantusi Lawr. Ann. Lyc. N. Y. 1860, 109.
Basilinna xanthusi Elliot, Class. & Synop. Troch. March, 1879, 227.

[B —, C 273, R 347, C 407.]

Hab. Lower California.

Genus **IACHE** Elliot.

Iache Elliot, Class. & Synop. Troch. March, 1879, 234. Type, *Cynanthus latirostris* Swains.

441. **Iache latirostris** (Swains.).
 Broad-billed Hummingbird.

Cynanthus latirostris Swains. Phil. Mag. 1827, 441.
Iache latirostris Elliot, Class. & Synop. Troch. March, 1879, 235.

[B —, C —, R 348, C 421.]

Hab. Southern Arizona and Western Mexico.

Order PASSERES. Perching Birds.

Suborder CLAMATORES. Songless Perching Birds.

Family TYRANNIDÆ. Tyrant Flycatchers.

Genus **MILVULUS** Swainson.

Milvulus Swainson, Zool. Journ. III. July, 1827, 165. Type, *Tyrannus savanna* Vieill. = *Muscicapa tyrannus* Linn.

[442.] **Milvulus tyrannus** (Linn.).
Fork-tailed Flycatcher.

Muscicapa tyrannus Linn. S. N. ed. 12, I. 1766, 325.
Milvulus tyrannus Bonap. Geogr. & Comp. List, 1838, 25.

[B 122, C 240, R 302, C 366.]

Hab. Mexico and southward throughout Central and most of South America. Accidental in the United States (Mississippi, Kentucky, New Jersey).

443. **Milvulus forficatus** (Gmel.).
Scissor-tailed Flycatcher.

Muscicapa forficata Gmel. S. N. I. i. 1788, 931.
Milvulus forficatus Swains. Classif. B. II. 1827, 225.

[B 123, C 241, R 301, C 367.]

Hab. Texas and Indian Territory, casually north to Kansas and Missouri; south to Central America. Accidental in Virginia, New Jersey, New England, Manitoba, and at York Factory, Hudson's Bay.

Genus **TYRANNUS** Cuvier.

Tyrannus Cuvier, Leç. d'An. Comp. I. 1799, tabl. ii. (*Cf.* Tabl. Elem. 1797, p. 201.) Type, *Lanius tyrannus* Linn.

444. Tyrannus tyrannus (LINN.).
Kingbird.

Lanius tyrannus LINN. S. N. ed. 10, I. 1758, 94.
Tyrannus tyrannus JORDAN, Man. Vert. ed. 4, 1884, 96.

[B 124, C 242, R 304, C 368.]

HAB. Eastern North America, from the British Provinces south to Central and South America. Rare west of the Rocky Mountains (Utah, Nevada, Washington Territory, etc.).

445. Tyrannus dominicensis (GMEL.).
Gray Kingbird.

Lanius tyrannus β. *dominicensis* GMEL. S. N. I. 1788, 302.
Tyrannus dominicensis RICHARDSON, Rep. Sixth Meet. Brit. Ass. V. 1837, 170.

[B 125, C 243, R 303, C 369.]

HAB. South Atlantic States (South Carolina, Georgia, Florida), West Indies, Atlantic coast of Central America, and Northern South America. Accidental in Massachusetts.

446. Tyrannus melancholicus couchii (BAIRD).
Couch's Kingbird.

Tyrannus couchii BAIRD, B. N. Am. 1858, 175.
Tyrannus melancholicus var. *couchii* COUES, Checkl. ed. 1, Dec. 1873, 51.

[B 128, 129, C 246, R 305, C 372.]

HAB. Southern border of the United States (Texas, Arizona), south to Guatemala.

447. Tyrannus verticalis SAY.
Arkansas Kingbird.

Tyrannus verticalis SAY, LONG'S Exp. II. 1823, 60.

[B 126, C 244, R 306, C 370.]

HAB. Western United States, from the Plains to the Pacific, south to Guatemala. Accidental in Maryland, New Jersey, New York, and Maine.

448. Tyrannus vociferans SWAINS.
Cassin's Kingbird.

Tyrannus vociferans SWAINS. Quart. Jour. Sci. XX. 1826, 273.

[B 127, C 245, R 307, C 371.]

HAB. Western United States, from the western border of the Plains to Southern California, south to Guatemala.

GENUS **PITANGUS** SWAINSON.

Pitangus SWAINSON, Zool. Journ. III. July, 1827, 165. Type, *Tyrannus sulphuratus* VIEILL.

449. Pitangus derbianus (KAUP).
Derby Flycatcher.

Saurophagus derbianus KAUP, P. Z. S. 1851, 44, pl. xxxvi.
Pitangus derbianus SCLATER, P. Z. S. 1856, 297.

[B —, C —, R 308, C 364.]

HAB. Valley of the Lower Rio Grande in Texas, south to Northern South America.

GENUS **MYIOZETETES** SCLATER.

Myiozetetes SCL. P. Z. S. 1859, 46. Type, *Muscicapa cayennensis* LINN.

[450.] Myiozetetes texensis (GIRAUD).
Giraud's Flycatcher.

Muscicapa texensis GIRAUD, Sixteen Texas B. 1841, pl. 1.
Myiozetetes texensis SCL. P. Z. S. 1859, 56.

[B —, C —, R 309, C —.]

HAB. "Texas" (GIRAUD), south to Central America and Northern South America.

GENUS **MYIODYNASTES** BONAPARTE.

Myiodynastes BONAP. Bull. Soc. Linn. Normandée, II. 1857, 35. Type, *Muscicapa audax* GMEL.

451. **Myiodynastes luteiventris** SCL.
   Sulphur-bellied Flycatcher.

   Myiodynastes luteiventris SCL. P. Z. S. 1859, 42 (ex BONAP. Compte Rend. XXXVIII. 1854, 657, nomen nudum).

   [B —, C —, R 310, C 365.]

   HAB. Southern Arizona, south to Costa Rica.

   GENUS **MYIARCHUS** CABANIS.

   Myiarchus CAB. Faun. Per. Aves, 1844-46, 152. Type, *Muscicapa ferox* GMEL.

452. **Myiarchus crinitus** (LINN.).
   Crested Flycatcher.

   Muscicapa crinita LINN. S. N. ed. 12, I. 1766, 325.
   Myiarchus crinitus LICHT. Nomencl. Mus. Berol. 1854, 16.

   [B. 130, C 247, R 312, C 373.]

   HAB. Eastern United States and Southern Canada, west to the Plains, south through Eastern Mexico to Costa Rica.

453. **Myiarchus mexicanus** (KAUP).
   Mexican Crested Flycatcher.

   Tyr[annula] mexicana KAUP, P. Z. S. 1851, 51.
   Myiarchus mexicanus LAWR. Ann. Lyc. N. Y. IX. May, 1869, 202.

   [B 132, C —, R 311, C 374.]

   HAB. Valley of the Lower Rio Grande in Texas, southward to Guatemala.

453 a. **Myiarchus mexicanus magister** RIDGW.
   Arizona Crested Flycatcher.

   Myiarchus mexicanus magister RIDGW. Pr. Biol. Soc. Wash. II. April 10, 1884, 90.

   [B —, C —, R —, C —.]

   HAB. Southern Arizona, south into Western Mexico.

454. Myiarchus cinerascens LAWR.
Ash-throated Flycatcher.

Tyrannula cinerascens LAWR. Ann. Lyc. N. Y. V. 1851, 121.
M[yiarchus] cinerascens LAWR. Ann. Lyc. N. Y. VII. May, 1860, 285.

[B 131, C 248, R 313, C 375.]

HAB. Western United States, north to Oregon, Nevada, Utah, and Colorado, south to Guatemala.

[455.] Myiarchus lawrenceii (GIR.).
Lawrence's Flycatcher.

Muscicapa lawrenceii GIRAUD, Sixteen Sp. Texas B. 1841, 9 (by actual counting, the text not being paged).
Myiarchus lawrencii BAIRD, B. N. Am. 1858, 181.

[B 133, C 248, R 314, C 376.]

HAB. "Texas" (GIRAUD) and Eastern Mexico.

455a. Myiarchus lawrencei olivascens RIDGW.
Olivaceous Flycatcher.

Myiarchus lawrencei olivascens RIDGW. Pr. Biol. Soc. Wash. II. April 10, 1884, 91.

[B —, C —, R —, C —.]

HAB. Arizona and Western Mexico.

GENUS **SAYORNIS** BONAPARTE.

Sayornis BONAP. Coll. Delattre, 1854, 87. Type, *Tyrannula nigricans* SWAINS.

456. Sayornis phœbe (LATH.).
Phœbe.

Muscicapa phœbe LATHAM, Ind. Orn. II. 1790, 489.
Sayornis phœbe STEJN. Auk, II. Jan. 1885, 51.

[B 135, C 252, R 315, C 379.]

HAB. Eastern North America, from the British Provinces south to Eastern Mexico and Cuba, wintering from the South Atlantic and Gulf States southward.

457. **Sayornis saya** (BONAP.).
    Say's Phœbe.

Muscicapa saya BONAP. Am. Orn. I. 1825, 20.
Sayornis sayus BAIRD, B. N. Am. 1858, 185.

[B 136, C 250, R 316, C 377.]

HAB. Western United States, from the Plains to the Pacific, south into Mexico.

458. **Sayornis nigricans** (SWAINS.).
    Black Phœbe.

Tyrannula nigricans SWAINS. Philos. Mag. I. May, 1827, 367.
Sayornis nigricans BONAP. Coll. Delattre, 1854, 87.

[B 134, C 251, R 317, C 378.]

HAB. Southwestern United States, from Texas through Southern New Mexico and Arizona to California, and northward along the coast to Oregon; south to Southern Mexico.

GENUS **CONTOPUS** CABANIS.

Contopus CAB. J. f. O. III. Nov. 1855, 479. Type, *Muscicapa virens* LINN.

459. **Contopus borealis** (SWAINS.).
    Olive-sided Flycatcher.

Tyrannus borealis SWAINS. F. B. A. II. 1831, 141, pl. 35.
Contopus borealis BAIRD, B. N. Am. 1858, 188.

[B 137, C 253, R 318, C 380.]

HAB. North America, breeding from the northern and the higher mountainous parts of the United States northward. In winter, south to Central America and Colombia.

460. **Contopus pertinax** CAB.
    Coues's Flycatcher.

Myiarchus pertinax LICHT. Nomen. Mus. Berol. 1854, 16 (nomen nudum).
Contopus pertinax CAB. Mus. Hein. II. Sept. 30, 1859, 72.

[B —, C 254, R 319, C 381.]

HAB. Southern Arizona, Mexico, and Guatemala.

461. Contopus virens (LINN.).
Wood Pewee.

Muscicapa virens LINN. S. N. ed. 12, I. 1766, 327.
Contopus virens CAB. J. f. O. III. Nov. 1855, 479.

[B 139, C 255, R 320, C 382.]

HAB. Eastern North America to the Plains, and from Southern Canada southward.

462. Contopus richardsonii (SWAINS.).
Western Wood Pewee.

Tyrannula richardsonii SWAINS. F. B. 'A. II. 1831, 146, pl. 46, lower fig.
Contopus richardsonii BAIRD, B. N. Am. 1858, 189.

[B 138, C 255 a, R 321, C 383.]

HAB. Western United States, from the Plains to the Pacific, south through Central America to Colombia.

GENUS **EMPIDONAX** CABANIS.

Empidonax CAB. J. f. O. 1855, 480. Type, *Tyrannula pusilla* SWAINS.

463. Empidonax flaviventris BAIRD.
Yellow-bellied Flycatcher.

Tyrannula flaviventris BAIRD (W. M. & S. F.), Pr. Ac. Nat. Sci. Phila. July, 1843, 283.
Empidonax flaviventris BAIRD, B. N. Am. 1858, 198.

[B 144, C 259, R 322, C 388.]

HAB. Eastern North America to the Plains, and from Southern Labrador south through Eastern Mexico to Panama, breeding from the Northern States northward.

464. Empidonax difficilis BAIRD.
Baird's Flycatcher.

Empidonax difficilis BAIRD, B. N. Am. 1858, 198 (in text).

[B 144 *a*, C 259, *part*, R 323, C 389.]

HAB. Western United States, from the Plains to the Pacific, south through Western Mexico to Costa Rica.

465. **Empidonax acadicus** (GMEL.).
   Acadian Flycatcher.

Muscicapa acadica GMEL. S. N. I. ii. 1788, 947.
Empidonax acadicus BAIRD, B. N. Am. 1858, 197.

[B 143, C 256, R 324, C 384.]

HAB. Eastern United States, chiefly southward, west to the Plains, south to Cuba and Costa Rica.

466. **Empidonax pusillus** (SWAINS.).
   Little Flycatcher.

Platyrhynchus pusillus SWAINS. Phil. Mag. I. May, 1827, 366.
Empidonax pusillus CABANIS, J. f. O. 1855, 480.

[B 141, C 257 *a*, R 325, C 386.]

HAB. Western North America, from the western border of the Plains to the Pacific, and from the Fur Countries south into Mexico.

466 *a*. **Empidonax pusillus traillii** (AUD.).
   Traill's Flycatcher.

Muscicapa traillii AUD. Orn. Biog. I. 1832, 236.
Empidonax pusillus var. *traillii* B. B. & R. Hist. N. Am. B. II. 1874, 369.

[B 140, C 257, R 325 *a*, C 385.]

HAB. Eastern North America, breeding from the Middle States (Southern Illinois and Missouri) northward; in winter south to Central America.

467. **Empidonax minimus** BAIRD.
   Least Flycatcher.

Tyrannula minima BAIRD (W. M. & S. F.), Pr. Ac. Nat. Sci. Phila. July, 1843, 284.
Empidonax minimus BAIRD, B. N. Am. 1858, 195.

[B 142, C 258, R 326, C 387.]

HAB. Eastern North America, south in winter to Central America. Breeds from the Northern States northward.

468. Empidonax hammondi (XANTUS).
Hammond's Flycatcher.

Tyrannula hammondi XANTUS, Pr. Ac. Nat. Sci. Phila. May, 1858, 117.
Empidonax hammondi BAIRD, B. N. Am. 1858, 199.

[B 145, C 260, R 327, C 390.]

HAB. Western North America, from the western border of the Plains westward, north to the Lesser Slave Lake, and south to Southern Mexico.

469. Empidonax obscurus (SWAINS.).
Wright's Flycatcher.

Tyrannula obscura SWAINS. Phil. Mag. I. May, 1827, 367.
Empidonax obscurus BAIRD, B. N. Am. 1858, 200.

[B 146, C 261, R 328, C 391.]

HAB. Western United States, north to Oregon and Montana, and south to Southern Mexico.

[470.] Empidonax fulvifrons (GIRAUD).
Fulvous Flycatcher.

Muscicapa fulvifrons GIRAUD, Sixteen Tex. B. 1841, pl. ii.
Empidonax fulvifrons SCL. P. Z. S. 1858, 301.

[B —, C —, R 329, C —.]

HAB. "Texas" (GIRAUD), and probably Northeastern Mexico.

470 a. Empidonax fulvifrons pygmæus (COUES).
Buff-breasted Flycatcher.

Empidonax pygmæus COUES, Ibis, 1865, 537.
Empidonax fulvifrons pygmæus RIDGW. Pr. U. S. Nat. Mus. VIII. 1885, 356.

[B —, C 262, R 329 a, C 392.]

HAB. Western New Mexico and Southern Arizona, south probably into Western Mexico.

GENUS **PYROCEPHALUS** GOULD.

Pyrocephalus GOULD, Zool. Voy. Beag. 1841, 44. Types, "*Pyrocephalus parvirostris* (GOULD), and *Muscicapa coronata* (AUCT.)."

471. **Pyrocephalus rubineus mexicanus** (SCL.).
Vermilion Flycatcher.

Pyrocephalus mexicanus SCL. P. Z. S. 1859, 45.
Pyrocephalus rubineus var. *mexicanus* COUES, Key, 1872, 177.

[B 147, C 263, R 330, C 394.]

HAB. Southern Arizona and valley of the Lower Rio Grande in Texas, south to Guatemala.

GENUS **ORNITHION** HARTLAUB.

Ornithion HARTLAUB, J. f. O. 1853, 35. Type, *O. inerme* HARTL.

472. **Ornithion imberbe** (SCL.).
Beardless Flycatcher.

Camptostoma imberbe SCL. P. Z. S. 1857, 203.
Ornithion imberbe LAWR. Ibis, 1876, 497.

[B —, C —, R 331, C 393.]

HAB. Valley of the Lower Rio Grande in Texas, south into Eastern Mexico.

472 a. **Ornithion imberbe ridgwayi** BREWST.
Ridgway's Flycatcher.

Ornithium imberbe ridgwayi BREWST. Bull. Nutt. Orn. Cl. VII. Oct. 1882, 208.

[B —, C —, R —, C —.]

HAB. Southern Arizona and Western Mexico.

Suborder OSCINES. Song Birds.

Family ALAUDIDÆ. Larks.

Genus ALAUDA Linnæus.

Alauda Linn. S. N. ed. 10, I. 1758, 165. Type, by elimination, *A. arvensis* Linn.

[473.] **Alauda arvensis** Linn.
Skylark.

Alauda arvensis Linn. S. N. ed. 10, I. 1758, 165.

[B —, C 55 *bis*, R 299, C 88.]

Hab. Europe and Asia. Accidental in Greenland and the Bermudas.

Genus OTOCORIS Bonaparte.

Otocoris Bonap. Faun. Ital. Ucc. Introd. 1839. Type, *Alauda alpestris* Linn.

474. **Otocoris alpestris** (Linn.).
Horned Lark.

Alauda alpestris Linn. S. N. ed. 10, 1758, 166.
Otocoris alpestris Bonap. Fauna Ital. Uccelli, Introd. 1839 (not paged).

[B 302, C 53, R 300, C 82.]

Hab. Northeastern North America, Greenland, and northern parts of the Old World; in winter south in the Eastern United States to the Carolinas, Illinois, etc.

474 *a*. **Otocoris alpestris leucolæma** (Coues).
Pallid Horned Lark.

Eremophila alpestris b. *leucolæma* Coues, B. N. W. 1875, 38 (part).
Otocoris alpestris leucolæma Stejn. Pr. U. S. Nat. Mus. V. June 5, 1882, 34.

[B —, C 53 *b*, R 300 *a*, C 83.]

HAB. Interior of British America, and Alaska, south in winter into Western United States.

474 *b*. Otocoris alpestris praticola HENSH.
Prairie Horned Lark.

O[*tocorys*] *alpestris praticola* HENSH. Auk, I. July, 1884, 264.

[B —, C —, R —, C —.]

HAB. Upper Mississippi Valley and the region of the Great Lakes.

474 *c*. Otocoris alpestris arenicola HENSH.
Desert Horned Lark.

O[*tocorys*] *alpestris arenicola* HENSH. Auk, I. July, 1884, 265.

[B —, C —, R —, C —.]

HAB. Rocky Mountain region and Great Basin of the United States.

474 *d*. Otocoris alpestris giraudi HENSH.
Texan Horned Lark.

Otocorys alpestris giraudi HENSH. Auk, I. July, 1884, 266.

[B —, C —, R —, C —.]

HAB. Eastern and Southeastern Texas.

474 *e*. Otocoris alpestris chrysolæma (WAGL.).
Mexican Horned Lark.

Alauda chrysolæma WAGL. Isis, 1831, 530.
Otocoris alpestris chrysolæma STEJN. Pr. U. S. Nat. Mus. V. June 5, 1882, 34.

[B —, C 53 *a*, R 300 *b*, C 84.]

HAB. Southern Arizona and Southern New Mexico, south into Mexico.

474 f. Otocoris alpestris rubea HENSH.
Ruddy Horned Lark.

O[*tocorys*] *alpestris rubeus* HENSH. Auk, I. July, 1884, 267.

[B —, C —, R —, C —.]

HAB. California.

474 g. Otocoris alpestris strigata HENSH.
Streaked Horned Lark.

O[*tocorys*] *alpestris strigata* HENSH. Auk, I. July, 1884, 267.

[B —, C —, R —, C —.]

HAB. Coast region of Washington Territory, Oregon, and British Columbia.

FAMILY **CORVIDÆ**. CROWS, JAYS, MAGPIES, ETC.

SUBFAMILY **GARRULINÆ**. MAGPIES AND JAYS.

GENUS **PICA** BRISSON.

Pica BRISS. Orn. II. 1760, 35. Type, *Corvus pica* LINN.

475. Pica pica hudsonica (SAB.).
American Magpie.

Corvus hudsonicus SAB. App. Frankl. Journ. 1823, 25, 671.
Pica pica hudsonica JORDAN, Man. Vert. ed. 4, 1884, 94.

[B 432, C 233, R 286, C 347.]

HAB. Northern and Western North America, casually east and south to Michigan (accidental in Northern Illinois in winter) and the Plains, and in the Rocky Mountains to New Mexico and Arizona, mainly replaced in California by the next species.

476. Pica nuttalli AUD.
Yellow-billed Magpie.

Pica nuttalli AUD. Orn. Biog. IV. 1838, 450, pl. 362.

[B 433, C 233 a, R 287, C 348.]

HAB. California.

GENUS **CYANOCITTA** STRICKLAND.

Cyanocitta STRICKL. Ann. Nat. Hist. XV. 1845, 261. Type, *Corvus cristatus* LINN.

477. Cyanocitta cristata (LINN.).
Blue Jay.

Corvus cristatus LINN. S. N. ed. 10, I. 1758, 106.
Cyanocitta cristata STRICKL. Ann. Nat. Hist. XV. 1845, 261.

[B 434, C 234, R 289, C 349.]

HAB. Eastern North America to the Plains, and from the Fur Countries south to Florida and Eastern Texas.

477 a. Cyanocitta cristata florincola COUES.
Florida Blue Jay.

Cyanocitta cristata florincola COUES, Key, ed. 2, 1884, 421.

[B —, C —, R —, C —.]

HAB. Florida.

478. Cyanocitta stelleri (GMEL.).
Steller's Jay.

Corvus stelleri GMEL. S. N. I. 1788, 370.
Cyanocitta stelleri STRICKL. Ann. N. Hist. XV. 1845, 261.

[B 435, C 235, R 290, C 350.]

HAB. Pacific coast of North America, from the Columbia River to Sitka, and northern Coast Range in California.

478 a. Cyanocitta stelleri frontalis (RIDGW.).
Blue-fronted Jay.

Cyanura stelleri var. *frontalis* RIDGW. Am. Journ. Sc. & Arts, 3d ser. V. Jan. 1873, 41.
Cyanocitta stelleri var. *frontalis* BOUCARD, Cat. Av. 1876, 279.

[B —, C 235 b, R 290 a, C 353.]

HAB. Sierra Nevada of California and Western Nevada, from Fort Crook to Fort Tejon.

478 b. Cyanocitta stelleri macrolopha (BAIRD).
Long-crested Jay.

Cyanocitta macrolopha BAIRD, Pr. Ac. Nat. Sci. Phila. Junè, 1854, 118.
Cyanocitta stelleri macrolopha COUES, Bull. Nutt. Orn. Cl. V. April, 1880, 98.

[B 436, C 235 a, R 290 b, 290 c, C 352.]

HAB. Central Rocky Mountains, from British America to New Mexico and Southern Arizona.

GENUS **APHELOCOMA** CABANIS.

Aphelocoma CABANIS, Mus. Hein. I. Oct. 15, 1851, 221. Type, *Garrulus californicus* VIG.

479. Aphelocoma floridana (BARTR.).
Florida Jay.

Corvus floridanus BARTR. Trav. Carol. 1791, 291.
Aphelocoma floridana CAB. Mus. Hein. I. 1851, 221.

[B 439, C 236, R 291, C 354.]

HAB. Florida.

480. Aphelocoma woodhousei (BAIRD).
Woodhouse's Jay.

Cyanocitta woodhousei BAIRD, B. N. Am. 1858, pl. 59.
Aphelocoma woodhousii RIDGW. Field and Forest, June, 1877, 208.

[B 438, C 236 a, R 292, C 355.]

HAB. Middle Province of the United States, north to Eastern Oregon, Idaho, Montana, and Wyoming, east to Colorado and New Mexico, west to Nevada and Arizona.

481. Aphelocoma californica (VIG.).
California Jay.

Garrulus californicus VIG. Zool. Beech. Voy. 1839, 21, pl. v.
A[phelocoma] californica CAB. Mus. Hein. I. Oct. 15, 1851, 221.

[B 437, C 236 *b*, R 293, C 356.]

HAB. Pacific coast region, including both slopes of the Sierra Nevada, from the Columbia River to Cape St. Lucas.

482. **Aphelocoma sieberii arizonæ** RIDGW.
Arizona Jay.

Cyanocitta ultramarina var. *arizonæ* RIDGW. Bull. Essex Inst. V. Dec. 1873, 199.
Aphelocoma sieberii arizonæ RIDGW. Pr. U. S. Nat. Mus. VIII. 1885, 355.

[B 440, C 237, R 295, C 357.]

HAB. Southern New Mexico and Arizona.

GENUS **XANTHOURA** BONAPARTE.

Xanthoura BONAP. Consp. Av. I. May 6, 1850, 380. Type, *Corvus yncas* BODD.

483. **Xanthoura luxuosa** (LESS.).
Green Jay.

Garrulus luxuosus LESS. Rev. Zool. 1839, 100.
Xanthoura luxuosa BONAP. Consp. Av. I. 1850, 380.

[B 442, C 238, R 296, C 358.]

HAB. Valley of the Lower Rio Grande in Texas, and southward into Eastern Mexico.

GENUS **PERISOREUS** BONAPARTE.

Perisoreus BONAP. Saggio, 1831, 43. Type, *Corvus infaustus* LINN.

484. **Perisoreus canadensis** (LINN.).
Canada Jay.

Corvus canadensis LINN. S. N. ed. 12, I. 1766, 158.
Perisoreus canadensis BONAP. Geog. & Comp. List, 1838, 27.

[B 443, C 239, R 297, C 359.]

HAB. Northern New England, Michigan, and Canada, northward to Arctic America.

484 a. Perisoreus canadensis capitalis BAIRD.
Rocky Mountain Jay.

Perisoreus canadensis var. *capitalis* "BAIRD MS." RIDGW. Bull. Essex Inst. V. Nov. 1873, 193.

[B —, C 239 b, R 297 a, C 362.]

HAB. Rocky Mountain region of the United States, south to New Mexico and Arizona.

484 b. Perisoreus canadensis fumifrons RIDGW.
Alaskan Jay.

Perisoreus canadensis fumifrons RIDGW. Pr. U. S. Nat. Mus. III. March 27, 1880, 5.

[B —, C —, R 297 b, C 360.]

HAB. Alaska.

484 c. Perisoreus canadensis nigricapillus RIDGW.
Labrador Jay.

Perisoreus canadensis nigricapillus RIDGW. Pr. U. S. Nat. Mus. V. June 5, 1882, 15.

[B —, C —, R —, C —.]

HAB. Coast district of Labrador, north to Ungava Bay.

485. **Perisoreus obscurus** (RIDGW.).
Oregon Jay.

Perisoreus canadensis var. *obscurus* RIDGW. Bull. Essex Inst. Nov. 1873, 194.
Perisoreus obscurus SHARPE, Brit. Mus. Cat. B. III. 1877, 105.

[B —, C 239 a, R 298, C 361.]

HAB. Northwest Coast, from the Sierra Nevada, in California, to British Columbia.

SUBFAMILY **CORVINÆ**. CROWS.

GENUS **CORVUS** LINNÆUS.

Corvus LINN. S. N. ed. 10, I. 1758, 105. Type, by elimination, *C. corax* LINN.

486. **Corvus corax sinuatus** (WAGL.).
American Raven.

Corvus sinuatus WAGLER, Isis, 1829, 748.
Corvus corax sinuatus RIDGW. Pr. U. S. Nat. Mus. VIII. 1885, 355.

[B 423, 424, C 226, R 280, C 338.]

HAB. Continent of North America, from the Arctic regions to Guatemala, but local and not common in the United States east of the Mississippi River.

487. **Corvus cryptoleucus** COUCH.
White-necked Raven.

Corvus cryptoleucus COUCH, Pr. Ac. Nat. Sci. Phila. April, 1854, 66.

[B 425, C 227, R 281, C 339.]

HAB. Southern border of the United States, from Texas to Southern California, north to Colorado, and south into Mexico.

488. **Corvus americanus** AUD.
American Crow.

Corvus americanus AUD. Orn. Biog. II. 1834, 317.

[B 426, C 228, R 282, C 340.]

HAB. North America, from the Fur Countries to Mexico.

488 *a*. **Corvus americanus floridanus** BAIRD.
Florida Crow.

Corvus americanus var. *floridanus* BAIRD, B. N. Am. 1858, 568.

[B 427, C 228 *a*, R 282 *a*, C 341.]

HAB. Florida.

489. Corvus caurinus BAIRD.
Northwest Crow.

Corvus caurinus BAIRD, B. N. Am. 1858, 569.

[B 428, C 228 *b*, R 282 *b*, C 342.]

HAB. Northwest coast, from California to Sitka.

490. Corvus ossifragus WILS.
Fish Crow.

Corvus ossifragus WILS. Am. Orn. V. 1812, 27, pl. 37, fig. 2.

[B 429, C 229, R 283, C 343.]

HAB. Atlantic coast, from Long Island to Florida.

GENUS **PICICORVUS** BONAPARTE.

Picicorvus BONAP. Consp. Av. I. 1850, 384. Type, *Corvus columbianus* WILS.

491. Picicorvus columbianus (WILS.).
Clarke's Nutcracker.

Corvus columbianus WILS. Am. Orn. III. 1811, 29, pl. 20, fig. 3.
Picicorvus columbianus BONAP. Consp. Av. I. 1850, 384.

[B 430, C 230, R 284, C 344.]

HAB. Western North America, from Arizona to Sitka, and east to the Plains.

GENUS **CYANOCEPHALUS** BONAPARTE.

Cyanocephalus BONAP. Oss. Stat. Zool. Eur. Vertebr. 1842, 17. Type, *Gymnorhinus cyanocephalus* WIED.

492. Cyanocephalus cyanocephalus (WIED).
Piñon Jay.

Gymnorhinus cyanocephalus WIED, Reise N. Amer. II. 1841, 21.
Cyanocephalus cyanocephalus STEJN. Auk. I. 1884, 230.

[B 431, C 231, R 285, C 345.]

HAB. Rocky Mountain region, westward to the Cascade range and Sierra Nevada, and from Mexico north into British America.

FAMILY **STURNIDÆ**. STARLINGS.

GENUS **STURNUS** LINNÆUS.

Sturnus LINN. S. N. ed. 10, I. 1758, 167. Type, by elimination, *S. vulgaris* LINN.

[493.] **Sturnus vulgaris** LINN.
Starling.

Sturnus vulgaris LINN. S. N. ed. 10, I. 1758, 167.

[B —, C —, R 279, C 363.]

HAB. Europe and Northern Asia; accidental in Greenland.

FAMILY **ICTERIDÆ**. BLACKBIRDS, ORIOLES, ETC.

GENUS **DOLICHONYX** SWAINSON.

Dolichonyx SWAINS. Phil. Mag. I. June, 1827, 435. Type, *Fringilla oryzivora* LINN.

494. **Dolichonyx oryzivorus** (LINN.).
Bobolink.

Fringilla oryzivora LINN. S. N. ed. 10, I. 1758, 179.
Dolichonyx oryzivorus SWAINS. Zool. Jour. III. 1827, 351.

[B 399, C 210, R 257, C 312.]

HAB. Eastern North America to the Great Plains; north to Southern Canada; south, in winter, to the West Indies and South America. Breeds from the Middle States northward, and winters south of the United States.

494 *a*. Dolichonyx oryzivorus albinucha RIDGW.
Western Bobolink.

Dolichonyx oryzivorus var. *albinucha* RIDGW. Bull. Essex Inst. V. Nov. 1873, 191.

[B —, C —, R —, C —.]

HAB. Dakota, westward to Utah and Nevada, north to Manitoba.

GENUS **MOLOTHRUS** SWAINSON.

Molothrus SWAINS. F. B. A. II. 1831, 277. Type, *Fringilla pecoris* GMEL. = *Oriolus ater* BODD.

495. Molothrus ater (BODD.).
    Cowbird.

Oriolus ater BODD. Tabl. Pl. Enlum. 1783, 37.
Molothrus ater GRAY, Handl. B. II. 1870, 36.

[B 400, C 211, R 258, C 313.]

HAB. United States, from the Atlantic to the Pacific, north into Southern British America, south, in winter, into Mexico.

495 a. Molothrus ater obscurus (GMEL.).
    Dwarf Cowbird.

Sturnus obscurus GMEL. S. N. I. ii. 1788, 804.
M[olothrus] ater var. *obscurus* COUES, B. N. W. 1874, 180, in text.

[B —, C 211 a, R 258 a, C 314.]

HAB. Southern United States, from Texas to Arizona and Lower California, south into Mexico.

496. Molothrus æneus (WAGL.).
    Bronzed Cowbird.

Psarocolius æneus WAGL. Isis, 1829, 758.
Molothrus æneus CAB. Mus. Hein. I. 1851, 192.

[B —, C —, R 259, C 315.]

HAB. Valley of the Lower Rio Grande in Texas, and southward.

GENUS **XANTHOCEPHALUS** BONAPARTE.

Xanthocephalus BONAP. Consp. Av. I. 1850, 431. Type, *Icterus icterocephalus* BONAP. = *I. xanthocephalus* BONAP.

497. **Xanthocephalus xanthocephalus** (BONAP.).
   Yellow-headed Blackbird.

Icterus xanthocephalus BONAP. Journ. Ac. Nat. Sci. Phila. V. 1826, 223.
Xanthocephalus xanthocephalus JORDAN, Man. Vert. ed. 4, 1884, 92.

[B 404, C 213, R 260, C 319.]

HAB. Western North America, from Wisconsin, Illinois, and Texas to the Pacific coast. Accidental in the Atlantic States (Massachusetts, South Carolina, Florida).

GENUS **AGELAIUS** VIEILLOT.

Agelaius VIEILL. Analyse, 1816, 33. Type, *Oriolus phœniceus* LINN.

498. **Agelaius phœniceus** (LINN.).
   Red-winged Blackbird.

Oriolus phœniceus LINN. S. N. ed. 12, I. 1766, 161.
Agelaius phœniceus SWAINS. F. B. A. II. 1831, 280.

[B 401, C 212, R 261, C 316.]

HAB. North America in general, from Great Slave Lake south to Costa Rica.

499. **Agelaius gubernator** (WAGL.).
   Bicolored Blackbird.

Psarocolius gubernator WAGL. Isis, IV. 1832, 281.
Agelaius gubernator BONAP. Geog. & Comp. List, 1838, 29.

[B 402, C 212 *a*, R 261 *a*, C 317.]

HAB. Pacific Province of the United States, south into Western Mexico.

500. **Agelaius tricolor** (NUTT.).
   Tricolored Blackbird.

Icterus tricolor "NUTT." AUD. Orn. Biog. V. 1839, pl. 388, fig. 1.
Agelaius tricolor BONAP. Geog. & Comp. List, 1838, 29.

[B 403, C 212 *b*, R 262, C 318.]

Genus STURNELLA Vieillot.

Sturnella Vieill.. Analyse, 1816, 34. Type, *Alauda magna* Linn.

501. Sturnella magna (Linn.).
   Meadowlark.

Alauda magna Linn. S. N. ed. 10, I. 1758, 167.
Sturnella magna Swains. Phil. Mag. I. 1827, 436.

[B 406, C 214, R 263, C 320.]

Hab. Eastern United States and Southern Canada to the Plains.

501 a. Sturnella magna mexicana (Scl.).
   Mexican Meadowlark.

Sturnella mexicana Scl. Ibis, 1861, 179.
Sturnella magna var. *mexicana* B. B. & R. Hist. N. Am. B. II. 1874, 172.

[B —, C —, R 263 a, C 321.]

Hab. Valley of the Lower Rio Grande, and Arizona, southward.

501 b. Sturnella magna neglecta (Aud.).
   Western Meadowlark.

Sturnella neglecta Aud. B. Am. VII. 1843, 339, pl. 487.
Sturnella magna var. *neglecta* Allen, Bull. M. C. Z. III. No. 2, July, 1872, 178.

[B 407, C 214 a, R 264, C 322.]

Hab. Western United States, from Wisconsin, Illinois, Iowa, Texas, etc., west to the Pacific coast.

Genus ICTERUS Brisson.

Subgenus ICTERUS.

Icterus Briss. Orn. II. 1760, 85. Type, by elimination, *Oriolus icterus* Linn.

ORDER PASSERES.

[502.] **Icterus icterus** (LINN.).
   Troupial.

   Oriolus icterus LINN. S. N. ed. 12, I. 1766, 161.
   Icterus icterus RIDGW. Pr. U. S. Nat. Mus. VIII. 1885, 355.

   [B 408, C —, R 265, C 323.]

HAB. West Indies (introduced) and Northern South America. Accidental at Charleston, S. C. (AUDUBON).

503. **Icterus audubonii** GIRAUD.
   Audubon's Oriole.

   Icterus audubonii GIRAUD, Sixteen Texas B. 1841, 3.

   [B 409, C 220, R 266, C 330.]

HAB. Valley of the Lower Rio Grande in Texas, and southward.

504. **Icterus parisorum** BONAP.
   Scott's Oriole.

   Icterus parisorum BONAP. P. Z. S. 1837, 109.

   [B 411, C 219, R 268, C 329.]

HAB. Southern border of the United States, from Texas to Lower California, and southward.

SUBGENUS **PENDULINUS** VIEILLOT.

Pendulinus VIEILL. Analyse, 1816, 33. Type, *Oriolus spurius* LINN.

505. **Icterus cucullatus** SWAINS.
   Hooded Oriole.

   Icterus cucullatus SWAINS. Phil. Mag. I. 1827, 436.

   [B 413, C 218, R 269, C 328.]

' HAB. Valley of the Lower Rio Grande in Texas, and southward through Eastern and Southern Mexico.

505 *a*. **Icterus cucullatus nelsoni** RIDGW.
   Arizona Hooded Oriole.

   Icterus cucullatus nelsoni RIDGW. Pr. U. S. Nat. Mus. Vol. VIII. No. 2, April 20, 1885, 19.

[B —, C —, R —, C —.]

HAB. Southern Arizona, west to San Diego, and south to Mazatlan and Cape St. Lucas.

506. **Icterus spurius** (LINN.).
Orchard Oriole.

Oriolus spurius LINN. S. N. ed. 12, I. 1766, 162.
Icterus spurius BONAP. Journ. Ac. Nat. Sci. Phila. III. 1823, 363.

[B 414, C 215, R 270, C 324.]

HAB. United States, west to the Plains, south, in winter, to Panama.

SUBGENUS **YPHANTES** VIEILLOT.

Yphantes VIEILL. Analyse, 1816, 33. Type, *Coracias galbula* LINN.

507. **Icterus galbula** (LINN.).
Baltimore Oriole.

Coracias galbula LINN. S. N. ed. 10, 1758, 108.
Icterus galbula COUES, Bull. Nutt. Orn. Cl. V. 1880, 98.

[B 415, C 216, R 271, C 326.]

HAB. Eastern United States, west nearly to the Rocky Mountains.

508. **Icterus bullocki** (SWAINS.).
Bullock's Oriole.

Xanthornus bullocki SWAINS. Phil. Mag. I. 1827, 436.
Icterus bullocki BONAP. Geog. & Comp. List, 1838, 29.

[B 416, C 217, R 272, C 327.]

HAB. Western United States, from the eastern base of the Rocky Mountains west to the Pacific coast.

GENUS **SCOLECOPHAGUS** SWAINSON.

Scolecophagus SWAINS. F. B. A. II. 1831, 286. Type, *Oriolus ferrugineus* GMEL. = *Turdus carolinus* MÜLL.

509. Scolecophagus carolinus (MÜLL.).
   Rusty Blackbird.

   Turdus carolinus MÜLLER, Syst. Nat. Suppl. 1776, 140.
   Scolecophagus carolinus RIDGW. Pr. U. S. Nat. Mus. VIII. 1885, 356.

   [B 417, C 221, R 273, C 331.]

HAB. Eastern North America, west to Alaska and the Plains. Breeds from Northern New England northward.

510. Scolecophagus cyanocephalus (WAGL.).
   Brewer's Blackbird.

   Psarocolius cyanocephalus WAGL. Isis, 1829, 758.
   Scolecophagus cyanocephalus CAB. Mus. Hein. I. 1851, 193.

   [B 418, C 222, R 274, C 332.]

HAB. Western North America, from the Plains to the Pacific, and from the Saskatchewan region south to the highlands of Mexico.

GENUS **QUISCALUS** VIEILLOT.

SUBGENUS **QUISCALUS**.

Quiscalus VIEILL. Anal. 1816, 36. Type, *Gracula quiscula* LINN.

511. Quiscalus quiscula (LINN.).
   Purple Grackle.

   Gracula quiscula LINN. S. N. ed. 10, 1758, 109.
   Quiscalus quiscula JORDAN, Man. Vert. ed. 4, 1884, 93.

   [B 421, C 225, R 278, C 335.]

HAB. Atlantic States, from Florida to Long Island.

511 a. Quiscalus quiscula aglæus (BAIRD).
   Florida Grackle.

   Quiscalus aglæus BAIRD, Am. Jour. Sci. & Arts, 1866, 84.
   Quiscalus quiscula aglæus STEJN. Auk, II. Jan. 1885, 43, foot-note.

   [B 422, C —, R 278 a, C 336.]

HAB. Florida.

511 b. Quiscalus quiscula æneus (RIDGW.).
    Bronzed Grackle.

Quiscalus æneus RIDGW. Pr. Ac. Nat. Sci. Phila. June, 1869, 134.
Quiscalus quiscula æneus STEJN. Auk, II. Jan. 1885, 43, foot-note.

[B —, C 225 a, R 278 b, C 337.]

HAB. From the Alleghanies and New England north and west to Hudson's Bay and the Rocky Mountains.

SUBGENUS **MEGAQUISCALUS** CASSIN.

Megaquiscalus CASS. Pr. Ac. Nat. Sci. Phila. 1866, 409. Type, *Quiscalus major* VIEILL.

512. Quiscalus macrourus SWAINS.
    Great-tailed Grackle.

Quiscalus macrourus SWAINS. Anim. in Menag. 1838, 299.

[B 419, C 223, R 275, C 333.]

HAB. Eastern Texas, south to Central America.

513. Quiscalus major VIEILL.
    Boat-tailed Grackle.

Quiscalus major VIEILL. N. Dict. d'Hist. Nat. XXVIII. 1819, 487.

[B 420, C 224, R 277, C 334.] •

HAB. Coast region of the South Atlantic and Gulf States, from North Carolina to Texas.

FAMILY **FRINGILLIDÆ**. FINCHES, SPARROWS, ETC.

GENUS **COCCOTHRAUSTES.** BRISSON.

Coccothraustes BRISS. Orn. III. 1760, 218. Type, *Loxia coccothraustes* LINN.

SUBGENUS **HESPERIPHONA** BONAPARTE.

Hesperiphona BONAP. Compt. Rend. XXXI. Sept. 1850, 424. Type, *Fringilla vespertina* COOPER.

514. **Coccothraustes vespertina** (Coop.).
　　Evening Grosbeak.

　　Fringilla vespertina Coop. Ann. Lyc. N. Y. I. ii. 1825, 220.
　　Coccothraustes vespertina Sw. & Rich. F. B. A. II. 1831, 269, pl. 68.

[B 303, C 136, R 165, C 189.]

Hab. Western North America, east to Lake Superior, and casually to Ohio and Ontario; from the Fur Countries south into Mexico.

Genus **PINICOLA** Vieillot.

Pinicola Vieill. Ois. Am. Sept. I. 1807, p. iv. Type, *P. rubra* Vieill. = *Loxia enucleator* Linn.

515. **Pinicola enucleator** (Linn.).
　　Pine Grosbeak.

　　Loxia enucleator Linn. S. N. ed. 10, I. 1758, 171.
　　Pinicola enucleator Cab. Mus. Hein. I. 1851, 167

[B 304, C 137, R 166, C 190.]

Hab. Northern portions of the Northern Hemisphere, breeding far north; in winter south, in North America, irregularly to the Northern United States. South in the Rocky Mountains to Colorado, and in the Sierra Nevada to California.

Genus **PYRRHULA** Brisson.

Pyrrhula Briss. Orn. III. 1760, 308. Type, *Loxia pyrrhula* Linn.

[516.] **Pyrrhula cassini** (Baird).
　　Cassin's Bullfinch.

　　Pyrrhula coccinea var. *cassini* Baird, Trans. Chicago Ac. Sci. I. 1869, 316.
　　Pyrrhula cassini Tristram, Ibis, 1871, 231.

[B —, C 138, R 167, C 191.]

Hab. Alaska and Siberia. (Known as American only from a single specimen, taken at Nulato, Jan. 10, 1867.)

GENUS **CARPODACUS** KAUP.

Carpodacus KAUP, Ent. Eur. Thierw. 1829, 161. Type, *Loxia erythrina* PALL.

517. Carpodacus purpureus (GMEL.).
Purple Finch.

Fringilla purpurea GMEL. S. N. I. ii. 1788, 923.
Carpodacus purpureus GRAY, Gen. B. II. 1844, 384.

[B 305, C 139, R 168, C 194.]

HAB. Eastern North America, from the Atlantic coast to the Plains. Breeds from the Middle States northward.

517 a. Carpodacus purpureus californicus BAIRD.
California Purple Finch.

Carpodacus californicus BAIRD, B. N. Am. 1858, 413.
Carpodacus purpureus var. *californicus* B. B. & R. Hist. N. Am. B. I. 1874, 465.

[B 306, C —, R 168 a, C —.]

HAB. Pacific coast region, from British Columbia south to Southern California.

518. Carpodacus cassini BAIRD.
Cassin's Purple Finch.

Carpodacus cassini BAIRD, Pr. Ac. Nat. Sci. Phila. June, 1854, 119.

[B 307, C 140, R 169, C 195.]

HAB. Western United States, from the eastern base of the Rocky Mountains to the Pacific coast, and south over the plateau region of Mexico.

519. Carpodacus frontalis (SAY).
House Finch.

Fringilla frontalis SAY, LONG'S Exp. II. 1824, 40.
Carpodacus frontalis GRAY, Gen. B. II. 1844, 384.

[B 308, C 141, R 170, C 196.]

HAB. Middle Province of the United States.

519 *a*. Carpodacus frontalis rhodocolpus (Cab.).
    Crimson House Finch.

Carpodacus rhodocolpus Cab. Mus. Hein. I. 1851, 166.
Carpodacus frontalis var. *rhodocolpus* Ridgw. Am. Jour. Sci. & Arts, V. Jan. 1873, 39.

[B —, C 141 *a*, R 170 *a*, C 197.]

Hab. Pacific coast region, from Oregon to Cape St. Lucas.

520. Carpodacus amplus Ridgw.
    Guadalupe House Finch.

Carpodacus amplus Ridgw. Bull. U. S. Geol. & Geog. Surv. Terr. II. No. 2, April 1, 1876, 187.

[B —, C —, R 171, C —.]

Hab. Guadalupe Island, Lower California.

Genus **LOXIA** Linnæus.

Loxia Linn. S. N. ed. 10, I. 1758, 171. Type, by elimination, *Loxia curvirostra* Linn.

521. Loxia curvirostra minor (Brehm).
    American Crossbill.

Crucirostra minor Brehm. Naumannia. 1853, 193.
Loxia curvirostra minor Ridgw. Pr. U. S. Nat. Mus. VIII. 1885, 354.

[B 318, C 143, R 172, C 199.]

Hab. Northern North America, resident sparingly south in the Eastern United States to Maryland and Tennessee, and in the Alleghanies; irregularly abundant in winter; resident south in the Rocky Mountains to Colorado.

521 *a*. Loxia curvirostra stricklandi Ridgw.
    Mexican Crossbill.

Loxia curvirostra stricklandi Ridgw. Pr. U. S. Nat. Mus. VIII. 1885, 354.

[B 318 *a*, C 143 *a*, R 172 *a*, C 200.]

Hab. Colorado, Southern Arizona, and highlands of Mexico.

522. Loxia leucoptera GMEL.
   White-winged Crossbill.

Loxia leucoptera GMEL. S. N. I. ii. 1788, 540.

[B 319, C 142, R 173, C 198.]

HAB. Northern parts of North America, south into the United States in winter. Breeds from Northern New England northward.

GENUS **LEUCOSTICTE** SWAINSON.

Leucosticte SWAINS. F. B. A. II. 1831, 265.   Type, *Linaria tephrocotis* SWAINS.

523. Leucosticte griseonucha (BRANDT).
   Aleutian Leucosticte.

Fringilla (Linaria) griseonucha BRANDT, Bull. Ac St. Pétersb. Nov. 1841, 36.
Leucosticte griseonucha BONAP. Consp. Av. I. 1850, 537.

[B 323, C 144 a, R 174, C 205.]

HAB. Aleutian Islands, including Kadiak, Unalashka, Prybilof, and Commander Islands.

524. Leucosticte tephrocotis SWAINS.
   Gray-crowned Leucosticte.

Linaria (Leucosticte) tephrocotis SWAINS. F. B. A. II. 1831, 255, pl. 50.
Leucosticte tephrocotis SWAINS. F. B. A. II. 1831, 494.

[B 322, C 144, R 175, C 203.]

HAB. Interior of British America, south in winter throughout the entire Rocky Mountain region of the United States, but most abundant on the eastern slope.

524 a. Leucosticte tephrocotis littoralis (BAIRD).
   Hepburn's Leucosticte.

Leucosticte littoralis BAIRD, Trans. Chicago Ac. Sci. I. i. 1869, 318, pl. 28, fig. 1.
Leucosticte tephrocotis var. *littoralis* COUES, Key, 1872, 130.

[B —, C —, R 175 *a*, C 204.]

HAB. In summer, probably the interior mountainous regions of British Columbia; in winter, northwest coast, from Kadiak southward, and eastward in the Rocky Mountain region to Colorado.

525. Leucosticte atrata RIDGW.
Black Leucosticte.

Leucosticte atrata RIDGW. American Sportsman, July 18, 1874, 241; Bull. U. S. Geol. & Geog. Surv. Terr. 2d ser. No. 2, May 11, 1875, 69.

[B —, C —, R 176, C 201.]

HAB. In winter, mountains of Colorado and Utah; summer range not known.

526. Leucosticte australis (ALLEN).
Brown-capped Leucosticte.

Leucosticte tephrocotis var. *australis* "ALLEN, MS." RIDGW. Bull. Essex Inst. V. Dec. 1873, 197.
Leucosticte australis RIDGW. Bull. U. S. Geol. & Geog. Surv. Terr. 2d ser. No. 2, May 11, 1875, 79.

[B —, C —, R 177, C 203.]

HAB. Mountains of Colorado, breeding above timber-line, descending into the valleys in winter; New Mexico.

GENUS **ACANTHIS** BECHSTEIN.

Acanthis BECHST. Orn. Tasch. Deutschl. 1803, 125. Type, *Fringilla linaria* LINN.

527. Acanthis hornemannii (HOLB.).
Greenland Redpoll.

Linota hornemannii HOLBÖLL, Naturh. Tidskr. IV. 1843, 398.
Acanthis hornemannii STEJN. Auk, I. April, 1884, 152.

[B 321, C —, R 178, C 209.]

HAB. Greenland and Eastern Arctic America.

527 a. Acanthis hornemannii exilipes (Coues).
Hoary Redpoll.

Ægiothus exilipes Coues, Pr. Ac. Nat. Sci. Phila. 1861, 385.
Acanthis hornemannii exilipes Stejn. Auk, I. April, 1884, 152.

[B —, C 146 *b*, R 178 *a*, C 210.]

Hab. Arctic America and Northeastern Asia.

528. Acanthis linaria (Linn.).
Redpoll.

Fringilla linaria Linn. S. N. ed. 10, I. 1758, 182.
Acanthis linaria Bonap. & Schleg. Mon. Lox. 1850, 48.

[B 320, C 146, 146 *a*, R 179, C 207.]

Hab. Northern portions of Northern Hemisphere, south irregularly in winter, in North America, to the Middle United States (Washington, D. C., Kansas, Southeastern Oregon).

528 a. Acanthis linaria holbœllii (Brehm).
Holbœll's Redpoll.

Linaria holbœllii Brehm, Handb. Vög. Deutschl. 1831, 280.
Acanthis linaria β. *holbœllii* Dubois, Consp. Av. Europ. 1871, 18.

[B —, C —, R 179 *a*, *part*, C 208, *part*.]

Hab. Northern portions of Northern Hemisphere, near the seacoast.

528 b. Acanthis linaria rostrata (Coues).
Greater Redpoll.

Ægiothus rostratus Coues, Pr. Ac. Nat. Sci. Phila. 1861, 378.
Acanthis linaria rostrata Stejn. Auk, I. April, 1884, 153.

[B —, C —, R 179 *a*, *part*, C 208, *part*.]

Hab. Greenland and Northeastern North America, south irregularly in winter to New England, New York, and Northern Illinois.

Genus **SPINUS** Koch.

Spinus Koch, Bayr. Zool. 1816, 233. Type, *Fringilla spinus* Linn.

529. **Spinus tristis** (LINN.).
   American Goldfinch.

   Fringilla tristis LINN. S. N. ed. 10, I. 1758, 181.
   Spinus tristis STEJN. Auk, I. Oct. 1884, 362.

   [B 313, C 149, R 181, C 213.]

   HAB. North America generally, breeding southward to the middle districts of the United States (to about the Potomac and Ohio Rivers, Kansas, and California), and wintering mostly south of the northern boundary of the United States.

530. **Spinus psaltria** (SAY).
   Arkansas Goldfinch.

   Fringilla psaltria SAY, LONG'S Exp. II. 1823, 40.
   Spinus psaltria STEJN. Auk, II. Oct. 1884, 362.

   [B 314, C 151, R 182, C 215.]

   HAB. Western United States, from the Plains to the Pacific, and from Colorado and Utah southward to Sonora.

530 a. **Spinus psaltria arizonæ** (COUES).
   Arizona Goldfinch.

   Chrysomitris mexicana var. *arizonæ* COUES, Pr. Ac. Nat. Sci. Phila. 1866, 82.
   Spinus psaltria arizonæ STEJN. Auk, I. Oct. 1884, 362.

   [B —, C 151 a, R 182 a, C 216.]

   HAB. Southern New Mexico and Southern Arizona, southward into Northern Mexico.

530 b. **Spinus psaltria mexicanus** (SWAINS.).
   Mexican Goldfinch.

   Carduelis mexicanus SWAINS. Phil. Mag. I. 1827, 435.
   Spinus psaltria mexicanus STEJN. Auk. I. Oct. 1884, 362.

   [B 315, C 159 b, R 182 b, C 217.]

   HAB. Valley of the Lower Rio Grande in Texas, southward through Mexico and Central America to Panama.

531. Spinus lawrencei (Cass.).
Lawrence's Goldfinch.

Carduelis lawrencei Cass. Pr. Ac. Nat. Sci. Phila. 1851, 105, pl. v.
Spinus lawrencei Stejn. Auk, II. Oct. 1884, 362.

[B 316, C 150, R 183, C 214.]

Hab. California; Arizona, in winter.

[532.] Spinus notatus (DuBus).
Black-headed Goldfinch.

Carduelis notata DuBus, Bull. Ac. Brux. XIV. pt. 2, 1847, 106.
Spinus notatus Stejn. Auk, I. Oct. 1884, 362.

[B 310, C —, R 184, C 218.]

Hab. Mexico; accidental in Kentucky (Audubon).

533. Spinus pinus (Wils.).
Pine Siskin.

Fringilla pinus Wils. Am. Orn. II. 1810, 133, pl. 17, fig. 1.
Spinus pinus Stejn. Auk, I. Oct. 1884, 362.

[B 317, C 148, R 185, C 212.]

Hab. North America generally, breeding mostly north of the United States and in the Rocky Mountain region; in winter south to the Gulf States and Mexico.

Genus **PLECTROPHENAX** Stejneger.

Plectrophenax Stejn. Pr. U. S. Nat. Mus. V. June 5, 1882, 33. Type, *Emberiza nivalis* Linn.

534. Plectrophenax nivalis (Linn.).
Snowflake.

Emberiza nivalis Linn. S. N. ed. 10, I. 1758, 176.
Plectrophenax nivalis Stejn. Pr. U. S. Nat. Mus. V. June 5, 1882, 33.

[B 325, C 152, R 186, C 219.]

HAB. Northern parts of the Northern Hemisphere, breeding in the arctic regions; in North America south in winter into the Northern United States, irregularly to Georgia, Southern Illinois, and Kansas.

535. Plectrophenax hyperboreus RIDGW.
McKay's Snowflake.

Plectrophenax hyperboreus RIDGW. Pr. U. S. Nat. Mus. VII. June 11, 1884, 68.

[B —, C —, R —, C —.]

HAB. Alaska.

GENUS CALCARIUS BECHSTEIN.

Calcarius BECHST. Taschb. Vög. Deutschl. 1803, 130. Type, *Fringilla lapponica* LINN.

536. Calcarius lapponicus (LINN.).
Lapland Longspur.

Fringilla lapponica LINN. S. N. ed. 10, I. 1758, 180.
Calcarius lapponicus STEJN. Pr. U. S. Nat. Mus. V. June 5, 1882, 33.

[B 326, C 153, R 187, C 220.]

HAB. Northern portions of the Northern Hemisphere, breeding far north; in North America south in winter to the Northern United States, irregularly to the Middle States, accidentally to South Carolina, and abundantly in the interior to Kansas and Colorado.

537. Calcarius pictus (SWAINS.).
Smith's Longspur.

Emberiza (Plectrophanes) picta SWAINS. F. B. A. II 1831, 250, pl. 49.
Calcarius pictus STEJN. Pr. U. S. Nat. Mus. V. June 5, 1882, 33.

[B 327, C 154, R 188, C 221.]

HAB. Interior of North America, from the Arctic coast to Illinois and Texas, breeding far north.

538. Calcarius ornatus (TOWNS.).
Chestnut-collared Longspur.

Plectrophanes ornatus TOWNS. Journ. Ac. Nat. Sci. Phila. VII. 1837, 189.
Calcarius ornatus STEJN. Pr. U. S. Nat. Mus. V. June 5, 1882, 33.

[B 328, 329, C 155, R 189, C 222.]

HAB. Interior of North America, from the Saskatchewan Plains south to Texas. Rare west of the Rocky Mountains. Accidental in Massachusetts.

Genus **RHYNCHOPHANES** BAIRD.

Rhynchophanes BAIRD, B. N. Am. 1858, 432 (in text). Type, *Plectrophanes mccownii* LAWR.

539. Rhynchophanes mccownii (LAWR.).
McCown's Longspur.

Plectrophanes mccownii LAWR. Ann. Lyc. N. Y. V. 1851, 122.
Rhynchophanes maccowni RIDGW. Field & Forest, II. May, 1877, 197.

[B 330, C 156, R 190, C 223.]

HAB. Interior of North America, from the Saskatchewan Plains south to Texas and Mexico; breeds from about the northern border of Western Kansas northward.

Genus **POOCÆTES** BAIRD.

Poocætes BAIRD, B. N. Am. 1858, 447. Type, *Fringilla graminea* GMEL.

540. Poocætes gramineus (GMEL.).
Vesper Sparrow.

Fringilla graminea GMEL. S. N. I. ii. 1788, 992.
Poocætes gramineus BAIRD, B. N. Am. 1858, 447.

[B 337, *part*, C 161, R 197, C 232.]

HAB. Eastern North America to the Plains, from Nova Scotia and Ontario southward; breeds from Virginia, Kentucky, and Missouri northward.

540 a. Poocætes gramineus confinis BAIRD.
Western Vesper Sparrow.

Poocætes gramineus var. *confinis* BAIRD, B. N. Am. 1858, 448 (in text).

[B 337, *part*, C 161 *a*, R 197 *a*, C 232.]

HAB. Western United States, from the Plains to the Pacific, south into Mexico.

GENUS **AMMODRAMUS** SWAINSON.

Ammodramus SWAINS. Zool. Journ. III. 1827, 348. Type, *Fringilla caudacuta* WILSON.

SUBGENUS **PASSERCULUS** BONAPARTE.

Passerculus BONAP. Geog. & Comp. List, 1838, 33. Type, *Fringilla savanna* WILS.

541. Ammodramus princeps (MAYN.).
Ipswich Sparrow.

Passerculus princeps MAYN. Am. Nat. VI. 1872, 637.
Ammodramus princeps RIDGW. Pr. U. S. Nat. Mus. VIII. 1885, 354.

[B —, C 158, R 192, C 225.]

HAB. Atlantic coast, from Nova Scotia south, in winter, to Virginia.

542. Ammodramus sandwichensis (GMEL.).
Sandwich Sparrow.

Emberiza sandwichensis GMEL. S. N. I. ii. 1788, 875.
Ammodramus sandwichensis RIDGW. Pr. U. S. Nat. Mus. VIII. 1885, 354.

[B 333, C 159 *b*, R 193, C 226.]

HAB. Northwest coast, from the Columbia River to Unalashka.

542 *a*. Ammodramus sandwichensis savanna (WILS.).
Savanna Sparrow.

Fringilla savanna WILS. Am. Orn. III. 1811, 55, pl. 22, fig. 2.
Ammodramus sandwichensis savanna RIDGW. Pr. U. S. Nat. Mus. VIII. 1885, 354.

[B 332, C 159, R 193 *a*, C 227.]

HAB. Eastern Province of North America, breeding from the Northern United States to Labrador and Hudson's Bay Territory.

542 b. **Ammodramus sandwichensis alaudinus** (BONAP.).
Western Savanna Sparrow.

Passerculus alaudinus BONAP. Compt. Rend. XXXVII. 1853, 918.
Ammodramus sandwichensis alaudinus RIDGW. Pr. U. S. Nat. Mus. VIII. 1885, 354.

[B 335, C —, R 193 b, C 229.]

HAB. Western North America, from the Plains to the Pacific coast region, north to the Arctic coast.

542 c. **Ammodramus sandwichensis bryanti** RIDGW.
Bryant's Marsh Sparrow.

Passerculus sandwichensis bryanti RIDGW. Pr. U. S. Nat. Mus. VII. Jan. 19, 1885, 517.
Ammodramus sandwichensis bryanti RIDGW. Pr. U. S. Nat. Mus. VIII. 1885, 354.

[B 334, *part*, C 159 a, *part*, R 194, *part*, C 228, *part*.]

HAB. Salt marshes about San Francisco Bay, probably south along the coast in winter.

543. **Ammodramus beldingi** RIDGW.
Belding's Marsh Sparrow.

Passerculus beldingi RIDGW. Pr. U. S. Nat. Mus. VII. Jan. 19, 1885, 516.
Ammodramus beldingi RIDGW. Pr. U. S. Nat. Mus. VIII. 1885, 354.

[B 334, *part*, C 159 a, *part*, R 194, *part*, C 228, *part*.]

HAB. Salt marshes of the Pacific coast, from Santa Barbara south to Todos Santos Island, Lower California.

544. **Ammodramus rostratus** CASS.
Large-billed Sparrow.

Emberiza rostrata CASS. Pr. Ac. Nat. Sci. Phila. 1852, 348.
Ammodromus rostratus CASS. Illustr. B. Cal. Tex. etc. 1855, 226, pl. 38.

[B 336, C 160, R 196, C 230.]

HAB. Coast of California, south in winter to Cape St. Lucas and Northwestern Mexico.

544 a. Ammodramus rostratus guttatus (LAWR.).
St. Lucas Sparrow.

Passerculus guttatus LAWR. Ann. Lyc. N. Y. VIII. 1867, 473.
Ammodramus rostratus guttatus RIDGW. Pr. U. S. Nat. Mus. VIII. 1885, 355.

[B —, C 160 a, R 195, C 231.]

HAB. Lower California.

SUBGENUS **CENTRONYX** BAIRD.

Centronyx BAIRD, B. N. Am. 1858, 440. Type, *Emberiza bairdii* AUD.

545. Ammodramus bairdii (AUD.).
Baird's Sparrow.

Emberiza bairdii AUD. B. Am. VII. 1843, 359, pl. 500.
Ammodromus bairdi GIEBEL, Thes. Orn. I. 1872, 328.

[B 331, C 157, 157 bis, R 191, C 224.]

HAB. Interior of North America, from the plains of the Red River and Saskatchewan south to Texas, New Mexico, and Arizona.

SUBGENUS **COTURNICULUS** BONAPARTE.

Coturniculus BONAP. Geog. & Comp. List, 1838, 32. Type, *Fringilla passerina* WILS.

546. Ammodramus savannarum passerinus (WILS.).
Grasshopper Sparrow.

Fringilla passerina WILS. Am. Orn. III. 1811, 76, pl. 26, fig. 5.
Ammodramus savannarum passerinus RIDGW. Pr. U. S. Nat. Mus. VIII. 1885, 355.

[B 338, C 162, R 198, C 234.]

HAB. Eastern United States and Southern Canada to the Plains, south to Florida, Cuba, Porto Rico, and coast of Central America.

546 a. **Ammodramus savannarum perpallidus** RIDGW.
    Western Grasshopper Sparrow.

> *Coturniculus passerinus* var. *perpallidus* "RIDGW. MS." COUES, Key, 1872, 137.
> *Ammodramus savannarum perpallidus* RIDGW. Pr. U. S. Nat. Mus. VIII. 1885, 355.

[B 338, *part*, C 162 a, R 198 a, C 235.]

HAB. Western United States, from the Plains to the Pacific coast, and the table lands of Mexico.

547. **Ammodramus henslowii** (AUD.).
    Henslow's Sparrow.

> *Emberiza henslowii* AUD. Orn. Biog. I. 1831, 360, pl. 77.
> *Ammodromus henslowi* GRAY, Gen. B. II. June, 1849, 374.

[B 339, C 163, R 199, C 236.]

HAB. Eastern United States, west to the Plains, north to Southern New England and Ontario.

548. **Ammodramus leconteii** (AUD.).
    Leconte's Sparrow.

> *Emberiza leconteii* AUD. B. Am. VII. 1843, 338, pl. 488.
> *Ammodromus leconteii* GRAY, Gen. B. II. June, 1849, 374.

[B 340, C 164, R 200, C 237.]

HAB. From the Plains eastward to Illinois, South Carolina, and Florida, and from Manitoba south to Texas.

SUBGENUS **AMMODRAMUS**.

> *Ammodramus* SWAINS. Zool. Jour. III. 1827, 348. Type, *Oriolus caudacutus* GMEL.

549. **Ammodramus caudacutus** (GMEL.).
    Sharp-tailed Sparrow.

> *Oriolus caudacutus* GMEL. S. N. I. i. 1788, 394.
> *Ammodramus caudacutus* SWAINS. Classif. B. II. 1837, 289.

[B 341, C 166, R 201, C 240.]

HAB. Salt marshes of the Atlantic coast, from Prince Edward Island and Nova Scotia to the Gulf States.

549 a. **Ammodramus caudacutus nelsoni** ALLEN.
Nelson's Sparrow.

Ammodromus caudacutus var. *nelsoni* ALLEN, Pr. Bost. Soc. Nat. Hist. XVII. March, 1875, 93.

[B —, C —, R 201 a, C 241.]

HAB. Fresh marshes of the Mississippi Valley region (Illinois, Kansas, etc.), and the Atlantic coast in its migrations (Lower Hudson Valley to Charleston, S. C.).

550. **Ammodramus maritimus** (WILS.).
Seaside Sparrow.

Fringilla maritima WILS. Am Orn. VII. 1811, 68, pl. 24, fig. 2.
Ammodramus maritima SWAINS. Classif. B. II. 1837, 289.

[B 342, C 165, R 202, C 238.]

HAB. Salt marshes of the Atlantic coast, from Massachusetts southward, and along the Gulf coast to the Rio Grande.

551. **Ammodramus nigrescens** RIDGW.
Dusky Seaside Sparrow.

Ammodromus maritimus var. *nigrescens* RIDGW. Bull. Essex Inst. V. Dec. 1873, 198.
Ammodramus nigrescens RIDGW. Pr. U. S. Nat. Mus. III. Aug. 24, 1880, 178.

[B —, C 165 a, R 203, C 239.]

HAB. Salt Lake, Southern Florida.

GENUS **CHONDESTES** SWAINSON.

Chondestes SWAINS. Phil. Mag. I. 1827, 435. Type, *C. strigatus* SWAINS.

552. Chondestes grammacus (Say).
   Lark Sparrow.

   Fringilla grammaca Say, Long's Exp. II. 1823, 139.
   Chondestes grammaca Bonap. Geog. & Comp. List, 1838, 32.

   [B 344, *part*, C 186, *part*, R 204, C 281, *part*.]

HAB. Mississippi Valley region, from Ohio, Illinois, and Michigan to the Plains, south to Eastern Texas. Accidental near the Atlantic coast (Massachusetts, Long Island, New Jersey, and Washington, D. C.).

552 a. Chondestes grammacus strigatus (Swains.).
   Western Lark Sparrow.

   Chondestes strigatus Swains. Phil. Mag. I. 1827, 435.
   Chondestes grammaca strigata Ridgw. Pr. U. S. Nat. Mus. III. Aug. 24, 1880, 179.

   [B 344, *part*, C 186, *part*, R 204 *a*, C 281, *part*.]

HAB. Western United States, from the Plains to the Pacific coast, south into Mexico.

GENUS **ZONOTRICHIA** SWAINSON.

Zonotrichia Swains. F. B. A. II. 1831, 493. Type, by elimination, *Emberiza leucophrys* Forst.

553. Zonotrichia querula (Nutt.).
   Harris's Sparrow.

   Fringilla querula Nutt. Man. I. 2d ed. 1840, 555.
   Zonotrichia querula Gamb. Journ. Ac. Nat. Sci. Phila. 2d ser. I. 1847, 51.

   [B 348, C 185, R 205, C 280.]

HAB. Middle United States, from Missouri and Iowa west to Middle Kansas and Dakota, and from Texas north to the Red River of the North.

554. Zonotrichia leucophrys (Forst.).
   White-crowned Sparrow.

   Emberiza leucophrys Forst. Philos. Trans. LXII. 1772, 382, 426.
   Z[*onotrichia*] *leucophrys* Swains. F. B. A. II. 1831, 493.

[B 345, C 183, R 206, C 276.]

HAB. North America at large, breeding chiefly in the Rocky Mountain region (including Sierra Nevada) and northeast to Labrador.

555. Zonotrichia intermedia RIDGW.
Intermediate Sparrow.

Zonotrichia leucophrys var. *intermedia* RIDGW. Bull. Essex Inst. V.
   Dec. 1873, 198.
Zonotrichia intermedia RIDGW. Field & Forest, May, 1877, 198.

[B 346, *part*, C 183 *b*, R 207 *a*, C 277.]

HAB. Western North America, from the Rocky Mountains to the Pacific, and from Mexico to Alaska. Breeds, so far as known, only north of the United States.

556. Zonotrichia gambeli (NUTT.).
Gambel's Sparrow.

Fringilla gambeli NUTT. Man. I. 2d ed. 1840, 556.
Zonotrichia gambeli GAMB. Journ. Ac. Nat. Sci. Phila. 2d ser. I.
   1847, 50.

[B 346, *part*, C 183 *a*, R 207, C 278.]

HAB. Pacific coast region, from Oregon southward.

557. Zonotrichia coronata (PALL.).
Golden-crowned Sparrow.

Emberiza coronata PALL. Zoog. Rosso-As. II. 1826, 44.
Zonotrichia coronata BAIRD, B. N. Am. 1858, 461.

[B 347, C 184, R 208, C 279.]

HAB. Pacific coast region, from Alaska to Southern California.

558. Zonotrichia albicollis (GMEL.).
White-throated Sparrow.

Fringilla albicollis GMEL. S. N. I. ii. 1788, 926.
Zonotrichia albicollis SWAINS. Classif. B. II. 1837, 288.

[B 349, C 182, R 209, C 275.]

HAB. Eastern North America, west to the Plains, north to Labrador and the Fur Countries. Breeds in Northern Michigan, Northern New York, and Northern New England, and winters from the Middle States southward.

Genus **SPIZELLA** Bonaparte.

Spizella BONAP. Saggio Distr. Met. 1832, 140.   Type, *Fringilla pusilla* WILS.

559. **Spizella monticola** (GMEL.).
Tree Sparrow.

Fringilla monticola GMEL. S N. I. ii. 1788, 912.
Spizella monticola BAIRD, B. N. Am. 1858, 472.

[B 357, *part*, C 177, *part*, R 210, *part*, C 268, *part*.]

HAB. Eastern North America, westward to the Plains, and from the Arctic Ocean south, in winter, to the Carolinas, Kentucky, and Eastern Kansas. Breeds north of the United States, east of the Rocky Mountains.

559 a. **Spizella monticola ochracea** BREWST.
Western Tree Sparrow.

Spizella monticola ochracea BREWST. Bull. Nutt. Orn. Club, VII. Oct. 1882, 228.

[B 357, *part*, C 177, *part*, R 210, *part*, C 268, *part*.]

HAB. Western North America, east to Dakota and Western Kansas, south in winter to New Mexico and Arizona, north to the arctic regions; breeds in Alaska.

560. **Spizella socialis** (WILS.).
Chipping Sparrow.

Fringilla socialis WILS. Am. Orn. II. 1810, 127, pl. 16, fig. 5.
Spizella socialis BONAP. Geog. & Comp. List, 1838, 33.

[B 359, *part*, C 178, R 211, C 269.]

HAB. Eastern North America, west to the Rocky Mountains, north to Great Slave Lake, and south to Eastern Mexico.

560 *a*. **Spizella socialis arizonæ** COUES.
    Western Chipping Sparrow.

Spizella socialis var. *arizonæ* COUES, Key, 1872, 143.

[B 359, *part*, C 178 *a*, R 211 *a*, C 270.]

HAB. Western United States, from the Rocky Mountains to the Pacific, south in winter to Middle and Western Mexico.

561. **Spizella pallida** (SWAINS.).
    Clay-colored Sparrow.

Emberiza pallida SWAINS. F. B. A. II. 1831, 251.
Spizella pallida BONAP. Geog. & Comp. List, 1838, 33.

[B 360, C 180, R 212, C 272.]

HAB. Interior of North America, from Illinois and Iowa west to the Rocky Mountains, Arizona, and Cape St. Lucas, and from Texas north to the Saskatchewan Plains.

562. **Spizella breweri** CASS.
    Brewer's Sparrow.

Spizella breweri CASS. Pr. Ac. Nat. Sci. Phila. Feb. 1856, 40.

[B 361, C 180 *a*, R 213, C 273.]

HAB. Western United States, from the eastern base of the Rocky Mountains to the Pacific coast. Accidental in Massachusetts.

563. **Spizella pusilla** (WILS.).
    Field Sparrow.

Fringilla pusilla WILS. Am. Orn. II. 1810, 121, pl. 16, fig. 2.
Spizella pusilla BONAP. Geog. & Comp. List, 1838, 33.

[B 358, C 179, R 214, C 271.]

HAB. Eastern United States and Southern Canada, west to the Plains.

564. **Spizella wortheni** RIDGW.
    Worthen's Sparrow.

Spizella wortheni RIDGW. Pr. U. S. Nat. Mus. VII. Aug. 22, 1884, 259.

[B —, C —, R —, C —.]

HAB. New Mexico and Western Texas.

565. Spizella atrigularis (CAB.).
Black-chinned Sparrow.

Spinites atrigularis CAB. Mus. Hein. I. 1851, 133.
Spizella atrigularis BAIRD, B. N. Am. 1858, 476.

[B 362, C 181, R 215, C 274.]

HAB. Southern border of the United States, from Texas to California, south into Mexico.

GENUS **JUNCO** WAGLER.

Junco WAGLER, Isis, 1831, 526. Type, *J. phæonotus* WAGL. = *Fringilla cinerea* SWAINS.

566. Junco aikeni RIDGW.
White-winged Junco.

Junco hyemalis var. *aikeni* RIDGW. Am. Nat. VII. Oct. 1873, 612, 614.
Junco aikeni RIDGW. Field & Forest, May, 1877, 198.

[B —, C 174 *a*, R 216, C 262.]

HAB. Colorado, north to the Black Hills, where it breeds.

567. Junco hyemalis (LINN.).
Slate-colored Junco.

Fringilla hyemalis LINN S. N. ed. 10, I. 1758, 183.
Junco hyemalis SCL. P. Z. S. 1857, 7.

[B 354, C 174, R 217. C 261.]

HAB. North America at large, but chiefly east of the Rocky Mountains, breeding from the higher parts of the Alleghanies and Northern New York and Northern New England northward. South in winter to the Gulf States.

567 *a*. Junco hyemalis oregonus (TOWNS.).
Oregon Junco.

Fringilla oregona TOWNS. Journ. Ac. Nat. Sci. Phila. VII. 1837, 188.
Junco hyemalis var. *oregonus* RIDGW. Am. Nat. VII. Oct. 1873, 612.

[B 352, C. 175, R 218, C 263.]

HAB. Western United States, northward to Alaska, east to the Plains, south, in winter, to New Mexico, Arizona, and Southern California. Accidental in Michigan and Massachusetts.

568. Junco annectens BAIRD.
Pink-sided Junco.

Junco annectens BAIRD, Orn. Cal. I. 1870, 564.

[B —, C —, R 219, C 264.]

HAB. Rocky Mountain region, from Arizona and New Mexico (in winter) north to Idaho and Montana.

569. Junco caniceps (WOODH.).
Gray-headed Junco.

Struthus caniceps WOODH. Pr. Ac. Nat. Sci. Phila. Dec. 1852, 202.
Junco caniceps BAIRD, B. N. Am. 1858, 468.

[B 353, C 176, R 220, C 265.]

HAB. Rocky Mountain region, from the Black Hills to the Wahsatch and Uintah Mountains, south to New Mexico and Arizona.

570. Junco cinereus palliatus RIDGW.
Arizona Junco.

Junco cinereus palliatus RIDGW. Auk, II. Oct. 1885, 364.

[B 350, *part*, C —, R 222, *part*, C 267, *part*.]

HAB. Mountains of Southern Arizona, and probably southward into Western Mexico.

570 a. Junco cinereus dorsalis HENRY.
Red-backed Junco.

Junco dorsalis HENRY, Pr. Ac. Nat. Sci. Phila. 1858, 117.
Junco cinereus dorsalis RIDGW. Pr. U. S. Nat. Mus. VIII. 1885, 355.

[B 351, C —, R 221, C 266.]

HAB. Mountains of New Mexico and Eastern Arizona.

571. Junco bairdi BELDING.
   Baird's Junco.

   Junco bairdi BELDING, Pr. U. S. Nat. Mus. VI. Oct. 5, 1883, 155.

   [B —, C —, R —, C —.]

HAB. Lower California.

572. Junco insularis RIDGW.
   Guadalupe Junco.

   Junco insularis RIDGW. Bull. U. S. Geol. & Geog. Surv. Terr. II. No. 2, April 1, 1876, 188.

   [B —, C —, R 223, C —.]

HAB. Guadalupe Island, Lower California.

GENUS **AMPHISPIZA** COUES.

Amphispiza COUES, B. Northwest, 1875, 234. Type, *Emberiza bilineata* CASS.

573. Amphispiza bilineata (CASS.).
   Black-throated Sparrow.

   Emberiza bilineata CASSIN, Pr. Ac. Nat. Sci. Phila. Oct. 1850, 104, pl. 3.
   Amphispiza bilineata COUES, B. Northwest, 1875, 234.

   [B 355, C 172, R 224, C 258.]

HAB. Western United States, from Western Texas and the Indian Territory west to California, north throughout the Great Basin, and south into Mexico.

574. Amphispiza belli (CASS.).
   Bell's Sparrow.

   Emberiza belli CASSIN, Pr. Ac. Nat. Sci. Phila. Oct. 1850, 104, pl. 4.
   Amphispiza bellii COUES, B. Northwest, 1875, 234.

   [B 356, C 173, R 225, C 259.]

HAB. California.

574 *a*. **Amphispiza belli nevadensis** (Ridgw.).
Sage Sparrow.

Poospiza belli var. *nevadensis* Ridgw. Bull. Essex Inst. V. Nov. 1873, 191.
Amphispiza bellii var. *nevadensis* Coues, B. Northwest, 1875, 234.

[B —, C 173 *a*, R 225 *a*, C 260.]

Hab. Southeastern Wyoming, Utah, and Nevada, south to Arizona and Mexico, and east to Colorado and New Mexico.

Genus **PEUCÆA** Audubon.

Peucæa Aud. Synop. 1839, 112. Type, *Fringilla bachmani* Aud.

575. **Peucæa æstivalis** (Licht.).
Pine-woods Sparrow.

Fringilla æstivalis Licht. Verz. Doubl. 1823, 25.
Peucæa æstivalis Cab. Mus. Hein. I. 1850, 132.

[B 370, *part*, C 170, *part*, R 226, C 251.]

Hab. Florida and Southern Georgia.

575 *a*. **Peucæa æstivalis bachmanii** (Aud.).
Bachman's Sparrow.

Fringilla bachmanii Aud. Orn. Biog. II. 1834, 366, pl. 165.
Peucæa æstivalis bachmani Brewst. Auk, II. Jan. 1885, 106.

[B 370, *part*, C 170, *part*, R 226 *a*, C 252.]

Hab. South Carolina and Alabama, west to Texas, and north to Southern Illinois and Southern Indiana.

576. **Peucæa arizonæ** Ridgw.
Arizona Sparrow.

Peucæa æstivalis var. *arizonæ* Ridgw. Am. Nat. VII. Oct. 1873, 615.
Peucæa arizonæ Ridgw. Pr. U. S. Nat. Mus. I. Aug. 15, 1878, 127.

[B —, C 170 *a*, R 227, C 253.]

Hab. Southern Arizona and Sonora.

577. **Peucæa mexicana** (Lawr.).
Mexican Sparrow.

Coturniculus mexicanus Lawr. Ann. Lyc. N. Y. VIII. May, 1867, 474. (Mts. of Colima.)
Peucæa mexicana Ridgw. Pr. U. S. Nat. Mus. VIII. No. 7, May 23, 1885, 99.

[B —, C —, R —, C —.]

Hab. Valley of the Lower Rio Grande in Texas south into Central and Western Mexico.

578. **Peucæa cassini** (Woodh.).
Cassin's Sparrow.

Zonotrichia cassini Woodh. Pr. Ac. Nat. Sci. Phila. April, 1852, 60.
Peucæa cassini Baird, B. N. Am. 1858, 458.

[B 371, C 170 bis, R 228, C 254.]

Hab. Plains of Kansas southward and westward, through Texas, New Mexico, and Arizona, into Mexico.

579. **Peucæa carpalis** Coues.
Rufous-winged Sparrow.

Peucæa carpalis Coues, Am. Nat. VII. June, 1873, 322.

[B —, C 171 bis, R 229, C 257.]

Hab. Arizona.

580. **Peucæa ruficeps** (Cass.).
Rufous-crowned Sparrow.

Ammodromus ruficeps Cass. Pr. Ac. Nat. Sci. Phila. Oct. 1852, 184.
Peucæa ruficeps Baird, B. N. Am. 1858, 486.

[B 372, C 171, R 230, C 255.]

Hab. Coast of California, south to Cape St. Lucas.

580 a. **Peucæa ruficeps boucardi** (Scl.).
Boucard's Sparrow.

Zonotrichia boucardi Sclater, P. Z. S. 1867, 1, pl. i.
Peucæa ruficeps boucardi Ridgw. Hist. N. Am. B. II. 1874, 38.

[B —, C —, R 230 a, C 256.]

HAB. Southern New Mexico and Southern Arizona, south into Mexico.

580 b. **Peucæa ruficeps eremœca** BROWN.
Rock Sparrow.

Peucæa ruficeps eremœca BROWN, Bull. Nutt. Orn. Cl. VII. Jan. 1882, 26.

[B —, C —, R —, C —.]

HAB. Southwestern Texas, south into Eastern Mexico.

GENUS **MELOSPIZA** BAIRD.

Melospiza BAIRD, B. N. Am. 1858, 478. Type, *Fringilla melodia* WILS. = *F. fasciata* GMEL.

581. **Melospiza fasciata** (GMEL.).
Song Sparrow.

Fringilla fasciata GMEL. S. N. I. 1788, 922.
Melospiza fasciata SCOTT, Am. Nat. X. 1876, 18.

[B 363, C 169, R 231, C 244.]

HAB. Eastern United States to the Plains, breeding from Virginia and the northern portion of the Lake States northward.

581 a. **Melospiza fasciata fallax** (BAIRD).
Desert Song Sparrow.

Zonotrichia fallax BAIRD, Pr. Ac. Nat. Sci. Phila. June, 1854, 119 (nec *Melospiza fallax* auctorum plurimorum !).
Melospiza fasciata fallax HENSH. Auk, I. July, 1884, 224.

[B 367, C 169 a, *part*, R 231 a, *part*, C 245, *part*.]

HAB. New Mexico and Arizona.

581 b. **Melospiza fasciata montana** HENSH.
Mountain Song Sparrow.

Melospiza fasciata montana HENSHAW, Auk, I. July, 1884, 224.

[B —, C 169 *a, part,* R 231 *a, part,* C 245, *part.*]

HAB. Colorado, Utah, Nevada, and northward.

581 *c.* Melospiza fasciata heermanni (BAIRD).
Heermann's Song Sparrow.

Melospiza heermanni BAIRD, B. N. Am. 1858, 478.
Melospiza fasciata δ. *heermanni* RIDGW. Bull. Nutt. Orn. Cl. III. April, 1878, 66.

[B 364, C 169 *d*, R 231 *b*, C 248.]

HAB. Interior of Southern California, east into Western Nevada.

581 *d.* Melospiza fasciata samuelis (BAIRD).
Samuels's Song Sparrow.

Ammodromus samuelis BAIRD, B. N. Am. 1858, 455.
Melospiza fasciata samuelis RIDGW. Pr. U. S. Nat. Mus. III. Aug. 24, 1880, 180.

[B 343, 365, C 169 *e*, R 231 *c*, C 249.]

HAB. Coast region of California.

581 *e.* Melospiza fasciata guttata (NUTT.).
Rusty Song Sparrow.

Fringilla guttata NUTTALL, Man. Orn. I. ed. 2, 1840, 581.
Melospiza fasciata β. *guttata* RIDGW. Bull. Nutt. Orn. Cl. III. April, 1878, 66.

[B —, C 169 *b*, R 231 *d*, C 246.]

HAB. Coast region of Oregon and Washington Territory, south in winter to San Francisco, California.

581 *f.* Melospiza fasciata rufina (BONAP.).
Sooty Song Sparrow.

Passerella rufina BONAP. Consp. Av. I. July 15, 1850, 477.
Melospiza fasciata rufina RIDGW. Pr. U. S. Nat. Mus. III. Aug. 24, 1880, 180.

[B 366, C 169 *c*, R 231 *e*, C 247.]

HAB. Coast region of British Columbia, north to Sitka.

582. **Melospiza cinerea** (GMEL.).
Aleutian Song Sparrow.

Fringilla cinerea GMEL. S. N. I. ii. 1788, 922.
Melospiza cinerea RIDGW. Pr. U. S. Nat. Mus. III. Aug. 24, 1880, 180.

[B —, C 169*f*, R 232, C 250.]

HAB. Aleutian and Prybilof Islands, and east to Fort Kenai, Alaska.

583. **Melospiza lincolni** (AUD.).
Lincoln's Sparrow.

Fringilla lincolni AUD. Orn. Biog. II. 1834, 539, pl. 193.
Melospiza lincolni BAIRD, B. N. Am. 1858, 482.

[B 368, C 167, R 234, C 242.]

HAB. North America at large, breeding chiefly north of the United States and in the higher parts of the Rocky Mountains; south, in winter, to Guatemala.

584. **Melospiza georgiana** (LATH.).
Swamp Sparrow.

Fringilla georgiana LATH. Ind. Orn I 1790, 460.
Melospiza georgiana RIDGW. Pr. U. S. Nat. Mus. VIII. 1885, 355.

[B 369, C 168, R 233, C 243.]

HAB. Eastern North America to the Plains, accidentally to Utah, north to the British Provinces, including Newfoundland and Labrador. Breeds from the Northern States northward, and winters in the Middle States and southward.

GENUS **PASSERELLA** SWAINSON.

Passerella SWAINS. Classif. B. II. 1837, 288. Type, *Fringilla iliaca* GMEL.

585. **Passerella iliaca** (MERR.).
Fox Sparrow.

Fringilla iliaca MERREM, "Beitr. zur besond. Gesch. der Vögel, II. 1786-87, 40, pl. x."
Passerella iliaca SWAINS. Classif. B. II. 1837, 288.

[B 374, C 188, R 235, C 282.]

HAB. Eastern North America, west to the Plains and Alaska (valley of the Yukon to the Pacific), and from the Arctic coast south to the Gulf States. Breeds north of the United States; winters chiefly south of the Potomac and Ohio Rivers.

585 a. Passerella iliaca unalaschcensis (GMEL.).
Townsend's Sparrow.

Emberiza unalaschcensis GMEL. S. N. I. ii. 1788, 875.
Passerella iliaca unalascensis RIDGW. Pr. U. S. Nat. Mus. III. Aug. 24, 1880, 181.

[B 375, C 189, R 235 a, C 283.]

HAB. Pacific coast region, from Kadiak south, in winter, to Southern California. Breeds north of the United States.

585 b. Passerella iliaca megarhyncha (BAIRD).
Thick-billed Sparrow.

Passerella megarhyncha BAIRD, B. N. Am. 1858, 925.
Passerella iliaca megarhyncha RIDGW. Pr. U. S. Nat. Mus. III. Aug. 24, 1880, 181.

[B 376 a, C —, R 235 b, C 285.]

HAB. Sierra Nevada and Coast Range, California.

585 c. Passerella iliaca schistacea (BAIRD).
Slate-colored Sparrow.

Passerella schistacea BAIRD, B. N. Am. 1858, 490.
Passerella iliaca var. *schistacea* ALLEN, Bull. M. C. Z. III. 1872, 168.

[B 376, C 189 a, R 235 c, C 284.]

HAB. Rocky Mountain region of the United States, east, in winter, to the Plains (Kansas), west to Nevada and California.

GENUS **EMBERNAGRA** LESSON.

Embernagra LESS. Traité, 1831, 465. Type, *E. dumetorum* LESS. = *Emberiza platensis* GMEL.

586. **Embernagra rufivirgata** Lawr.
   Texas Sparrow.

   Embernagra rufivirgata Lawr. Ann. Lyc. N. Y. V. May, 1851, 112, pl. 5, fig. 2.

   [B 373, C 209, R 236, C 311.]

Hab. Valley of the Lower Rio Grande in Texas and Eastern Mexico.

Genus **PIPILO** Vieillot.

Pipilo Vieill. Analyse, 1816, 32. Type, *Fringilla erythrophthalma* Linn.

587. **Pipilo erythrophthalmus** (Linn.).
   Towhee.

   Fringilla erythrophthalma Linn. S. N. ed. 10, I. 1758, 180.
   Pipilo erythrophthalmus Vieill. Gal. Ois. I. 1824, 109, pl. 80.

   [B 391, C 204, R 237, C 301.]

Hab. Eastern United States and Southern Canada, west to the Plains.

587 *a*. **Pipilo erythrophthalmus alleni** Coues.
   White-eyed Towhee.

   Pipilo erythrophthalmus var. *alleni* Coues, Am. Nat. V. Aug. 1871, 366.

   [B —, C 204 *a*, R 237 *a*, C 302.]

Hab. Florida.

588. **Pipilo maculatus arcticus** (Swains.).
   Arctic Towhee.

   Pyrgita (*Pipilo*) *arctica* Swains. F. B. A. II. 1831, 260, pls. 51, 52.
   Pipilo maculatus var. *arcticus* Coues, Key, 1872, 152.

   [B 393, C 205 *a*, R 238, C 304.]

Hab. Plains of the Platte, Upper Missouri, Yellowstone, and Saskatchewan Rivers, west to the eastern slope of the Rocky Mountains, south in winter to Kansas, Colorado, and Texas.

588 a. Pipilo maculatus megalonyx (BAIRD).
Spurred Towhee.

Pipilo megalonyx BAIRD, B. N. Am. 1858, 515.
Pipilo maculatus var. *megalonyx* COUES, Key, 1872, 152.

[B 394, C 205 *b*, R 238 *a*, C 305.]

HAB. Rocky Mountain region of the United States, west to the Sierra Nevada and Southern California.

588 b. Pipilo maculatus oregonus (BELL).
Oregon Towhee.

Pipilo oregonus BELL, Ann. Lyc. N. Y. V. 1852, 6.
Pipilo ma.ulatus var. *oregonus* COUES, Key, 1872, 152.

[B 392, C 205, R 238 *b*, C 303.]

HAB. Pacific coast region, from Washington Territory south to San Francisco, California.

589. Pipilo consobrinus RIDGW.
Guadalupe Towhee.

Pipilo maculatus consobrinus RIDGW. Bull. U. S. Geol. & Geog. Surv. Terr. II. No. 2, April 1, 1876, 189.
Pipilo consobrinus RIDGW. Bull. Nutt. Orn. Club, II. July, 1877, 60.

[B —, C —, R 238 *c*, C —.]

HAB. Guadalupe Island, Lower California.

590. Pipilo chlorurus (TOWNS.).
Green-tailed Towhee.

Fringilla chlorura "TOWNS." AUD. Orn. Biog. V. 1839, 336.
Pipilo chlorurus BAIRD, B. N. Am. 1858, 519.

[B 398, C 208, R 239, C 310.]

HAB. Interior Plateau region of the United States, from the western border of the Plains to the Sierra Nevada, from about lat. 40° south into Mexico.

591. **Pipilo fuscus mesoleucus** (BAIRD).
    Cañon Towhee.

    Pipilo mesoleucus BAIRD, Pr. Ac. Nat. Sci. Phila. June, 1854, 119.
    Pipilo fuscus var. *mesoleucus* RIDGW. Bull. Essex Inst. V. Nov. 1873. 183.

        [B 397, C 206, R 240, C 306.]

HAB. Southern border of the United States, from the valley of the Upper Rio Grande west to the valley of the Gila, south into Western Mexico.

591 *a*. **Pipilo fuscus albigula** (BAIRD).
    Saint Lucas Towhee.

    Pipilo albigula BAIRD, Pr. Ac. Nat. Sci. Phila. Nov. 1859, 305.
    Pipilo fuscus var. *albigula* COUES, Key, 1872, 152.

        [B —, C 206 *a*, R 240 *a*, C 307.]

HAB. Lower California.

591 *b*. **Pipilo fuscus crissalis** (VIG.).
    Californian Towhee.

    Fringilla crissalis VIG. Zool. Blos. 1839, 19.
    Pipilo fuscus var. *crissalis* COUES, Key, 1872, 153.

        [B 396, C 206 *b*, R 240 *b*, C 308.]

HAB. California.

592. **Pipilo aberti** BAIRD.
    Abert's Towhee.

    Pipilo aberti BAIRD, STANSBURY'S Rep. Exped. Utah, 1852, 325.

        [B 395, C 207, R 241, C 309.]

HAB. New Mexico and Arizona, north into Southern Colorado and Utah.

GENUS **CARDINALIS** BONAPARTE.

    Cardinalis BONAP. P. Z. S. 1837, 111. Type, *C. virginianus* BONAP.
    = *Loxia cardinalis* LINN.

593. Cardinalis cardinalis (LINN.).
  Cardinal.

  Loxia cardinalis LINN. S. N. ed. 10, 1758, 172.
  Cardinalis cardinalis LICHT. Nomencl. Mus. Berol. 1854, 44.

  [B 390, C 203, R 242, C 299.]

HAB. Eastern United States, north to New Jersey and the Ohio Valley (casually farther), west to the Plains.

593 a. Cardinalis cardinalis superbus RIDGW.
  Arizona Cardinal.

  Cardinalis cardinalis superbus RIDGW. Auk, II. Oct. 1883, 344.

  [B —, C 203 a, *part,* R 242 a, *part,* C 300, *part.*]

HAB. Arizona and Western Mexico.

593 b. Cardinalis cardinalis igneus (BAIRD).
  Saint Lucas Cardinal.

  Cardinalis igneus BAIRD, Pr. Ac. Nat. Sci. Phila. 1859, 305.
  Cardinalis cardinalis igneus STEJN. Auk, I. 1884, 171.

  [B —, C 203 a, *part,* R 242 a, *part,* C 300, *part.*]

HAB. Lower California.

GENUS **PYRRHULOXIA** BONAPARTE.

  Pyrrhuloxia BONAP. Consp. Av. I. 1850, 500. Type, *Cardinalis sinuatus* BONAP.

594. Pyrrhuloxia sinuata BONAP.
  Texan Cardinal.

  Cardinalis sinuatus BONAP. P. Z. S. 1837, 111.
  Pyrrhuloxia sinuata BONAP. Consp. Av. I. 1850, 500.

  [B 389, C 202, R 243, C 298.]

HAB. Southern border of the United States, from the valley of the Lower Rio Grande westward and southward.

Genus **HABIA** Reichenbach.

Habia Reich. Syst. Av. June 1, 1850, pl. lxxviii. Type, *Guiraca melanocephala* Swains.

595. **Habia ludoviciana** (Linn.).
Rose-breasted Grosbeak.

Loxia ludoviciana Linn. S. N. ed. 12, I. 1766, 306.
Habia ludoviciana Stejn. Auk, I. Oct. 1884, 367.

[B 380, C 193, R 244, C 289.]

Hab. Eastern United States and Southern Canada, west to the eastern border of the Plains, south, in winter, to Cuba, Central America, and Northern South America.

596. **Habia melanocephala** (Swains.).
Black-headed Grosbeak.

Guiraca melanocephala Swains. Philos. Mag. I. 1827, 438.
Habia melanocephala Stejn. Auk, I. Oct. 1884, 367.

[B 381, C 194, R 245, C 290.]

Hab. Western United States, from Middle Kansas to the Pacific coast, and south into Mexico.

Genus **GUIRACA** Swainson.

Guiraca Swains. Zool. Jour. III. Nov. 1827, 350. Type, *Loxia cærulea* Linn.

597. **Guiraca cærulea** (Linn.).
Blue Grosbeak.

Loxia cærulea Linn. S. N. ed. 10, I. 1758, 175.
Guiraca cærulea Swains. Phil. Mag. I. 1827, 438.

[B 382, C 195, R 246, C 291.]

Hab. Southern half of the United States, from the Atlantic to the Pacific, south into Mexico.

Genus **PASSERINA** Vieillot.

Passerina Vieill. Analyse, 1816, 30.   Type, by elimination, *Tanagra cyanea* Linn.

598. Passerina cyanea (Linn.).
   Indigo Bunting.

   Tanagra cyanea Linn. S. N. ed. 12, I. 1766, 315.
   Passerina cyanea Vieill. Nouv. Dict. d'Hist. Nat. XXV. 1817, 7.

   [B 387, C 199, R 248, C 295.]

   Hab. Eastern United States, south in winter to Veragua.

599. Passerina amœna (Say).
   Lazuli Bunting.

   Emberiza amœna Say, Long's Exp. II. 1823, 47.
   Passerina amœna Gray, Handl. II. 1870, 97.

   [B 386, C 200, R 249, C 296.]

   Hab. Western United States, from the Plains to the Pacific, south into Mexico.

600. Passerina versicolor (Bonap.).
   Varied Bunting.

   Spiza versicolor Bonap. P. Z. S. 1837, 120.
   Passerina versicolor Gray, Handl. II. 1870, 97.

   [B 385, C 197, R 250, C 293.]

   Hab. From the valley of the Lower Rio Grande in Texas and Lower California southward to Guatemala. Accidental in Southern Michigan.

601. Passerina ciris (Linn.).
   Painted Bunting.

   Emberiza ciris Linn. S. N. ed. 10, I. 1758, 179.
   Passerina ciris Vieill. Nouv. Dict. d'Hist. Nat. XXV. 1817, 17.

   [B 384, C 196, R 251; C 292.]

   Hab. South Atlantic and Gulf States, north to North Carolina and Southern Illinois, and south to Panama.

Genus SPOROPHILA Cabanis.

Sporophila Cabanis, Fauna Peruana, 1844, 211.

602. Sporophila morelleti (Bonap.).
Morellet's Seed-eater.

Spermophila morelleti "Pucheran," Bonap. Consp. Av. I, 1850, 497.
Sporophila morelleti Cabanis, Mus. Hein. I. 1851, 150.

[B 388, C 200, R 252, C 296.]

Hab. Valley of the Lower Rio Grande in Texas, south through Mexico to Costa Rica.

Genus EUETHEIA Reichenbach.

Euetheia Reich. Av. Syst. Nat. Knacker, "June 1, 1850," pl. lxxix. Type, *Emberiza lepida* Linn.

603. Euetheia bicolor (Linn.).
Grassquit.

Fringilla bicolor Linn. S. N. ed. 12, I. 1766, 324.
Euethia bicolor Gundlach, J. f. O. XXII. 1874, 312.

[B —, C 201, R 253, C 297.]

Hab. West Indies. Accidental or casual in Southern Florida.

Genus SPIZA Bonaparte.

Spiza Bonap. Journ. Ac. Nat. Sci. Phila. IV. i. Aug. 1824, 45. Type, *Emberiza americana* Gmel.

604. Spiza americana (Gmel.).
Dickcissel.

Emberiza americana Gmel. S. N. I. ii. 1788, 872.
Spiza americana Ridgw. Pr. U. S. Nat. Mus. III. March 27, 1880, 3.

[B 378, C 191, R 254, C 287.]

Hab. Eastern United States to the Rocky Mountains, north to Massachusetts, New York, Wisconsin, and Minnesota, and south in winter through Central America to Northern South America.

Genus **CALAMOSPIZA** Bonaparte.

Calamospiza Bonap. Geog. & Comp. List, 1838, 30. Type, *Fringilla bicolor* Towns. = *Calamospiza melanocorys* Stejn.

605. Calamospiza melanocorys Stejn.
Lark Bunting.

Calamospiza melanocorys Stejn. Auk, II. Jan. 1885, 49.

[B 377, C 190, R 256, C 286.]

Hab. From the Plains of Dakota and Middle Kansas west to the Rocky Mountains, less commonly thence to the Pacific, and south to Northern Mexico and Lower California. Accidental in Massachusetts.

Family **TANAGRIDÆ**. Tanagers.

Genus **EUPHONIA** Desmarest.

Euphonia Desm. Hist. Nat. Tang. 1805, —. Type, *Pipra musica* Gmel. ?

606. Euphonia elegantissima (Bonap.).
Blue-headed Euphonia.

Pipra elegantissima Bonap. P. Z. S. 1837, 112.
Euphonia elegantissima Gray, Gen. B. App. 1849, 17.

[B 224, C —, R 160, C —.]

Hab. Eastern Mexico, and south to Veragua. Texas (Giraud).

Genus **PIRANGA** Vieillot.

Piranga Vieill. Ois. Am. Sept. I. 1807, p. iv. Type, *Muscicapa rubra* Linn.

607. Piranga ludoviciana (Wils.).
Louisiana Tanager.

Tanagra ludoviciana Wils. Am. Orn. III. 1811, 27, pl. 20, fig. 1.
Pyranga ludoviciana Richardson, Rep. Brit. Ass. Adv. Sci. V. 1837, 175.

[B 223, C 110, R 162, C 158.]

HAB. Western United States, from the Great Plains to the Pacific. In winter south to Guatemala.

608. **Piranga erythromelas** VIEILL.
Scarlet Tanager.

Pyranga erythromelas VIEILL. Nouv. Dict. d'Hist. Nat. XXVIII. 1819, 293 (= *Pyranga rubra* AUCT., nec *Fringilla rubra* LINN.).

[B 220, C 107, R 161, C 154.]

HAB. Eastern United States, west to the Plains, and north to Southern Canada. In winter the West Indies, Central America, and Northern South America.

609. **Piranga hepatica** SWAINS.
Hepatic Tanager.

Pyranga hepatica SWAINS. Phil. Mag. I. 1827, 438.

[B 222, C 109, R 163, C 157.]

HAB. Southern New Mexico and Southern Arizona southward.

610. **Piranga rubra** (LINN.).
Summer Tanager.

Fringilla rubra LINN. S. N. ed. 10, I. 1758, 181.
Piranga rubra VIEILL. Ois. Am. Sept. I. 1807, p. iv.

[B 221, C 108, R 164, C 155.]

HAB. Eastern United States, to the Plains, north to Southern New Jersey and Southern Illinois, casually north to Connecticut and Ontario, and accidentally to Nova Scotia. In winter, Cuba, Central America, and Northern South America.

610 *a*. **Piranga rubra cooperi** RIDGW.
Cooper's Tanager.

Pyranga cooperi RIDGW. Pr. Ac. Nat. Sci. Phila. 1869, 130.
Piranga rubra cooperi RIDGW. Pr. U. S. Nat. Mus. VIII. 1885, 354.

[B —, C 108 *a*, R 164 *a*, C 156.]

HAB. New Mexico and Arizona, south into Western Mexico.

FAMILY HIRUNDINIDÆ. SWALLOWS.

GENUS **PROGNE** BOIE.

Progne BOIE, Isis, 1826, 971. Type, *Hirundo subis* LINN.

611. Progne subis (LINN.).
Purple Martin.

Hirundo subis LINN. S. N. ed. 10, I. 1758, 192.
Progne subis BAIRD, Rev. Am. B. I. May, 1865, 274.

[B 231, C 117, R 152, C 165.]

HAB. Temperate North America, south to Mexico.

GENUS **PETROCHELIDON** CABANIS.

Petrochelidon CAB. Mus. Hein. I. 1850, 47. Type, *Hirundo melanogastra* SWAINS.

612. Petrochelidon lunifrons (SAY).
Cliff Swallow.

Hirundo lunifrons SAY, LONG'S Exp. II. 1823, 47.
Petrochelidon lunifrons BAIRD, Rev. Am. B. I. May, 1865, 288.

[B 226, C 114, R 153, C 162.]

HAB. North America at large, and south to Brazil and Paraguay.

GENUS **CHELIDON** FORSTER.

Chelidon FORST. Synop. Cat. Brit. B. 1817, 55. Type, *Hirundo rustica* LINN.

613. Chelidon erythrogaster (BODD.).
Barn Swallow.

Hirundo erythrogaster BODD. Tabl. P. E. 1783, 45.
Chelidon erythrogastra STEJN. Pr. U. S. Nat. Mus. V. June 5, 1882, 31.

[B 225, C 111, R 154, C 159.]

HAB. North America in general, from the Fur Countries southward to the West Indies, Central America, and South America.

GENUS **TACHYCINETA** CABANIS.

Tachycineta CAB. Mus. Hein. I. 1850, 48.   Type, *Hirundo thalassina* SWAINS.

614. Tachycineta bicolor (VIEILL.).
   Tree Swallow.

Hirundo bicolor VIEILL. Ois. Am. Sept. I. 1807, 61, pl. 31.
Tachycineta bicolor CAB. Mus. Hein. I. 1850, 48.

[B 227, C 112, R 155, C 160.]

HAB. North America at large, from the Fur Countries southward, in winter, to the West Indies and Central America.

615. Tachycineta thalassina (SWAINS.).
   Violet-green Swallow.

Hirundo thalassinus SWAINS. Phil. Mag. I. 1827, 366.
Tachycineta thalassina CAB. Mus. Hein. I. 1850, 48.

[B 228, C 113, R 156, C 161.]

HAB. Western United States, from the eastern base of the Rocky Mountains to the Pacific, south to Guatemala.

GENUS **CLIVICOLA** FORSTER.

Clivicola FORST. Synop. Cat. Brit. B. 1817, 55.   Type, *Hirundo riparia* LINN.

616. Clivicola riparia (LINN.).
   Bank Swallow.

Hirundo riparia LINN. S. N. ed. 10, I. 1758, 192.
Clivicola riparia STEJN. Pr. U. S. Nat. Mus. V. 1882, 32.

[B 229, C 115, R 157, C 163.]

HAB. Northern Hemisphere; in America, south to the West Indies, Central America, and Northern South America.

Genus **STELGIDOPTERYX** Baird.

Stelgidopteryx Baird, B. N. Am. 1858, 312. Type, *Hirundo serripennis* Aud.

617. Stelgidopteryx serripennis (Aud.).
Rough-winged Swallow.

Hirundo serripennis Aud. Orn. Biog. IV. 1838, 593.
Stelgidopteryx serripennis Baird, B. N. Am. 1858, 312.

[B 230, C 116, R 158, C 164.]

Hab. United States at large (in the Eastern States north to Connecticut), south to Guatemala.

Family **AMPELIDÆ**. Waxwings, etc.

Subfamily **AMPELINÆ**. Waxwings.

Genus **AMPELIS** Linnæus.

Ampelis Linn. S. N. ed. 12, I. 1766, 297. Type, by elimination, *A. garrulus* Linn.

618. Ampelis garrulus Linn.
Bohemian Waxwing.

Lanius garrulus Linn. S. N. ed. 10, I. 1758, 95.
Ampelis garrulus Linn. S. N. ed. 12, I. 1766, 297.

[B 232, C 118, R 150, C 166.]

Hab. Northern parts of the Northern Hemisphere. In North America, south in winter, irregularly, to the Northern United States.

619. Ampelis cedrorum (Vieill.).
Cedar Waxwing.

Bombycilla cedrorum Vieill. Ois. Am. Sept. I. 1807, 88, pl. 57.
Ampelis cedrorum Gray, Gen. B. I. 1846, 278.

[B 233, C 119, R 151, C 167.]

HAB. North America at large, from the Fur Countries southward. In winter south to Guatemala and the West Indies.

SUBFAMILY **PTILIOGONATINÆ**.

GENUS **PHAINOPEPLA** SCLATER.

Phainopepla SCL. P. Z. S. 1858, 543. Type, *Ptiliogonys nitens* SWAINS.

620. **Phainopepla nitens** (SWAINS.).
   Phainopepla.

Ptiliogonys nitens SWAINS. Anim. in Menag. 1838, 285.
Phainopepla nitens SCL. P. Z. S. 1858, 543.

[B 234, C 120, R 26, C 168.]

HAB. Southwestern United States, from Southwestern Texas westward to California, north to Southern Utah and Nevada, and south into Mexico.

FAMILY **LANIIDÆ**. SHRIKES.

GENUS **LANIUS** LINNÆUS.

Lanius LINN. S. N. ed. 10, I. 1758, 93. Type, by elimination, *L. excubitor* LINN.

621. **Lanius borealis** VIEILL.
   Northern Shrike.

Lanius borealis VIEILL. Ois. Am. Sept. I. 1807. 90. pl. 50.

[B 236, C 134, R 148, C 186.]

HAB. Northern North America, south in winter to the middle portions of the United States (Washington, D. C., Kentucky, Kansas, Colorado, Arizona, Northern California).

622. Lanius ludovicianus LINN.
   Loggerhead Shrike.

   Lanius ludovicianus LINN. S. N. ed. 12, I. 1766, 134.

   [B 237, C 135, R 149, C 187.]

   HAB. Florida, the Carolinas, and the Gulf States east of Texas.

622 a. Lanius ludovicianus excubitorides (SWAINS.).
   White-rumped Shrike.

   Lanius excubitorides SWAINS. Fauna Bor. Am. II. 1831, 115, pl. 34.
   Lanius ludovicianus var. *excubitoroides* COUES, Key, 1872, 125.

   [B 238, C 135 a, R 149 a, C 188.]

   HAB. Western United States, east to the Middle and New England States, breeding as far north as Northern New York and Northern New England. Rare or local east of the Alleghanies.

FAMILY **VIREONIDÆ**. VIREOS.

GENUS **VIREO** VIEILLOT.

SUBGENUS **VIREOSYLVA** BONAPARTE.

Vierosylva BONAP. Geog. & Comp. List, 1838, 26. Type, *Muscicapa olivacea* LINN.

[623.] Vireo altiloquus barbatulus (CAB.).
   Black-whiskered Vireo.

   Phyllomanes barbatulus CAB. J. f. O. 1855, 467.
   Vireo altiloquus var. *barbatulus* COUES, Key, 1872, 120.

   [B 243, C 123, R 137, C 172.]

   HAB. Bahamas, Cuba, and Southern Florida.

624. Vireo olivaceus (LINN.).
   Red-eyed Vireo.

   Muscicapa olivacea LINN. S. N. ed. 12, I. 1766, 327.
   Vireo olivaceus BONAP. Ann. Lyc. N. Y. II. 1826, 71.

[B 240, C 122, R 135, C 170.]

HAB. Eastern North America, to the Rocky Mountains, north to the arctic regions.

625. **Vireo flavoviridis** (CASS.).
Yellow-green Vireo.

Vireosylvia flavoviridis CASS. Pr. Ac. Nat. Sci. Phila. V. Feb. 1851, 152.
Vireo flavoviridis BAIRD, B. N. Am. 1858, 332.

[B 241, C —, R 136, C 171.]

HAB. Valley of the Lower Rio Grande in Texas, southward to Panama. Accidental at Godbout, Province of Quebec.

626. **Vireo philadelphicus** (CASS.).
Philadelphia Vireo.

Vireosylvia philadelphica CASS. Pr. Ac. Nat. Sci. Phila. V. Feb. 1851, 153, pl. 10, fig. 2.
Vireo philadelphicus BAIRD, B. N. Am. 1858, 335.

[B 244, C 124, R 138, C 173.]

HAB. Eastern North America, north to Hudson's Bay; south, in winter, to Costa Rica.

627. **Vireo gilvus** (VIEILL.).
Warbling Vireo.

Muscicapa gilva VIEILL. Ois. Am. Sept. I. 1807, 65, pl. 34.
Vireo gilvus BONAP. Journ. Ac. Nat. Sci Phila. IV. 1824, 176.

[B 245, C 125, 125 a, R 139, 139 a, C 174, 175.]

HAB. North America in general, from the Fur Countries to Mexico.

SUBGENUS **LANIVIREO** BAIRD.

Lanivireo BAIRD, Rev. Am. B. I May, 1866, 345. Type, *Vireo flavifrons* VIEILL.

628. **Vireo flavifrons** VIEILL.
Yellow-throated Vireo.

Vireo flavifrons VIEILL. Ois. Am. Sept. I. 1807, 85, pl. 54.

[B 252, C 126, R 140, C 176.]

HAB. Eastern United States; south, in winter, to Costa Rica.

629. Vireo solitarius (WILS.).
Blue-headed Vireo.

Muscicapa solitaria WILS. Am. Orn. II. 1810, 43, pl. 17, fig. 6.
Vireo solitarius VIEILL. Nouv. Dict. d'Hist. Nat. XXXVI. 1819, 103.

[B 250, C 127, R 141, C 177.]

HAB. Eastern United States to the Plains. In winter, south to Mexico and Guatemala.

629 a. Vireo solitarius cassinii (XANTUS).
Cassin's Vireo.

Vireo cassinii XANT. Pr. Ac. Nat. Sci. Phila. 1858, 117.
Vireo solitarius var. *cassini* HENSH. Rep. Orn. Spec. (Wheeler's Exp.), 1874, 105.

[B 251, C —, R 141 a, C 178.]

HAB. Western United States; confined to the Pacific slope during the breeding season.

629 b. Vireo solitarius plumbeus (COUES).
Plumbeous Vireo.

Vireo plumbeus COUES, Pr. Ac. Nat. Sci. Phila. 1866, 74.
Vireo solitarius var. *plumbeus* ALLEN, Bull. M. C. Z. III. 1872, 176.

[B —, C 127 a, R 141 b, C 179.]

HAB. Western United States, from the eastern base of the Rocky Mountains westward, south into Mexico in winter.

SUBGENUS **VIREO** VIEILLOT.

Vireo VIEILL. Ois. Am. Sept. I. 1807, 83. Type, *V. musicus* VIEILL. = *Muscicapa noveboracensis* GMEL.

630. Vireo atricapillus WOODH.
Black-capped Vireo.

Vireo atricapillus WOODH. Pr. Ac. Nat. Sci. Phila. 1852, 60.

[B 427, C 133, R 142, C 185.]

HAB. Mexico and Texas, and north to Kansas.

631. **Vireo noveboracensis** (GMEL.).
White-eyed Vireo.

Muscicapa noveboracensis GMEL. S. N. I. ii. 1788, 947.
Vireo noveboracensis BONAP. Journ. Ac. Nat. Sci. Phila. IV. 1824, 176.

[B 248, C 129, R 143, C 181.]

HAB. Eastern United States, west to the Rocky Mountains; south, in winter, to Guatemala. Resident in the Bermudas.

632. **Vireo huttoni** CASS.
Hutton's Vireo.

Vireo huttoni CASS. Pr. Ac. Nat. Sci. Phila. 1851, 150, pl. 10, fig. 1.

[B 249, C 130, R 144, C 182.]

HAB. California.

632 a. *Vireo huttoni stephensi* BREWST.
Stephens's Vireo.

Vireo huttoni stephensi BREWST. Bull. Nutt. Orn. Club, VII. July, 1882, 142.

[B —, C —, R —, C —.]

HAB. Arizona, Western Mexico, and Lower California.

633. **Vireo bellii** AUD.
Bell's Vireo.

Vireo bellii AUD. B. Am. VII. 1844, 333, pl. 485.

[B 246, C 131, R 145, C 183.]

HAB. Middle portion of the United States, from Illinois and Iowa west to the eastern base of the Rocky Mountains, south into Mexico.

633 a. *Vireo bellii pusillus* (COUES).
Least Vireo.

Vireo pusillus COUES, Pr. Ac. Nat. Sci. Phila. 1866, 76.
Vireo bellii pusillus RIDGW. Pr. U. S. Nat. Mus. VIII. 1885, 354.

[B —, C 132, R 146, C 184.]

HAB. Arizona and California, south to Cape St. Lucas, and throughout Western Mexico.

634. **Vireo vicinior** COUES.
Gray Vireo.

Vireo vicinior COUES, Pr. Ac. Nat. Sci. Phila. 1866, 75.

[B —, C 128, R 147, C 180.]

HAB. Western Texas, New Mexico, Arizona, and Southern California.

FAMILY **CŒREBIDÆ.** HONEY CREEPERS.

GENUS **CERTHIOLA** SUNDEVALL.

Certhiola SUND. Vet. Ak. Handl. Stockh. 1835, 99. Type, *Certhia flaveola* LINN.

635. **Certhiola bahamensis** REICH.
Bahama Honey Creeper.

Certhiola bahamensis REICH. Handb. I. 1853, 253.

[B 301, C 106, R 159, C 153.]

HAB. Bahamas, and the Keys of the southeastern coast of Florida.

FAMILY **MNIOTILTIDÆ.** WOOD-WARBLERS.

GENUS **MNIOTILTA** VIEILLOT.

Mniotilta VIEILL. Analyse, 1816, 45. Type, *Motacilla varia* LINN.

636. **Mniotilta varia** (LINN.).
Black and White Warbler.

Motacilla varia LINN. S. N. ed. 12, I. 1766, 333.
Mniotilta varia VIEILL. Nouv. Dict. d'Hist. Nat. XXI. 1818, 230.

[B 167, C 57, R 74, 74 a, C 91, 92.]

HAB. Eastern United States to the Plains, north to Fort Simpson, south, in winter, to Central America and the West Indies.

Genus **PROTONOTARIA** BAIRD.

Protonotaria BAIRD, B. N. Am. 1858, 239. Type, *Motacilla citrea* BODD.

637. Protonotaria citrea (BODD.).
   Prothonotary Warbler.

Motacilla citrea BODD. Tabl. P. E. 1783. 44.
Protonotaria citrea BAIRD, B. N. Am. 1858, 239.

[B 169, C 59, R 75, C 95.]

HAB. Eastern United States, chiefly southward; in winter, Cuba and Central America.

Genus **HELINAIA** AUDUBON.

Helinaia AUD. Synop. 1839, 66. Type, *Sylvia swainsonii* AUD.

638. Helinaia swainsonii AUD.
   Swainson's Warbler.

Sylvia swainsonii AUD. Orn. Biog. II. 1834, 563, pl. 198.
Helinaia swainsonii AUD. Synop. 1839, 66.

[B 179, C 61, R 76, C 97.]

HAB. Southeastern United States (South Carolina, Georgia, Florida, Louisiana, Texas) and Jamaica.

Genus **HELMITHERUS** RAFINESQUE.

Helmitherus RAFIN. Journ. de Phys. LXXXVIII. 1819, 417. Type, *Motacilla vermivora* GMEL.

639. Helmitherus vermivorus (GMEL.).
   Worm-eating Warbler.

Motacilla vermivora GMEL. S. N. I. ii. 1788, 951.
Helmitheros vermivora BONAP. Consp. Av. I. April 20, 1850, 314.

[B 178, C 60, R 77, C 96.]

HAB. Eastern United States, north to Southern New York and Southern New England, south, in winter, to Cuba and Central America.

GENUS **HELMINTHOPHILA** RIDGWAY.

Helminthophila RIDGW. Bull. Nutt. Orn. Club, VII. Jan. 1882, 53. Type, *Sylvia ruficapilla* WILS.

640. **Helminthophila bachmani** (AUD.).
Bachman's Warbler.

Sylvia bachmani AUD. Orn. Biog. II. 1834, 483, pl. 183.
Helminthophila bachmani RIDGW. Bull. Nutt. Orn. Club, VII. Jan. 1882, 53.

[B 182, C 64, R 78, C 103.]

HAB. South Carolina and Georgia; Cuba, in winter. No recent record of its occurrence.

641. **Helminthophila pinus** (LINN.).
Blue-winged Warbler.

Certhia pinus LINN. S. N. ed. 12, I. 1766, 187.
Helminthophila pinus RIDGW. Bull. Nutt. Orn. Club, VII. Jan. 1882, 53.

[B 180, C 62, R 79, C 98.]

HAB. Eastern United States, from Southern New York and Southern New England southward. In winter, Mexico and Guatemala.

642. **Helminthophila chrysoptera** (LINN.).
Golden-winged Warbler.

Motacilla chrysoptera LINN. S. N. ed. 12, I. 1766, 333.
Helminthophila chrysoptera RIDGW. Bull. Nutt. Orn. Club, VII. Jan. 1882, 53.

[B 181, C 63, R 81, C 102.]

HAB. Eastern United States; Central America in winter.

643. **Helminthophila luciæ** (COOPER).
   Lucy's Warbler.

   Helminthophaga luciæ COOPER, Pr. Cal. Ac. Sci. July, 1862, 120.
   Helminthophila luciæ RIDGW. Bull. Nutt. Orn. Club, VII. Jan. 1882, 54.

   [B —, C 65, R 83, C 104.]

   HAB. Valleys of the Colorado and Gila Rivers in Arizona and California.

644. **Helminthophila virginiæ** (BAIRD).
   Virginia's Warbler.

   Helminthophaga virginiæ BAIRD, B. N. Am. ed. 1860, Atlas, p. xi. foot-note, pl. 79, fig. 1.
   Helminthophila virginiæ RIDGW. Bull. Nutt. Orn. Club, VII. Jan. 1882, 54.

   [B —, C 66, R 84, C 105.]

   HAB. Rocky Mountain region of the United States, from Colorado, Utah, and Nevada southward.

645. **Helminthophila ruficapilla** (WILS.).
   Nashville Warbler.

   Sylvia ruficapilla WILS. Am. Orn. III. 1811, 120, pl. 27, fig. 3.
   Helminthophila ruficapilla RIDGW. Bull. Nutt. Orn. Club, VII. Jan. 1882, 54.

   [B 183, *part*, C 67, *part*, R 85, *part*, C 106, *part*.]

   HAB. Eastern North America to the Plains, north to the Fur Countries, breeding from the Northern United States northward. Mexico in winter.

645 *a*. **Helminthophila ruficapilla gutturalis** RIDGW.
   Calaveras Warbler.

   Helminthophaga ruficapilla var. *gutturalis* RIDGW. in Hist. N. Am. B. I. Jan. 1874, 191.
   Helminthophila ruficapilla gutturalis RIDGW. Pr. U. S. Nat. Mus. VIII. 1885, 354.

   [B 183, *part*, C 67, *part*, R 85, *part*, C 106, *part*.]

   HAB. Western United States, from the Rocky Mountains to the Pacific.

646. Helminthophila celata (Say).
   Orange-crowned Warbler.

   Sylvia celata Say, Long's Exp. I. 1823, 169.
   Helminthophila celata Ridgw. Bull. Nutt. Orn. Club, VII. Jan. 1882, 54.

   [B 184, *part*, C 68, R 86, C 107.]

   Hab. Eastern North America (rare, however, in the Northeastern United States), breeding as far northward as the Yukon and Mackenzie River districts, and southward through the Rocky Mountains, and wintering in the South Atlantic and Gulf States and Mexico.

646 a. Helminthophila celata lutescens (Ridgw.).
   Lutescent Warbler.

   Helminthophaga celata var. *lutescens* Ridgw. Am. Jour. Sci. & Arts, 1872, 457.
   Helminthophila celata lutescens Brewst. Bull. Nutt. Orn. Club, VII. April, 1882, 85.

   [B 184, *part*, C 68 *a*, R 86 *a*, C 108.]

   Hab. Pacific coast of North America, eastward, during migrations, to the Rocky Mountains, and northward to Kadiak, Alaska.

647. Helminthophila peregrina (Wils.).
   Tennessee Warbler.

   Sylvia peregrina Wils. Am. Orn. III. 1811, 83, pl. 25, fig. 2.
   Helminthophila peregrina Ridgw. Bull. Nutt. Orn. Club, VII. Jan. 1882, 54.

   [B 185, C 69, R 87, C 109.]

   Hab. Eastern North America, breeding from Northern New York and Northern New England northward to Hudson's Bay Territory; Central America in winter.

Genus **COMPSOTHLYPIS** Cabanis.

Compsothlypis Cab. Mus. Hein. I. 1850, 20. Type, *Parus americanus* Linn.

ORDER PASSERES. 305

648. Compsothlypis americana (LINN.).
Parula Warbler.

Parus americanus LINN. S. N. ed. 10, I. 1758, 190.
Compsothlypis americana CAB. Mus. Hein. I. 1850, 20.

[B 168, C 58, R 88, C 93.]

HAB. Eastern United States, west to the Plains, north to Canada, and south in winter to the West Indies and Central America.

649. Compsothlypis nigrilora (COUES).
Sennett's Warbler.

Parula nigrilora COUES, Bull. U. S. Geol. & Geog. Surv. Terr. IV. 1878, 11.
Compsothlypis nigrilora STEJN. Auk, I. April, 1884, 170.

[B —, C —, R 89 a, C 94.]

HAB. Valley of the Lower Rio Grande in Texas.

GENUS **DENDROICA** GRAY.

SUBGENUS **PERISSOGLOSSA** BAIRD.

Perissoglossa BAIRD, Rev. Am. B. I. April, 1865, 180. Type, *Motacilla tigrina* GMEL.

650. Dendroica tigrina (GMEL.).
Cape May Warbler.

Motacilla tigrina GMEL. S. N. I. ii. 1788. 985.
Dendroica tigrina BAIRD, B. N. Am. 1858, 286.

[B 206, C 85, R 90, C 126.]

HAB. Eastern North America, north to Hudson's Bay Territory, west to the Plains. Breeds from Northern New England northward, and also in Jamaica; winters in the West Indies.

SUBGENUS **PEUCEDRAMUS** COUES.

Peucedramus COUES, in Zool. Wheeler's Exp. 1876, 202. Type, *Sylvia olivacea* GIRAUD.

651. Dendroica olivacea (GIRAUD).
Olive Warbler.

Sylvia olivacea GIRAUD, Sixteen Sp. Tex. B. 1841, 29, pl. 7, fig. 2.
Dendroica olivacea BAIRD, B. N. Am. 1858, 305.

[B —, C —, R 92, C 110.]

HAB. Southern New Mexico, Arizona, Mexico, and Guatemala. Texas (GIRAUD).

SUBGENUS **DENDROICA** GRAY.

Dendroica GRAY, List Gen. B. App. 1842, 8. Type, *Motacilla coronata* LINN.

652. Dendroica æstiva (GMEL.).
Yellow Warbler.

Motacilla æstiva GMEL. S. N. I. ii. 1788, 996.
Dendroica æstiva BAIRD, B. N. Am. 1858, 282.

[B 203, C 70, R 93, C 111.]

HAB. North America at large, south in winter to Central America and Northern South America.

653. Dendroica bryanti castaneiceps RIDGW.
Mangrove Warbler.

Dendroica bryanti castaneiceps RIDGW. Pr. U. S. Nat. Mus. VIII. Sept. 2, 1885, 350.

[B —, C —, R —, C —.]

HAB. Western Mexico, and Cape St. Lucas, Lower California.

654. Dendroica cærulescens (GMEL.).
Black-throated Blue Warbler.

Motacilla cærulescens GMEL. S. N. I. 1788, 960.
Dendroica cærulescens BAIRD, Rev. Am. B. 1865, 186.

[B 193, C 76, R 94, C 117.]

HAB. Eastern North America to the Plains, breeding from Northern New England and Northern New York northward, and in the Alleghanies to Northern Georgia; West Indies in winter.

655. Dendroica coronata (LINN.).
Myrtle Warbler.

Motacilla coronata LINN. S. N. ed. 12, I. 1766, 333.
Dendroica coronata GRAY, List Gen. B. App. 1842, 8.

[B 194, C 78, R 95, C 119.]

HAB. Eastern North America, chiefly, straggling more or less commonly westward to the Pacific; breeds from the Northern United States northward, and winters from the Middle States and the Ohio Valley southward to the West Indies and Central America.

656. Dendroica auduboni (TOWNS.).
Audubon's Warbler.

Sylvia auduboni TOWNS. Journ. Ac. Nat. Sci. Phila. VII. 1837, 191.
Dendroica audubonii BAIRD, B. N. Am. 1858, 273.

[B 195, C 79, R 96, C 120.]

HAB. Western United States, east to the western border of the Plains; south in winter to Guatemala. Accidental in Massachusetts.

657. Dendroica maculosa (GMEL.).
Magnolia Warbler.

Motacilla maculosa GMEL. S. N. I. ii. 1788, 984.
Dendroica maculosa BAIRD, B. N. Am. 1858, 284.

[B 204, C 84, R 97, C 125.]

HAB. Eastern North America to the base of the Rocky Mountains, breeding from Northern New England, Northern New York, and Northern Michigan, to Hudson's Bay Territory. In winter, Bahamas, Cuba, and Central America.

658. Dendroica cærulea (WILS.).
Cerulean Warbler.

Sylvia cærulea WILS. Am. Orn. II. 1810, 141, pl. 17, fig. 5.
Dendroica cærulea BAIRD, B. N. Am. 1858, 280.

[B 201, C 77, R 98, C 118.]

HAB. Eastern United States and Southern Canada to the Plains. Rare or casual east of Central New York and the Alleghanies. Cuba (rare) and Central America in winter.

659. Dendroica pensylvanica (LINN.).
Chestnut-sided Warbler.

Motacilla pensylvanica LINN. S. N. ed. 12, I. 1766, 333.
Dendroica pennsylvanica BAIRD, B. N. Am. 1858, 279.

[B 200, C 83, R 99, C 124.]

HAB. Eastern United States and Southern Canada, west to the Plains, breeding southward to Central Illinois and in the Appalachian highlands probably to Northern Georgia. Visits the Bahamas and Central America in winter.

660. Dendroica castanea (WILS.).
Bay-breasted Warbler.

Sylvia castanea WILS. Am. Orn. II. 1810, 97, pl. 14, fig. 4.
Dendroica castanea BAIRD, B. N. Am. 1858, 276.

[B 197, C 82, R 100, C 123.]

HAB. Eastern North America, north to Hudson's Bay. Breeds from Northern New England and Northern Michigan northward; winters in Central America.

661. Dendroica striata (FORST.).
Black-poll Warbler.

Muscicapa striata FORST. Philos. Trans. LXII. 1772, 406, 428.
Dendroica striata BAIRD, B. N. Am. 1858, 280.

[B 202, C 81, R 101, C 122.]

HAB. Eastern North America to the Rocky Mountains, north to Greenland, the Barren Grounds, and Alaska, breeding from Northern New England northward. South in winter to Northern South America.

662. Dendroica blackburniæ (GMEL.).
Blackburnian Warbler.

Motacilla blackburniæ GMEL. S. N. I. ii. 1788, 977.
Dendroica blackburniæ BAIRD, B. N. Am. 1858, 274.

[B 196, C 80, R 102, C 121.]

HAB. Eastern North America to the Plains, breeding from the northern and more elevated parts of the Eastern United States northward; in winter, south to the Bahamas, Central America, and Northern South America.

663. **Dendroica dominica** (LINN.).
Yellow-throated Warbler.

Motacilla dominica LINN. S. N. ed. 12, I. 1766, 334.
Dendroica dominica BAIRD, Rev. Am. B. I. 1865, 209.

[B 209, *part*, C 88, R 103, C 129.]

HAB. Southeastern United States, north to the Middle States, and rarely to Southern New England; south to the West Indies.

663 a. **Dendroica dominica albilora** BAIRD.
Sycamore Warbler.

Dendroica dominica var. *albilora* "BAIRD," RIDGW. Am. Nat. VII. Oct. 1873, 606.

[B 209, *part*, C 88 a, R 103 a, C 130.]

HAB. Mississippi Valley, west to the Plains, and north to Lake Erie and Southern Michigan; in winter south to Southern Mexico, Hondurus, and Guatemala. Accidental in South Carolina.

664. **Dendroica graciæ** COUES.
Grace's Warbler.

Dendroica graciæ "COUES MSS." BAIRD, Rev. Am. B. I. Apr. 1865, 210.

[B —, C 87, R 104, C 128.]

HAB. Southern New Mexico and Arizona, and southward.

665. **Dendroica nigrescens** (TOWNS.).
Black-throated Gray Warbler.

Sylvia nigrescens TOWNS. Journ. Ac. Nat. Sci. Phila. VII, 1837, 191.
Dendroica nigrescens BAIRD, B. N. Am. 1858, 270.

[B 192, C 75, R 105, C 116.]

HAB. Western United States, north to Colorado and Oregon, migrating into Mexico in winter.

666. Dendroica chrysoparia SCL. & SALV.
Golden-cheeked Warbler.

Dendrœca chrysoparia SCL. & SALV. P. Z. S. 1860, 298.

[B —, C 74, R 106, C 115.]

HAB. Southwestern Texas, and southward to Guatemala.

667. Dendroica virens (GMEL.).
Black-throated Green Warbler.

Motacilla virens GMEL. S. N. I. ii. 1788, 985.
Dendroica virens BAIRD, B. N. Am. 1858, 267.

[B 189, C 71, R 107, C 112.]

HAB. Eastern North America to the Plains, north to Hudson's Bay Territory, breeding from the Northern United States northward. In winter, south to Cuba and Panama. Accidental in Greenland and Europe.

668. Dendroica townsendi (NUTT.).
Townsend's Warbler.

Sylvia townsendi "NUTT." TOWNS. Journ. Ac. Nat. Sci. Phila. VII. 1837, 191.
Dendroica townsendi BAIRD, B. N. Am. 1858, 269.

[B 191, C 73, R 108, C 114.]

HAB. Western North America, east to Western Colorado, north to Sitka, south into Mexico, and in winter to Guatemala. Accidental near Philadelphia.

669. Dendroica occidentalis (TOWNS.).
Hermit Warbler.

Sylvia occidentalis TOWNS. Journ. Ac. Nat. Sci. Phila. VII. 1837, 190.
Dendroica occidentalis BAIRD, B. N. Am. 1858, 268.

[B 190, C 72, R 109, C 113.]

HAB. Western United States, from the Rocky Mountains to the Pacific coast, and from Washington Territory southward; in winter, to Guatemala.

670. **Dendroica kirtlandi** BAIRD.
 Kirtland's Warbler.

 Sylvicola kirtlandi BAIRD, Ann. Lyc. N. Y. V. 1852, 216, pl. 6.
 Dendroica kirtlandi BAIRD, B. N. Am. 1858, 249.

   [B 205, C 89, R 110, C 131.]

 HAB. Eastern United States (Ohio, Missouri, Michigan, Wisconsin), and the Bahamas in winter.

671. **Dendroica vigorsii** (AUD.).
 Pine Warbler.

 Sylvia vigorsii AUD. Orn. Biog. I. 1832, 153, pl. 30.
 Dendroica vigorsii STEJN. Auk, II. Oct. 1885, 343.

   [B 198, C 91, R 111, C 134.]

 HAB. Eastern United States, to the Plains, north to Ontario and New Brunswick, wintering in the South Atlantic and Gulf States, and the Bahamas.

672. **Dendroica palmarum** (GMEL.).
 Palm Warbler.

 Motacilla palmarum GMEL. S. N. I. ii. 1788, 951.
 Dendroica palmarum BAIRD, B. N. Am. 1858, 288.

   [B 208, *part*, C 90, *part*, R 113, C 132.]

 HAB. Northern interior to Great Slave Lake; in winter and in migrations, Mississippi Valley and Gulf States, including Western and Southern Florida, and the West Indies. Casual in the Atlantic States.

672*a*. **Dendroica palmarum hypochrysea** RIDGW.
 Yellow Palm Warbler.

 Dendrœca palmarum hypochrysea RIDGW. Bull. Nutt. Orn. Club, I. Nov. 1876, 85.

   [B 208, *part*, C 90, *part*, R 113 *a*, C 133.]

 HAB. Atlantic States, north to Hudson's Bay. Breeds from New Brunswick and Nova Scotia northward; winters in the South Atlantic and Gulf States.

673. **Dendroica discolor** (Vieill.).
Prairie Warbler.

Sylvia discolor Vieill. Ois. Am. Sept. I. 1807, 37, pl. 98.
Dendroica discolor Baird, B. N. Am. 1858, 290.

[B 210, C 86, R 114, C 127.]

Hab. Eastern United States to the Plains, north to Michigan and Southern New England. Winters in Southern Florida and the West Indies.

Genus **SEIURUS** Swainson.

Seiurus Swains. Phil. Mag. I. May, 1827, 369. Type, *Motacilla aurocapilla* Linn.

674. **Seiurus aurocapillus** (Linn.).
Oven-bird.

Motacilla aurocapilla Linn. S. N. ed. 12, I. 1766, 334.
Seiurus aurocapillus Swains. Zool. Journ. III. 1827, 171.

[B 186, C 92, R 115, C 135.]

Hab. Eastern North America, north to Hudson's Bay Territory and Alaska, breeding from Kansas, the Ohio Valley, and Virginia northward. In winter, Southern Florida, the West Indies, and Central America.

675. **Seiurus noveboracensis** (Gmel.).
Water-Thrush.

Motacilla noveboracensis Gmel. S. N. I. ii. 1788, 958.
Seiurus noveboracensis Bonap. Geog. & Comp. List, 1838, 21.

[B 187, *part*, C 93, *part*, R 116, C 136.]

Hab. Eastern United States to Illinois, and northward to Arctic America, breeding from the Northern United States northward. South in winter to the West Indies and Northern South America.

675a. Seiurus noveboracensis notabilis (Grinn.).
Grinnell's Water-Thrush.

Seiurus nævius notabilis "Grinnell," Ridgw. Pr. U. S. Nat. Mus. II. 1880, 12.
Seiurus noveboracensis notabilis Ridgw. Pr. U. S. Nat. Mus. VIII. 1885, 354.

[B 187, *part*, C 93, *part*, R 116 *a*, C 137.]

HAB. United States from Illinois westward to California, and north into British America. Winters from the southern border of the United States southward to Northern South America.

676. **Seiurus motacilla** (VIEILL.).
 Louisiana Water-Thrush.

Turdus motacilla VIEILL. Ois. Am. Sept. II. 1807, 9, pl. 65.
Seiurus motacilla BONAP. Consp. Av. I. 1850, 306.

[B 188, C 94, R 117, C 138.]

HAB. Eastern United States, north to Southern New England and Michigan, west to the Plains. In winter, West Indies, Southern Mexico, and Central America.

GENUS **GEOTHLYPIS** CABANIS.

SUBGENUS **OPORORNIS** BAIRD.

Oporornis BAIRD, B. N. Am. 1858, 246. Type, *Sylvia agilis* WILS.

677. **Geothlypis formosa** (WILS.).
 Kentucky Warbler.

Sylvia formosa WILS. Am. Orn. III. 1811, 85, pl. 25, fig. 3.
Geothlypis formosa RIDGW. Pr. U. S. Nat. Mus. VIII. 1885, 354.

[B 175, C 96, R 119, C 140.]

HAB. Eastern United States, west to the Plains, and north to Southern New England and Southern Michigan. In winter, West Indies and Central America.

678. **Geothlypis agilis** (WILS.).
 Connecticut Warbler.

Sylvia agilis WILS. Am. Orn. V. 1812, 64, pl. 39, fig. 4.
Geothlypis agilis GREGG, Pr. Elmira Acad. 1870, — (p. 7 of reprint).

[B 174, C 95, R 118, C 139.]

HAB. Eastern North America, breeding north of the United States.

SUBGENUS **GEOTHLYPIS** CABANIS.

Geothlypis CAB. Wiegm. Archiv, 1847, i. 316, 349. Type, *Turdus trichas* LINN.

679. **Geothlypis philadelphia** (WILS.).
Mourning Warbler.

Sylvia philadelphia WILS. Am. Orn. II. 1810, 101, pl. 14, fig. 6.
Geothlypis philadelphia BAIRD, B. N. Am. 1858, 243.

[B 172, C 98, R 120, C 142.]

HAB. Eastern North America to the Plains, breeding from the mountainous portions of Pennsylvania, New England, and New York, and Northern Michigan northward. Central America and Northern South America in winter.

680. **Geothlypis macgillivrayi** (AUD.).
Macgillivray's Warbler.

Sylvia macgillivrayi AUD. Orn. Biog. V. 1839, 75, pl. 399, figs. 4, 5.
Geothlypis macgillivrayi BAIRD, B. N. Am. 1858, 244.

[B 173, C 99, R 121, C 143.]

HAB. Western United States, from the eastern foothills of the Rocky Mountains to the Pacific coast, north into British Columbia. Mexico and Central America in winter.

681. **Geothlypis trichas** (LINN.).
Maryland Yellow-throat.

Turdus trichas LINN. S. N. ed. 12, I. 1766, 293.
Geothlypis trichas CAB. Mus. Hein. I. 1850, 16.

[B 170, *part*, C 97, *part*, R 122, *part*, C 141, *part*.]

HAB. Eastern United States, mainly east of the Alleghanies, north to Ontario and Nova Scotia, breeding from Georgia northward. In winter, South Atlantic and Gulf States, and the West Indies.

681 a. **Geothlypis trichas occidentalis** BREWST.
Western Yellow-throat.

Geothlypis trichas occidentalis BREWST. Bull. Nutt. Orn. Club, VIII. July, 1883, 159

[B 170, *part*, C 97, *part*, R 122, *part*, C 141, *part*.]

HAB. United States, from the Mississippi Valley west to the Pacific coast, south, in winter, to Central America.

682. Geothlypis beldingi RIDGW.
Belding's Yellow-throat.

Geothlypis beldingi RIDGW. Pr. U. S. Nat. Mus. V. Sept. 5, 1882, 344.

[B —, C —, R —, C —.]

HAB. Lower California.

GENUS ICTERIA VIEILLOT.

Icteria VIEILL. Ois. Am. Sept. I. 1807, pp. iii., 85. Type, *Muscicapa viridis* GMEL. = *Turdus virens* LINN.

683. Icteria virens (LINN.).
Yellow-breasted Chat.

Turdus virens LINN. S. N. ed. 10, I. 1758, 171.
Icteria virens BAIRD, Rev. Am. B. I. 1865, 228.

[B 176, C 100, R 123, C 144.]

HAB. Eastern United States to the Plains, north to Ontario and Southern New England, south, in winter, to Eastern Mexico and Guatemala.

683 a. Icteria virens longicauda (LAWR.).
Long-tailed Chat.

Icteria longicauda LAWR. Ann. Lyc. N. Y. VI. 1853, 4.
Icteria virens var. *longicauda* COUES, Key, 1872, 108.

[B 177, C 100 a, R 123 a, C 145.]

HAB. Western United States, from the Plains to the Pacific, south into Mexico.

GENUS SYLVANIA NUTTALL.

Sylvania NUTT. Man. Land Birds, I. 1832, 290. Type, by elimination, *Muscicapa selbii* AUD. = *Motacilla mitrata* GMEL.

684. Sylvania mitrata (GMEL.).
   Hooded Warbler.

   Motacilla mitrata GMEL. S. N. I. ii. 1788, 977.
   Sylvania mitrata NUTT. Man. Land B. ed. 1840, 333.

   [B 211, C 101, R 124, C 146.]

HAB. Eastern United States, west to the Plains, north and east to Michigan, Southern New York, and Southern New England. In winter, West Indies, Eastern Mexico, and Central America.

685. Sylvania pusilla (WILS.).
   Wilson's Warbler.

   Muscicapa pusilla WILS. Am. Orn. III. 1811, 103, pl. 26, fig. 4.
   Sylvania pusilla NUTT. Man. Land B. ed. 1840, 335.

   [B 213, *part*, C 102, R 125, C 147.]

HAB. Eastern North America, west to and including the Rocky Mountains, north to Hudson's Bay Territory and Alaska. Breeds chiefly north of the United States, migrating south to Eastern Mexico and Central America.

685 a. Sylvania pusilla pileolata (PALL.).
   Pileolated Warbler.

   Motacilla pileolata PALL. Zoog. Rosso-As. I. 1826, 497.
   Sylvania pusilla pileolata RIDGW. Pr. U. S. Nat. Mus. VIII. 1885, 354.

   [B 213, *part*, C 102 a, R 125 a, C 148.]

HAB. Western North America, from the Great Basin to the Pacific, north to Alaska (Kadiak), and south, in winter, to Costa Rica.

686. Sylvania canadensis (LINN.).
   Canadian Warbler.

   Muscicapa canadensis LINN. S. N. ed. 12, I. 1766, 327.
   Sylvania canadensis RIDGW. Pr. U. S. Nat. Mus. VIII. 1885, 354.

   [B 214, 215, C 103, R 127, C 149.]

HAB. Eastern North America, westward to the Plains, and north to Newfoundland, Southern Labrador, and Lake Winnipeg, south, in winter, to Central America and Northern South America.

Genus **SETOPHAGA** Swainson.

Setophaga Swains. Phil. Mag. I. May, 1827, 368. Type, *Motacilla ruticilla* Linn.

687. **Setophaga ruticilla** (Linn.).
American Redstart.

Motacilla ruticilla Linn. S. N. ed. 10, I. 1758, 186.
Setophaga ruticilla Swains. Phil. Mag. I. May, 1827, 368.

[B 217, C 104, R 128, C 152.]

Hab. North America, north to Fort Simpson, west regularly to the Great Basin, casually to the Pacific coast, breeding from the middle portion of the United States northward. In winter, the West Indies, and from Southern Mexico through Central America to Northern South America.

688. **Setophaga picta** Swains.
Painted Redstart.

Setophaga picta Swains. Zool. Illustr. 2d ser. I. 1829, pl. 3.

[B 218, C 105, R 129, C 151.]

Hab. Southern Arizona, south through Mexico to Guatemala.

[689.] **Setophaga miniata** Swains.
Red-bellied Redstart.

Setophaga miniata Swains. Phil. Mag. I. 1827, 368.

[B 219, C —, R 130, C —.]

Hab. Mexico and Guatemala. Texas (Giraud).

Genus **CARDELLINA** Du Bus.

Cardellina Du Bus. Esq. Orn. 1850, pl. 25. Type, *C. amicta* Du Bus = *Muscicapa rubrifrons* Giraud.

690. **Cardellina rubrifrons** (Giraud).
Red-faced Warbler.

Muscicapa rubrifrons Giraud, Sixteen Sp. Texas B. 1841, pl. 7, fig. 1.
Cardellina rubrifrons Scl. P. Z. S. 1855, 66.

[B —, C —, R 131, C 150.]

HAB. Southern Arizona, through Mexico, to Guatemala. Texas (GIRAUD).

GENUS **ERGATICUS** BAIRD.

Ergaticus BAIRD, Rev. Am. B. I. May, 1865, 264   Type, *Setophaga rubra* SWAINS.

[691.] **Ergaticus ruber** (SWAINS.).
Red Warbler.

Setophaga rubra SWAINS. Phil. Mag. I. 1827, 368.
Ergaticus ruber SCL. & SAL. Nom. Neotr. 1873, 11.

[B 216, C —, R 132, C —.]

HAB. Mexico. Texas (GIRAUD).

GENUS **BASILEUTERUS** CABANIS.

Basileuterus CAB. in SCHOMB. Guiana, III. 1848, 666.   Type, *Sylvia vermivora* VIEILL. = *Setophaga auricapilla* SWAINS.

[692.] **Basileuterus culicivorus** (LICHT.).
Brasher's Warbler.

Sylvia culicivora LICHT. Preis-Verzeich. 1830, no. 78.
Basileuterus culicivorus BONAP. Conspr Av. I. 1850, 313.

[B —, C —, R 133, C —.]

HAB. Mexico and Central America. Texas (GIRAUD).

[693.] **Basileuterus belli** (GIRAUD).
Bell's Warbler.

Muscicapa belli GIRAUD, Sixteen Sp. Texas B. 1841, pl. 4, fig. 1.
Basileuterus belli SCL. P. Z. S. 1855, 65.

[B —, C —, R 134, C —.]

HAB. Mexico and Guatemala. Texas (GIRAUD).

Family MOTACILLIDÆ. Wagtails.

Genus MOTACILLA Linnæus.

Motacilla Linn. S. N. ed. 10, I. 1758, 184. Type, by elimination, *M. alba* Linn.

[694.] **Motacilla alba** Linn.
Whlte Wagtail.

Motacilla alba Linn. S. N. ed. 10, I. 1758, 185.

[B —, C —, R 69, C 86.]

Hab. Northern Europe and Northern Asia, south, in winter, to North Africa and India. Accidental in Greenland.

[695.] **Motacilla ocularis** Swinh.
Swinhoe's Wagtail.

Motacilla ocularis Swinh. Ibis, Jan. 1860, 55.

[B —, C —, R —, C —.]

Hab. Eastern Asia. Accidental in Lower California. Aleutian Islands?

Genus BUDYTES Cuvier.

Budytes Cuv. Règne An. I. 1817, 371. Type, *Motacilla flava* Linn.

696. **Budytes flavus leucostriatus** (Hom.).
Siberian Yellow Wagtail.

Budytes leucostriatus Homeyer, J. f. O. 1878, 128.
Budytes flavus leucostriatus Stejn. Orn. Expl. Kamtsch. 1885, 280.

[B —, C 54, R 70, C 87.]

Hab. Alaska and Northern Siberia to China, wintering in the Moluccas.

Genus ANTHUS Bechstein.

Subgenus ANTHUS.

Anthus Bechst. Gem. Naturg. Deutschl. III. 1807, 704. Type, by elimination, *A. aquaticus* = *Alauda spinoletta* Linn.

697. Anthus pensilvanicus (LATH.).
   American Pipit.

   Alauda pensilvanica LATH. Synop. Suppl. I. 1787, 287.
   Anthus pensilvanicus THIENEM. Rhea, II. 1849, 171.

   [B 165, C 55, R 71, C 89.]

HAB. North America at large, breeding in the higher parts of the Rocky Mountains and subarctic districts, and wintering in the Gulf States, Mexico, and Central America. Accidental in Europe.

[**698.**] **Anthus pratensis** (LINN.).
   Meadow Pipit.

   Alauda pratensis LINN. S. N. ed. 10, I. 1758, 166.
   Anthus pratensis BECHST. Gem. Naturg. Deutschl. III. 1807, 732.

   [B —, C 55 *bis*, R 72, C 88.]

HAB. Europe, straggling to Greenland (and Alaska?).

[**699.**] **Anthus cervinus** (PALLAS).
   Red-throated Pipit.

   Motacilla cervina PALLAS, Zoog. Rosso-As. I. 1826, 511.
   Anthus cervinus KEYS. & BLAS. Wirb. Eur. I. 1840, p. xlviii.

   [B —, C —, R —, C —.]

HAB. Northern parts of the Old World. Accidental in Lower California. St. Michael's and Aleutian Islands, Alaska?

SUBGENUS **NEOCORYS** SCLATER.

Neocorys SCL. P. Z. S. 1857, 5. Type, *Alauda spragueii* AUD.

700. Anthus spragueii (AUD.).
   Sprague's Pipit.

   Alauda spragueii AUD. B. Am. VII. 1843, 335, pl. 486.
   Anthus spraguei BAIRD, Rev. Am. B. I. Oct. 1864, 155.

   [B 166, C 56, R 73, C 90.]

HAB. Interior plains of North America, breeding from Central Dakota northward to the Saskatchewan district, and from the Red River westward (probably to the Rocky Mountains). South in winter to Southern Mexico.

Family CINCLIDÆ. Dippers.

Genus CINCLUS Bechstein.

Cinclus BECHST. Orn. Taschenb. Deutschl. 1802, 205. Type, *Sturnus cinclus* LINN.

701. Cinclus mexicanus SWAINS.
American Dipper.

Cinclus mexicanus SWAINS. Phil. Mag. I. 1827, 368.

[B 164, C 19, R 19, C 30.]

HAB. The mountainous parts of Central and Western North America, from the Yukon Valley and Unalashka to Guatemala; east, in the United States, to the eastern base of the Rocky Mountains.

Family TROGLODYTIDÆ. Wrens, Thrashers, etc.

Subfamily MIMINÆ. Thrashers.

Genus OROSCOPTES Baird.

Oroscoptes BAIRD, B. N. Am. 1858, 346. Type, *Orpheus montanus* TOWNS.

702. Oroscoptes montanus (TOWNS.).
Sage Thrasher.

Orpheus montanus TOWNS. Journ. Ac. Nat. Sci. Phila. VII. 1837, 193.
Oroscoptes montanus BAIRD, B. N. Am. 1858, 347.

[B 255, C 7, R 10, C 14.]

HAB. Western United States, from the western part of the Plains to the Pacific.

Genus **MIMUS** Boie.

Mimus Boie, Isis, Oct. 1826, 972.   Type, *Turdus polyglottos* Linn.

703. Mimus polyglottos (Linn.).
Mockingbird.

Turdus polyglottos Linn. S. N. ed. 10, I. 1758, 169.
Mimus polyglottus Bonap. Geog. & Comp. List, 1838, 17.

[B 253, 253 *a*, C 8, R 11, C 15.]

Hab.   United States, south into Mexico.   Rare from New Jersey, the Valley of the Ohio, Colorado, and California northward.

Genus **GALEOSCOPTES** Cabanis.

Galeoscoptes Cab. Mus. Hein. I. 1850, 82.   Type, *Muscicapa carolinensis* Linn.

704. Galeoscoptes carolinensis (Linn.).
Catbird.

Muscicapa carolinensis Linn. S. N. ed. 12, I. 1766, 328.
Galeoscoptes carolinensis Cab. Mus. Hein. I. 1850, 82.

[B 254, C 9, R 12, C 16.]

Hab.   Eastern United States and British Provinces, west to and including the Rocky Mountains; occasional on the Pacific coast. Winters in the Southern States, Cuba, and Middle America to Panama.   Accidental in Europe.

Genus **HARPORHYNCHUS** Cabanis.

Subgenus **METHRIOPTERUS** Reichenbach.

Methriopterus Reich. Syst. Nat. 1850, pl. iv.   Type, *Turdus rufus* Linn.

705. Harporhynchus rufus (Linn.).
Brown Thrasher.

Turdus rufus Linn. S. N. ed. 10, I. 1758, 169.
Harporhynchus rufus Cab. Mus. Hein. I. 1850, 82.

ORDER PASSERES. 323

[B 261, 261 a, C 10, R 13, C 17.]

HAB. Eastern United States, west to the Rocky Mountains, north to Southern Maine, Ontario, and Manitoba, south to the Gulf States, including Eastern Texas. Accidental in Europe.

706. **Harporhynchus longirostris** (LAFR.).
    Long-billed Thrasher.

Orpheus longirostris LAFR. Rev. Zool. 1838, 55.
Harporhynchus longirostris CAB. Mus. Hein. I. 1850, 81.

[B 260, C 10 a, R 13 a, C 18.]

HAB. Eastern Mexico, north to the Valley of the Rio Grande in Texas.

707. **Harporhynchus curvirostris** (SWAINS.).
    Curve-billed Thrasher.

Orpheus curvirostris SWAINS. Phil. Mag. III. 1827, 369.
Harporhynchus curvirostris CAB. Mus. Hein. I. 1850, 81.

[B 259, 259 a, C —, R 15, C 19.]

HAB. Eastern Mexico, extending into the southern border of Texas and Eastern New Mexico.

707 a. **Harporhynchus curvirostris palmeri** RIDGW.
    Palmer's Thrasher.

Harporhynchus curvirostris var. *palmeri* "RIDGW." COUES, Key, 1872, 351.

[B —, C 11, R 15 a, C 20.]

HAB. Southern Arizona, south into Sonora (Guaymas).

708. **Harporhynchus bendirei** COUES.
    Bendire's Thrasher.

Harporhynchus bendirei COUES, Am. Nat. VII. 1873, 330.

[B —, C 11 bis, R 14 a, C 21.]

HAB. Southern Arizona, south into Sonora (Guaymas), and north, at least casually, to Colorado (Colorado Springs).

709. Harporhynchus cinereus XANTUS.
St. Lucas Thrasher.

Harporhynchus cinereus XANTUS, Pr. Ac. Nat. Sci. Phila. 1859, 298.

[B —, C 12, R 14, C 22.]

HAB. Lower California.

SUBGENUS **HARPORHYNCHUS** CABANIS.

Harporhynchus CAB. Wiegm. Archiv, 1848, i. 98. Type, *Harpes redivivus* GAMB.

710. Harporhynchus redivivus (GAMB.).
Californian Thrasher.

Harpes rediviva GAMB. Pr. Ac. Nat. Sci. Phila. 1845, 264.
Harporhynchus redivivus CAB. Wiegm. Archiv, 1848, i. 98.

[B 256, C 13, R 16, C 23.]

HAB. Coast region of California, and Lower California.

711. Harporhynchus lecontei (LAWR.).
Leconte's Thrasher.

Toxostoma lecontei LAWR. Ann. Lyc. N. Y. V. 1852, 121.
Harporhynchus lecontii BONAP. Notes Coll. Delattre, 1854, 39.

[B 257, C 13 a, R 16 a, C 24.]

HAB. Valleys of the Gila and Lower Colorado Rivers, south into Sonora.

712. Harporhynchus crissalis (HENRY).
Crissal Thrasher.

Toxostoma crissalis HENRY, Pr. Ac. Nat. Sci. Phila. 1858, 117.
Harporhynchus crissalis BAIRD, B. N. Am. 1858, 350.

[B 258, C 14, R 17, C 25.]

HAB. Southwestern United States, from New Mexico to Utah and Southern California.

ORDER PASSERES.

SUBFAMILY **TROGLODYTINÆ**. WRENS.

GENUS **CAMPYLORHYNCHUS** SPIX.

Campylorhynchus SPIX, Av. Bras. I. 1824, 77.   Type, *C. scolopaceus* SPIX = *Turdus variegatus* GMEL.

713. **Campylorhynchus brunneicapillus** (LAFR.).
Cactus Wren.

Picolaptes brunneicapillus LAFR. Mag. de Zool. 1835, 61, pl. 47.
Campylorhynchus brunneicapillus GRAY, Gen. B. I. 1847, 159.

[B 262, C 43, R 56, C 63.]

HAB.   Southern border of the United States, from Texas to Southern California, and south into Northern Mexico.

714. **Campylorhynchus affinis** XANTUS.
St. Lucas Cactus Wren.

Campylorhynchus affinis XANTUS, Pr. Ac. Nat. Sci. Phila. 1859, 298.

[B —, C 44, R 57, C 64.]

HAB.   Lower California.

GENUS **SALPINCTES** CABANIS.

Salpinctes CAB. Wiegm. Archiv, 1847, i. 323.   Type, *Troglodytes obsoletus* SAY.

715. **Salpinctes obsoletus** (SAY).
Rock Wren.

Troglodytes obsoletus SAY, LONG'S Exp. II. 1823, 4.
Salpinctes obsoletus CAB. Wiegm. Archiv, 1847, i. 323.

[B 264, C 45, R 58, C 65.]

HAB.   Western United States, from the western border of the Plains to the Pacific.

716. Salpinctes guadeloupensis RIDGW.
Guadalupe Rock Wren.

Salpinctes obsoletus guadeloupensis RIDGW. Bull. U. S. Geol. & Geog. Surv. Terr. II. No. 2, April, 1876, 185.
Salpinctes guadalupensis RIDGW. Bull. Nutt. Orn. Club, II. July, 1877, 60.

[B —, C —, R 58 a, C —.]

HAB. Guadalupe Island, Lower California.

GENUS **CATHERPES** BAIRD.

Catherpes BAIRD, B. N. Am. 1858, 357. Type, *Thryothorus mexicanus* SWAINS.

[717.] Catherpes mexicanus (SWAINS.).
White-throated Wren.

Thryothorus mexicanus SWAINS. Zool. Ill. 2d ser. I. 1829, pl. 11.
Catherpes mexicanus BAIRD, B. N. Am. 1858, 356.

[B 263, C —, R 59, C 66.]

HAB. Mexico. Texas (GIRAUD).

717 a. Catherpes mexicanus conspersus RIDGW.
Cañon Wren.

Catherpes mexicanus var. *conspersus* RIDGW. Am. Nat. VII. Oct. 1873, 602.

[B 263, *part*, C 46, R 59 a, C 67.]

HAB. Southwestern United States, from Western Texas and Colorado to the Pacific.

GENUS **THRYOTHORUS** VIEILLOT.

SUBGENUS **THRYOTHORUS**.

Thryothorus VIEILL. Analyse, 1816, 45. Type, *Troglodytes arundinaceus* VIEILL. = *Sylvia ludoviciana* LATH.

718. Thryothorus ludovicianus (LATH.).
Carolina Wren.

Sylvia ludoviciana LATH. Ind. Orn. II. 1790, 548.
Thryothorus ludovicianus BONAP. Geog. & Comp. List, 1838, 11.

[B 265, C 47, R 60, C 68.]

HAB. Eastern United States (rare toward the northern border), west to the Plains. Rare in Southern New England.

718 a. Thryothorus ludovicianus miamensis RIDGW.
Florida Wren.

Thryothorus ludovicianus var. *miamensis* RIDGW. Am. Nat. IX. Aug. 1875, 469.

[B 265, *part*, C 47, *part*, R 60 b, C 69.]

HAB. Southern Florida.

SUBGENUS **THRYOMANES** SCLATER.

Thryomanes SCL. Cat. Am. B. 1861, 22. Type, *Troglodytes bewickii* AUD.

719. Thryothorus bewickii (AUD.).
Bewick's Wren.

Troglodytes bewickii AUD. Orn. Biog. I. 1831, 96, pl. 18.
Thriothorus bewickii BAIRD, B. N. Am. 1858, 363.

[B 267, C 48, R 61, C 71.]

HAB. Eastern United States, to Eastern Texas and the eastern border of the Plains; north to New Jersey and Minnesota.

719 a. Thryothorus bewickii spilurus (VIG.).
Vigors's Wren.

Troglodytes spilurus VIG. Zool. Voy. Bloss. 1839, 18, pl. 4, fig. 1.
Thryothorus bewickii var. *spilurus* BAIRD, Rev. Am. B. I. 1864, 126.

[B —, C 48 b, R 61 a, C 73.]

HAB. Pacific coast region of North America, from British Columbia southward to Lower California and Western Mexico.

719 b. Thryothorus bewickii bairdi (Salv. & Godm.).
Baird's Wren.

Thryothorus bairdi Salv. & Godm. Biol. Centr.-Am. Aves, April, 1880, 95.
Thryothorus bewickii bairdi Ridgw. Pr. U. S. Nat. Mus. VIII. 1885, 354.

[B —, C 48 a, R 61 b, C 72.]

Hab. Southern Texas and Arizona, north to Middle Kansas, Colorado, and Southern Utah, south into Mexico.

720. Thryothorus brevicaudus Ridgw.
Guadalupe Wren.

Thryomanes brevicauda Ridgw. Bull. U. S. Geol. & Geog. Surv. Terr. II. No. 2, April 1, 1876, 186.
Thryothorus brevicaudus Ridgw. Pr. U. S. Nat. Mus. VIII. 1885, 354.

[B —, C —, R 62, C —.]

Hab. Guadalupe Island, Lower California.

Genus **TROGLODYTES** Vieillot.

Subgenus **TROGLODYTES**.

Troglodytes Vieill. Ois. Am. Sept. II. 1807, 52. Type, *T. aëdon* Vieill.

721. Troglodytes aëdon Vieill.
House Wren.

Troglodytes aëdon Vieill. Ois. Am. Sept. II. 1807, 52, pl. 107.

[B 270, 272, C 49, R 63, C 74.]

Hab. Eastern United States, and Southern Canada west to Indiana and Louisiana.

721 a. Troglodytes aëdon parkmanii (Aud.).
Parkman's Wren.

Troglodytes parkmanii Aud. Orn. Biog. V. 1839, 310.
Troglodytes ædon var. *parkmanni* Coues, Key, 1872, 87.

[B 271, C 49 a, R 63 a, C 75.]

HAB. Western North America, from Texas, Illinois, Minnesota, and Manitoba westward; north to Great Slave Lake, south to Jalapa, Mexico, and Lower California.

SUBGENUS **ANORTHURA** RENNIE.

Anorthura RENNIE, MONT. Orn. Dict. ed. 2, 1831, 570. Type, *Motacilla troglodytes* LINN.

722. **Troglodytes hiemalis** VIEILL.
Winter Wren.

Troglodytes hiemalis VIEILL. Nouv. Dict. d'Hist. Nat. XXXIV. 1819, 514.

[B 273, C 50, R 65, C 76.]

HAB. Eastern North America generally, breeding from the northern parts of the United States northward, and wintering from about its southern breeding limit southward.

722 a. **Troglodytes hiemalis pacificus** BAIRD.
Western Winter Wren.

Troglodytes hyemalis var. *pacificus* BAIRD, Rev. Am. B. I. Sept. 1864, 145.

[B 273, *part*, C 50, *part*, R 65 a, C 77.]

HAB. Pacific coast, from Sitka to Southern California; south, in winter, to Mexico.

723. **Troglodytes alascensis** BAIRD.
Alaskan Wren.

Troglodytes alascensis BAIRD, Trans. Chic. Ac. Sci. I. 1869, 315, pl. 30, fig. 3.

[B —, C 50 a, R 66, C 78.]

HAB. Aleutian and Pribylof Islands, Alaska.

GENUS **CISTOTHORUS** CABANIS.

SUBGENUS **CISTOTHORUS**.

Cistothorus CAB. Mus. Hein. I. 1850, 77. Type, *Troglodytes stellaris* LICHT.

724. Cistothorus stellaris (Licht.).
   Short-billed Marsh Wren.

   Troglodytes stellaris Licht. in Naum. Vög. Deutschl. III. 1823, tab. ad p. 724.
   Cistothorus stellaris Cab. Mus. Hein. I. 1850, 77.

   [B 269, C 52, R 68, C 81.]

Hab. Eastern United States and Southern British Provinces, west to the Plains. Winters in the Gulf States and southward.

Subgenus **TELMATODYTES** Cabanis.

Telmatodytes Cab. Mus. Hein. I. 1850, 78. Type, *Certhia palustris* Wils.

725. Cistothorus palustris (Wils.).
   Long-billed Marsh Wren.

   Certhia palustris Wils. Am. Orn. II. 1810, 58, pl. 12, fig. 4.
   Cistothorus (Telmatodytes) palustris Baird, B. N. Am. 1858, 364.

   [B 268, C 51, R 67, 67 a, C 79, 80.]

Hab. Southern British America and the United States, south, in winter, to Guatemala.

Family **CERTHIIDÆ**. Creepers.

Genus **CERTHIA** Linnæus.

Certhia Linn. S. N. ed. 10, I. 1758, 118. Type, by elimination, *C. familiaris* Linn.

726. Certhia familiaris americana (Bonap.).
   Brown Creeper.

   Certhia americana Bonap. Geog. & Comp. List, 1838, 11.
   Certhia familiaris var. *americana* Ridgw. Bull. Essex Inst. V. 1873, 180.

   [B 275, C 42, R 55, C 62.]

Hab. North America in general, breeding from the northern and more elevated parts of the United States northward, migrating southward in winter.

726 a. **Certhia familiaris mexicana** (GLOG.).
    Mexican Creeper.

    Certhia mexicana GLOG. Handb. 1834, 381.
    Certhia familiaris var. *mexicana* B. B. & R. Hist. N. Am. B. I. 1874, 128.

[B 276, C —, R 55 a, C —.]

HAB. Guatemala, Mexico, and Southern Arizona.

FAMILY **PARIDÆ**. NUTHATCHES AND TITS.

SUBFAMILY **SITTINÆ**. NUTHATCHES.

GENUS **SITTA** LINNÆUS.

Sitta LINN. S. N. ed. 10, I. 1758, 115. Type, *S. europæa* LINN.

727. **Sitta carolinensis** LATH.
    White-breasted Nuthatch.

    Sitta carolinensis LATH. Ind. Orn. I. 1790, 262.

[B 277, C 38, R 51, C 57.]

HAB. Southern British Provinces and Eastern United States to the Rocky Mountains.

727 a. **Sitta carolinensis aculeata** (CASS.).
    Slender-billed Nuthatch.

    Sitta aculeata CASS. Pr. Ac. Nat. Sci. Phila. Oct. 1856, 254.
    Sitta canadensis var. *aculeata* ALLEN, Bull. M. C. Z. III. No. 6, July, 1872, 161.

[B 278, C 38 a, R 51 a, C 58.]

HAB. Western North America, east to the Plains, and south into Mexico.

728. **Sitta canadensis** LINN.
    Red-breasted Nuthatch.

    Sitta canadensis LINN. S. N. ed. 12, 1. 1766, 177.

[B 279, C 39, R 52, C 59.]

HAB. North America at large, breeding mostly north of the United States, migrating south in winter.

729. Sitta pusilla LATH.
Brown-headed Nuthatch.

Sitta pusilla LATH. Ind. Orn. I. 1790, 263.

[B 280, C 40, R 53, C 60.]

HAB. South Atlantic and Gulf States; casual (?) in Ohio, Michigan, Missouri, etc.

730. Sitta pygmæa VIG.
Pygmy Nuthatch.

Sitta pygmæa VIG. Zool. Beechey's Voy. 1839, 25, pl. 4.

[B 281, C 41, R 54, C 61.]

HAB. Western United States, from New Mexico and Colorado to Southern California and Washington Territory.

SUBFAMILY **PARINÆ**. TITMICE.

GENUS **PARUS** LINNÆUS.

SUBGENUS **LOPHOPHANES** KAUP.

Lophophanes KAUP, Entw. Gesch. Eur. Thierw. 1829, 92. Type, *Parus cristatus* LINN.

731. Parus bicolor LINN.
Tufted Titmouse.

Parus bicolor LINN. S. N. ed. 12, I. 1766, 340.

[B 285, C 27, R 36, C 40.]

HAB. Eastern United States to the Plains, but rare towards the northern border, being a straggler merely to Southern New England.

732. Parus atricristatus CASS.
Black-crested Titmouse.

Parus atricristatus CASS. Pr. Ac. Nat. Sci. Phila. 1850, 103, pl. 2.

[B 286, C 29, R 37, C 42.]

HAB. Southeastern Texas and Eastern Mexico.

733. **Parus inornatus** GAMB.
Plain Titmouse.

Parus inornatus GAMB. Pr. Ac. Nat. Sci. Phila. Aug. 1845, 265.

[B 287, *part*, C 28, *part*, R 38, *part*, C 41, *part*.]

HAB. California and Western Oregon.

733 *a*. **Parus inornatus griseus** RIDGW.
Gray Titmouse.

Lophophanes inornatus griseus RIDGW. Pr. U. S. Nat. Mus. V. Sept. 5, 1882, 344.
Parus inornatus griseus RIDGW. Pr. U. S. Nat. Mus. VIII. 1885, 354.

[B 287, *part*, C 28, *part*, R 38, *part*, C 41, *part*.]

HAB. New Mexico and Colorado to Arizona and Nevada.

733 *b*. **Parus inornatus cineraceus** RIDGW.
Ashy Titmouse.

Lophophanes inornatus cineraceus RIDGW. Pr. U. S. Nat. Mus. VI. Oct. 5, 1883, 154.
Parus inornatus cineraceus RIDGW. Pr. U. S. Nat. Mus. VIII. 1885, 354.

[B —, C —, R —, C —.]

HAB. Lower California.

734. **Parus wollweberi** (BONAP.).
Bridled Titmouse.

Lophophanes wollweberi BONAP. Compt. Rend. XXXI. Sept. 1850, 478.
Parus wollweberi HENRY, Pr. Ac. Nat. Sci. Phila. 1855, 309.

[B 288, C 30, R 39, C 43.]

HAB. Western Texas, Southern New Mexico, Southern Arizona, and southward.

SUBGENUS **PARUS** LINNÆUS.

Parus LINN. S. N. ed. 10, I. 1758, 189. Type, by elimination, *P. major* LINN.

735. Parus atricapillus LINN.
Chickadee.

Parus atricapillus LINN. S. N. ed. 12, I. 1766, 341.

[B 290, C 31, R 41, C 44.]

HAB. Eastern North America, north of the Potomac and Ohio Valleys.

735 a. Parus atricapillus septentrionalis (HARRIS).
Long-tailed Chickadee.

Parus septentrionalis HARRIS, Pr. Ac. Nat. Sci. Phila. 1845, 300.
Parus atricapillus var. *septentrionalis* ALLEN, Bull. M. C. Z. III. 1872, 174.

[B 289, 289 a, C 31 a, R 41 a, C 45.]

HAB. Rocky Mountain Plateau region, east to Manitoba and the Plains.

735 b. Parus atricapillus occidentalis (BAIRD).
Oregon Chickadee.

Parus occidentalis BAIRD, B. N. Am. 1858, 391.
Parus atricapillus var. *occidentalis* COUES, Key, 1872, 81.

[B 291, C 31 c, R 41 b, C 46.]

HAB. Pacific coast region of North America, from Northern California northward.

736. Parus carolinensis AUD.
Carolina Chickadee.

Parus carolinensis AUD. Orn. Biog. II. 1834, 474, pl. 160.

[B 293, C 31 b, R 42, C 47.]

HAB. Southeastern States, north to New Jersey and Illinois, west to Missouri, the Indian Territory, and Eastern Texas.

[737.] **Parus meridionalis** Scl.
    Mexican Chickadee.

    Parus meridionalis Scl. P. Z. S. 1856, 293.

$$[\text{B }292,\ \text{C}\text{ —},\ \text{R }43,\ \textbf{C 879.}]$$

Hab. Mexico, north to Southern Arizona.

738. **Parus gambeli** Ridgw.
    Mountain Chickadee.

    Parus gambeli Ridgw. MS.

$$[\text{B }294,\ \text{C }32,\ \text{R }40,\ \text{C }48.]$$

Hab. Mountainous parts of the Western United States, from the Rocky Mountains to the Sierra Nevada.

739. **Parus cinctus obtectus** (Cab.).
    Siberian Chickadee.

    Parus (Pœcila) obtectus Cab. J. f. O. 1871, 237.
    Parus cinctus obtectus Ridgw. Pr. U. S. Nat. Mus. VIII. 1885, 354.

$$[\text{B —},\ \text{C —},\ \text{R }44,\ \text{C }52.]$$

Hab. Northern Alaska and Eastern Siberia.

740. **Parus hudsonicus** Forst.
    Hudsonian Chickadee.

    Parus hudsonicus Forst. Phil. Trans. LXII. 1772, 383, 430.

$$[\text{B }296,\ \text{C }33,\ \text{R }45,\ \text{C }49.]$$

Hab. Northern North America, from the more elevated parts of the Northern United States (Northern New England, Northern New York, Northern Michigan, etc.) northward.

741. **Parus rufescens** Towns.
    Chestnut-backed Chickadee.

    Parus rufescens Towns. Journ. Ac. Nat. Sci. Phila. VII. ii. 1837, 190.

[B 295, *part*, C 34, *part*, R 46, C 50.]

HAB. Northwest coast of North America, from the Columbia River northward.

741 *a*. **Parus rufescens neglectus** RIDGW.
Californian Chickadee.

Parus rufescens β. *neglectus* RIDGW. Pr. U. S. Nat. Mus. I. April 25, 1879, 485.

[B 295, *part*, C 34, *part*, R 46 *a*, C 51.]

HAB. Coast region of middle and southern portions of California.

SUBFAMILY **CHAMÆINÆ**. WREN-TITS AND BUSH-TITS.

GENUS **CHAMÆA** GAMBEL.

Chamæa GAMB. Pr. Ac. Nat. Sci. Phila. 1847, 154. Type, *Parus fasciatus* GAMB.

742. **Chamæa fasciata** GAMB.
Wren-Tit.

Parus fasciatus GAMB. Pr. Ac. Nat. Sci. Phila. Aug. 1845, 265.
Chamæa fasciata GAMB. Pr. Ac. Nat. Sci. Phila. 1847, 154.

[B 274, *part*, C 26, *part*, R 35, *part*, C 39, *part*.]

HAB. Coast region of California.

742 *a*. **Chamæa fasciata henshawi** RIDGW.
Pallid Wren-Tit.

Chamæa fasciata henshawi RIDGW. Pr. U. S. Nat. Mus. V. June 5, 1882, 13.

[B 274, *part*, C 26, *part*, R 35, *part*, C 39, *part*.]

HAB. Interior of California, including the western slope of the Sierra Nevada.

GENUS **PSALTRIPARUS** BONAPARTE.

Psaltriparus BONAP. Compt. Rend. XXXI. 1850, 478. Type, *Parus melanotis* HARTL.

743. Psaltriparus minimus (Towns.).
Bush-Tit.

Parus minimus Towns. Journ. Ac. Nat. Sci. Phila. VII. ii. 1837, 190.
Psaltriparus minimus Bonap. Compt. Rend. XXXVIII. 1854, 62.

[B 298, *part*, C 35, *part*, R 47, *part*, C 53, *part*.]

Hab. Pacific coast region, from Northern California to Washington Territory.

743 a. Psaltriparus minimus californicus Ridgw.
Californian Bush-Tit.

Psaltriparus minimus californicus Ridgw. Pr. Biol. Soc. Wash. II. April 10, 1884, 89.

[B 298, *part*, C 35, *part*, R 47, *part*, C 53, *part*.]

Hab. California, except the northern coast district.

743 b. Psaltriparus minimus grindæ (Belding).
Grinda's Bush-Tit.

Psaltriparus grindæ Beld. Pr. U. S. Nat. Mus. VI. Oct. 5, 1883, 155.
Psaltriparus minimus grindæ Ridgw. Pr. U. S. Nat. Mus. VIII. 1885, 354.

[B —, C —, R —, C —.]

Hab. Lower California.

744. Psaltriparus plumbeus Baird.
Lead-colored Bush-Tit.

Psaltria plumbea Baird, Pr. Ac. Nat. Sci. Phila. June, 1854, 118.
Psaltriparus plumbeus Baird, B. N. Am. 1858, 398.

[B 299, C 36, R 48, C 54.]

Hab. New Mexico and Arizona, north to Eastern Oregon and Western Wyoming.

[745.] Psaltriparus melanotis (Hartl.).
Black-eared Bush-Tit.

Parus melanotis Hartl. Rev. Zool. 1844, 216.
Psaltriparus melanotis Bonap. Compt. Rend. XXXVIII. 1854, 62.

[B 297, C —, R 49, C 55.]

HAB. Eastern Mexico and Guatemala, north to the Rio Grande Valley; East Humboldt Mountains, Nevada (?).

GENUS **AURIPARUS** BAIRD.

Auriparus BAIRD, Rev. Am. B. I. July, 1864, 85. Type, *Ægithalus flaviceps* SUND.

746. **Auriparus flaviceps** (SUND.).
Verdin.

Ægithalus flaviceps SUND. Öfv. Vet. Ak. Förh. VII. 1850, 129.
Auriparus flaviceps BAIRD, Rev. Am. B. I. July, 1864, 85.

[B 300, C 37, R 50, C 56.]

HAB. Southern border of the United States, from the Valley of the Rio Grande to Arizona, Mexico, and Lower California.

FAMILY **SYLVIIDÆ**. WARBLERS, KINGLETS, GNATCATCHERS.

SUBFAMILY **SYLVIINÆ**. WARBLERS.

GENUS **PHYLLOPSEUSTES** MEYER.

Phyllopseustes MEYER, Vög. Lifl. Estl. 1815, 122. Type, *Sylvia sibilatrix* BECHST.

747. **Phyllopseustes borealis** (BLAS.).
Kennicott's Willow Warbler.

Phyllopneuste borealis BLASIUS, Naumannia, 1858, 313.
Phyllopseustes borealis MEVES, J. f. O. 1875, 429.

[B —, C 20, R 34, C 32.]

HAB. Northeastern Asia and Alaska.

ORDER PASSERES. 339

SUBFAMILY REGULINÆ. KINGLETS.

GENUS **REGULUS** CUVIER.

Regulus CUV. Leç. d'Anat. Comp. I. 1799-1800, tab. ii. Type, *Motacilla regulus* LINN.

748. **Regulus satrapa** LICHT.
Golden-crowned Kinglet.

Regulus satrapa LICHT. Verz. Doubl. 1823, 35.

[B 162, *part*, C 22, *part*, R 33, C 34.]

HAB. North America generally, breeding in the northern and elevated parts of the United States and northward, migrating south in winter to Guatemala.

748 a. Regulus satrapa olivaceus BAIRD.
Western Golden-crowned Kinglet.

Regulus satrapa var. *olivaceus* BAIRD, Rev. Am. B. I. July, 1864, 65 (in text under *R. satrapa*).

[B 162, *part*, C 22, *part*, R 33 a, C 35.]

HAB. Pacific coast region of North America, from California northward.

749. **Regulus calendula** (LINN.).
Ruby-crowned Kinglet.

Motacilla calendula LINN. S. N. ed. 12, I. 1766, 337.
Regulus calendula LICHT. Verz. Doubl. 1823, 35.

[B 161, C 21, R 30, C 33.]

HAB. North America, south to Guatemala, north to the Arctic coast, breeding mostly north of the United States.

750. **Regulus obscurus** RIDGW.
Dusky Kinglet.

Regulus calendula obscurus RIDGW. Bull. U. S. Geol. & Geog. Surv. Terr. II. No. 2, April 1, 1876, 184.
Regulus obscurus RIDGW. Bull. Nutt. Orn. Club, II. July, 1877, 59.

[B —, C —, R 31, C —.]

HAB. Guadalupe Island, Lower California.

SUBFAMILY **POLIOPTILINÆ**. GNATCATCHERS.

GENUS **POLIOPTILA** SCLATER.

Polioptila SCL. P. Z. S. 1855, 11. Type, *Motacilla cærulea* LINN.

751. Polioptila cærulea (LINN.).
Blue-gray Gnatcatcher.

Motacilla cærulea LINN. S. N. ed. 12, I. 1766, 337.
Polioptila cærulea SCL. P. Z. S. 1855, 11.

[B 282, C 23, R 27, C 36.]

HAB. Middle and southern portions of the United States, from the Atlantic to the Pacific, south, in winter, to Guatemala, Cuba, and the Bahamas; rare north toward the Great Lakes, Southern New York, and Southern New England, straggling north to Massachusetts and Maine.

752. Polioptila plumbea BAIRD.
Plumbeous Gnatcatcher.

Polioptila plumbea BAIRD, Pr. Ac. Nat. Sci. Phila. June, 1854, 118.

[B 283, C 25, R 28, C 38.]

HAB. Western Texas to Arizona and eastern coast of Lower California.

753. Polioptila californica BREWST.
Black-tailed Gnatcatcher.

Polioptila californica BREWST. Bull. Nutt. Orn. Club, VI. April, 1881, 103.

[B 284, C 24, R 29, C 37.]

HAB. Southern California and Pacific coast of Lower California.

FAMILY **TURDIDÆ**. THRUSHES, SOLITAIRES, STONECHATS, BLUEBIRDS, ETC.

SUBFAMILY **MYADESTINÆ**. SOLITAIRES.

GENUS **MYADESTES** SWAINSON.

Myadestes SWAINS. Nat. Libr. XIII. Flycatchers, 1838, 132. Type, *M. genibarbis* SWAINS.

754. **Myadestes townsendii** (AUD.).
Townsend's Solitaire.

Ptiliogonys townsendii AUD. Orn. Biog. V. 1839, 206, pl. 419, fig. 2.
Myiadestes townsendi CAB. Wiegm. Archiv, 1847, i. 208.

[B 235, C 121, R 25, C 169.]

HAB. Western United States, from the Plains westward to the Pacific coast.

SUBFAMILY **TURDINÆ**. THRUSHES.

GENUS **TURDUS** LINNÆUS.

SUBGENUS **HYLOCICHLA** BAIRD.

Hylocichla BAIRD, Rev. Am. B. I. June, 1864, 12. Type, *Turdus mustelinus* GMEL.

755. **Turdus mustelinus** GMEL.
Wood Thrush.

Turdus mustelinus GMEL. S. N. I. ii. 1788, 817.

[B 148, C 3, R 1, C 6.]

HAB. Eastern United States to the Plains, north to Southern Michigan, Ontario, and Massachusetts, south, in winter, to Guatemala and Cuba.

756. Turdus fuscescens STEPH.
Wilson's Thrush.

Turdus fuscescens STEPH. Gen. Zool. X. i. 1817, 182.

[B 151, C 6, R 2, C 7.]

HAB. Eastern United States to the Plains, north to Manitoba, Ontario, Anticosti, and Newfoundland.

756 a. Turdus fuscescens salicicolus (RIDGW.).
Willow Thrush.

Hylocichla fuscescens salicicola RIDGW. Pr. U. S. Nat. Mus. IV. April 6, 1882, 374.
Turdus fuscescens salicicola COUES, Key, ed. 2, 1884, 246.

[B —, C —, R —, C —.]

HAB. Rocky Mountain region of the United States, east to Dakota.

757. Turdus aliciæ BAIRD.
Gray-cheeked Thrush.

Turdus aliciæ BAIRD, B. N. Am. 1858, 217.

[B 154, C 5 a, R 3, C 12.]

HAB. Eastern North America, west to the Plains, Alaska, and Eastern Siberia, north to the Arctic coast, south, in winter, to Costa Rica. Breeds chiefly north of the United States.

757 a. Turdus aliciæ bicknelli (RIDGW.).
Bicknell's Thrush.

Hylocichla aliciæ bicknelli RIDGW. Pr. U. S. Nat. Mus. IV. April 6, 1882, 377.
Turdus aliciæ bicknelli COUES, Key, ed. 2, 1884, 248.

[B 154, *part*, C 5 a, *part*, R 3, *part*, C 12, *part*.]

HAB. In summer, mountainous parts of the Northeastern States (Catskills, White Mountains, etc.) and Nova Scotia, migrating south in winter.

758. **Turdus ustulatus** (NUTT.).
Russet-backed Thrush.

Turdus ustulatus NUTT. Man. Orn. Land B. ed. 2, 1840, 830 (*cestulatus*, err. typ. p. 400).

[B 152, C 5 *b*, R 4, C 11.]

HAB. Pacific coast region of North America, from Alaska to California, south in winter to Guatemala.

758 *a*. **Turdus ustulatus swainsonii** (CAB.).
Olive-backed Thrush.

Turdus swainsonii CAB. Fauna Per. 1845–46, 187.
Turdus ustulatus β. swainsoni RIDGW. Field & Forest, II. May, 1877, 195.

[B 153, C 5, R 4 *a*, C 13.]

HAB. Eastern North America, and westward to the Upper Columbia River and East Humboldt Mountains, straggling to the Pacific coast. Breeds mostly north of the United States.

759. **Turdus aonalaschkæ** GMEL.
Dwarf Hermit Thrush.

Turdus aonalaschkæ GMEL. S N. I. ii. 1788, 808.

[B 150, C 4 *b*, R 5, C 8.]

HAB. Pacific coast region, from Alaska to Lower California, east, during migrations, to Nevada and Arizona. Breeds from California northward.

759 *a*. **Turdus aonalaschkæ auduboni** (BAIRD).
Audubon's Hermit Thrush.

Turdus auduboni BAIRD, Rev. Am. B. June, 1864, 16.
Turdus aonalaschkæ auduboni RIDGW. Pr. U. S. Nat. Mus. Vol. 3, March 27, 1880, 1.

[B 149 *a*, C 4 *a*, R 5 *a*, C 9.]

HAB. Rocky Mountain region, from near the northern border of the United States south into Mexico.

759 *b*. **Turdus aonalaschkæ pallasii** (CAB.).
Hermit Thrush.

Turdus pallasii CAB. Wiegm. Archiv. 1847, i 205.
Turdus aonalaschkæ pallasi RIDGW. Pr. U. S. Nat. Mus. III. March 27, 1880, 1.

[B 149, C 4, R 5 b, C 10.]

HAB. Eastern North America, breeding from the Northern United States northward, and wintering from the Northern States southward.

SUBGENUS **TURDUS** LINNÆUS.

Turdus LINN. S. N. ed. 10, I. 1758, 168. Type, by elimination *T. viscivorus* LINN.

[760.] **Turdus iliacus** LINN.
Red-winged Thrush.

Turdus iliacus LINN. S. N. ed. 10, I. 1758, 168.

[B —, C —, R 6, C 4.]

HAB. Northern parts of the Old World; accidental in Greenland.

GENUS **MERULA** LEACH.

Merula LEACH, Syst. Cat. Brit. Mam. & B. 1816, 20. Type, *Turdus merula* LINN.

761. **Merula migratoria** (LINN.).
American Robin.

Turdus migratorius LINN. S. N. ed. 12, I. 1766, 292.
Merula migratoria SWAINS. Phil. Mag. I. 1827, 368.

[B 155, *part*, C 1, *part*, R 7, C 1.]

HAB. Eastern North America to the Rocky Mountains, including Eastern Mexico and Alaska. Breeds from near the southern border of the United States northward to the Arctic coast; winters from Southern Canada and the Northern States (irregularly) southward.

761 a. **Merula migratoria propinqua** RIDGW.
Western Robin.

T[*urdus*] *propinquus* RIDGW. Bull. Nutt. Orn. Club, II. Jan. 1877, 9.
Merula migratoria propinqua RIDGW. Pr. U. S. Nat. Mus. III. Aug. 24, 1880, 166.

[B 155, *part*, C 1, *part*, R 7 *a*, C 2.]

Hab. Western United States, from the eastern base of the Rocky Mountains westward.

762. **Merula confinis** (Baird).
    St. Lucas Robin.

Turdus confinis Baird, Rev. Am. B. I. June, 1864, 29.
Merula confinis Ridgw. Pr. U. S. Nat. Mus. III. Aug. 24, 1880, 166.

[B —, C 1 *a*, R 8, C 3.]

Hab. Lower California.

Genus **HESPEROCICHLA** Baird.

Hesperocichla Baird, Rev. Am. B. I. June, 1864, 12. Type, *Turdus nævius* Gmel.

763. **Hesperocichla nævia** (Gmel.).
    Varied Thrush.

Turdus nævius Gmel. S. N. I. ii. 1788, 817.
Hesperocichla nævia Ridgw. Pr. U. S. Nat. Mus. III. Aug. 24, 1880, 166.

[B 156, C 2, R 9, C 5.]

Hab. Pacific coast of North America, from Bering's Strait to California. Accidental in the Eastern States (New Jersey, Long Island, and Massachusetts).

Genus **CYANECULA** Brehm.

Cyanecula Brehm, Isis, 1828, 1280. Type, *Motacilla suecica* Linn.

[764.] **Cyanecula suecica** (Linn.).
    Red-spotted Bluethroat.

Motacilla suecica Linn. S. N. ed. 10, I. 1758, 187.
Cyanecula suecica Brehm, Isis, 1828, 1280.

[B —, C —, R 20, C 31.]

Hab. Northern parts of the Old World; casual in Alaska.

Genus **SAXICOLA** Bechstein.

Saxicola Bechst. Orn. Taschb. 1803, 216. Type, *Motacilla œnanthe* Linn.

765. Saxicola œnanthe (Linn.).
Wheatear.

Motacilla œnanthe Linn. S. N. ed. 10, I. 1758, 186.
Saxicola œnanthe Bechst. Orn. Taschb. 1803, 217.

[B 157, C 15, R 21, C 26.]

Hab. Europe, North Africa, Asia, Alaska, Greenland, and Labrador, straggling southward to Nova Scotia, Maine, Long Island, and the Bermudas.

Genus **SIALIA** Swainson.

Sialia Swains. Phil. Mag. I. May, 1827, 369. Type, *Motacilla sialis* Linn.

766. Sialia sialis (Linn.).
Bluebird.

Motacilla sialis Linn. S. N. ed. 10, I. 1758, 187.
Sialia sialis Haldem. Trego's Geog. Penn. 1843, 77.

[B 158, C 16, R 22, C 27.]

Hab. Eastern United States to the eastern base of the Rocky Mountains, north to Manitoba, Ontario, and Nova Scotia, south, in winter, from the Middle States to the Gulf States and Cuba. Bermudas, resident.

766 a. Sialia sialis azurea (Swains.).
Azure Bluebird.

Sialia azurea Swains. Phil. Mag. I. 1827, 369.
Sialia sialis var. *azurea* B. B. & R. Hist. N. Am. B. I. Jan. 1874, 62.

[B —, C —, R —, C —.]

Hab. Southern Arizona and Eastern Mexico.

767. Sialia mexicana Swains.
Western Bluebird.

Sialia mexicana Swains. Fauna Bor. Am. II. 1831, 202.

[B 159, C 17, R 23, C 28.]

HAB. Western United States, from the eastern base of the Rocky Mountains to the Pacific coast, south to Southern Mexico.

768. **Sialia arctica** (SWAINS.).
Mountain Bluebird.

Erythaca (Sialia) arctica SWAINS. Fauna Bor. Am. II. 1831, 209, pl. 39.
Sialia arctica NUTT. Man. Land B. 1834, 573.

[B 160, C 18, R 24, C 29.]

HAB. Western North America (chiefly the interior), from the western parts of the Plains to the Pacific, north to Great Slave Lake, south to Mexico.

HYPOTHETICAL LIST.[1]

FAMILY **PODICIPIDÆ**.

1. **Æchmophorus clarkii** (LAWR.).
   Clark's Grebe.

   Podiceps clarkii LAWR. in BAIRD's B. N. Am. 1858, 895.
   Æchmophorus clarkii COUES, Pr. Ac. Nat. Sci. Phila. 1862, 229.

   [B 705, C 608 a, R 730, C 846.]

   Probably the female of *Æ. occidentalis* (LAWR.). (*Cf.* HENSHAW, Bull. Nutt. Orn. Club, VI. 1881, pp. 214-218; B. B. & R., Water B. N. Am. II. p. 423; and especially BRYANT, Auk, II. 1885, pp. 313, 314.)

FAMILY **ALCIDÆ**.

2. **Cepphus motzfeldi** (BENICK.).
   Black-winged Guillemot.

   Uria motzfeldi BENICK. Isis, Aug. 1824, 889.
   Cepphus motzfeldi STEJN. Pr. U. S. Nat. Mus. VII. Aug. 5, 1884, 210.

   [B —, C —, R —, C —.]

   North American, but its specific validity not satisfactorily established. (*Cf.* STEJN. *l. c.*, and Water B. N. Am. II. 1884, pp. 497, 498).

---

[1] Consisting of species which have been recorded as North American, but whose status as North American birds is doubtful, either from lack of positive evidence of their occurrence within the prescribed limits of the present Check-List, or from absence of satisfactory proof of their validity as species.

3. **Cepphus carbo** PALL.
   Sooty Guillemot.

   Cepphus carbo PALL. Zoog. Rosso-As. II. 1826, 350.

   [B 728, C 633, R 762, C 873.]

   No evidence of its occurrence in North America. (*Cf.* STEJN. Proc. U. S. Nat. Mus. VII. 1884, pp. 225-227.)

   FAMILY **LARIDÆ**.

4. **Xema (Creagrus) furcata** (NEB.).
   Swallow-tailed Gull.

   Larus furcatus NEB. Voy. 'Venus,' Atlas, pl. 10 (1846).
   Xema furcatum COUES, Key, 1872, 317.

   [B 679, C 559, R 678, C 791.]

   In all probability erroneously accredited to North America. Only three examples are known, — the type, said to be from Monterey, Cal., one from the Galapagos, and one from the coast of Peru.

   FAMILY **PROCELLARIIDÆ**.

5. **Puffinus kuhlii** (BOIE).
   Cinereous Shearwater.

   Procellaria kuhlii BOIE, Isis, 1835, 257.
   Puffinus kuhlii BONAP. Consp. II. 1856, 202.

   [B 651, C 596, R 708, C 831.]

   An Eastern Atlantic species, of which no American specimens are known to exist in collections.

6. **Oceanodroma hornbyi** (GRAY).
   Hornby's Petrel.

   Thalassidroma hornbyi GRAY, P. Z. S. 1853, 62.
   Oceanodroma hornbyi BONAP. Consp. II. 1856, 195.

   [B 641, C 592, R 727, C 827.]

A very distinct species, of which only one specimen has been obtained, the alleged locality being the "northwest coast of America."

Family PHALACROCORACIDÆ.

7. **Phalacrocorax perspicillatus** PALL.
Pallas's Cormorant.

Phalacrocorax perspicillatus PALL. Zoog. Rosso-As. II. 1826, 305.

[B 621, C 533, R 648, C 756.]

Believed, on good evidence, to be now extinct, as it unquestionably is in the locality (Bering Island) where originally discovered. Only three specimens are known to exist in collections, — one each being in the St Petersburgh, Leyden, and British Museums. Even if existing, it has no valid claim to a place in the North American fauna. (*Cf.* STEJN. Pr. U. S. Nat. Mus. VI. 1883, p. 65.)

Family ANATIDÆ.

8. **Chen cærulescens** (LINN.).
Blue Goose.

Anas cærulescens LINN. S. N. ed. 10, I. 1758, 224.
Chen cærulescens RIDGW. Pr. U. S. Nat. Mus. III. Aug. 24, 1880, 202.

[B 564, C 479, R 590, C 694.]

Possibly a race of *C. hyperboreus* (PALL.). (*Cf.* B. B. & R. Water B. N. Am. I. 1884, 437 ; RIDGW. Auk, I. 1884, 240.)

Family ARDEIDÆ.

9. **Ardea wuerdemanni** BAIRD.
Würdemann's Heron.

Ardea würdemanni BAIRD, B. N. Am. 1858, 669.

[B 488, C 450, R 486, *part*, C 656, *part*.]

Believed to be either the colored phase of *A. oceidentalis* AUD., or an abnormal specimen of *A. wardi* RIDGW. (*Cf.* RIDGW. Bull. U. S. Geol. & Geog. Surv. Terr. IV. No. 1, 1878, pp. 229-236; Bull. Nutt. Orn. Club, VII. 1882, pp. 1-6; Auk, I. 1884, pp. 161-163; Water B. N. Am. I. 1884, pp. 7-13.)

10. **Ardea (Dichromanassa) pealei** BONAP.
    Peale's Egret.

Ardea pealei BONAP. Ann. Lyc. N. Y. II. 1826, 154.

[B 482, C 355, *part*, R 491, *part*, C 661, *part*.]

Supposed to be the white phase of *A. rufa* BODD., but possibly entitled to recognition as a local or geographical race.

FAMILY **SCOLOPACIDÆ**.

11. **Tringa (Actodromas) cooperi** BAIRD.
    Cooper's Sandpiper.

Tringa cooperi BAIRD, B. N. Am. 1858, 716.

[B 527, C 422, R 535, C 618.]

Known only from the single specimen from which the species was originally described, taken on Long Island, in May, 1833, and still extant in the National Museum. The status of the species is in doubt.

FAMILY **CATHARTIDÆ**.

GENUS **GYPAGUS** VIEILLOT.

Gypagus VIEILL. Analyse, 1816, 21. Type, by elimination, *Vultur papa* LINN.

12. **Gypagus papa** (LINN.).
    King Vulture.

Vultur papa LINN. S. N. ed. 10, I. 1758, 86.
Gypagus papa VIEILL. Nouv. Dict. d'Hist. Nat. XXXVI. 1819, 456.

[B —, C —, R —, C —.]

Recorded as occurring on the Rio Verde, Arizona, but its identity not satisfactorily determined. (*Cf.* Coues, Bull. Nutt. Orn. Club, VI. 1881, p. 248.)

13. **Cathartes burrovianus** Cass.
Burroughs's Turkey Vulture.

Cathartes burrovianus Cass. Pr. Ac. Nat. Sci. Phila. II. 1845, 212.

[B 4, C —, R —, C —.]

Hab. Mexico and Eastern South America. Reported as having been seen near Brownsville, Texas. (*Cf.* Dresser, Ibis, 1865, p. 322.)

Family FALCONIDÆ.

14. **Buteo cooperi** Cass.
Cooper's Henhawk.

Buteo cooperi Cass. Pr. Ac. Nat. Sci. Phila. VIII. 1856, 253.

[B 29, C 349, R 437, C 514.]

Probably the light phase of *B. harlani* Aud. (*Cf.* Ridgw. Auk, I. 1884, pp. 253, 254; Ib. II. 1885, pp. 165, 166.)

15. **Buteo fuliginosus** Scl.
Little Black Hawk.

Buteo fuliginosus Scl. P. Z. S. 1858, 356.

[B —, C —, R —, C —.]

Hab. Tropical America; Florida (accidental?). Said to be the melanistic phase of *B. brachyurus* Vieill. (*Cf.* Ridgw. Bull. Nutt. Orn. Club, VI. Oct. 1881, pp. 207–214.)

Genus RHYNCHOPSITTA Bonaparte.

Rhynchopsitta Bonap. Rev. et Mag. Zool. VI. 1854, 149. Type, *Macrocercus pachyrhynchus* Swains.

16. **Rhynchopsitta pachyrhyncha** (SWAINS.).
Thick-billed Parrot.

Macrocercus pachyrhynchus SWAINS. Phil. Mag. 1827, 439.
Rhynchopsitta pachyrhyncha BONAP. Rev. et Mag. Zool. VI. 1854, 149.

[B 64, C —, R 391, C —.]

HAB. Mexico. There is said to be a specimen in "the collection of the Philadelphia Academy of Natural Sciences, labelled Rio Grande, Texas, J. W. Audubon," but there is doubt as to whether the specimen was really taken within the limits of the United States. (*Cf.* BAIRD, Birds N. Am. 1858, p. 66, foot-note.) Its occurrence in Texas is not improbable.

FAMILY **FRINGILLIDÆ**. FINCHES, SPARROWS, ETC.

17. **Acanthis brewsterii** (RIDGW.).
Brewster's Linnet.

Ægiothus (*flavirostris* var.) *brewsterii* RIDGW. Am. Nat. July, 1872, 433.
Acanthis brewsterii RIDGW. Pr. U. S. Nat. Mus. VIII. 1885, 354.

[B —, C 147, R 180, C 211.]

The type-specimen, taken at Waltham, Mass., remains unique. It cannot be identified with any known species, but may be a hybrid between *Acanthis linaria* and *Spinus pinus*. (*Cf.* BREWST. Bull. Nutt. Orn. Club, VI. 1881, p. 225.)

18. **Spiza townsendii** (AUD.).
Townsend's Bunting.

Emberiza townsendii AUD. Orn. Biog. II. 1834, 183.
Spiza townsendi RIDGW. Pr. U. S. Nat. Mus. III. Aug. 24, 1880, 182.

[B 379, C 192, R 255, C 288.]

The original specimen, taken May 11, 1833, in Chester County, Pa., by Mr. J. K. Townsend, remains unique. Its peculiarities cannot be accounted for by hybridism, nor probably by individual variation.

Family VIREONIDÆ. Vireos.

Genus HYLOPHILUS Temminck.

Hylophilus Temm. Pl. Col. III. Livr. 29, 1823, text, and pl. 173, fig. 1. Type, *H. thoracicus* Temm.

19. Hylophilus decurtatus (Bonap.).
Short-winged Hylophilus.

Sylvicola decurtata Bonap. P. Z. S. 1837, 118.
Hylophilus decurtatus Baird, Rev. Am. B. I. 1866, 380.

[B —, C —, R —, C —.]

Hab. Mexico and Central America, to Isthmus of Panama. Southern Texas? (*Helinai brevipennis* Giraud, Ann. Lyc. N. Y. 1850, 40. "Mexico and Texas.")

Family MNIOTILTIDÆ. Wood-Warblers.

20. Helminthophila lawrencei (Herrick).
Lawrence's Warbler.

Helminthophaga lawrencei Herrick, Pr. Ac. Nat. Sci. Phila. 1874, 220, pl. 15.
Helminthophila lawrencei Ridgw. Bull. Nutt. Orn. Club, VII. Jan. 1882, 53.

[B —, C —, R 80, C 99.]

Two specimens have been taken in New Jersey. Supposed to be a hybrid between *H. pinus* and *H. chrysoptera*. (*Cf.* Ridgw. Ibis, 1876, p. 169, and Brewst. Bull. Nutt. Orn. Club, VI. 1881, pp. 218-225.)

21. Helminthophila leucobronchialis (Brewst.).
Brewster's Warbler.

Helminthophaga leucobronchialis Brewst. Bull. Nutt. Orn. Club, I. Jan. 1876, 1, plate.
Helminthophila leucobronchialis Ridgw. Bull. Nutt. Orn. Club, VII. Jan. 1882, 53.

[B —, C —, R 82, C 100.]

Known from numerous specimens, taken in Southern New England, Lower Hudson Valley, New Jersey, Virginia, Michigan, etc. Supposed to be a hybrid between *H. pinus* and *H. chrysoptera*, but possibly a distinct species. (*Cf.* BREWST. Bull. Nutt. Orn. Club, VI. 1881, pp 218–225 ; RIDGW. Auk, II. Oct. 1885, pp. 359–363.)

22. Helminthophila cincinnatiensis (LANGD.).
Cincinnati Warbler.

Helminthophaga cincinnatiensis LANGD. Jour. Cinc. Soc. N. H July, 1880, 119, 120, pl. 4.
Helminthophila cincinnatiensis RIDGW. Pr. U. S. Nat. Mus. VIII. 1885, 354.

[B —, C —, R —, C 101.]

One specimen taken near Cincinnati, Ohio. Probably a hybrid between *H. pinus* and *Geothlypis* (*Oporornis*) *formosa*. (*Cf.* RIDGW. Bull. Nutt. Orn. Club, V. 1880, p. 237.)

23. Dendroica (Perissoglossa?) carbonata (AUD.).
Carbonated Warbler.

Sylvia carbonata AUD. Orn. Biog. I. 1831, 308, pl. 60.
Dendroica carbonata BAIRD, B. N. Am. 1858, 287.
Perissoglossa carbonata B. B. & R. Hist. N. Am. B. I. Jan. 1874, 214.

[B 207, C —, R 91, C —.]

Known only from Audubon's plate and description of two specimens killed near Henderson, Kentucky, in May, 1811.

24. Dendroica montana (WILS.).
Blue Mountain Warbler.

Sylvia montana WILS. Am. Orn. V. 1812, 113, pl. 44, fig. 2.
Dendroica montana BAIRD, B. N. Am. 1858, 278.

[B 199, C —, R 112, C —.]

Known only from the works of Wilson and Audubon. Taken in the Blue Mountains of Virginia. Not as yet satisfactorily identified with any other species.

25. Sylvania (?) microcephala RIDGW.
Small-headed Warbler.

Sylvania microcephala RIDGW. Pr. U. S. Nat. Mus. VIII. 1885, 354. (= *Muscicapa minuta* WILS. Am. Orn. VI. 1812, 62, pl. 1, fig. 5.) (Nec GMEL., 1788.)

[B 212, C —, R 126, C —.]

Known only from the works of Wilson and Audubon. Claimed to have been taken in New Jersey and Kentucky.

FAMILY **SYLVIIDÆ**. WARBLERS.

26. Regulus cuvieri AUD.
Cuvier's Kinglet.

Regulus cuvieri AUD. Orn. Biog. I. 1832, 288, pl. 55.

[B 163, C —, R 32, C —.]

Known only from Audubon's description and figure of the original specimen, killed in June, 1812, on the banks of the Schuylkill River, in Pennsylvania.

THE FOSSIL BIRDS OF NORTH AMERICA.

A. — JURASSIC.

1. **Laopteryx priscus** MARSH.

    Laopteryx priscus MARSH, Am. Journ. Sci. XXI. 1881, 341.

    Upper Jurassic beds of Wyoming.

B. — CRETACEOUS.[1]

2. **Apatornis celer** MARSH.

    Ichthyornis celer MARSH, Am. Journ. Sci. V. 1873, 74.
    Apatornis celer MARSH, Am. Journ. Sci. V. 1873, 162.

    Middle Cretaceous of Western Kansas.

3. **Baptornis advenus** MARSH.

    Baptornis advenus MARSH, Am. Journ. Sci. XIV. 1877, 86.

    Cretaceous of Western Kansas, in the same beds with Odontornithes and Pteranodontia.

---

[1] The genera alphabetically arranged.

4. Graculavus velox MARSH.

Graculavus velox MARSH, Am. Journ. Sci. III. 1872, 363.

Greensand of the middle marl bed, or Upper Cretaceous, near Hornerstown, New Jersey.

5. Graculavus pumilus MARSH.

Graculavus pumilus MARSH, Am. Journ. Sci. III. 1872, 364.

Greensand of the middle marl bed, or Upper Cretaceous, near Hornerstown, New Jersey.

6. Hesperornis regalis MARSH.

Hesperornis regalis MARSH, Am. Journ. Sci. III. 1872, 56.

Pteranodon beds of Western Kansas.

7. Hesperornis crassipes MARSH.

Lestornis crassipes MARSH, Am. Journ. Sci. XI. 1876, 509.
Hesperornis crassipes MARSH, Odontornithes, 1880, 196, figs. 40 a–d, pls. vii, xvii.

Yellow chalk of the Pteranodon beds, Western Kansas.

8. Hesperornis gracilis MARSH.

Hesperornis gracilis MARSH, Am. Journ. Sci. XI. 1876, 510.

Yellow chalk of the Pteranodon beds, Western Kansas.

9. Ichthyornis dispar MARSH.

Ichthyornis dispar MARSH, Am. Journ. Sci. IV. 1872, 344.

Pteranodon beds, Middle Cretaceous, Northwestern Kansas.

10. Ichthyornis agilis MARSH.

Graculavus agilis MARSH, Am. Journ. Sci. V. 1873, 230.
Ichthyornis agilis MARSH, Odontornithes, 1880, 197.

Pteranodon beds, Middle Cretaceous, Western Kansas.

11. Ichthyornis anceps MARSH.

Graculavus anceps MARSH, Am. Journ. Sci. III. 1872, 364.
Ichthyornis anceps MARSH, Odontornithes, 1880, 198.

Gray shale of the Middle Cretaceous, Smoky Hill River, Western Kansas.

12. Ichthyornis lentus MARSH.

Graculavus lentus MARSH, Am. Journ. Sci. XIV. 1877, 253.
Ichthyornis lentus MARSH, Odontornithes, 1880, 198.

Middle Cretaceous beds, near Fort McKinney, Texas.

13. Ichthyornis tener MARSH.

Ichthyornis tener MARSH, Odontornithes, 1880, 198, pl. xxx. fig. 8.

Pteranodon beds, Middle Cretaceous, Wallace County, Kansas.

14. Ichthyornis validus MARSH.

Ichthyornis validus MARSH, Odontornithes, 1880, 198, pl. xxx. figs. 11–14.

Yellow chalk of the Middle Cretaceous, near Solomon River, Northwestern Kansas.

15. Ichthyornis victor MARSH.

Ichthyornis victor MARSH, Am. Journ. Sci. XI. 1876, 511.

Middle Cretaceous of Kansas, in various localities.

16. Laornis edvardsianus MARSH.

Laornis edvardsianus MARSH, Pr. Ac. Nat. Sci. Phila. 1870, 5.

Middle marl bed, Upper Cretaceous, Birmingham, New Jersey.

17. Palæotringa littoralis MARSH.

Palæotringa littoralis MARSH, Pr. Ac. Nat. Sci. Phila. 1870, 5.

Greensand of the Upper Cretaceous, near Hornerstown, New Jersey.

18. **Palæotringa vagans** MARSH.

Palæotringa vagans MARSH, Am. Journ. Sci. III. 1872, 365.

Greensand of the Upper Cretaceous, near Hornerstown, New Jersey.

19. **Palæotringa vetus** MARSH.

Scolopax MORTON, Syn. Organic Remains of the Cret. U. S. 1834, 32.
Palæotringa vetus MARSH, Pr. Ac. Nat. Sci. Phila. 1870, 5.

Lower marl bed of the Cretaceous formation, near Arneytown, New Jersey.

20. **Telmatornis priscus** MARSH.

Telmatornis priscus MARSH, Pr. Ac. Nat. Sci. Phila. 1870, 5.

Middle marl bed of the Upper Cretaceous, near Hornerstown, New Jersey.

21. **Telmatornis affinis** MARSH.

Telmatornis affinis MARSH, Pr. Ac. Nat. Sci. Phila. 1870, 5.

Middle marl beds of the Upper Cretaceous, near Hornerstown, New Jersey.

C.—TERTIARY.

SUBCLASS RATITÆ.

22. **Gastornis giganteus** (COPE).

Diatryma gigantea COPE, Pr. Ac. Nat. Sci. Phila. 1876, 11.
Gastornis giganteus COUES, Key N. A. Birds, 2d ed. 1884, 825.

Wahsatch Epoch, Eocene of New Mexico.

Subclass CARINATÆ.

Order PYGOPODES.

23. Uria antiqua (Marsh).

Catarractes antiqua Marsh, Am. Journ. Sci. XLIX. 1870, 213.
Uria antiqua Coues, MS.

Miocene of North Carolina.

24. Uria affinis (Marsh).

Catarractes affinis Marsh, Am. Journ. Sci. IV. 1872, 259.
Uria affinis Coues, MS.

Post-pliocene of Maine.

Order TUBINARES.

25. Puffinus conradii Marsh.

Puffinus conradii Marsh, Am. Journ. Sci. XLIX. 1870, 212.

Miocene of Maryland.

Order STEGANOPODES.

26. Sula loxostyla Cope.

Sula loxostyla Cope, Tr. Amer. Philos. Soc. XIV. 1870, 236.

Miocene of North Carolina.

27. Phalacrocorax idahensis (Marsh).

Graculus idahensis Marsh, Am. Journ. Sci. XLIX. 1870, 216.
Phalacrocorax idahensis Coues, Key N. A. Birds, 2d ed. 1884, 824.

Pliocene of Idaho.

28. **Phalacrocorax micropus** (Cope).

> *Graculus micropus* Cope, Bull. U. S. Geol. Surv. Terr. IV. No. 2, 1878, 386.
> *Phalacrocorax micropus* Coues, Key N. A. Birds, 2d ed. 1884, 824.

Pliocene of Oregon.

Order ANSERES.

29. **Cygnus paloregonus** Cope.

> *Cygnus paloregonus* Cope, Bull. U. S. Geol. Surv. Terr. IV. No. 2, 1878, 388.

Pliocene of Oregon.

30. **Branta hypsibates** (Cope).

> *Anser hypsibates* Cope, Bull. U. S. Geol. Surv. Terr. IV. No. 2, 1878, 387.
> *Branta hypsibates* Coues, MS.

Order PALUDICOLÆ.

31. **Grus haydeni** Marsh.

> *Grus haydeni* Marsh, Am. Journ. Sci. XLIX. 1870, 214.

Pliocene of Nebraska.

32. **Grus proavus** Marsh.

> *Grus proavus* Marsh, Am. Journ. Sci. IV. 1872, 261.

Post-pliocene of New Jersey.

33. **Aletornis nobilis** Marsh.

> *Aletornis nobilis* Marsh, Am. Journ. Sci. IV. 1872, 256.

Eocene of Wyoming.

34. **Aletornis pernix** Marsh.

Aletornis pernix Marsh, Am. Journ. Sci. IV. 1872, 256.

Eocene of Wyoming.

35. **Aletornis venustus** Marsh.

Aletornis venustus Marsh, Am. Journ. Sci. IV. 1872, 257.

Eocene of Wyoming.

36. **Aletornis gracilis** Marsh.

Aletornis gracilis Marsh, Am. Journ. Sci. IV. 1872, 258.

Eocene of Wyoming.

37. **Aletornis bellus** Marsh.

Aletornis bellus Marsh, Am. Journ. Sci. IV. 1872, 258.

Eocene of Wyoming.

Order LIMICOLÆ.

38. **Charadrius sheppardianus** Cope.

Charadrius sheppardianus Cope, Bull. U. S. Geol. Surv. Terr. VI. No. 1, 1881, 83.

(Formation and locality not given.)

Order GALLINÆ.

39. **Meleagris antiquus** Marsh.

Meleagris antiquus Marsh, Am. Journ. Sci. II. 1871, 126.

Miocene of Colorado.

40. Meleagris altus MARSH.

Meleagris altus MARSH, Pr. Ac. Nat. Sci. Phila. 1870, 11.

Post-pliocene of New Jersey.

41. Meleagris celer MARSH.

Meleagris celer MARSH, Am. Journ. Sci. 1872, 261.

Post-pliocene of New Jersey.

ORDER RAPTORES.

42. Palæoborus umbrosus (COPE).

Cathartes umbrosus COPE, Pr. Ac. Nat. Sci. Phila. 1874, 151.
Palæoborus umbrosus COUES, Key N. A. Birds, 2d ed. 1884, 822.

Pliocene of New Mexico.

43. Bubo leptosteus MARSH.

Bubo leptosteus MARSH, Am. Journ. Sci. II. 1871, 126.

Lower Tertiary of Wyoming.

44. Aquila danana MARSH.

Aquila danana MARSH, Am. Journ. Sci. II. 1871, 125.

Pliocene of Nebraska.

ORDER COCCYGES.

45. Uintornis lucaris MARSH.

Uintornis lucaris MARSH, Am. Journ. Sci. IV. 1872, 259.

Lower Tertiary formation of Wyoming.

Order PASSERES.

46. **Palæospiza bella** ALLEN.

Palæospiza bella ALLEN, Bull. U. S. Geol. Surv. Terr. IV. No. 2, 1878, 443, pl. i. figs. 1, 2.

Insect-bearing shales of Florissant, Colorado.

INDEX.

ACANTHIS, 259.
    brewsterii, 354.
    hornemannii, 259.
    hornemannii exilipes, 260.
    linaria, 260.
    linaria holbœllii, 260.
    linaria rostrata, 260.
Accipiter, 186.
    atricapillus, 186.
    atricapillus striatulus, 186.
    cooperi, 186.
    velox, 186.
Accipitrinæ, 184.
Actitis, 158.
    macularia, 158.
Actochelidon, 92.
Actodromas, 150, 352.
Æchmophorus, 73.
    clarkii, 349.
    occidentalis, 73.
Ægialitis, 161, 162.
    dubia, 162.
    hiaticula, 162.
    meloda, 162.
    meloda circumcincta, 163.
    mongola, 163.
    montana, 164.
    nivosa, 163.
    semipalmata, 162.
    vocifera, 161.
    wilsonia, 163.
Æsalon, 195.
Æstrelata, 102.
    fisheri, 103.
    gularis, 102.
    hasitata, 102.
Agelaius, 249.
    gubernator, 249.
    phœniceus, 249.
    tricolor, 249.
Aix, 117.

Aix sponsa, 118.
Ajaja, 131.
    ajaja, 131.
Alauda, 238.
    arvensis, 238.
Alaudidæ, 238.
Albatross, Black-footed, 97.
    Short-tailed, 97.
    Sooty, 98.
    Yellow-nosed, 98.
Alca, 83.
    torda, 83.
Alcedinidæ, 209.
Alcidæ, 76, 349.
Alcinæ, 82.
Alcyones, 209.
Alectorides, 364.
Aletornis bellus, 365.
    gracilis, 365.
    nobilis, 364.
    pernix, 365.
    venustus, 365.
Alle, 84.
    alle, 84.
Allinæ, 84.
Amazilia, 226.
    cerviniventris, 227.
    fuscicaudata, 227.
Ammodramus, 265, 268.
    bairdii, 267.
    beldingi, 266.
    caudacutus, 268.
    caudacutus nelsoni, 269.
    henslowii, 268.
    leconteii, 268.
    maritimus, 269.
    nigrescens, 269.
    princeps, 265.
    rostratus, 266.
    rostratus guttatus, 267.
    sandwichensis, 265.

Ammodramus sandwichensis alaudinus, 266.
   sandwichensis bryanti, 266.
   sandwichensis savanna, 265.
   savannarum passerinus, 267.
   savannarum perpallidus, 268.
Ampelidæ, 294.
Ampelinæ, 294.
Ampelis, 294.
   cedrorum, 294.
   garrulus, 294.
Amphispiza, 276.
   belli, 276.
   belli nevadensis, 277.
   bilineata, 276.
Anas, 114.
   americana, 116.
   boschas, 114.
   carolinensis, 116.
   crecca, 116.
   cyanoptera, 117.
   discors, 116.
   fulvigula, 115.
   obscura, 115.
   penelope, 115.
   strepera, 115.
Anatidæ, 113, 351.
Anatinæ, 114.
Ancylocheilus, 152.
Anhinga, 108.
   anhinga, 108.
Anhingidæ, 108.
Ani, 206.
   Groove-billed, 207.
Anorthura, 329.
Anous, 96
   stolidus, 96.
Anser, 126.
   albifrons, 126.
   albifrons gambeli, 126.
Anseres, 113, 364.
Anserinæ, 125.
Anthus, 319.
   cervinus, 320.
   pensilvanicus, 320.
   pratensis, 320.
   spragueii, 320.
Antrostomus, 219.
   carolinensis, 219.
   vociferus, 219.
   vociferus arizonæ, 219.
Apatornis celer, 359.
Aphelocoma, 242.
   californica, 242.
   floridana, 242.

Aphelocoma sieberii arizonæ, 243.
   woodhousei, 242.
Aphriza, 164.
   virgata, 164.
Aphrizidæ, 164.
Aphrizinæ, 164.
Aquila, 192.
   chrysaëtos, 192.
   danana, 366.
Aramidæ, 139.
Aramus, 139.
   giganteus, 139.
Archibuteo, 191.
   ferrugineus, 191.
   lagopus, 191.
   lagopus sancti-johannis, 191.
Arctonetta, 122.
   fischeri, 122.
Ardea, 135.
   candidissima, 136.
   cinerea, 135.
   cœrulea, 137.
   egretta, 136.
   herodias, 135.
   occidentalis, 135.
   pealei, 352.
   rufa, 136.
   tricolor ruficollis, 137.
   virescens, 137.
   wardi, 135.
   wuerdemanni, 351.
Ardeidæ, 134, 351.
Ardeinæ, 135.
Ardetta, 134.
Arenaria, 164.
   interpres, 165.
   melanocephala, 165.
Arenariinæ, 164.
Arquatella, 149.
Asio, 198.
   accipitrinus, 198.
   wilsonianus, 198.
Astur, 186.
Asturina, 191.
   plagiata, 191.
Asyndesmus, 216.
Atthis, 226.
Auk, Great, 84.
   Razor-billed, 83.
Auklet, Cassin's, 78.
   Crested, 79.
   Least, 79.
   Paroquet, 78.
   Rhinoceros, 78.
   Whiskered, 79.

Auriparus flaviceps, 338.
Avocet, American, 146.
Aythya, 118.
    affinis, 119.
    americana, 118.
    collaris, 119.
    marila nearctica, 119.
    vallisneria, 118.

BALDPATE, 116.
Baptornis advenus, 359.
Bartramia, 157.
    longicauda, 157.
Basileuterus, 318.
    belli, 318.
    culicivorus, 318.
Basilinna, 227.
    xantusi, 227.
Bird, Red billed Tropic, 107.
    Surf, 164.
    Yellow-billed Tropic, 106.
Bittern, American, 134.
    Least, 134.
Blackbird, Bicolored, 249.
    Brewer's, 253.
    Red-winged, 249.
    Rusty, 253.
    Tricolored, 249.
    Yellow-headed, 249.
Bluebird, 346.
    Azure, 346.
    Mountain, 347.
    Western, 346.
Bluethroat, Red-spotted, 345.
Bobolink, 247.
    Western, 247.
Bob-white, 167.
    Florida, 167.
    Grayson's, 168.
    Masked, 168.
    Texan, 167.
Bonasa, 172.
    umbellus, 172.
    umbellus sabini, 173.
    umbellus togata, 172.
    umbellus umbelloides, 172.
Booby, 107.
    Blue-faced, 107.
    Red-footed, 108.
Botaurinæ, 134.
Botaurus, 134.
    exilis, 134.
    lentiginosus, 134.
Brachyramphus, 80.

Brachyramphus craveri, 81.
    hypoleucus, 81.
    kittlitzii, 81.
    marmoratus, 80.
Brant, 127.
    Black, 128.
Branta, 126.
    bernicla, 127.
    canadensis, 126.
    canadensis hutchinsii, 127.
    canadensis minima, 127.
    canadensis occidentalis, 127.
    hypsibates, 364.
    leucopsis, 128.
    nigricans, 128.
Bubo, 202.
    leptosteus, 366.
    virginianus, 202.
    virginianus arcticus, 203.
    virginianus saturatus, 203.
    virginianus subarcticus, 202.
Bubonidæ, 198.
Budytes, 319.
    flavus leucostriatus, 319.
Bullfinch, Cassin's, 255.
Bulweria, 103.
    bulweri, 103.
Bunting, Indigo, 288.
    Lark, 290.
    Lazuli, 288.
    Painted, 288.
    Townsend's, 354.
    Varied, 288.
Bush-Tit, 337.
    Black-eared, 337.
    Californian, 337.
    Grinda's, 337.
    Lead-colored, 337.
Buteo, 187.
    abbreviatus, 189.
    albicaudatus, 189.
    borealis, 187.
    borealis calurus, 188.
    borealis kriderii, 188.
    borealis lucasanus, 188.
    brachyurus, 190.
    buteo, 187.
    cooperi, 353.
    fuliginosus, 353.
    harlani, 188.
    latissimus, 190.
    lineatus, 188.
    lineatus alleni, 189.
    lineatus elegans, 189.
    swainsoni, 189.

Buteola, 190.
Butorides, 137.
Buzzard, European, 187.

CALAMOSPIZA, 290.
   melanocorys, 290.
Calcarius, 263.
   lapponicus, 263.
   ornatus, 263.
   pictus, 263.
Calidris, 153.
   arenaria, 153.
Callipepla, 169.
   californica, 169.
   californica vallicola, 169.
   gambeli, 170.
   squamata, 169.
   squamata castanogastris, 169.
Calothorax, 226.
Calypte, 224.
Campephilus, 210.
   principalis, 210.
Camptolaimus, 121.
   labradorius, 121.
Campylorhynchus, 325.
   affinis, 325.
   brunneicapillus, 325.
Canachites, 171.
Canvas-back, 118.
Caprimulgi, 219.
Caprimulgidæ, 219.
Caracara, Audubon's, 196.
   Guadalupe, 196.
Cardellina, 317.
   rubrifrons, 317.
Cardinal, 286.
   Arizona, 286.
   Saint Lucas, 286.
   Texan, 286.
Cardinalis, 285.
   cardinalis, 286.
   cardinalis igneus, 286.
   cardinalis superbus, 286.
Carinatæ, 363.
Carpodacus, 256.
   amplus, 257.
   cassini, 256.
   frontalis, 256.
   frontalis rhodocolpus, 257.
   purpureus, 256.
   purpureus californicus, 256.
Catbird, 322.
Catharista, 183.
   atrata, 183.

Cathartes, 183.
   aura, 183.
   burrovianus, 353.
Cathartidæ, 182, 352.
Catherpes, 326.
   mexicanus, 326.
   mexicanus conspersus, 326.
Centrocercus, 176.
   urophasianus, 176.
Centronyx, 267.
Centurus, 217.
Ceophlœus, 215.
   pileatus, 215.
Cepphi, 75.
Cepphus, 81.
   carbo, 350.
   columba, 82.
   grylle, 81.
   mandtii, 82.
   motzfeldi, 349.
Cerorhinca, 78.
   monocerata, 78.
Certhia, 330.
   familiaris americana, 330.
   familiaris mexicana, 331.
Certhiidæ, 330.
Certhiola, 300.
   bahamensis, 300.
Ceryle, 209.
   alcyon, 209.
   cabanisi, 209.
Chachalaca, 178.
Chætura, 222.
   pelagica, 222.
   vauxii, 222.
Chæturinæ, 221.
Chamæa, 336.
   fasciata, 336.
   fasciata henshawi, 336.
Chamæinæ, 336.
Charadriidæ, 160.
Charadrius, 160.
   apricarius, 160.
   dominicus, 161.
   dominicus fulvus, 161.
   sheppardianus, 365.
   squatarola, 160.
Charitonetta, 120.
   albeola, 120.
Chat, Long-tailed, 315.
   Yellow-breasted, 315.
Chaulelasmus, 115.
Chelidon, 292.
   erythrogaster, 292.
Chen, 125.

Chen cærulescens, 351.
    hyperborea, 125.
    hyperborea nivalis, 125.
    rossii, 126.
Chickadee, 334.
    Californian, 336.
    Carolina, 334.
    Chestnut-backed, 335.
    Hudsonian, 335.
    Long-tailed, 334.
    Mexican, 335.
    Mountain, 335.
    Oregon, 334.
    Siberian, 335.
Chloroceryle, 209.
Chondestes, 269.
    grammacus, 270.
    grammacus strigatus, 270.
Chordeiles, 220.
    virginianus, 220.
    virginianus henryi, 221.
    virginianus minor, 221.
    texensis, 221.
Chuck-will's-widow, 219.
Ciceronia, 79.
Ciconiæ, 133.
Ciconiidæ, 133.
Ciconiinæ, 133.
Cinclidæ, 321.
Cinclus, 321.
    mexicanus, 321.
Circus, 185.
    hudsonius, 185.
Cistothorus, 329.
    palustris, 330.
    stellaris, 330.
Clamatores, 228.
Clangula, 120.
    hyemalis, 120.
Clivicola, 293.
    riparia, 293.
Coccothraustes, 254.
    vespertina, 255.
Coccyges, 206, 366.
Coccyginæ, 207.
Coccyzus, 207.
    americanus, 208.
    erythrophthalmus, 208.
    minor, 207.
Cœligena, 223.
    clemenciæ, 223.
Cœrebidæ, 300.
Colaptes, 217.
    auratus, 217.
    cafer, 218.

Colaptes cafer saturatior, 218.
    chrysoides, 218.
    rufipileus, 218.
Colinus, 167.
    graysoni, 168.
    ridgwayi, 168.
    virginianus, 167.
    virginianus floridanus, 167.
    virginianus texanus, 167.
Columba, 178.
    fasciata, 178.
    flavirostris, 179.
    leucocephala, 179.
Columbæ, 178.
Columbidæ, 178.
Columbigallina, 181.
    passerina, 181.
Colymbus, 73.
    auritus, 74.
    dominicus, 74.
    holbœlii, 73.
    nigricollis californicus, 74.
Compsohalieus, 110.
Compsothlypis, 304.
    americana, 305.
    nigrilora, 305.
Contopus, 233.
    borealis, 233.
    pertinax, 233.
    richardsonii, 234.
    virens, 234.
Conurus, 205.
    carolinensis, 206.
Coot, American, 144.
    European, 144.
Cormorant, 109.
    Baird's, 111.
    Brandt's, 110.
    Double-crested, 109.
    Farallone, 110.
    Florida, 109.
    Mexican, 110.
    Pallas's, 351.
    Pelagic, 111.
    Red-faced, 111.
    Violet-green, 111.
    White-crested, 110.
Corvidæ, 240.
Corvinæ, 245.
Corvus, 245.
    americanus, 245.
    americanus floridanus, 245.
    caurinus, 246.
    corax sinuatus, 245.
    cryptoleucus, 245.

Corvus ossifragus, 246.
Coturnicops, 142.
Coturniculus, 267.
Cowbird, 248.
    Bronzed, 248.
    Dwarf, 248.
Cracidæ, 178.
Crake, Corn, 143.
    Spotted, 141.
Crane, Little Brown, 139.
    Sandhill, 139.
    Whooping, 139.
Creagrus, 350.
Creciscus, 142.
Creeper, Bahama Honey, 300.
    Brown, 330.
    Mexican, 331.
Crex, 143.
    crex, 143.
Crossbill, 257.
    American, 257.
    Mexican, 257.
    White-winged, 258.
Crotophaga, 206.
    ani, 206.
    sulcirostris, 207.
Crotophaginæ, 206.
Crow, American, 245.
    Fish, 246.
    Florida, 245.
    Northwest, 246.
Crymophilus, 145.
    fulicarius, 145.
Cuckoo, Black-billed, 208.
    Mangrove, 207.
    Yellow-billed, 208.
Cuculi, 206.
Cuculidæ, 206.
Curlew, Bristle-thighed, 159.
    Eskimo, 159.
    Hudsonian, 159.
    Long-billed, 158.
Cyanecula, 345.
    suecica, 345.
Cyanocephalus, 246.
    cyanocephalus, 246.
Cyanocitta, 241.
    cristata, 241.
    cristata florincola, 241.
    stelleri, 241.
    stelleri frontalis, 241.
    stelleri macrolopha, 242.
Cyclorrhynchus, 78.
    psittaculus, 78.
Cygninæ, 129.

Cygnus paloregonus, 364.
Cymodroma, 105.
    grallaria, 106.
Cypseli, 221.
Cypseloides, 221.
    niger, 222.
Cyrtonyx, 170.
    montezumæ, 170.
Cyrtopelicanus, 112.

DAFILA, 117.
    acuta, 117.
Daption, 103.
    capensis, 103.
Dendragapus, 170.
    canadensis, 171.
    franklinii, 172.
    obscurus, 170.
    obscurus fuliginosus, 171.
    obscurus richardsonii, 171.
Dendrocygna, 128.
    autumnalis, 129.
    fulva, 129.
Dendroica, 305, 306.
    æstiva, 306.
    auduboni, 307.
    blackburniæ, 308.
    bryanti castaneiceps, 306.
    cærulea, 307.
    cærulescens, 306.
    carbonata, 356.
    castanea, 308.
    chrysoparia, 310.
    coronata, 307.
    discolor, 312.
    dominica, 309.
    dominica albilora, 309.
    graciæ, 309.
    kirtlandi, 311.
    maculosa, 307.
    montana, 356.
    nigrescens, 309.
    occidentalis, 310.
    olivacea, 306.
    palmarum, 311.
    palmarum hypochrysea, 311.
    pensylvanica, 308.
    striata, 308.
    tigrina, 305.
    townsendi, 310.
    vigorsii, 311.
    virens, 310.
Dichromanassa, 136, 352.
Dickcissel, 289.

Diomedea, 97.
    albatrus 97.
    nigripes, 97.
Diomedeidæ, 97.
Dipper, American, 321.
Dolichonyx, 247.
    oryzivorus, 247.
    oryzivorus albinucha, 247.
Dove, Ground, 181.
    Inca, 181.
    Mourning, 180.
    White-fronted, 180.
    White-winged, 180.
    Zenaida, 180.
Dovekie, 84.
Dowitcher, 148.
    Long-billed, 148.
Dryobates, 210.
    borealis, 212.
    nuttallii, 212.
    pubescens, 211.
    pubescens gairdnerii, 211.
    scalaris, 212.
    scalaris lucasanus, 212.
    stricklandi, 213.
    villosus, 210.
    villosus audubonii, 211.
    villosus harrisii, 211.
    villosus leucomelas, 210.
Duck, American Scaup, 119.
    Black, 115.
    Florida, 115.
    Harlequin, 121.
    Labrador, 121.
    Lesser Scaup, 119.
    Masked, 125.
    Ring-necked, 119.
    Ruddy, 124.
    Rufous-crested, 118.
    Steller's, 121.
    Wood, 118.
Dunlin, 151.
Dysporus, 108.
Dytes, 74.

EAGLE, Bald, 193.
    Golden, 192.
    Gray Sea, 192.
    Harpy, 192.
Ectopistes, 179.
    migratorius, 179.
Egret, American, 136.
    Peale's, 352.
    Reddish, 136.

Eider, 122.
    American, 122.
    King, 123.
    Pacific, 123.
    Spectacled, 122.
Elanoides, 184.
    forficatus, 184.
Elanus, 184.
    leucurus, 184.
Embernagra, 282.
    rufivirgata, 283.
Empidonax, 234
    acadicus, 235.
    difficilis, 234.
    flaviventris, 234.
    fulvifrons, 236.
    fulvifrons pygmæus, 236.
    hammondi, 236.
    minimus, 235.
    obscurus, 236.
    pusillus, 235.
    pusillus traillii, 235.
Engyptila, 180.
    albifrons, 180.
Eniconetta, 121.
    stelleri, 121.
Ereunetes, 152.
    occidentalis, 153.
    pusillus, 153.
Ergaticus, 318.
    ruber, 318.
Erismatura, 124.
    rubida, 124.
Euetheia, 289.
    bicolor, 289.
Eugenes, 223.
    fulgens, 223.
Euphonia, 290.
    elegantissima, 290.
Euphonia, Blue-headed, 290.
Eurynorhynchus, 152.
    pygmæus, 152.

FALCO, 193.
    columbarius, 195.
    columbarius suckleyi, 195.
    fusco-cœrulescens, 195.
    islandus, 193.
    mexicanus, 194.
    peregrinus anatum, 194.
    peregrinus pealei, 194.
    richardsonii, 195.
    rusticolus, 193.
    rusticolus gyrfalco, 193.

Falco rusticolus obsoletus, 194.
  sparverioides, 196.
  sparverius, 196.
Falcon, Aplomado, 195.
  Peale's, 194.
  Prairie, 194.
Falcones, 184.
Falconidæ, 184, 353.
Falconinæ, 193.
Finch, California Purple, 256.
  Cassin s Purple, 256.
  Crimson House, 257.
  Guadalupe House, 257.
  House, 256.
  Purple, 256.
Flamingo, American, 130.
Flicker, 217.
  Gilded, 218.
  Guadalupe, 218.
  Northwestern, 218.
  Red-shafted, 218.
Florida, 137.
Flycatcher, Acadian, 235.
  Arizona Crested, 231.
  Ash-throated, 232.
  Baird's, 234.
  Beardless, 237.
  Buff-breasted, 236.
  Coues's, 233.
  Crested, 231.
  Derby, 230.
  Fork-tailed, 228.
  Fulvous, 236.
  Giraud's, 230.
  Hammond's, 236.
  Lawrence's, 232.
  Least, 235.
  Little, 235.
  Mexican Crested, 231.
  Olivaceous, 232.
  Olive-sided, 233.
  Ridgway's, 237.
  Scissor-tailed, 228.
  Sulphur-bellied, 231.
  Traill's, 235.
  Vermilion, 237.
  Wright's, 236.
  Yellow-bellied, 234.
Fratercula, 77
  arctica, 77.
  arctica glacialis, 77.
  corniculata, 77.
Fraterculinæ, 76.
Fregata, 113.
  aquila, 113.

Fregatidæ, 113.
Fringillidæ, 254, 354.
Fulica, 144.
  americana, 144.
  atra, 144.
Fulicinæ, 144.
Fuligula, 119.
Fulmar, 99.
  Giant, 98.
  Lesser, 99.
  Pacific, 99.
  Rodger's, 99.
  Slender-billed, 100.
Fulmarus, 99.
  glacialis, 99.
  glacialis glupischa, 99.
  glacialis minor, 99.
  glacialis rodgersii, 99.
  glacialoides, 100.

GADWALL, 115.
Galeoscoptes, 322.
  carolinensis, 322.
Gallinæ, 167, 365.
Gallinago, 147.
  delicata, 148.
  gallinago, 147.
Gallinula, 144.
  galeata, 144.
Gallinule, Florida, 144.
  Purple, 143.
Gallinulinæ, 143.
Gannet, 108.
Garrulinæ, 240.
Garzetta, 136.
Gastornis giganteus, 362.
Gavia, 86.
  alba, 86.
Gelochelidon, 92.
  nilotica, 92.
Geococcyx, 207.
  californianus, 207.
Geothlypis, 313, 314.
  agilis, 313.
  beldingi, 315.
  formosa, 313.
  macgillivrayi, 314.
  philadelphia, 314.
  trichas, 314.
  trichas occidentalis, 314.
Geotrygon, 181.
  martinica, 182.
Glaucidium, 204.
  gnoma, 204.

INDEX.

Glaucidium phalænoides, 205.
Glaucionetta, 119.
    clangula americana, 120.
    islandica, 120.
Glottis, 155.
Gnatcatcher, Black-tailed, 340.
    Blue-gray, 340.
    Plumbeous, 340.
Godwit, Black-tailed, 154.
    Hudsonian, 154.
    Marbled, 153.
    Pacific, 154.
Golden-eye, American, 120.
    Barrow's, 120.
Goldfinch, American, 261.
    Arizona, 261.
    Arkansas, 261.
    Black-headed, 262.
    Lawrence's, 262.
    Mexican, 261.
Goose, American White-fronted, 126
    Barnacle, 128.
    Blue, 351.
    Cackling, 127.
    Canada, 126.
    Emperor, 128.
    Greater Snow, 125.
    Hutchins's, 127.
    Lesser Snow, 125.
    Ross's Snow, 126.
    White-cheeked, 127.
    White-fronted, 126.
Goshawk, American, 186.
    Mexican, 191.
    Western, 186.
Grackle, Boat-tailed, 254.
    Bronzed, 254.
    Florida, 253.
    Great-tailed, 254.
    Purple, 253.
Graculavus pumilus, 360.
    velox, 360.
Grassquit, 289.
Grebe, American Eared, 74.
    Clark's, 349.
    Holbœll's, 73.
    Horned, 74.
    Pied-billed, 75.
    St. Domingo, 74.
    Western, 73.
Green-shank, 155.
Grosbeak, Black-headed, 287.
    Blue, 287.
    Evening, 255.
    Pine, 255.

Grosbeak, Rose-breasted, 287.
Grouse, Canada, 171.
    Canadian Ruffed, 172.
    Columbian Sharp-tailed, 176.
    Dusky, 170.
    Franklin's, 172.
    Gray Ruffed, 172.
    Oregon Ruffed, 173.
    Prairie Sharp-tailed, 176.
    Richardson's, 171.
    Ruffed, 172.
    Sage, 176.
    Sharp-tailed, 176.
    Sooty, 171.
Grues, 138.
Gruidæ, 138.
Grus, 138.
    americana, 139.
    canadensis, 139.
    haydeni, 364.
    mexicana, 139.
    proavus, 364.
Guara, 131.
    alba, 131.
    rubra, 132.
Guillemot, Black, 81.
    Black-winged, 349.
    Mandt's, 82.
    Pigeon, 82.
    Sooty, 350.
Guiraca, 287.
    cærulea, 287.
Gull, American Herring, 89.
    Bonaparte's, 91.
    California, 89.
    Franklin's, 91.
    Glaucous, 87.
    Glaucous-winged, 87.
    Great Black-backed, 88.
    Herring, 89.
    Heermann's, 90.
    Iceland, 87.
    Ivory, 86.
    Kumlien's, 88.
    Laughing, 90.
    Mew, 90.
    Nelson's, 88.
    Pallas's, 89.
    Ring-billed, 90.
    Ross's, 91.
    Sabine's, 91.
    Short-billed, 90.
    Siberian, 89.
    Slaty-backed, 88.
    Swallow-tailed, 350.

Gull, Western, 88.
Gypagus, 352.
　　papa, 352.
Gyrfalcon, 193.
　　Black, 194.
　　Gray, 193.
　　White, 193.

HABIA, 287.
　　ludoviciana, 287.
　　melanocephala, 287.
Hæmatopodidæ, 165.
Hæmatopus, 165.
　　bachmani, 166.
　　ostralegus, 165.
　　palliatus, 165.
Haliplana, 95.
Halocyptena, 103.
　　microsoma, 104.
Haliæetus, 192.
　　albicilla, 192.
　　leucocephalus, 193.
Harporhynchus, 322, 324.
　　bendirei, 323.
　　cinereus, 324.
　　crissalis, 324.
　　curvirostris, 323.
　　curvirostris palmeri, 323.
　　lecontei, 324.
　　longirostris, 323.
　　redivivus, 324.
　　rufus, 322.
Hawk, American Rough-legged, 191.
　　American Sparrow, 196.
　　Broad-winged, 190.
　　Cooper's, 186.
　　Cuban Sparrow, 196.
　　Duck, 194.
　　Florida Red shouldered, 189.
　　Harlan's, 188.
　　Harris's, 187.
　　Krider's, 188.
　　Little Black, 353.
　　Marsh, 185.
　　Mexican Black, 190.
　　Pigeon, 195.
　　Red-bellied, 189.
　　Red-shouldered, 188.
　　Red-tailed, 187.
　　Rough-legged, 191.
　　Sharp-shinned, 186.
　　Short-tailed, 190.
　　Swainson's, 189.
　　White-tailed, 189.

Hawk, Zone-tailed, 189.
Helinaia, 301.
　　swainsonii, 301.
Helminthophila, 302.
　　bachmani, 302.
　　celata, 304.
　　celata lutescens, 304.
　　chrysoptera, 302.
　　cincinnatiensis, 356.
　　lawrencei, 355.
　　leucobronchialis, 355.
　　luciæ, 303.
　　peregrina, 304.
　　pinus, 302.
　　ruficapilla, 303.
　　ruficapilla gutturalis, 303.
　　virginiæ, 303.
Helmitherus, 301.
　　vermivorus, 301.
Hen, Heath, 175.
　　Lesser Prairie, 175.
　　Prairie, 175.
Henhawk, Cooper's, 353.
Herodias, 136.
Herodii, 134.
Herodiones, 131.
Heron, Black-crowned Night, 138.
　　European Blue, 135.
　　Great Blue, 135.
　　Great White, 135.
　　Green, 137.
　　Little Blue, 137.
　　Louisiana, 139.
　　Snowy, 136.
　　Ward's, 135.
　　Würdemann's, 351.
　　Yellow-crowned Night, 138.
Hesperiphona, 254.
Hesperocichla, 345.
　　nævia, 345.
Hesperornis crassipes, 360.
　　gracilis, 360.
　　regalis, 360.
Heteractitis, 156.
　　incana, 156.
Hierofalco, 193.
Himantopus, 146.
　　mexicanus, 146.
Hirundinidæ, 292.
Histrionicus, 121.
　　histrionicus, 121.
Hummingbird, Allen's, 225.
　　Anna's, 225.
　　Black-chinned, 224.
　　Blue-throated, 223.

INDEX.

Hummingbird, Broad-billed, 227.
    Broad-tailed, 225.
    Buff-bellied, 227.
    Calliope, 226.
    Costa's, 224.
    Heloise's, 226.
    Lucifer, 226.
    Rieffer's, 227.
    Rivoli, 223.
    Ruby-throated, 224.
    Rufous, 225.
    Xantus's, 227.
Hydranassa, 136.
Hydrochelidon, 95.
    leucoptera, 96.
    nigra surinamensis, 96.
Hylocichla, 341.
Hylophilus, 355.
    decurtatus, 355.
Hylophilus, Short-winged, 355.

IACHE, 227.
    latirostris, 227.
Ibides, 131.
Ibididæ, 131.
Ibis, Glossy, 132.
    Scarlet, 132.
    White, 131.
    White-faced Glossy, 132.
    Wood, 133.
Ichthyornis agilis, 360.
    anceps, 361.
    dispar, 360.
    lentus, 361.
    tener, 361.
    validus, 361.
    victor, 361.
Icteria, 315.
    virens, 315.
    virens longicauda, 315.
Icteridæ, 247.
Icterus, 250.
    audubonii, 251.
    bullocki, 252.
    cucullatus, 251.
    cucullatus nelsoni, 251.
    galbula, 252.
    icterus, 250.
    parisorum, 251.
    spurius, 252.
Ictinia, 185.
    mississippiensis, 185.
Ionornis, 143.
    martinica, 143.

JABIRU, 133.
Jacana, 166.
    gymnostoma, 166.
Jaçana, Mexican, 166.
Jacanidæ, 166.
Jaeger, Parasitic, 85.
    Pomarine, 85.
    Long-tailed, 85.
Jay, Alaskan, 244.
    Arizona, 243.
    Blue, 241.
    Blue-fronted, 241.
    California, 242.
    Canada, 243.
    Florida, 242.
    Florida Blue, 241.
    Green, 243.
    Labrador, 244.
    Long-crested, 242.
    Oregon, 244.
    Piñon, 246.
    Rocky Mountain, 244.
    Steller's, 241.
    Woodhouse's, 242.
Junco, 274.
    aikeni, 274.
    annectens, 275.
    bairdi, 276.
    caniceps, 275.
    cinereus dorsalis, 275.
    cinereus palliatus, 275.
    hyemalis, 274.
    hyemalis oregonus, 274.
    insularis, 276.
Junco, Arizona, 275.
    Baird's, 276.
    Gray-headed, 275.
    Guadalupe, 276.
    Oregon, 274.
    Pink-sided, 275.
    Red-backed, 275.
    Slate-colored, 274.
    White-winged, 274.

KILLDEER, 161.
Kingbird, 229.
    Arkansas, 229.
    Cassin's, 230.
    Couch's, 229.
    Gray, 229.
Kingfisher, Belted, 209.
    Texan, 209.
Kinglet, Cuvier's, 357.
    Dusky, 339.

Kinglet, Golden-crowned, 339.
    Ruby-crowned. 339.
    Western Golden-crowned, 339.
Kite, Everglade, 185.
    Mississippi, 185.
    Swallow-tailed, 184.
    White-tailed, 184.
Kittiwake, 86.
    Pacific, 86.
    Red-legged, 87.
Knot, 149.

LAGOPUS, 173.
    lagopus, 173.
    lagopus alleni, 173.
    leucurus, 174.
    rupestris, 173.
    rupestris atkhensis, 174.
    rupestris nelsoni, 174.
    rupestris reinhardti, 174.
    welchi, 174.
Laniidæ, 295.
Lanius, 295.
    borealis, 295.
    ludovicianus, 296.
    ludovicianus excubitorides, 296.
Lanivireo, 297.
Laopteryx priscus, 359.
Laornis edvardsianus, 361.
Lapwing, 160.
Laridæ, 86, 350.
Larinæ, 86.
Lark, Desert Horned, 239.
    Horned, 238.
    Mexican Horned, 239.
    Pallid Horned, 238.
    Prairie Horned, 239.
    Ruddy Horned, 240.
    Streaked Horned, 240.
    Texan Horned, 239.
Larus, 87.
    affinis, 89.
    argentatus, 89.
    argentatus smithsonianus, 89.
    atricilla, 90.
    brachyrhynchus, 90.
    cachinnans, 89.
    californicus, 89.
    canus, 90.
    delawarensis, 90.
    franklinii, 91.
    glaucescens, 87.
    glaucus, 87.
    heermanni, 90.

Larus kumlieni, 88.
    leucopterus, 87.
    marinus, 88.
    nelsoni, 88.
    occidentalis, 88.
    philadelphia, 91.
    schistisagus, 88.
Leptopelicanus, 112.
Leucosticte, 258.
    atrata, 259.
    australis, 259.
    griseonucha, 258.
    tephrocotis, 258.
    tephrocotis littoralis, 258.
Leucosticte, Aleutian, 258.
    Black, 259.
    Brown-capped, 259.
    Gray-crowned, 258.
    Hepburn's, 258.
Limicolæ, 145, 365.
Limosa, 153.
    fedoa, 153.
    hæmastica, 154.
    lapponica baueri, 154.
    limosa, 154.
Limpkin, 140.
Linnet, Brewster's, 354.
Longipennes, 84.
Longspur, Chestnut-collared, 263.
    Lapland, 263.
    McCown's, 264.
    Smith's, 263.
Loon, 75.
    Black-throated, 76.
    Pacific, 76.
    Red-throated, 76.
    Yellow-billed, 75.
Lophodytes, 114.
    cucullatus, 114.
Lophophanes, 332.
Lophortyx, 169.
Loxia, 257.
    curvirostra minor, 257.
    curvirostra stricklandi, 257.
    leucoptera, 258.
Lunda, 76.
    cirrhata, 77.

MACROCHIRES, 219.
Macrorhamphus, 148.
    griseus, 148.
    scolopaceus, 148.
Magpie, American, 240.
    Yellow-billed, 240.

INDEX.

Mallard, 114
Man-o'-War Bird, 113.
Mareca, 115.
Martin, Purple, 292.
Meadowlark, 250.
    Mexican, 250.
    Western, 250.
Megalestris, 84.
    skua, 85.
Megaquiscalus, 254.
Megascops, 200.
    asio, 200.
    asio bendirei, 201.
    asio floridanus, 200.
    asio kennicottii, 201.
    asio maxwelliæ, 201.
    asio mccallii, 201.
    asio trichopsis, 202.
    flammeolus, 202.
Melanerpes, 216.
    aurifrons, 217.
    carolinus, 217.
    erythrocephalus, 216.
    formicivorus angustifrons, 216.
    formicivorus bairdi, 216.
    torquatus, 216.
    uropygialis, 217.
Melanitta, 123.
Meleagrinæ, 177.
Meleagris, 177.
    altus, 366.
    antiquus, 365.
    celer, 366.
    gallopavo, 177.
    gallopavo mexicana, 177.
Melopelia, 180.
    leucoptera, 181
Melospiza, 279.
    cinerea, 281.
    fasciata, 279.
    fasciata fallax, 279.
    fasciata guttata, 280.
    fasciata heermanni, 280.
    fasciata montana, 279.
    fasciata rufina, 280.
    fasciata samuelis, 280.
    georgiana, 281.
    lincolni, 281.
Merganser, 113.
    americanus, 113.
    serrator, 114.
Merganser, American, 113.
    Hooded, 114.
    Red-breasted, 114.
Merginæ, 113.

Merlin, Black, 195.
    Richardson's, 195.
Merula, 344.
    confinis, 345.
    migratoria, 344.
    migratoria propinqua, 344.
Methriopterus, 222.
Micrathene, 205.
    whitneyi, 205.
Micropalama, 148.
    himantopus, 149.
Micropodidæ, 221.
Micropodinæ, 222.
Micropus, 222.
    melanoleucus, 223.
Milvulus, 228.
    forficatus, 228.
    tyrannus, 228.
Miminæ, 321.
Mimus, 322.
    polyglottos, 322.
Mniotilta, 300.
    varia, 300.
Mniotiltidæ, 300, 355.
Mockingbird, 322.
Molothrus, 248.
    æneus, 248.
    ater, 248.
    ater obscurus, 248.
Motacilla, 319.
    alba, 319.
    ocularis, 319.
Motacillidæ, 319.
Murre, 82.
    Brünnich's, 83.
    California, 82.
    Pallas's, 83.
Murrelet, Ancient, 80.
    Craveri's, 81.
    Kittlitz's, 81.
    Marbled, 80.
    Temminck's, 80.
    Xantus's, 81.
Myadestes, 341.
    townsendii, 341.
Myadestinæ, 341.
Mycteria, 133.
    americana, 133.
Myiarchus, 231.
    cinerascens, 232.
    crinitus, 231.
    lawrenceii, 232.
    lawrenceii olivascens, 232.
    mexicanus, 231.
    mexicanus magister, 231.

Myiozetetes, 230.
    texensis, 230.
Myiodynastes, 230.
    luteiventris, 231.

NEOCORYS, 320.
Netta, 118.
    rufina, 118.
Nettion, 116.
Nighthawk, 220.
    Cuban, 221.
    Texan, 221.
    Western, 221.
Noddy, 96.
Nomonyx, 125.
    dominicus, 125.
Numenius, 158.
    borealis, 159.
    hudsonicus, 159.
    longirostris, 158.
    phæopus, 159.
    tahitiensis, 159.
Nutcracker, Clarke's, 246.
Nuthatch, Brown-headed, 332.
    Pygmy, 332.
    Red-breasted, 331.
    Slender-billed, 331.
    White-breasted, 331.
Nyctala, 200.
    acadica, 200.
    tengmalmi richardsoni, 200.
Nyctea, 203.
    nyctea, 203.
Nyctherodius, 138.
Nycticorax, 137.
    nycticorax nævius, 138.
    violaceus, 138.
Nyctidromus, 220.
    albicollis, 220.

OCEANITES, 105.
    oceanicus, 105.
Oceanitinæ, 105.
Oceanodroma, 104.
    furcata, 104.
    homochroa, 105.
    hornbyi, 350.
    leucorhoa, 104.
    melania, 105.
Ochthodromus, 163.
Odontoglossæ, 130.
Oidemia, 123.
    americana, 123.
    deglandi, 124.

Oidemia fusca, 124.
    perspicillata, 124.
Old-squaw, 120.
Olor, 129.
    buccinator, 130.
    columbianus, 129.
    cygnus, 129.
Oporornis, 313.
Oreortyx, 168.
    pictus, 168.
    pictus plumiferus, 168.
Oriole, Audubon's, 251.
    Arizona Hooded, 251.
    Baltimore, 252.
    Bullock's, 252.
    Hooded, 251.
    Orchard, 252.
    Scott's, 251.
Ornithion, 237.
    imberbe, 237.
    imberbe ridgwayi, 237.
Oroscoptes, 321.
    montanus, 321.
Ortalis, 178.
    vetula maccali, 178.
Oscines, 238.
Osprey, American, 197.
Ossifraga, 98.
    gigantea, 98.
Otocoris, 238.
    alpestris, 238.
    alpestris arenicola, 239.
    alpestris chrysolæma, 239.
    alpestris giraudi, 239.
    alpestris leucolæma, 238.
    alpestris praticola, 239.
    alpestris rubea, 240.
    alpestris strigata, 240.
Oven-bird, 312.
Owl, American Barn, 197.
    American Hawk, 204.
    American Long-eared, 198.
    Arctic Horned, 203.
    Barred, 198.
    Burrowing, 204.
    California Screech, 201.
    Dusky Horned, 203.
    Elf, 205.
    Ferruginous Pygmy, 205.
    Flammulated Screech, 202.
    Florida Barred, 199.
    Florida Burrowing, 204.
    Florida Screech, 200.
    Great Gray, 199.
    Great Horned, 202.

INDEX. 383

Owl, Hawk, 203.
    Kennicott's Screech, 201.
    Lapp, 199.
    Mexican Screech, 202.
    Pygmy, 204.
    Richardson's, 200.
    Rocky Mountain Screech, 201.
    Saw-whet, 200.
    Screech, 200.
    Short-eared, 198.
    Snowy, 203.
    Spotted, 199.
    Texan Screech, 201.
    Western Horned, 202.
Oxyechus, 161.
Oyster-catcher, 165.
    American, 165.
    Black, 166.

PALÆOBORUS umbrosus, 366.
Palæospiza bella, 367.
Palæotringa littoralis, 362.
    vagans, 362.
    vetus, 362.
Paludicolæ, 138.
Pandion, 197.
    haliaëtus carolinensis, 197.
Pandioninæ, 197.
Parabuteo, 187.
    unicinctus harrisi, 187.
Parauque, 220.
Paridæ, 331.
Parinæ, 332.
Paroquet, Carolina, 206.
Parrot, Thick-billed, 354.
Partridge, California, 169.
    Chestnut-bellied Scaled, 169.
    Gambel's, 170.
    Massena, 170.
    Mountain, 170.
    Plumed, 168.
    Scaled, 169.
    Valley, 169.
Parus, 332, 334.
    atricapillus, 334.
    atricapillus occidentalis, 334.
    atricapillus septentrionalis, 334.
    atricristatus, 332.
    bicolor, 332.
    carolinensis, 334.
    cinctus obtectus, 335.
    gambeli, 335.
    hudsonicus, 335.
    inornatus, 333.

Parus inornatus cineraceus, 333.
    inornatus griseus, 333.
    meridionalis, 335.
    rufescens, 335.
    rufescens neglectus, 336.
    wollweberi, 333.
Passerculus, 265.
Passerella, 281.
    iliaca, 281.
    iliaca megarhyncha, 282.
    iliaca schistacea, 282.
    iliaca unalaschensis, 282.
Passeres, 228, 367.
Passerina, 288.
    amœna, 288.
    ciris, 288.
    cyanea, 288.
    versicolor, 288.
Pavoncella, 157.
    pugnax, 157.
Pediocætes, 175.
    phasianellus, 176.
    phasianellus campestris, 176.
    phasianellus columbianus, 176.
Pelagodroma, 106.
    marina, 106.
Pelecanidæ, 112.
Pelecanus, 112.
    californicus, 112.
    erythrorhynchos, 112.
    fuscus, 112.
Pelican, American White, 112.
    Brown, 112.
    California Brown, 112.
Pelidna, 151.
Pelionetta, 124.
Pendulinus, 251.
Penelopes, 178.
Penelopinæ, 178.
Perdicinæ, 167.
Perisoreus, 243.
    canadensis, 243.
    canadensis capitalis, 244.
    canadensis fumifrons, 244.
    canadensis nigricapillus, 244.
    obscurus, 244.
Perissoglossa, 305, 356.
Petrel, Ashy, 105.
    Black, 105.
    Black-capped, 102.
    Bulwer's, 103.
    Fisher's, 103.
    Fork-tailed, 104.
    Hornby's, 350.
    Leach's, 104.

Petrel, Least, 104.
   Peale's, 102.
   Pintado, 103.
   Stormy, 104.
   White-bellied, 106.
   White-faced, 106.
   Wilson's, 105.
   Petrochelidon, 292.
   lunifrons, 292.
Peucæa, 277.
   æstivalis, 277.
   æstivalis bachmanii, 277.
   arizonæ, 277.
   carpalis, 278.
   cassini, 278.
   mexicana, 278.
   ruficeps, 278.
   ruficeps boucardi, 278.
   ruficeps eremœca, 279.
Peucedramus, 305.
Pewee, Western Wood, 234.
   Wood, 234.
Phaëthon, 106.
   æthereus, 107.
   flavirostris, 106.
Phaëthontidæ, 106.
Phainopepla, 295.
   nitens, 295.
Phalacrocoracidæ, 109, 351.
Phalacrocorax, 109.
   carbo, 109.
   dilophus, 109.
   dilophus albociliatus, 110.
   dilophus cincinatus, 110.
   dilophus floridanus, 109.
   idahensis, 363.
   mexicanus, 110.
   micropus, 364.
   pelagicus, 111.
   pelagicus resplendens, 111.
   pelagicus robustus, 111.
   penicillatus, 110.
   perspicillatus, 351.
   urile, 111.
Phalænoptilus, 220.
   nuttalli, 220.
Phalarope, Northern, 145.
   Red, 145.
   Wilson's, 146.
Phalaropodidæ, 145.
Phalaropus, 145.
   lobatus, 145.
   tricolor, 146.
Phalerinæ, 78.
Phaleris, 79.

Phasiani, 167.
Phasianidæ, 177.
Philacte, 128.
   canagica, 128.
Philohela, 147.
   minor, 147.
Phœbe, 232.
   Black, 233.
   Say's, 233.
Phœbetria, 98.
   fuliginosa, 98.
Phœnicopteridæ, 130.
Phœnicopterus, 130.
   ruber, 130.
Phyllopseustes, 338.
   borealis, 338.
Pica, 240.
   nuttalli, 240.
   pica hudsonica, 240.
Pici, 210.
Picidæ, 210.
Picoides, 213.
   americanus, 214.
   americanus alascensis, 214.
   americanus dorsalis, 214.
   arcticus, 213.
Picicorvus, 246.
   columbianus, 246.
Pigeon, Band-tailed, 178.
   Passenger, 179.
   Red-billed, 179.
   White-crowned, 179.
Pinicola, 255.
   enucleator, 255.
Pintail, 117.
Pipilo, 283.
   aberti, 285.
   chlorurus, 284.
   consobrinus, 284.
   erythrophthalmus, 283.
   erythrophthalmus alleni, 283.
   fuscus albigula, 285.
   fuscus crissalis, 285.
   fuscus mesoleucus, 285.
   maculatus arcticus, 283.
   maculatus megalonyx, 284.
   maculatus oregonus, 284.
Pipit, American, 320.
   Meadow, 320.
   Red-throated, 320.
   Sprague's, 320.
Piranga, 290.
   erythromelas, 291.
   hepatica, 291.
   ludoviciana, 290.

Piranga rubra, 291.
    rubra cooperi, 291.
Pitangus, 230.
    derbianus, 230.
Plataleidæ, 131.
Plautus, 83.
    impennis, 84.
Plectrophenax, 262.
    hyperboreus, 263.
    nivalis, 262.
Plegadis, 132.
    autumnalis, 132.
    guarauna, 132.
Plover, American Golden, 161.
    Belted Piping, 163.
    Black-bellied, 160.
    Golden, 160.
    Little Ring, 162.
    Mongolian, 163.
    Mountain, 164.
    Pacific Golden, 161.
    Piping, 162.
    Ring, 162.
    Semipalmated, 162.
    Snowy, 163.
    Wilson's, 163.
Podasocys, 164.
Podiceps, 74.
Podicipedes, 73.
Podicipidæ, 73, 349.
Podilymbus, 75.
    podiceps, 75.
Polioptila, 340.
    cærulea, 340.
    californica, 340.
    plumbea, 340.
Polioptilinæ, 340.
Polyborus, 196.
    cheriway, 196.
    lutosus, 196.
Poocætes, 264.
    gramineus, 264.
    gramineus confinis, 264.
Poor-will, 220.
Porzana, 141.
    carolina, 142.
    jamaicensis, 142.
    jamaicensis coturniculus, 143.
    noveboracensis, 142.
    porzana, 141.
Priocella, 100.
Priofinus, 102.
Procellaria, 104.
    pelagica, 104.
Procellariidæ, 98, 350.

Procellariinæ, 98.
Progne, 292.
    subis, 292.
Protonotaria, 301.
    citrea, 301.
Psaltriparus, 336.
    melanotis, 337.
    minimus, 337.
    minimus californicus, 337.
    minimus grindæ, 337.
    plumbeus, 337.
Pseudogryphus, 182.
    californianus, 183.
Psittaci, 205.
Psittacidæ, 205.
Ptarmigan, Allen's, 173.
    Nelson's, 174.
    Reinhardt's, 174.
    Rock, 173.
    Turner's, 174.
    Welch's, 174.
    White-tailed, 174.
    Willow, 173.
Ptiliogonatinæ, 295.
Ptychoramphus, 78.
    aleuticus, 78.
Puffin. 77.
    Horned. 77.
    Large-billed, 77.
    Tufted, 77.
Puffinus, 100.
    auduboni, 101.
    borealis, 100.
    cinereus, 102.
    conradii, 363.
    creatopus, 101.
    gavia, 101.
    griseus, 101.
    kuhlii, 350.
    major, 100.
    puffinus, 100.
    stricklandi, 101.
    tenuirostris, 102.
Pygopodes, 73, 363.
Pyrocephalus, 237.
    rubineus mexicanus, 237.
Pyrrhula, 255.
    cassini, 255.
Pyrrhuloxia, 286.
    sinuata, 286.

QUAIL-DOVE, Blue-headed, 182.
    Key West, 182.
Querquedula, 116.

Quiscalus, 253.
   macrourus, 254.
   major, 254.
   quiscula, 253.
   quiscula æneus, 253.
   quiscula aglæus, 253.

RAIL, Belding's, 140.
   Black, 142.
   California Clapper, 140.
   Clapper, 141.
   Farallone, 143.
   King, 140.
   Louisiana Clapper, 141.
   Virginia, 141.
   Yellow, 142.
Ralli, 139.
Rallidæ, 140.
Rallinæ, 140.
Rallus, 140.
   beldingi, 140.
   elegans, 140.
   longirostris crepitans, 141.
   longirostris saturatus, 141.
   obsoletus, 140.
   virginianus, 141.
Raptores, 182, 366.
Raven, American, 245.
   White-necked, 245.
Ratitæ, 362.
Recurvirostra, 146.
   americana, 146.
Recurvirostridæ, 146.
Redhead, 118.
Redpoll, 260.
   Greenland, 259.
   Greater, 260.
   Hoary, 260.
   Holbœll's, 260.
Redstart, American, 317.
   Painted, 317.
   Red-bellied, 317.
Red-tail, St. Lucas, 188.
   Western, 188.
Regulinæ, 339.
Regulus, 339.
   calendula, 339.
   cuvieri, 357.
   obscurus, 339.
   satrapa, 339.
   satrapa olivaceus, 339.
Rissa, 86.
   brevirostris, 87.
   tridactyla, 86.

Rissa tridactyla pollicaris, 86.
Road-runner, 207.
Robin, American, 344.
   St. Lucas, 345.
   Western, 344.
Rostrhamus, 185.
   sociabilis, 185.
Rough-leg, Ferruginous, 191.
Ruff, 157.
Rhodostethia, 91.
   rosea, 91.
Rhyacophilus, 155.
Rhynchodon, 194.
Rhynchofalco, 195.
Rhynchophanes, 264.
   mccownii, 264.
Rhynchopsitta, 353.
   pachyrhynca, 354.
Rynchopidæ, 96.
Rynchops, 96.
   nigra, 97.

SALPINCTES, 325.
   guadeloupensis, 326.
   obsoletus, 325.
Sanderling, 153.
Sandpiper, Aleutian, 150.
   Baird's, 151.
   Bartramian, 157.
   Buff-breasted, 158.
   Cooper's, 352.
   Curlew, 152.
   Green, 156.
   Least, 151.
   Pectoral, 150.
   Prybilof, 150.
   Purple, 149.
   Red-backed, 152.
   Semipalmated, 153.
   Sharp-tailed, 150.
   Solitary, 156.
   Spoon-bill, 152.
   Spotted, 158.
   Stilt, 149.
   Western, 153.
   White-rumped, 151.
Sapsucker, Red-breasted, 215.
   Red-naped, 215.
   Williamson's, 215.
   Yellow-bellied, 214.
Sarcorhamphi, 182.
Saxicola, 346.
   œnanthe, 345.
Sayornis, 232.

INDEX.

Sayornis nigricans, 233.
    phœbe, 232.
    saya, 233.
Scardafella, 181.
    inca, 181.
Scolecophagus, 252.
    carolinus, 253.
    cyanocephalus, 253.
Scolopacidæ, 147, 352.
Scolopax, 147.
    rusticola, 147.
Scoter, American, 123.
    Surf, 124.
    Velvet, 124.
    White-winged, 124.
Seed-eater, Morellet's, 289.
Seiurus, 312.
    aurocapillus, 312.
    motacilla, 313.
    noveboracensis, 312.
    noveboracensis notabilis, 312.
Selasphorus, 225.
Setophaga, 317.
    miniata, 317.
    picta, 317.
    ruticilla, 317.
Shearwater, Audubon's, 101.
    Black-tailed, 102.
    Black-vented, 101.
    Cinereous, 350.
    Cory's, 100.
    Dark-bodied, 101.
    Greater, 100.
    Manx, 100.
    Pink-footed, 101.
    Slender-billed, 102.
    Sooty, 101.
Shoveller, 117.
Shrike, Loggerhead, 296.
    Northern, 295.
    White-rumped, 296.
Sialia, 346.
    arctica, 347.
    mexicana, 346.
    sialis, 346.
    sialis azurea, 346.
Simorhynchus, 79.
    cristatellus, 79.
    pusillus, 79.
    pygmæus, 79.
Siskin, Pine, 262.
Sitta, 331.
    canadensis, 331.
    carolinensis, 331.
    carolinensis aculeata, 331.

Sitta pusilla, 332.
    pygmæa, 332.
Sittinæ, 331.
Skimmer, Black, 97.
Skua, 85.
Skylark, 238.
Snipe, European, 147.
    Wilson's, 148.
Snowflake, 262.
    McKay's, 263.
Solitaire, Townsend's, 341.
Somateria, 122.
    dresseri, 122.
    mollissima, 122.
    spectabilis, 123.
    v-nigra, 123.
Sora, 142.
Sparrow, Aleutian Song, 281.
    Arizona, 277.
    Bachman's, 277.
    Baird's, 267.
    Belding's Marsh, 266.
    Bell's, 276.
    Black-chinned, 274.
    Black-throated, 276.
    Boucard's, 278.
    Brewer's, 273.
    Bryant's Marsh, 266.
    Cassin's, 278.
    Chipping, 272.
    Clay-colored, 273.
    Desert Song, 279.
    Dusky Seaside, 269.
    Field, 273.
    Fox, 281.
    Gambel's, 271.
    Golden-crowned, 271.
    Grasshopper, 267.
    Harris's, 270.
    Heermann's, 280.
    Henslow's, 268.
    Intermediate, 271.
    Ipswich, 265.
    Large-billed, 266.
    Lark, 270.
    Leconte's, 268.
    Lincoln's, 281.
    Mexican, 278.
    Mountain Song, 279.
    Nelson's, 269.
    Pine-woods, 277.
    Rock, 279.
    Rufous-crowned, 278.
    Rufous-winged, 278.
    Rusty Song, 280.

Sparrow, Sage, 277.
  St. Lucas, 267.
  Samuels's Song, 280.
  Sandwich, 265.
  Savanna, 265.
  Seaside, 269.
  Sharp-tailed, 268.
  Slate-colored, 282.
  Song, 279.
  Sooty Song, 280.
  Swamp, 281.
  Texas, 283.
  Thick-billed, 282.
  Townsend's, 282.
  Tree, 272.
  Vesper, 264.
  Western Chipping, 273.
  Western Grasshopper, 268.
  Western Lark, 270.
  Western Savanna, 266.
  Western Tree, 272.
  Western Vesper, 264.
  White-crowned, 270.
  White-throated, 271.
  Worthen's, 273.
Spatula, 117.
  clypeata, 117.
Speotyto, 204.
  cuniculara floridana, 204.
  cunicularia hypogæa, 204.
Sphyrapicus, 214.
  ruber, 215.
  thyroideus, 215.
  varius, 214.
  varius nuchalis, 215.
Spinus, 260.
  lawrencei, 262.
  notatus, 262.
  pinus, 262.
  psaltria, 261.
  psaltria arizonæ, 261.
  psaltria mexicanus, 261.
  tristis, 261.
Spiza, 289.
  americana, 289.
  townsendi, 354.
Spizella, 272.
  atrigularis, 274.
  breweri, 273.
  monticola, 272.
  monticola ochracea, 272.
  pallida, 273.
  pusilla, 273.
  socialis, 272.
  socialis arizonæ, 273.

Spizella wortheni, 273.
Spoonbill, Roseate, 131.
Sporophila, 289.
  morelleti, 289.
Squatarola, 160.
Starling, 247.
Starnœnas, 182.
  cyanocephala, 182.
Steganopodes, 106, 363.
Steganopus, 145.
Stelgidopteryx, 294.
  serripennis, 294.
Stellula, 226.
Stercorariidæ, 84.
Stercorarius, 85.
  longicaudus, 85.
  parasiticus, 85.
  pomarinus, 85.
Sterna, 92, 93.
  aleutica, 94.
  anæthetus, 95.
  antillarum, 95.
  dougalli, 94.
  elegans, 93.
  forsteri, 94.
  fuliginosa, 95.
  hirundo, 94.
  maxima, 93.
  paradisæa, 94.
  sandvicensis acuflavida, 93.
  trudeaui, 93.
  tschegrava, 92.
Sterninæ, 92.
Sternula, 95.
Stilt, Black-necked, 146.
Streptoceryle, 209.
Striges, 197.
Strigidæ, 197.
Strix, 197.
  pratincola, 197.
Sturnella, 250.
  magna, 250.
  magna mexicana, 250.
  magna neglecta, 250.
Sturnidæ, 247.
Sturnus, 247.
  vulgaris, 247.
Sula, 107.
  bassana, 108.
  cyanops, 107.
  loxostyla, 363.
  piscator, 108.
  sula, 107.
Sulidæ, 107.
Surnia, 203.

Surnia ulula, 203.
    ulula caparoch, 204.
Swallow, Bank, 293.
    Barn, 292.
    Cliff, 292.
    Rough-winged, 294.
    Tree, 293.
    Violet-green, 293.
Swan, Trumpeter, 130.
    Whistling, 129.
    Whooping, 129.
Swift, Black, 222.
    Chimney, 222.
    Vaux's, 222.
    White-throated, 223.
Sylvania, 315.
    canadensis, 316.
    microcephala, 356.
    mitrata, 316.
    pusilla, 316.
    pusilla pileolata, 316.
Sylviidæ, 338, 357.
Sylviinæ, 338.
Symphemia, 156.
    semipalmata, 156.
Synthliboramphus, 80.
    antiquus, 80.
    wumizusume, 80.
Syrnium, 198.
    nebulosum, 198.
    nebulosum alleni, 199.
    occidentale, 199.

TACHYCINETA, 293.
    bicolor, 293.
    thalassina, 293.
Tanager, Cooper's, 291.
    Hepatic, 291.
    Louisiana, 291.
    Scarlet, 291.
    Summer, 291.
Tanagridæ, 290.
Tantalinæ, 133.
Tantalus, 133.
    loculator, 133.
Tatler, Wandering, 156.
Teal, Blue-winged, 116.
    Cinnamon, 117.
    European, 116.
    Green-winged, 116.
Telmatodytes, 330.
Telmatornis affinis, 362.
    priscus, 362.
Tern, Aleutian, 94.

Tern, Arctic, 94.
    Black, 96.
    Bridled, 95.
    Cabot's, 93.
    Caspian, 92.
    Common, 94.
    Elegant, 93.
    Forster's, 94.
    Gull-billed, 92.
    Least, 95.
    Roseate, 94.
    Royal, 93.
    Sooty, 93.
    Trudeau's, 93.
    White-winged Black, 96.
Tetraonidæ, 167.
Tetraoninæ, 170.
Thalasseus, 92.
Thalassogeron, 97.
    culminatus, 98.
Thrasaëtus, 192.
    harpyia, 192.
Thrasher, Bendire's, 323.
    Brown, 322.
    Californian, 324.
    Crissal, 324.
    Curve-billed, 323.
    Leconte's, 324.
    Long-billed, 323.
    Palmer's, 323.
    Sage, 321.
    St. Lucas, 324.
Thrush, Audubon's Hermit, 343.
    Bicknell's, 342.
    Dwarf Hermit, 343.
    Gray-cheeked, 342.
    Hermit, 343.
    Olive-backed, 343.
    Red-winged, 344.
    Russet-backed, 343.
    Varied, 345.
    Willow, 342.
    Wilson's, 342.
    Wood, 341.
Thryomanes, 327.
Thryothorus, 326.
    bewickii, 327.
    bewickii bairdi, 328.
    bewickii spilurus, 327.
    brevicaudus, 328.
    ludovicianus, 327.
    ludovicianus miamensis, 327.
Tinnunculus, 196.
Titmouse, Ashy, 333.
    Black-crested, 332.

Titmouse, Bridled, 333.
　Gray, 333.
　Plain, 333.
　Tufted, 333.
Totanus, 154.
　flavipes, 155.
　melanoleucus, 155.
　nebularius, 155.
　ochropus, 156.
　solitarius, 156.
Towhee, 283.
　Abert's, 283.
　Arctic, 283.
　Californian, 285.
　Cañon, 285.
　Green-tailed, 284.
　Guadalupe, 284.
　Oregon, 284.
　Saint Lucas, 285.
　Spurred, 284.
　White-eyed, 283.
Tree-duck, Black-bellied, 129.
　Fulvous, 129.
Tringa, 149.
　acuminata, 150.
　alpina, 151.
　alpina pacifica, 152.
　bairdii, 151.
　canutus, 149.
　cooperi, 352.
　couesi, 151.
　ferruginea, 152.
　fuscicollis, 151.
　maculata, 150.
　maritima, 149.
　minutilla, 151.
　ptilocnemis, 150.
Trochili, 223.
Trochilidæ, 223.
Trochilus, 224.
　alexandri, 224.
　alleni, 225.
　anna, 225.
　calliope, 226.
　colubris, 224.
　costæ, 224.
　heloisa, 226.
　lucifer, 226.
　platycercus, 225.
　rufus, 225.
Troglodytes, 328.
　aëdon, 328.
　aëdon parkmanii, 328.
　alascensis, 329.
　hiemalis, 329.

Troglodytes hiemalis pacificus, 329.
Troglodytidæ, 321.
Troglodytinæ, 325.
Trogon, 208.
　ambiguus, 208.
Trogon, Coppery-tailed, 208.
Trogones, 208.
Trogonidæ, 208.
Troupial, 251.
Tryngites, 157.
　subruficollis, 158.
Tubinares, 97, 363.
Turdidæ, 341.
Turdinæ, 341.
Turdus, 341, 344.
　aliciæ, 342.
　aliciæ bicknelli, 342.
　aonalaschkæ, 343.
　aonalaschkæ auduboni, 343.
　aonalaschkæ pallasi, 343.
　fuscescens, 342.
　fuscescens salicicolus, 342.
　iliacus, 344.
　mustelinus, 341.
　ustulatus, 343.
　ustulatus swainsoni, 343.
Turkey, Mexican, 177.
　Wild, 177.
Turnstone, 165.
　Black, 165.
Tympanuchus, 175.
　americanus, 175.
　cupido, 175.
　pallidicinctus, 175.
Tyrannidæ, 228.
Tyrannus, 228.
　dominicensis, 229.
　melancholicus couchii, 229.
　tyrannus, 229.
　verticalis, 229.
　vociferans, 230.

Uintornis lucaris, 366.
Ulula, 199.
　cinerea, 199.
　cinerea lapponica, 199.
Uria, 82.
　affinis, 363.
　antiqua, 363.
　lomvia, 83.
　lomvia arra, 83.
　troile, 82.
　troile californica, 82.
Urile, 111.

Urinator, 75.
  adamsii, 75.
  arcticus, 76.
  imber, 75.
  lumme, 76.
  pacificus, 76.
Urinatoridæ, 75.
Urubitinga, 190.
  anthracina, 190.

VANELLUS, 160.
  vanellus, 160.
Verdin, 338.
Vireo, 296, 298.
  altiloquus barbatulus, 296.
  atricapillus, 298.
  bellii, 299.
  bellii pusillus, 299.
  flavifrons, 297.
  flavoviridis, 297.
  gilvus, 297.
  huttoni, 299.
  huttoni stephensi, 299.
  noveboracensis, 299.
  olivaceus, 296.
  philadelphicus, 297.
  solitarius, 298.
  solitarius cassinii, 298.
  solitarius plumbeus, 298.
  vicinior, 300.
Vireo, Bell's, 299.
  Black-capped, 298.
  Black-whiskered, 296.
  Blue-headed, 298.
  Cassin's, 298.
  Gray, 300.
  Hutton's, 299.
  Least, 299.
  Philadelphia, 297.
  Plumbeous, 298.
  Red-eyed, 296.
  Stephens's, 299.
  Warbling, 297.
  White-eyed, 299.
  Yellow-green, 297.
  Yellow-throated, 297.
Vireonidæ, 296, 355.
Vireosylva, 296.
Vulture, Black, 183.
  Burroughs's Turkey, 353.
  California, 183.
  King, 352.
  Turkey, 183.

WAGTAIL, Siberian Yellow, 319.
  Swinhoe's, 319.
  White, 319.
Warbler, Audubon's, 307.
  Bachman's, 302.
  Bay-breasted, 308.
  Bell's, 318.
  Black and White, 300.
  Blackburnian, 308.
  Black-poll, 308.
  Black-throated Blue, 306.
  Black-throated Gray, 309.
  Black-throated Green, 310.
  Blue Mountain, 356.
  Blue-winged, 302.
  Brasher's, 318.
  Brewster's, 355.
  Calaveras, 303.
  Canadian, 316.
  Cape May, 305.
  Carbonated, 356.
  Cerulean, 307.
  Chestnut-sided, 308.
  Cincinnati, 356.
  Connecticut, 313.
  Golden-cheeked, 310.
  Golden-winged, 302.
  Grace's, 309.
  Hermit, 310.
  Hooded, 316.
  Kennicott's Willow, 338.
  Kentucky, 313.
  Kirtland's, 311.
  Lawrence's, 355.
  Lucy's, 303.
  Lutescent, 304.
  Macgillivray's, 314.
  Magnolia, 307.
  Mangrove, 306.
  Mourning, 314.
  Myrtle, 307.
  Nashville, 303.
  Olive, 306.
  Orange-crowned, 304.
  Palm, 311.
  Parula, 305.
  Pileolated, 316.
  Pine, 311.
  Prairie, 312.
  Prothonotary, 301.
  Red, 318.
  Red-faced, 318.
  Sennett's, 305.
  Small-headed, 356.
  Swainson's, 301.

Warbler, Sycamore, 309.
    Tennessee, 304.
    Townsend's, 310.
    Virginia's, 303.
    Wilson's, 316.
    Worm-eating, 301.
    Yellow, 306.
    Yellow Palm, 311.
    Yellow-throated, 309.
Water-Thrush, 312.
    Grinnell's, 312.
    Louisiana, 313.
Waxwing, Bohemian, 294.
    Cedar, 294.
Wheatear, 346.
Whimbrel, 159.
Whip-poor-will, 219.
    Stephens's, 219.
Widgeon, 115.
Willet, 156.
Woodcock, American, 147.
    European, 147.
Woodpecker, Alaskan Three-toed, 214.
    Alpine Three-toed, 214.
    American Three-toed, 214.
    Arctic Three-toed, 213.
    Californian, 216.
    Downy, 211.
    Gairdner's, 211.
    Gila, 217.
    Golden-fronted, 217.
    Hairy, 210.
    Harris's, 211.
    Ivory-billed, 210.
    Lewis's, 216.
    Narrow-fronted, 216.
    Northern Hairy, 210.
    Nuttall's, 212.
    Pileated, 215.
    Red-bellied, 217.
    Red-cockaded, 212.
    Red-headed, 216.
    Saint Lucas, 212.
    Southern Hairy, 211.
    Strickland's, 213.
    Texan, 212.
    White-headed, 213.
    Williamson's, 215.
Wren, Alaskan, 329.
    Baird's, 328.

Wren, Bewick's, 327.
    Cactus, 325.
    Cañon, 326.
    Carolina, 327.
    Florida, 327.
    Guadalupe, 328.
    Guadalupe Rock, 326.
    House, 328.
    Long-billed Marsh, 340.
    Parkman's, 328.
    Rock, 325.
    St. Lucas Cactus, 325.
    Short-billed Marsh, 330.
    Vigors's, 327.
    White-throated, 326.
    Winter, 329.
    Western Winter, 329.
Wren-Tit, 336.
    Pallid, 336.

XANTHOCEPHALUS, 248.
    xanthocephalus, 249.
Xanthoura, 243.
    luxuosa, 243.
Xema, 91.
    furcata, 350.
    sabinii, 91.
Xenopicus, 213.
    albolarvatus, 213.

YELLOW-LEGS, 155.
    Greater, 155.
Yellow-throat, Belding's, 315.
    Maryland, 314.
    Western, 314.
Yphantes, 252.

ZENAIDA, 180.
    zenaida, 180.
Zenaidura, 179.
    macroura, 180.
Zonotrichia albicollis, 271.
    coronata, 271.
    gambeli, 271.
    intermedia, 271.
    leucophrys, 270.
    querula, 270.

www.ingramcontent.com/pod-product-compliance
Lightning Source LLC
Chambersburg PA
CBHW030425300426
44112CB00009B/850